P9-DHG-208

Second Edition

Reading and the Middle School Student

Strategies to Enhance Literacy

TOURO COLLEGE LIBRARY
Kings Hwy

Judith L. Irvin
Florida State University
College of Education

WITHDRAWN

Allyn and Bacon
Boston • London • Toronto • Sydney • Tokyo • Singapore

KH

Vice President and Publisher, Education: Nancy Forsyth
Senior Series Editor: Virginia Lanigan
Editorial Assistant: Kris Lamarre
Production Coordinator: Christopher H. Rawlings
Editorial-Production Service: Shepherd, Inc.
Composition and Prepress Buyer: Linda Cox
Manufacturing Buyer: Suzanne Lareau
Cover Administrator: Suzanne Harbison

Copyright © 1998, 1990 by Allyn & Bacon
A Viacom Company
160 Gould Street
Needham Heights, MA 02194

All rights reserved. No part of the material protected by this copyright notice may be reproduced or utilized in any form or by any means, electronic or mechanical, including photocopying, recording, or by any information storage and retrieval system, without written permission from the copyright owner.

Library of Congress Cataloging-in-Publication Data

Irvin, Judith L., 1947–
Reading and the middle school student: strategies to enhance literacy/by Judith L. Irvin.—2nd ed.
p. cm.
Includes bibliographical references and index.
ISBN 0–205–16379–3
1. Reading (Elementary)—United States. 2. Reading (Middle school)—United States. 3. Content area readimg—United States.
I. Title.
LB1573. I73 1997
372. 4'0973—dc21 97–1535
CIP

Printed in the United States of America

10 9 8 7 06 05 04

11/22/04

Contents

Preface

Reading and the Middle School Student: Strategies to Enhance Literacy is a book for prospective and practicing teachers, administrators, program specialists, and resource teachers concerned with improving the literacy abilities of middle level learners. The last three decades have been a time of renewed interest in middle level education. Also, current research and theory in reading education/learning have contributed to what educators know about the most exciting ways for students to improve their literacy abilities. The powerful and exciting implications for instruction that result from this renewed interest and fine research motivated me to write and revise this book. It seemed to me that teachers deserve to receive the benefits of research and theory in a readable, usable form. Additionally, middle level students deserve instruction chosen because it is research-based and known to facilitate improved literacy learning.

Those working with young adolescents are aware of the importance of knowledge about the physical, social, emotional, cognitive, and moral developmental tasks of this age group. I hope that prospective, as well as experienced teachers, administrators, and resource and reading specialists will find ways of using the information in this book to improve instruction and programs for middle level students.

Prospective middle level teachers will appreciate the discussion of the basic processes of literacy instruction and motivational techniques, student work, and step-by-step assessment procedures. Numerous strategies are recommended for the instruction of vocabulary, comprehension, study skills, and the use of literature across the curriculum. Veteran teachers will find the discussion of recent research findings readable and useful to update their knowledge in such areas as developmental tasks of early adolescence, motivation, underachievement, and strategic learning. This book serves as a handy reference for learning strategies and for the recent young adult book titles that have been added to the chapter on literature.

The book is divided into two parts: what educators need to know to make instructional decisions and what they need to know to make programmatic decisions. The chapters in the first section include new views of learning and instruction, and strategies that enhance learning. The chapters included in the second part of the book give information on the history and philosophy of the middle school movement, detail components of successful reading programs, and describe exemplary literacy programs.

Personally, I have long-standing interest and considerable experience with middle grades students, teachers, and schools. Writing and revising this book has strengthened my commitment to improved literacy learning for middle level students. I sincerely hope that the information contained in these pages is helpful to those educators who share my commitment.

Chapter 1

Literacy Learning for Middle Grades Students

Middle schools teem with language. Students eagerly relate stories of last night's events or triumphs on succeeding levels of a video game. Mounds of notes are passed, read, answered, and sometimes collected throughout a normal day. Young adolescents read, write, speak, listen, and think enthusiastically and for appropriate reasons. They wish to communicate.

Vygotsky (1962) maintained that the nature of language learning shifts in early adolescence to encompass more of a social context; that is, language proficiency parallels the growth in the overall psychological and social development of students aged 10 to 14. As students become more psychologically astute and socially aware, their language accommodates these new interests and abilities. Ideally, these new social interests should also be reflected in their academic pursuits. Young adolescents actually strive to make sense of their learning by relating it to their new social interests and psychological awareness.

In fact, it is impossible to get middle level students to stop communicating as can be seen in the figures on the next few pages. But, how is it that Tammy's (Figure 1.1) sixth period teacher cannot seem to get her to write a full page on Mesopotamia when she can write abundantly on the love lives of Andy, Amy (who really is nobody important), Erika, and Alex?

Teachers know how students feel about reading the assigned "stuff" (Figure 1.2), but they continue to teach day after day hoping that students will share their love for learning. The "Secret Admirer" (Figure 1.3) can, at a later date, use his romantic feelings for Pammy to understand literature or events in history just as Paula (Figure 1.4) will be able to use her experience with friendship to understand much of what she reads later in life. For example, when Paula reads a story about divided loyalties between two friends, she will relate the story to her previous experience with friendship. Reading the story will then add to her store of experience and equip her to resolve difficulties in her own relationships.

So, how do teachers get the heartbeat of the hallway into the classroom and maximize its potential for language learning? Early adolescence provides one of the last chances to

Amanda —

Guess what. Andy broke-up with me. I'm really mad!!! But Amy (this girl, nobody important) told me that Andy said he still really liked me but he never sees me so he wanted to break up but also he said that he was not going to go with any body else because he still likes me. I don't understand why he won't go with me if he likes me (oh well) see, now I like Andy now that he broke-up with me. (what a bummer!) Erika is going with Alex. Well, not yet but in a few minutes as soon as Alex asks her, but he got sent to the office so it might take a while longer. I kind of like Alex too but I like Andy and Alex is going with Erika and doesn't like me. (oh yeah I'm writing this in 6th period its 1:55pm. gotta go)

Tammy

FIGURE 1.1

help students become independent, confident producers and comprehenders of language. Students who do not develop the ability to use language in an academic setting by the time they leave middle school often drop out or experience failure in high school. If teachers could somehow capture the excitement and necessity of student communication and relate it to the content they want students to learn, perhaps educators would find the key to motivation and success for middle grades students.

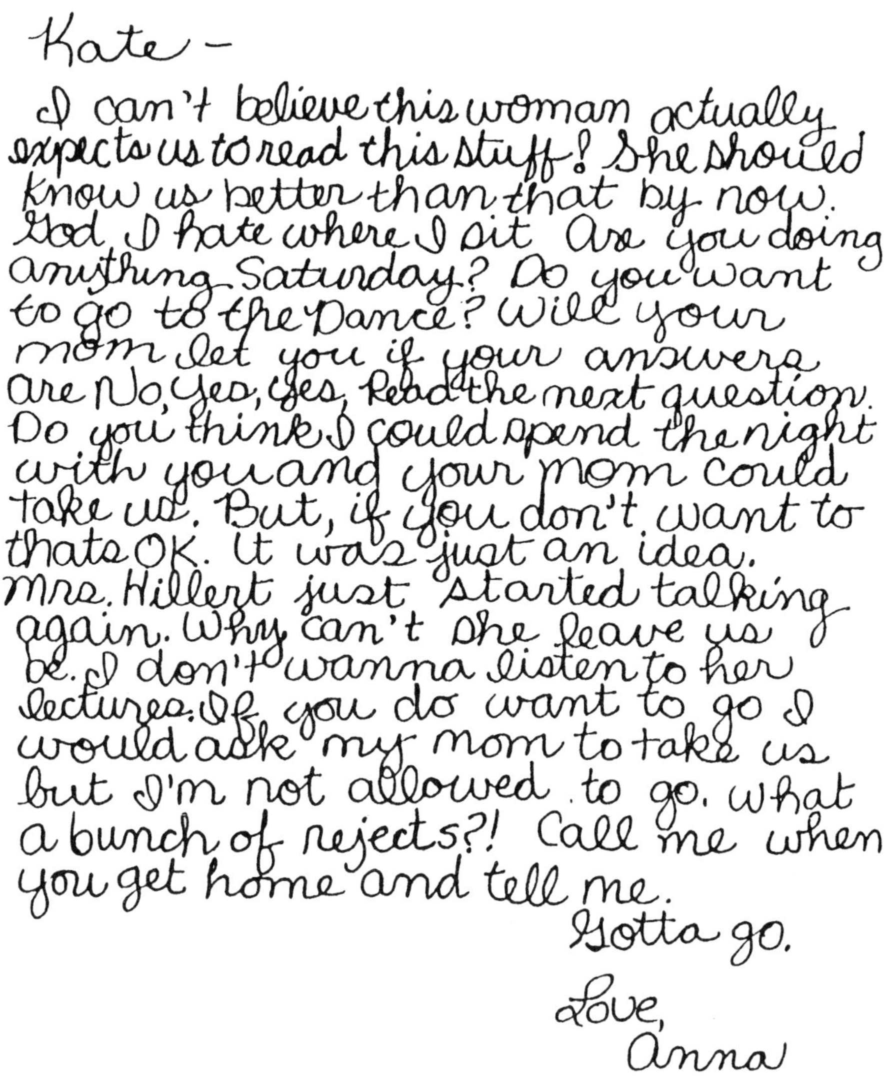

Kate -

I can't believe this woman actually expects us to read this stuff! She should know us better than that by now. God I hate where I sit. Are you doing anything Saturday? Do you want to go to the Dance? Will your mom let you if your answers are No, Yes, Yes, Read the next question. Do you think I could spend the night with you and your mom could take us. But, if you don't want to thats OK. It was just an idea. Mrs. Hillert just started talking again. Why can't she leave us be. I don't wanna listen to her lectures. If you do want to go I would ask my mom to take us but I'm not allowed to go. What a bunch of rejects?! Call me when you get home and tell me.

Gotta go.

Love,
Anna

FIGURE 1.2

Literacy as a Social Event

In the past, learning theorists have considered the psychological and linguistic aspects of literacy, but only more recently have focused on the social aspects of reading and writing. Although no one would dispute that dialogue in the classroom doorway is a social event, reading a play, discussing a chapter in a social studies book, and writing a story can also

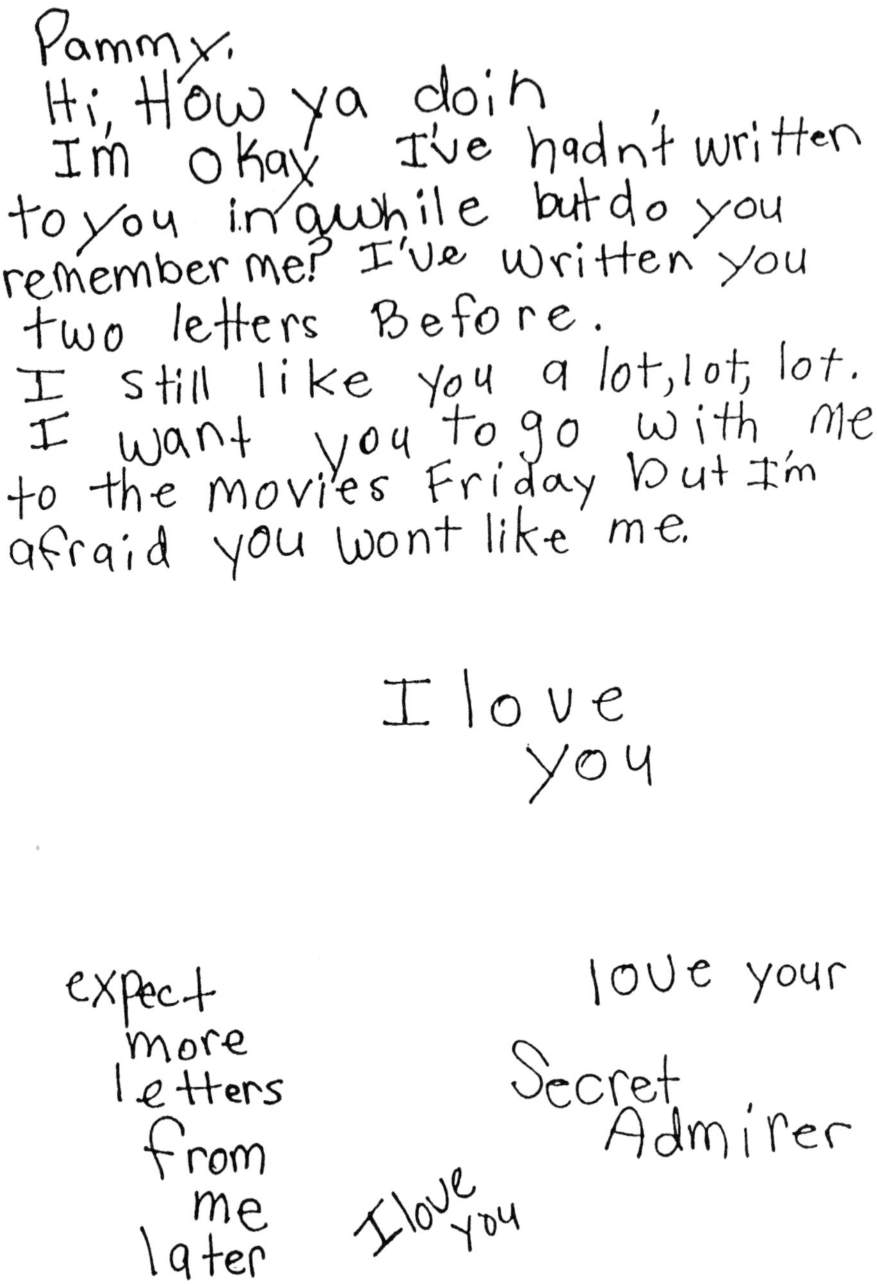

Pammy,
Hi, How ya doin
I'm okay I've hadn't written to you in awhile but do you remember me? I've written you two letters Before.
I still like you a lot, lot, lot.
I want you to go with me to the movies Friday but I'm afraid you wont like me.

I love
you

expect
more
letters
from
me
later

love your
Secret
Admirer

I love
you

FIGURE 1.3

Lynne,

I am writing you because you keep begging me so much. I asked Ms. Harris about our tests she said she have everything graded. I can't wait to join your Girl Scout troop. I bet you, me, and Karen have lots of fun.

(Best Friend Always)

Paula

P.S. Tell me the funny thing you said you had to tell me in your letter. Oh yeah, I forgot I am going to pay you your cookie money FRIDAY! tomorrow!

Paula

Sorry
o
Sloppy

Long
Letter
Later

Friends
Forever

FIGURE 1.4

be social events. Passing notes during class creates an opportunity to interact socially. Conversely, reading can serve as a barrier to social activity when a student hides behind a book to avoid social interaction.

Just as speakers and listeners interact in social situations, readers and writers can interact through text. "When readers understand a text, an exchange of meaning has taken place. Writers have succeeded in speaking to readers" (Nystrand & Himley, 1984, p. 198). To understand a social studies chapter concerning another culture, students must possess and activate information about how people behave politically, economically, spiritually, and socially. After reading and understanding the text, students can add this information to their store of social knowledge and apply it to a new learning situation. To understand a piece of literature, students must activate what they know about people and their relationships (Bruce, 1981).

"In responding as members of an interpretive community, readers share certain strategies and conventions valued by the group" (Beach, 1993, p. 106). As students gain experience socially, they learn acceptable responses while reading or listening; that is, they learn the norms of the "interpretive community." As students become more proficient with abstract thinking, they are better able to perceive themselves as members of the community and internalize socially acceptable responses. Of course, families and communities help to shape roles, perceptions, and attitudes of students. When students are allowed and encouraged to read and write about things that are congruent with their home culture, they may read and write more and with more sophistication (Moll & Diaz, 1987).

Intense interest in themselves and social interactions, emotional ups and downs, and a new capacity for analytical thought can be used to help young adolescents become more literate. Many teachers unfortunately view these manifestations as interruptions to instruction, whereas other teachers recognize them as opportunities to capitalize on student strengths and interests to facilitate learning.

It is within school that most people become literate. Young adolescents are still developing an understanding of appropriate responses to reading, listening, or viewing and, as stated, families and communities shape their understandings. Literacy learning is a complex process that is influenced by cognition and motivation. Equally important, however, is the social context within which students understand and respond to literacy events.

Philosophical Transformations

In the last fifteen years, reading educators have witnessed a remarkable transformation in the philosophical foundation of the field. This transformation has been pervasive, including the fundamental beliefs of educators regarding how children become literate, the day-to-day learning activities, and the materials designed to teach reading. In the last decade, teachers have received staff development in such areas as whole language, cooperative learning, authentic assessment, inquiry teaching, problem solving, literature-based instruction, higher order thinking, process writing, integrated instruction, learning styles, strategic teaching, and test-taking abilities. This list is not exhaustive but points to a philosophical focusing that embraces process learning, child-centered approaches, context-rich and authentic environments, and collaboration.

A few concepts are essential to understand this new movement in education. This section contains a quick overview of whole language, whole learning, social constructivism, reader response, schema theory, strategic learning, metacognition, and scaffolding. Although this attempt to clarify these key concepts in literacy learning is ambitious, hopefully it will serve as a quick reference. These concepts will be elaborated on and applied throughout this book.

Whole Language

Whole language as a movement began in the early 1980s and has successfully discredited the subskills orientation to reading instruction rooted in behaviorist psychological principals (Grundin, 1994). "Whole language literacy instruction is the simultaneous, integrated teaching of reading, writing, speaking, and listening within a context that is meaningful to the language learner" (Baumann, 1985, p. 5). Whole language philosophy has transformed elementary reading curriculum (generally delivered through thematic units), instruction (teacher facilitates and students discover), assessment (authentic and portfolios), and materials (more real literature and fewer worksheets). Whole language can be summarized in the following tenets:

- Reading, writing, speaking, and listening should be based on similar principles and processes.
- Language should not be taught in a fragmented manner.
- Working on one aspect of language (e.g., reading) automatically helps other aspects such as spelling, grammar, punctuation, and other language skills.
- Language is a meaning-centered activity and, above all, is meant to make sense.
- Language is learned through use. A person learns to read by reading, to write by writing, and to speak by speaking (Goodman, Smith, Meredith, & Goodman, 1987).

Whole language philosophy influenced the development of an approach called *Reading/Writing Workshop* implemented in many middle level schools (Atwell, 1987; Rief, 1992). Student choice of literature with authentic and shared process writing experiences makes this approach viable for young adolescents. The key component of whole language is that language learning is kept "whole."

Whole Learning

In the elementary grades, themes are used to organize the curriculum. One or two teachers can naturally integrate literature and social studies or science themes. Whole language, in a more departmentalized middle level school, seems to refer only to the language arts curriculum. Whole learning embodies whole language philosophy but implies a more interdisciplinary or integrated curriculum. Whole learning "challenges traditional, fragmented, skill and drill, pitcher-into-vessel transmission approaches [and] includes words and phrases such as the following: social constructivism, student- or learner-centered approaches; integrated, integrative, interdisciplinary, multi-disciplinary, holistic, or thematic curriculum" (Pace, 1995, p. 13).

Social Constructivism

The theory of social constructivism suggests that individuals "make meaning" from text (or speech, or viewing) and that the social and cultural context heavily influences the interpretations. This view is consistent with whole language philosophy in which active engagement with the text is an essential element for comprehension. Individuals construct meaning based on their knowledge, experience, cultural background, and social context. Students "construct" knowledge through reading, writing, and working on projects in collaborative groups.

Reader Response

Constuctivism supports the reader response theory, which suggests that "readers have a wide range of responses to literary works and encourages teachers to promote and accept a range of responses" (Graves & Graves, 1994) including drawing, writing a story, retelling, and so forth. Just as readers construct their own understandings of text, they may respond in a variety of ways.

Schema Theory

Meaningful learning occurs when a student relates new information to what is already known; that is, it is nearly impossible to learn new information that has no connection to what is already known. Schemata comprise all of the information and the experience that the reader has stored in memory. A particular schema, then, represents all the associations that come to mind when a person reads about a certain subject. For example, you probably have a schema for the object labeled "computers." You have a mental picture of what does or does not characterize a computer. You also bring to that basic picture many other associations. If you are a "user," your schema of computers may be merged with positive feelings of limitless possibilities. If the computer revolution has left you behind with your yellow legal pads and typewriter, you may have feelings of anxiety or frustration as you approach a computer. A person's schema determines the sum total of all thoughts about and reactions toward a certain subject. Readers cannot separate their schemata from what they read; thus, their schemata influence the interpretation of what they read.

Thelen (1986) likened schema to a file folder. Everyone has a unique and personal way of organizing cognitive structures (the cabinet). The schemata are the ideas contained within the file folders. Learners must be shown where and how new material fits into the existing structures. Because each reader has a unique organization, it is important that teachers help students engage their schemata to connect new information to what is already known. For this process to occur, students must be able to determine what is known and what is *not* known.

Strategic Learning

Suppose that during a racquetball game you hit a straight shot down the right side of the court and your opponent misses the ball. The point is yours. This well-placed shot may have been luck, or it may have been the result of a strategy. Before you hit the ball, you noted that your opponent was standing in the middle of the court and you remembered that she is left-handed with a weak backhand. You hit the ball deliberately and strategically.

This analogy can be applied to reading. Strategic reading involves analyzing the reading task, establishing a purpose for reading, and then selecting strategies for this purpose (Paris, Lipson, & Wixson, 1983). A strategy is a conscious effort on the part of the reader to attend to comprehension while reading, listening, or participating in any learning event. It may be helpful to distinguish between the term "strategies" and the more traditional term "skills."

- Strategies emphasize intentional and deliberate plans; skills are more automatic.
- Strategies emphasize reasoning and cognitive sophistication; skills are associated with lower levels of thinking and learning.
- Strategies are flexible and adaptable; skills connote consistency in application across tasks.
- Strategies imply an awareness or reflection on what they are doing while learning; skills imply an automatic response to learning (Dole, Duffy, Roehler, & Pearson, 1991, p. 242).

An emerging skill can become a strategy when it is used intentionally (Paris, Wasik, & Turner, 1991). Strategic learners know whether they understand what they read or what they hear and are willing to use any of a number of available strategies to help them understand better. Over a period of years, efficient learners may develop many strategies to help them construct meaning.

Metacognition

Learning is often referred to as a cognitive event. It is that, but it is also a metacognitive event. Cognition refers to using the knowledge possessed; metacognition refers to a person's awareness and understanding of that knowledge. "Cognition refers to having the skills; metacognition refers to awareness of and conscious control over those skills" (Stewart & Tei, 1983, p. 36).

Students may thumb through a difficult text while thinking about a school party; *knowing* they are not paying attention to the text is a metacognitive event. Strategic readers would do something—refocus and pay attention, close the book for later, or begin to take notes to organize their thoughts. Good readers who have developed metacognitive awareness do *something;* less proficient readers plow merrily (or not so merrily) along without stopping to assess, question, or correct the condition.

Proficient readers monitor their own comprehension and are able to apply strategies to help them understand, such as rereading, reading ahead, or searching their prior knowledge to make sense of text. In other words, they know when what they are reading is making sense, and they know what to do when it is not. Good listeners also know when speech does not make sense to them; they ask questions, take notes, and increase their concentration as they listen. Metacognition develops as a student matures, usually during adolescence, but it can be taught and strengthened by explicit instruction and practice even at earlier ages (Palincsar & Brown, 1983).

Scaffolding

"A Scaffolded Reading Experience is a set of prereading, during-reading, and postreading activities specifically designed to assist a particular group of students in successfully reading, understanding, learning from, and enjoying a particular selection" (Graves & Graves, 1994). A scaffold is a temporary structure that supports a person for a particular task that could not be performed without it, such as training wheels for a child's bicycle.

If a person believes that a student gets better at reading by reading and writing by writing, then repeated and successful reading and writing are necessary. When teachers design instruction to provide enough support to ensure a successful reading or writing experience, they are scaffolding.

Purpose and Overview of the Book

Reading this book should assist educators in applying current research and theory in the field of literacy to teaching and learning in the middle grades. "Literacy" as used throughout this book refers to any reading, writing, speaking, or listening event. The focus of this book is primarily on reading, which is only one of the four language systems and should be learned within the context of writing, speaking, listening, and thinking. Although topics such as the writing process and higher order thinking are not specifically addressed in this book, most educators certainly recognize the necessity for integrating the instruction of all language systems with the development of thinking abilities.

The book is divided into two parts: (1) what educators need to know to make instructional decisions and (2) what educators need to know to make programmatic decisions.

Making Instructional Decisions

To make the best decisions concerning instruction, teachers need (1) a thorough knowledge of their content area(s); (2) an intimate understanding of students—how they feel, think, and react; (3) an understanding of the nature of the language and literacy learning process; and (4) a knowledge of how and when to apply instructional learning strategies to teach both process and content. Through an understanding of content, of students, of the learning process, and of strategies that facilitate growth, educators can draw on students' natural desires to communicate and thereby improve their ability to read, write, speak, listen, and think.

Content

Because teachers in middle level schools have presumably mastered knowledge of the content they teach (social studies, science, literature), for the purposes of this book, knowledge of content will not be addressed.

Students

Recent advances in psychology, medicine, and education have yielded new knowledge about the physiology and psychology of young adolescents. Because this period is a unique time of life, it is imperative that middle level educators understand the special characteristics of young adolescents. Chapter 2 describes these characteristics so that teachers can plan instruction that meets student needs. The implications for instruction described at the end of the chapter provide a basis for the strategies suggested throughout the remainder of the book.

Nature of the Learning Process

During the last decade, educators have witnessed unprecedented advances in knowledge of the basic processes involved in reading, teaching, and learning. A study by the National Assessment of Educational Progress (1985, p. 8) reported that

> *There has been a conceptual shift in the way many researchers and teachers think about reading, which gives students a much more active role in the learning and reading comprehension process. This shift is reflected in changes from packaged reading programs to experiences with books and from concentration on isolated skills to practical reading and writing activities.*

The more teachers understand the learning process, the better they will be able to evaluate and improve the learning environments they create. The following statement from *Becoming a Nation of Readers* (Anderson, Hiebert, Scott, & Wilkinson, 1985, p. 3) helps educators understand that educators now have the tools to improve learning for students.

> *The knowledge is now available to make worthwhile improvements in reading throughout the United States. If the practices seen in the classrooms of the best teachers in the best schools could be introduced everywhere, improvements in reading would be dramatic.*

In Chapter 3, the nature of the learning process and suggested instructional methods are discussed. In Chapter 4, the issue of student motivation and underachievement is addressed. In Chapter 5, Lorraine Gerhart describes the environment for the new assessment and provides sample student work for both performance assessment and portfolios. In Chapter 6, factors relating to student interest and to the demands of text are discussed. In Chapter 7, Carol Lynch-Brown presents innovative ways to foster intensive and extensive reading through literature.

Effective Learning Strategies

Literacy instruction is designed to help students become more independent learners. The role of the teacher in this process is to model, guide, and provide for practice. Learning strategies help students to make sense of their reading and writing. In Chapters 8 through 11, many strategies are presented on developing vocabulary and improving reading comprehension.

Making Programmatic Decisions

The way a school is organized can help or hinder literacy instruction. Aspects of middle school organization lend themselves well to improved reading and writing instruction. An historical perspective of the middle school movement serves as a background for a description of current practices in the middle level reading program and the description of exemplary practices found currently in middle level schools and districts.

Middle Level Schools

In addition to advances in knowledge of reading and learning, the last two decades have also brought a transformation within the middle school movement. The middle school concept has matured and become more focused. Middle level educators seem more sensitive to their students' sometimes tumultuous struggle to leave childhood behind as they enter young adulthood. A new definition and a new impetus for middle level education are presented and issues in middle level education are discussed in Chapter 12.

The Reading Program

Traditionally, reading instruction in the middle level school has been delivered in a separate class labeled "reading" and writing has been the exclusive domain of the language arts teacher. In Chapter 13, a discussion of traditional practices in reading instruction is presented as well as new trends toward integration and whole learning. Recommended components of a successful reading program at the middle level are presented.

Exemplary Practices

The gap between current research and theory and current practice disturbs most educators. One step toward bridging that gap is to study schools that are actually implementing a program that is consistent with current research and theory. Five programs are described in detail in Chapter 14. Programs were selected because they had a commitment to literacy learning for all students, had building and administrative support, maintained a middle school organization, and focused on a commitment to teach reading across the content areas and foster wide reading through literature.

Any experienced teacher knows that teaching in the middle grades is never boring—often frustrating—but never boring. Young adolescents are alive with language. Somehow that excitement evaporates when they enter a classroom. Teachers must find the connection between the students' need to communicate and their own need to educate.

Summary

The middle level school provides the last chance for educators to help students become proficient readers and writers. Students who are confident in their ability to read and write hold the key to independent learning. What is necessary to enable students to achieve this goal? Teachers must understand their content; understand the physical, emotional, social, intellectual, and moral needs of students; and understand the nature of learning and the teaching of language. Beyond this, those making administrative decisions must understand how to organize the learning environment for the teaching of reading and writing at the middle level. Finally, educators must find ways to capitalize on young adolescents' natural desire to use language in the way in which it was intended—as a means of communication.

References

Anderson, R.C., Hiebert, E.H., Scott, J.A., & Wilkinson, I.A.G. (1985). *Becoming a Nation of Readers: The Report of the Commission on Reading.* Champaign, IL: Center for the Study of Reading.

Atwell, N. (1987). *In the Middle: Writing, Reading, and Learning with Adolescents.* Portsmouth, NH: Boynton/Cook.

Baumann, J.F. (1985). *Whole Language Instruction and Basal Readers.* Occasional paper in reading and language arts (No. 20). Needham Heights, MA: Silver Burdett & Ginn.

Beach, R. (1993). *A Teacher's Introduction to Reader-Response Theories.* Urbana, IL: National Council of Teachers of English.

Bruce, B.C. (1981). *A Social Interaction Model of Reading* (Technical Report No. 218). ED 208 363. Champaign, IL: Center for the Study of Reading.

Dole, J.A., Duffy, G.G., Roehler, L.R., & Pearson, P.D. (1991). Moving from the old to the new: Research on reading comprehension instruction. *Review of Educational Research, 61*(2), 239–264.

Goodman, K.S., Smith, E.B., Meredith, R., & Goodman, Y.M. (1987). *Language and Thinking in School: A Whole-Language Curriculum.* Katonah, NY: Owen.

Graves, M.F. & Graves, B.B. (1994). *Scaffolding Reading Experiences.* Norwood, MA: Christopher-Gordon Publishers.

Grundin, H.U. (1994). If it ain't whole, it ain't language—or back to the basics of freedom and dignity. In F. Lehr & J. Osborn (Eds.), *Reading, Language and Literacy: Instruction for the 21st Century* (pp. 77–100). Hillsdale, NJ: Lawrence Erlbaum Associates.

Moll, L. & Diaz, R. (1987). Teaching writing as communication: The use of ethnographic findings in classroom practice. In D. Bloome (Ed.), *Literacy and Schooling* (pp. 193–221). Norwood, NJ: Ablex.

National Assessment of Educational Progress. (1985). *The Reading Report Card.* Princeton, NJ: Educational Testing Service.

Nystrand, M. & Himley, M. (1984). Written text as social interaction. *Theory into Practice, 23*(3), 198–207.

Pace, G. (1995). Whole learning and a holistic vision of the middle school: Principles that guide practice. In G. Pace (Ed.), *Whole Learning in the Middle School: Evolution and Transition* (pp. 11–26). Norwood, MA: Christopher-Gordon Publishers.

Palincsar, A.S. & Brown, A.L. (1983). *Reciprocal teaching of comprehension-monitoring activities* (Technical Report No. 269). Champaign, IL: Center for the Study of Reading.

Paris, S., Lipson, M.Y., & Wixson, K.K. (1983). Becoming a strategic reader. *Contemporary Educational Psychology, 8*(3), 293–316.

Paris, S.G., Wasik, B.A., & Turner, J.C. (1991). The development of strategic readers. In R. Barr, M. Kamil, P.B. Mosenthal, & P.D. Pearson (Eds.), *Handbook of Reading Research* (pp. 143–166). Chicago: National Reading Conference.

Rief, L. (1992). *Seeking Diversity: Language Arts with Adolescents.* Portsmouth, NH: Heinemann.

Stewart, O. & Tei, O. (1983). Some implications of metacognition for reading instruction. *Journal of Reading, 27*(1), 36–43.

Thelen, J.N. (1986). Vocabulary instruction and meaningful learning. *Journal of Reading, 29*(7), 603–609.

Vygotsky, L.S. (1962). *Thought and Language.* Cambridge: MIT Press.

Chapter 2

The Young Adolescent

Anyone who has walked the halls of a middle level school has probably encountered flying arms and legs, changing voices, and behavior that ranges from childish to mature. Within any middle grades classroom, it is common to find students varying in height from six to eight inches and in weight as much as forty to sixty pounds. More extreme differences are not uncommon. This variety in physical growth is further compounded by a wide range of emotional maturity, intellectual ability, attentiveness, and interest. To make life still more interesting, individual students, reacting to changes in their bodies, may not even display the same behavior from day to day. These factors make the middle level school a fascinating place in which to teach.

Knowledge of the rapid and profound changes that young adolescents experience may help teachers understand, if not fully endorse, the behavior they display. With the onset of puberty, students undergo a series of swift and dramatic physical changes. With these physical changes come changes in intellectual capacity and in emotional stability. Many students begin to develop the ability to think abstractly. Most middle level teachers know too well that students' emotions tend to run high at this age and are often unpredictable. This period of life is also characterized by a new sense of social awareness in which students move from the security of the family to an added dependence on relationships with their peers. Coping with and adapting to these new experiences are often difficult for young adolescents as Figure 2.1 illustrates.

In this chapter, the physical, social, emotional, cognitive, and moral development of middle grades students will be examined, as well as the way in which our culture influences children's development to maturity. Finally, implications for instruction will be drawn from these factors for the benefit of the teachers of these interesting students.

Physical Development

With the exception of the period from birth to age 3, more changes occur during early adolescence (approximately 10 to 14 years of age) than at any other time in a person's life.

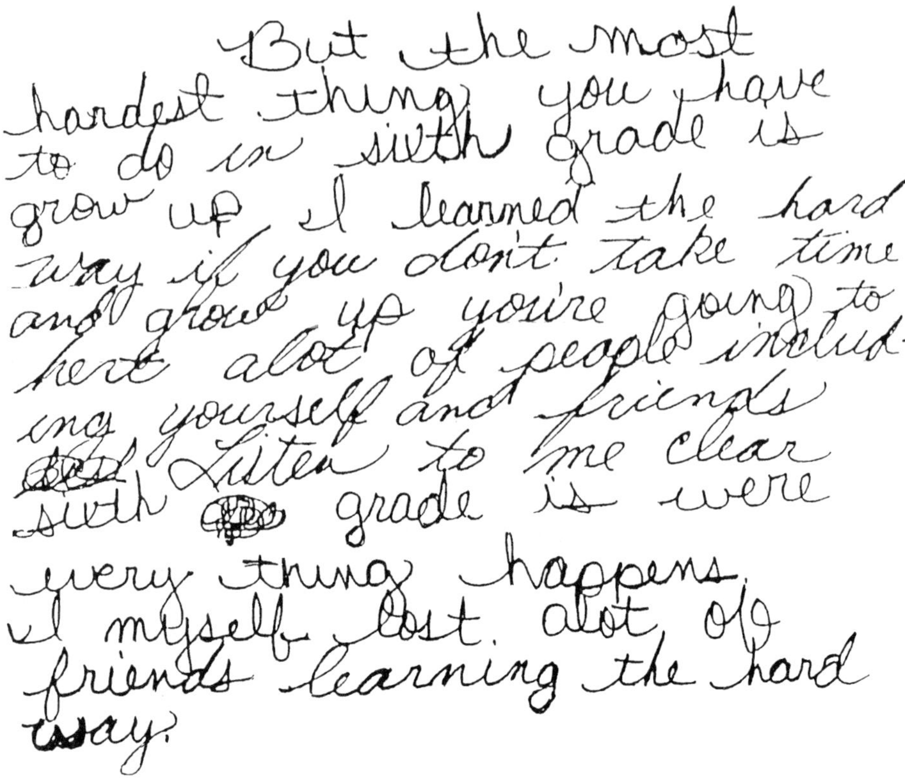

But the most
hardest thing you have
to do in sixth grade is
grow up I learned the hard
way if you don't take time
and grow up you're going to
hert alot of people including yourself and friends
Listen to me clear
sixth grade is were
very thing happens.
I myself lost alot of
friends learning the hard
way.

FIGURE 2.1

Consider how most adults would react if they were to undergo three years of radical changes in stature, sexual development and interest, and other bodily changes. Add to this list the fact that they will tend to be moody, physically awkward, and have numerous skin blemishes. Under such circumstances, most adults would likely become egocentric and self-conscious just as most young adolescents do. A sixth-grade student clarifies some of the issues of physical development in Figure 2.2.

The most dramatic and obvious changes are those associated with rapid physical growth and development. Puberty is preceded by a growth spurt with marked increase in height, weight, heart rate, lung capacity, and muscular strength. Bone grows faster than muscle, which may leave bones unprotected by muscles and tendons. Middle level students often have problems with coordination as a result of this rapid growth; thus, they are often characterized as awkward. Although all young adolescents experience this growth spurt, girls tend to undergo these changes approximately two years earlier than boys.

Sexual maturation is the other obvious physical change to which young adolescents must adjust. The average age at onset of puberty shows a trend toward earlier occurrence due to improvements in nutrition and general health care (Brooks-Gunn & Reiter, 1990). Physical changes are viewed as a cultural event that marks a transition clearly visible to peers and adults. Whenever young people experience these changes, the appearance of

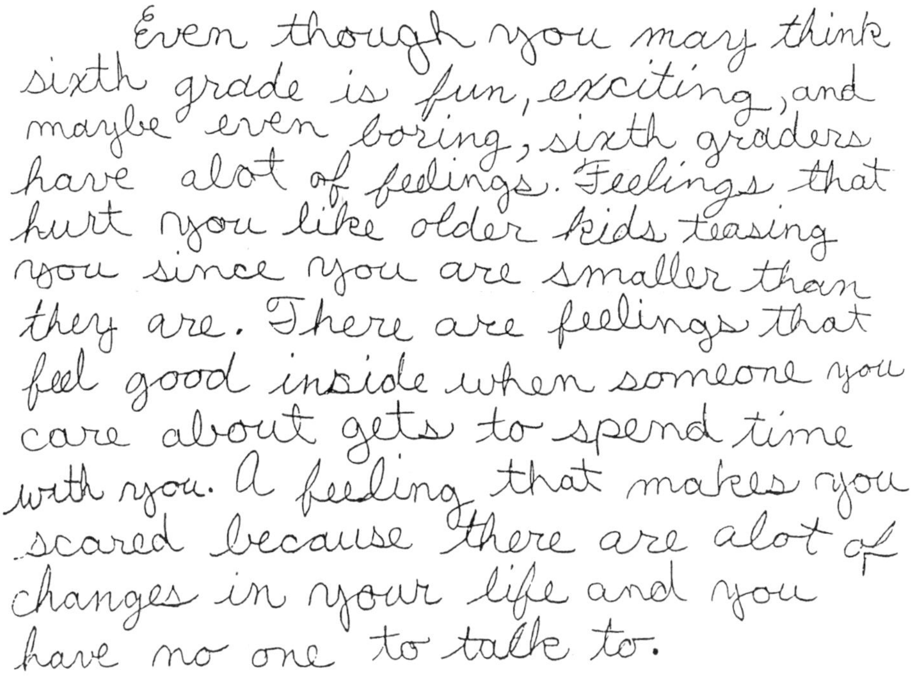

Even though you may think sixth grade is fun, exciting, and maybe even boring, sixth graders have alot of feelings. Feelings that hurt you like older kids teasing you since you are smaller than they are. There are feelings that feel good inside when someone you care about gets to spend time with you. A feeling that makes you scared because there are alot of changes in your life and you have no one to talk to.

FIGURE 2.2

secondary sex characteristics often makes them self-conscious about their bodies. Being off time with respect to maturation is what generally causes concern in young adolescents. Rice (1990) described the following off time maturation patterns.

- Early maturing boys are large for their age, stronger, more muscular, and better coordinated than late maturing boys. They are often treated like adults and chosen for leadership roles. Early sexual maturation thrusts them into heterosexual relationships at an early age.
- Late maturing boys suffer socially induced feelings of inferiority because coordination and size play a significant role in social acceptance. Late maturers sometimes overcompensate by becoming overly dependent on others or overly eager for status and attention. These negative attitudes may persist into adulthood long after the physical differences and their social importance have disappeared (*Youth: Transition to Adulthood,* 1974).
- Early maturing girls have difficulty adjusting to unwanted attention, especially if they are still in elementary school (Blyth, Simmons, & Zakin, 1985; Simmons, Blyth, & McKinney, 1983). Early maturing girls tend to associate with older peers who look more like them; thus, trying on more adult behaviors earlier such as dating, smoking, and drinking (Savin-Williams & Berndt, 1990). These girls may have a less positive body image than other girls, at least during the middle school years.

- Late maturing girls are often treated like little girls and are envious of the attention experienced by early maturers. They do have the advantage of observing changes relatively unnoticed and do not receive as much criticism from parents and other adults (Rice, 1990, p. 159–163).

Whether on or off time, most educators agree that, at this age, physical differences between students should be minimized by adults and in the school setting. Group showers and competitive sports, for example, merely accentuate the differences in physical ability and development. Information concerning the variability of growth spurts may be used to provide some reassurance for these students. It is helpful for students to realize that their development, whether early or late, is normal. Many teachers have found that books about adolescent development are helpful to students. Making an entry in a journal after each reading gives students an opportunity to identify with characters and to realize that "they are not the only ones."

A less obvious but fundamental physical change is the rate of basal metabolism. Young adolescents may be restless and active one minute and listless the next. Students at this age alternate between periods of great physical activity and fatigue. Understanding these different levels of activity may help teachers deal appropriately with the student who seems to fall asleep every afternoon as well as the student who never sits still. Activities in the classroom should be changed periodically; students simply cannot be expected to maintain quiet attention for forty to fifty minutes.

While students are attempting to adjust to these profound physical changes, changes in their relationships with parents and peers may compound the problem. If teachers understand the nature of these relationships, they may perhaps facilitate a smoother transition into new social situations.

Social Development

Those who live and work with young adolescents know that peers and social relationships are of extreme importance. Friendships are vital at this age, especially same-sex relationships. Feeling comfortable and secure with peers of the same sex at ages 10 to 12 helps adolescents progress toward opposite sex relationships that come later. Because rejection by peers represents a major crisis, students at this age spend much of their time trying to figure out ways to win acceptance by their peers. Figure 2.3 illustrates this point.

Notes such as these are common. The trying out of social situations is a part of social learning. Some experiences are fleeting, some agonizing, and some thoughtful; all are necessary because having friends helps to expand a person's world. "Friends allow us to compare families, contrast values, and take risks. Their reactions to our dress, our jokes, our athletic ability, and our appearance allow us to measure our ability in these areas" (Milgram, 1992).

Socialization is a developmental task of early adolescence. Savin-Williams & Berndt (1990) concluded that students who have "satisfying and harmonious friendships typically report positive self-esteem, a good understanding of other people's feelings, and relatively

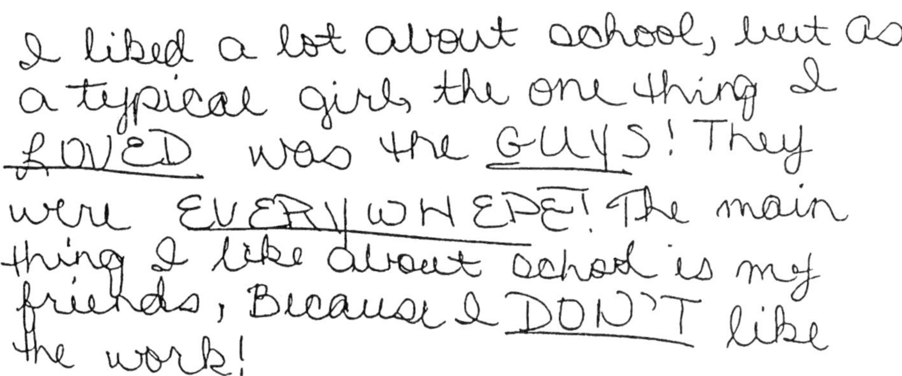

FIGURE 2.3

little loneliness" (p. 288). Additionally, those students "tend to behave appropriately in school, are motivated to do well, and often receive high grades" (p. 290). Adults often ridicule the time and intensity of phone conversations, frenzied note passing, and frequent broken hearts, but these interactions are "critical interpersonal bridges that move them toward psychological growth and social maturity" (p. 277).

A myth about the negative influence of peer groups has developed over the years. Recent research shows that young adolescents "do not routinely acquiesce to peer pressure. In fact, they are more likely to follow adults' than peers' advice in matters affecting their long-term future and they actually rely on their own judgment more often than that of either peers or parents" (Brown, 1990, p. 174). Peer groups usually reinforce rather than contradict the values of parents. It is not surprising that young adolescents tend to form friendships similar to the relationships they have with their families. Brown further concluded that students "seek out the peer group best suited to meeting their needs for emotional support and exploration or reaffirmation of their values and aspirations" (p. 180). Crowds, peer groups, and cliques are a natural part of middle school life. Figure 2.4 shows a sixth grade student's perception of social organization.

Students do not select a crowd as much as they are thrust into one by virtue of their personality, background, interests, and reputation among peers (Brown, 1990). A peer group is a place for trying out roles and ideas and serves as a validation of a student's value within a social unit beyond the family. Clasen and Brown (1987) argued that "teachers and administrators can have substantial impact on peer groups if they increase their awareness of school crowds and their norms" (p. 22). Students need many opportunities to experience success in socially acceptable ways so that the peer group reinforces prosocial activities.

Many parents feel rejected by their children's heightened interest in and growing dependence on their peers. This new attachment, however, does not occur at the expense of, but rather in addition to, parental affection. Hill (1980) asserted that research findings suggest that "authoritative parenting with its blend of nonsuffocating affection and moderate control provides a secure familial base for developing social competence in relation to peers and a degree of independence prior to adolescence" (p. 45). Although new peer

I sort of like middle school. It has it's bad parts of course. The most I like about 6th Grade is friends. The sort of friends you make is incredible skinheads, Geeks, morons, jocks, everybody, especially when your new they really treat you like your popular. In fact when I walk down the halls practicaly half the people know me. They all yell "hi."

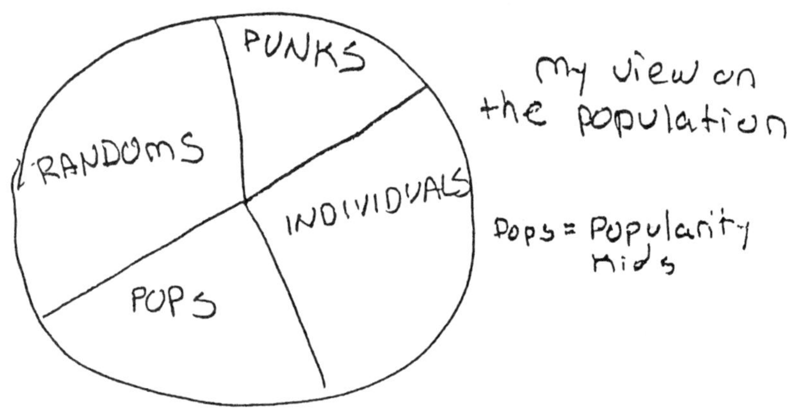

FIGURE 2.4

associations are vital to the young adolescent's social and emotional maturity, the family remains important to the young adolescent as Figure 2.5 illustrates.

Student relationships with both family and peers at this time can either augment or diminish a positive self-concept. Social validation is important for young adolescents to build and maintain a positive self-concept (Milgram, 1985). It is therefore imperative that educators recognize the developmental needs of young adolescents and provide opportunities for appropriate socialization. Teachers in middle level schools who accommodate rather than deny this socialization facilitate growth in this important developmental task.

Emotional Development

Perhaps because of the cumulative physical, social, and psychological changes experienced by young adolescents, adults have traditionally viewed early adolescence as a time of turbulence and disruption (Hill, 1980). Recent information, however (Brooks-

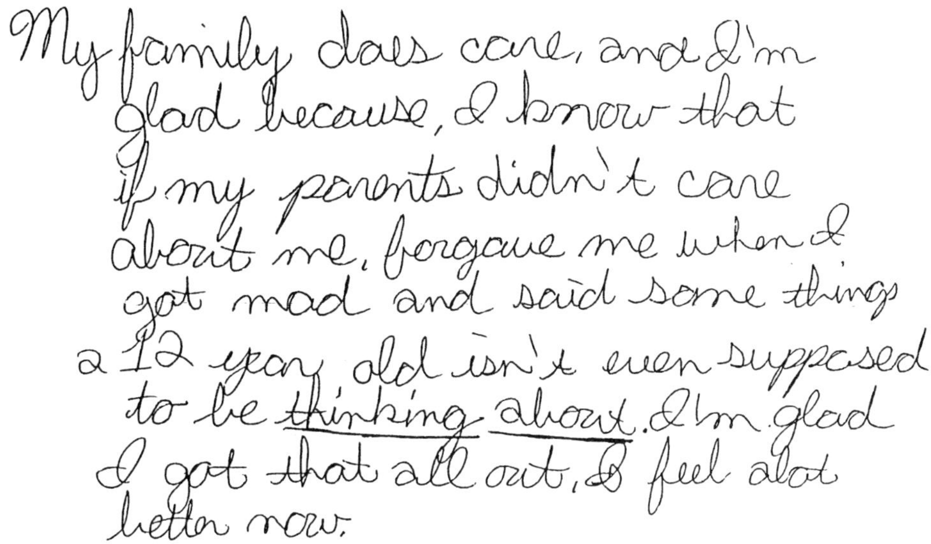

My family does care, and I'm glad because, I know that if my parents didn't care about me, forgave me when I got mad and said some things a 12 year old isn't even supposed to be thinking about. I'm glad I got that all out, I feel alot better now.

FIGURE 2.5

Gunn & Reiter, 1990; Hauser & Bowlds, 1990; Offer, Ostrov, & Howard, 1989; Scales, 1991; Steinberg, 1990), clearly indicates that it is a small percentage of students (less than 20 percent) who exhibit signs of serious disturbance and need adult intervention. Although the changes experienced are stressful for most young people, Dorman and Lipsitz (1981) argued that adults should "distinguish between behavior that is distressing (annoying to others) and behavior that is disturbed (harmful to the young person exhibiting the behavior)" (p. 4). When adults expect irresponsible behavior, they may, indeed, exacerbate the occurrence.

Emotions, both happy and sad, run high at this age. A teacher may observe the same girl happy and giggling at one minute, and sad and tearful the next minute. These extremes in emotion, probably caused by hormonal activity, are normal experiences and are heightened by the young adolescents' feelings of confusion about the changes within themselves and about their place within the social group. Figure 2.6 illustrates this point.

Changes in intellectual functioning may be the partial cause of emotional changes. "The advent of formal operational thought is considered by most to be a prerequisite for adolescent self-reflection. The very ability to think about one's thinking, to reflect on internal events, does not become fully developed until this period" (Harter, 1990, p. 362). During the middle years, young adolescents recognize that they are the potential focus of another's attention. For the first time in their development, they are able to take the other person's perspective. This new perspective leads to an egocentrism when they "assume themselves to be a focus of *most* other people's perspectives *much* of the time" (Keating, 1990, p. 71). The emergence of formal thinking is necessary to complete two essential developmental tasks: development of a positive self-esteem and attainment of personal autonomy.

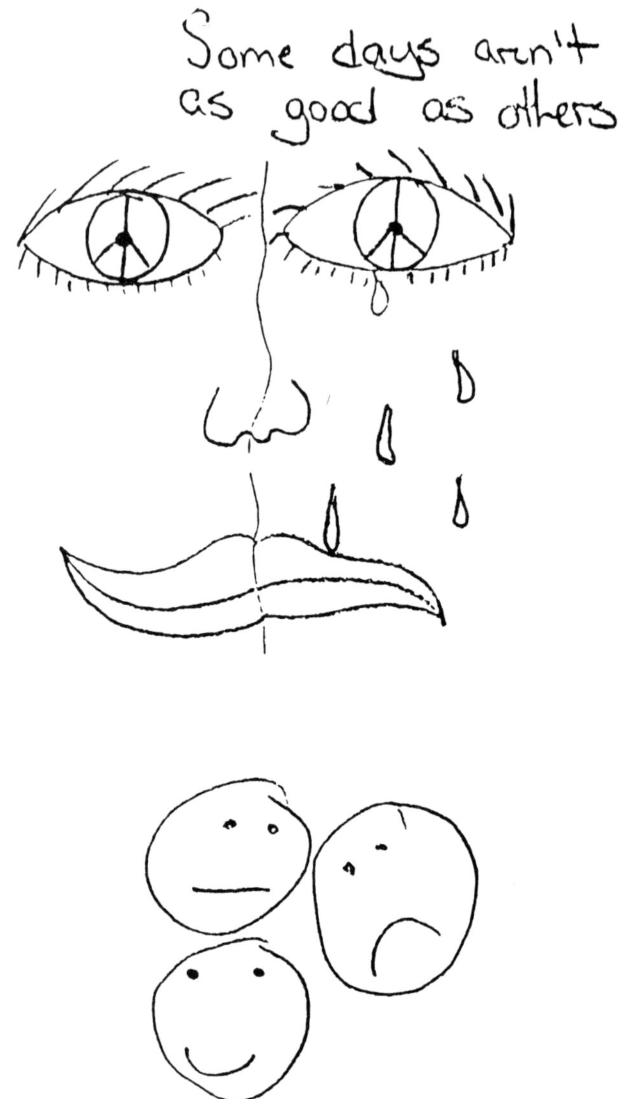

FIGURE 2.6

Self-Esteem and Self-Concept

The development of a personal identity is difficult until children move beyond concrete levels of thinking that enable them to be self-conscious and introspective. Beane and Lipka (1986) distinguished between self-concept and self-esteem. A *self-concept* is a description of roles and attributes (I am tall, I am the baby of the family). *Self-esteem* is the evaluation of one's self-concept (I like being tall, I don't get much attention in my family). The development of a positive self-esteem takes reflection, introspection, comparisons with others, and a sensitivity to the opinions of other people. These processes only become possible with the advent of formal thinking.

Self-esteem declines at age 11 and reaches a low point between 12 and 13 (Brack, Orr, & Ingersoll, 1988; Harter, 1990). Students, especially girls, who shift to a large, impersonal junior high school at the seventh grade exhibit long-term negative effects on their self-esteem (Simmons & Blyth, 1987) particularly because of the interruption of peer groups. "Schools that emphasize competition, social comparison, and ability self-assessment" can deteriorate students' academic motivation and self-esteem (Wigfield & Eccles, 1994).

Youth from a cultural minority have an especially difficult time forming an identity when the values of their culture may clash with the values and standards of the dominant culture. Having successful role models and negotiating a balance between the two value systems can help these youth form a positive self-esteem (Spencer & Dornbusch, 1990).

In a thorough review of relevant literature on self-esteem, Kohn (1994) questioned the value of programs designed to enhance self-esteem. Educators would do better to treat students with "respect [rather] than shower them with praise" (p. 282). "When members of a class meet to make decisions and solve problems, they get the self-esteem building message that their voices count, they experience a sense of belonging to a community, and they hone their ability to reason and analyze" (p. 279). A meaningful curriculum (Beane & Lipka, 1986); a safe, intellectual challenge (Wigfield & Eccles, 1994); and meaningful success experiences (Kohn, 1994) lead to the long lasting development of positive self-esteem.

Personal Autonomy

Another developmental task that sometimes leads to emotional trauma is a young adolescent's need to establish autonomy. The onset of adolescence is a time for major realignments in relationships with adults both at home and at school. Steinberg (1990) took a sociobiological perspective of "intergenerational conflict" (family fighting). He suggested that "bickering and squabbling at puberty is an atavism that ensures that adolescents will spend time away from the family of origin and mate outside the natal group" (p. 269). Disagreement becomes a vehicle to inform parents about changing self-conceptions and expectations and an opportunity to shed the view that parents can do no wrong. Of course, this low level conflict must begin with an already strong emotional bond between parents and children. If relationships are not strong before puberty, and often stepchildren and stepparents have a particularly rough time, this fighting can become destructive as Figure 2.7 illustrates.

Although Steinberg did not address bickering outside the family, the need for autonomy and control remains strong at school as well. Teachers, then, become the target of student frustration as shown in Figure 2.8.

Young adolescents are treated like children one minute, adults another. Their ambiguous status in society and their new powers of reasoning cause them frustration that occasionally leads to their lashing out at adults. Although much of young adolescent behavior appears

My mom as slaped me
arcoss my face. two
Times and I know
my sisters barly been
toched!! I dont like
school at all I
want ta go back
to my old shool,
friends, dad, dog,
and my house.
Part (4/5) is becuse
I dont like my
stepdad at all
he does the same
thing just becuse
my sister's perfect,
older, a knows mou
he yells at me
all the time and
someday Im
going ta yell
at him back!!!
Thats whats
not getting
me good grades
at my old schol
I got good
grades!

FIGURE 2.7

They call this back talk. Why I think someone should let them know how it feels because I sure will lay it own them. They think they're big shots but for all I care they can go to ##@?!. Teachers should give there money to charity and we should get the 71% increase on student salaries. Teachers should be fired & we hired.

FIGURE 2.8

rejecting, this is not the time for adults to alienate themselves. "Current research . . . indicates that early separation and emotional emancipation from family or significant adults can have a negative effect on adolescents" (Irwin & Vaughn, 1988, p. 12). Early separation results in an increased risk of susceptibility to negative peer influences and participation in unhealthy, even risky, behaviors.

The onset of formal thinking triggers a host of emotional tasks to be completed, not the least of which is the development of a positive self-esteem and some degree of autonomy from parents and teachers. New cognitive capacities often lead to difficulty in controlling and applying them. The by-products of this difficulty are emotional turmoil, erratic behavior, and egocentrism. Although these characteristics are troublesome for adults and students alike, they are a natural part of the transition to adulthood.

Cognitive Development

An understanding of the cognitive changes that take place in students is of paramount importance in planning a meaningful curriculum and establishing appropriate classroom practices. This age is characterized by a new capacity for thought. Students are moving from the *concrete* stage (able to think logically about real experiences) to the *formal* stage (able to consider "what ifs," think reflectively, and reason abstractly). This intellectual change is gradual and may occur at different times for different students, but generally begins at age 12 and is not firmly established until approximately age 15. Students may even shift back and forth from the concrete to the abstract, although it is important to remember that not all young adolescents, not even all adults, achieve this capacity.

Cognitive growth is intricately linked to social and emotional development. In fact, this new capacity for abstract thinking helps young adolescents make sense of new social demands, new feelings, and an emerging self-concept. The note written by Tammy

(Chapter 1, Figure 1.1) is an example of the sometimes complex social interactions young adolescents struggle with every day. Working out the love lives of Andy, Amy, Alex, and Erika takes an understanding of acceptable preteen behavior, the individual personalities involved, and the range of feelings elicited from such interactions. Social and emotional growth and cognitive functioning work hand in hand to facilitate the development of all areas. Abstract thinking is developed as young people struggle to make sense of their feelings, the behavior of others, and their place within a social context.

The cognitive activity known as *metacognition* actually regulates and controls social and emotional activity, and provides "the ability to monitor one's own cognitive activity for consistency, [and] for gaps in information that need to be filled" (Keating, 1990, p. 75). It is important to remember, however, that these new metacognitive abilities for young adolescents represent "*potential* accomplishments rather than typical everyday thinking" (p. 65). Most students display formal thinking consistently at age 15 or 16. Until that time, during early adolescence, students are practicing this new ability. Like any new skill, formal reasoning must be practiced repeatedly in a safe, encouraging environment.

Young adolescents often have difficulty with such tasks as analyzing political cartoons and understanding metaphors. Students do, however, need to personalize the abstract. Figure 2.9 is an example of a sixth grade student explaining his experiences in metaphoric language.

This practice helps students make the transition to consistent formal reasoning. Inferential leaps should be small, sometimes minuscule for young adolescents to "get" to the level of abstract thinking. For example, one middle grades teacher knew from past experience that *Johnny Tremain* (Forbes, 1943), although a classic and a favorite of hers, caused students difficulty because it introduced such concepts as apprenticeship and revolution (Simpson, 1986). She read the book aloud. After discussing a chapter, students made entries in their response journals for five to ten minutes. She received comments such as: "I liked writing in journals because I can tell you how I feel about the story even if I don't share it out loud" (p. 49). Johnny's perspective, historical and personal, came to be appreciated by these students. Through the discussion and the journal writing, Johnny's time, place, and struggle became real. Some teachers report that journal writing is a way to help students make "the small inferential leaps" to more abstract thoughts.

Strahan and Toepfer (1984) hypothesized that "latent formal thinkers" may solve problems if given a second try and a moderate amount of prompting. Perhaps Simpson's strategy of having students listen to, discuss, and write about *Johnny Tremain* allowed the potential "latent formal thinkers" a chance to explore abstract thought in a success-oriented way.

The young adolescent is egocentric; but the emerging formal thinker is, for the first time, able to consider the thoughts of others. Discussion and debate help students consider issues that are important to them and resolve conflicting viewpoints; they are forced to reexamine their own views in light of the views of others. Students may, for the first time, conceive of what might be possible or what might occur rather than merely what is. This process of social interaction enables young adolescents to mature both socially and intellectually.

PEACE

I think sixth grade was like finding a new bend in the road and walking along it. Most of the time it was a pretty easy road but every once and a wile. I would get a blister or would trip up. Like the time our 6th weeks project came out in geography. I was looking through it felling pretty good untill suddenly a whole page of true/false questions came up! Ahhhhh! I hate those things. But also on this road there are good things like when you get back a paper and it has a big red A on it! That feels good! One thing I've learned (amoungst other things) is that take advantage of every situation and try to do your best. You can't do anybetter. Also I've learned that no matter what the teacher says, a C is just as good as an A if that C is something you did your best on. Over all, I think sixth grade has been a pretty smooth road that other people shall find and have the same mistakes I did at first. I know I'm not the only one. The flower of success is at the end.

FIGURE 2.9

I would like to ask the teacher(s) reading this paper some questions, and would appreciate it if the answers were sent to E period L.A.

Where does the universe end?
If there is no other life in space, where do U.F.O's come from?
Why do clocks "tick"?
Why does Elvis only hang out a 7-Elevens?
Who and where is God?
What-s the meaning of life?
Why is the education system so hard-pressed on "grades"?
Who invented the wheel?
Why don't they invent a toaster oven that flies?
Why is there racism and sexism?
Why is there communism?
Who invented the baseball?
Why can't we send all of our garbadge and nuclear weapons into the sun?
What is on the other side of a black hole?
Why is love "blind"?
How do we think?
How do we "be"?

FIGURE 2.10

Moral Development

The development of character is intricately linked to socioemotional and cognitive growth. A new capacity for abstract thinking allows the "what ifs," but social and emotional growth provide the context for the answers. "Character develops within a social web or environment" (Leming, 1993, p. 69). Figure 2.10 presents the musings of one middle school student.

Reference groups such as families, peer groups, and television are particularly important as students seek to understand their place in the world (Rice, 1990). Young adolescents form lifelong self-concepts and identities. "Middle school students can be helped to think about who they are and who they want to be, to form identities as self-respecting, career minded persons" (Davis, 1993, p. 32).

Throughout the years, attempts at values education have come and gone. "Schools in the earliest days of our republic tackled character education head on—through discipline, the teacher's example, and the daily school curriculum" (Lickona, 1993, p. 6). Consensus supporting character education began to erode in the early twentieth century and it was not until the 1970s that character education returned in the form of values clarification and Kohlberg's moral dilemma discussions. Interest in values education decreased until recently when character education and service learning gave impetus to a new interest in the moral development of children.

Some criticize efforts to teach values by saying that "no research . . . shows a direct connection between values and behavior" (Lockwood, 1993, p. 73); yet, others maintain that "moral education that is merely intellectual misses the crucial emotional side of character, which serves as the bridge between judgment and action" (Lickona, 1993, p. 9). It is clear that educators feel a rebirth of moral education in schools, which may be due to the decline of family influence on students and the potent impact of the media on youth.

The state of Maryland requires service learning experience of all incoming ninth grade students (Howard, 1993). Many school districts are following their lead. Young adolescents benefit from opportunities to make contributions to their communities and their schools through service. Within the classroom, values may be explored and discussed. Leming (1993) stated that "those interested in character education have long believed that morally inspiring literature should be a part of any character education program" (p. 69).

Young adolescents will acquire a value system with or without the help of parents and teachers. At a stage of development when students are emerging as reflective citizens, educators can still help students to be consciously aware of constructive values, to think logically about consequences, to empathize with others, and to make personal commitments to constructive values and behavior (Davis, 1993).

Cultural Influences on Young Adolescent Development

Families, neighborhoods, economic conditions, and the historical era are factors that influence a gracious or awkward transition into adulthood. In fact, in times of economic depression, teenagers are portrayed as "immature, psychologically unstable, and in need of prolonged participation in the educational system" (Enright, Levy, Harris, & Lapsley, 1987, p. 541). When society has large manpower needs, the image of youth is quite the reverse. During wartime, "the psychological competence of youth is emphasized and the duration of education is recommended to be more retracted than in depression" (p. 541). Adolescence, then, seems closely tied to the structure and condition of adult society (Modell & Goodman, 1990).

Parents often make the following comments: "I wasn't doing that when I was in junior high school," "My mother would have never allowed such behavior," "These kids are 11 going on 18!" or "Kids these days just aren't what they used to be." Although these kinds of comments may reflect a sentiment of annoyance, they are, in part, accurate because of dramatic shifts in our social milieu. Changes in families, diversity issues, and media will be discussed briefly in this section as they relate to early adolescence.

Families

Indisputably, the nature of the family has changed in the past few decades. Yet, today's young people (1) still have respect for their parents (Atkinson, 1988), (2) are in widespread agreement with parental values (Allison & Lerner, 1993; National Association of Secondary School Principals, 1984), and (3) turn to parents for guidance and share parental values on major issues (Rutter, 1980). Although peers become more influential during this time, "in no grade does the influence of peers outweigh the influence of parents" (Benson, 1985, p. 3).

Families are being redefined as the rate of divorce and remarriage, latchkey kids, blended families, and mothers who work outside the home rises. Although these conditions cause educators much concern and certainly demand readjustment in how schools interact with families, authors of a twelve-year longitudinal study of nonconventional families reported that "in spite of considerable instability and other potential risk conditions in nonconventional families' lives, most of their children do as well or better in school than a comparison group of conventional families" (Weisner & Garnier, 1992, p. 605). Two factors that seemed to enhance school achievement were strong commitment to their nonconventional family lifestyles and long-term family stability. Middle level schools must find creative ways to support families and accommodate emerging lifestyles as they work with young adolescents experiencing significant changes in their lives.

Diversity

Family conditions, socioeconomic status, and ethnicity are important factors in the young adolescent experience (Feldman & Elliott, 1990). Lipsitz (1983) supported this conclusion by further asserting that "adolescence is culturally determined and defined" (p. 9). The culturally diverse context of schools provides a microcosm of society and students with an opportunity to learn social skills necessary to negotiate societal demands.

Youth from a cultural minority often have difficulty in school during the middle grades for two major reasons. First, "minority youth are well aware of the values of the majority culture and its standards of performance, achievement, and beauty" (Spencer &Dornbusch, 1990, p. 123). "Minorities whose cultural frames of reference are oppositional to the cultural frame of reference of American mainstream culture have greater difficulty crossing cultural boundaries at school to learn" (Ogbu, 1992, p. 5). It appears that school, in whatever setting, represents majority culture.

Second, early and later adolescence is a crucial time for forming self-identity. Youth from a cultural minority often find themselves immersed in the standards of the mainstream culture. Given young adolescents' sensitivity to peer evaluations, the conflict between majority culture and their own often creates tension for students working on the development task of positive self-identity. In a study focused on Asian, African, Mexican, and Caucasian American students to determine stages of ethnic identity development,

Phinney (1989) found that students belonging to a cultural minority experienced a similar need to deal with their ethnicity in a predominately Caucasian American society. In an analysis of cultural and gender diversity literature, Manning (1993) concluded that young adolescents' "expanding social world and their increasing ability to understand others' perspectives contribute to early adolescence being an ideal time during which to teach appreciation and acceptance of all people" (p. 16).

Media

Cultural and gender diversity and changes in lifestyle are reflected continually in the media. Most people acquire a "wide variety of information, ideas, attitudes, and behaviors from the mass media, particularly from television" (Fine, Mortimer, & Roberts, 1990). The way in which young adolescents are influenced by such media as radio, music, videos, and television depends on the needs and concerns of each individual.

Young adolescents spend a significant portion of their time involved with mass media. Two approaches to neutralizing the deleterious health effects (particularly alcohol and tobacco) of mass media are to (1) censor (such as banning tobacco advertisements on television), and (2) teach young people to "gain conscious control over the way they process media messages" (Firth & Firth, 1993, p. 422). It appears that early adolescence is an opportune time to help students process media and make healthy life choices.

The transmission of traditional values is an important component of education at home and in school, but neither parents nor teachers can predict the future needs of young people. Today's society is changing rapidly in terms of technology, cultural values, and socially acceptable lifestyles. Educators cannot predict the future but can understand the problems faced by young adolescents growing up in today's society. By helping students to negotiate these problems, teachers will enable their students to encounter the problems of the future with courage and determination.

Implications for Curriculum and Instruction

It is easier to ride a horse in the direction it's already heading.

This old Japanese proverb provides guidance for middle level educators attempting to meet the needs of young adolescents through their educational programs, curriculum, and instruction. The Center for Early Adolescence (Davidson & Pulver, 1991) summarized the seven developmental needs of young adolescents.

1. Positive social interaction with adults and peers
2. Structure and clear limits
3. Competence and achievement
4. Creative expression
5. Physical activity
6. Meaningful participation in their families, schools, and communities
7. Self-definition

The strategies suggested in this book have two elements in common: they accommodate the needs of the young adolescent and they facilitate the development of reading and writing ability. These strategies are helpful for students at any stage of their educational experience; however, using these strategies helps to develop learning processes that students need to make a smooth transition into the high school. The strategies suggested in this book provide students with

1. the opportunity to work in groups (social needs);
2. a vehicle for connecting new information to what is already known, thus helping students to feel more confident about learning new material (cognitive and emotional needs);
3. experiences in abstract thinking that may help students move gradually from the concrete to the abstract levels of reasoning (cognitive and moral needs);
4. an opportunity to move and change activities (physical needs);
5. successful experiences, which help students feel better about themselves as learners (emotional needs); and
6. motivation to learn because these strategies involve elements designed to heighten students' curiosity about the subject (emotional and cognitive needs).

Summary

Understanding the characteristics of the middle grades student is a prerequisite to making informed decisions about a reading program or instructional practices. The onset of adolescence brings with it a profound set of physical, social, emotional, and intellectual changes. More than at any other stage of life, the young adolescent is in a state of flux. Rapid physical growth is accompanied by sexual maturation and changes in basal metabolism. An increased social awareness gives rise to an increased emphasis on peer relations. Emotions, stirred by hormonal and psychological changes, run high and many young adolescents begin to experiment with abstract thinking. Middle level students need to move and change activities frequently, to engage in positive social interaction with peers, to move slowly from the concrete to the abstract, and to gain confidence and emotional stability through success and the development of self-worth.

References

Allison, K.W. & Learner, R.M. (1993). Adolescents and the family. In R.M. Lerner (Ed.), *Early Adolescence: Perspectives on Research, Policy, and Intervention* (pp. 17–25). Hillsdale, NY: Lawrence Erlbaum Associates.

Atkinson, R. (1988). Respectful, dutiful teenagers. *Psychology Today, 22,* 22–26.

Beane, J.A. & Lipka, R.P. (1986). *Self-Concept, Self-Esteem, and the Curriculum.* New York: Teachers College Press.

Benson, P.L. (1985). New picture of families emerges from research. *Common Focus, 6,* 3.

Blyth, D., Simmons, R., & Zakin, D. (1985). Satisfaction with body image for early adolescent females: The impact of pubertal timing within different school environments. *Journal of Youth and Adolescence, 14*(3), 207–225.

Brack, C.J., Orr, D.P., & Ingersoll, G. (1988). Pubertal maturation and adolescent self-esteem. *Journal of Adolescent Health Care, 9,* 280–285.

Brooks-Gunn, J. & Reiter, E.O. (1990). The role of pubertal processes. In S.S. Feldman & G.R. Elliott (Eds.), *At the Threshold: The Developing Adolescent* (pp. 16–53). Cambridge, MA: Harvard University Press.

Brown, B.B. (1990). Peer groups and peer cultures. In S.S. Feldman & G.R. Elliott (Eds.), *At the Threshold: The Developing Adolescent* (pp. 171–196). Cambridge, MA: Harvard University Press.

Clasen, D.R. & Brown, B.B. (1987). Understanding peer pressure in the middle school. *Middle School Journal, 19*(1), 21–23.

Davidson, J. & Pulver, R. (1991). *Literacy Assessment for the Middle Grades.* Carrboro, NC: Center for Early Adolescence.

Davis, G.A. (1993). Creative teaching of moral thinking: Fostering awareness and commitment. *Middle School Journal, 24*(4), 32–33.

Dorman, G. & Lipsitz, J. (1981). Early adolescent development. In G. Dorman (Ed.), *Middle Grades Assessment Program.* Carrboro, NC: Center for Early Adolescence.

Enright, R.D., Levy, V.M., Harris, D., & Lapsley, D.K. (1987). Do economic conditions influence how theorists view adolescents? *Journal of Youth and Adolescence, 16*(6), 541–559.

Feldman, S.S. & Elliott, G.R. (Eds.). (1990). *At the Threshold: The Developing Adolescent.* Cambridge, MA: Harvard University Press.

Fine, G.A., Mortimer, J.T., & Roberts, D.F. (1990). Leisure, work, and the mass media. In S.S. Feldman & G.R. Elliott (Eds.), *At the Threshold: The Developing Adolescent* (pp. 225–252). Cambridge, MA: Harvard University Press.

Firth, M. & Firth, K. (1993). Creating meaning from media messages: Participatory research and adolescent health. In R.M. Lerner (Ed.), *Early Adolescence: Perspectives on Research, Policy, and Intervention* (pp. 419–430). Hillsdale, NJ: Lawrence Erlbaum Associates.

Forbes, E. (1943). *Johnny Tremain.* New York: Dell Publishing Company.

Harter, S. (1990). Self and identity development. In S.S. Feldman & G.R. Elliott (Eds.), *At the Threshold: The Developing Adolescent* (pp. 352–387). Cambridge, MA: Harvard University Press.

Hauser, S.T. & Bowlds, M.K. (1990). Stress, coping, and adaptation. In S.S. Feldman & G.R. Elliott (Eds.), *At the Threshold: The Developing Adolescent* (pp. 388–413). Cambridge, MA: Harvard University Press.

Hill, J.P. (1980). *Understanding Early Adolescence: A Framework.* Carrboro, NC: Center for Early Adolescence.

Howard, M.B. (1993). Service learning: Character education applied. *Educational Leadership, 51*(3), 42.

Irwin, C.E. & Vaughn, E. (1988). Psychosocial context of adolescent development. *Journal of Adolescent Health Care, 9,* 11S–19S.

Keating, D. (1990). Adolescent thinking. In S.S. Feldman & G.R. Elliott (Eds.), *At the Threshold: The Developing Adolescent* (pp. 54–89). Cambridge, MA: Harvard University Press.

Kohn, A. (1994). The truth about self-esteem. *Phi Delta Kappan, 75*(1), 272–283.

Leming, J.S. (1993). In search of effective character education. *Educational Leadership, 51*(3), 63–71.

Lickona, T. (1993). The return of character education. *Educational Leadership, 51*(3), 6–11.

Lipsitz, J. (1983). *Making It the Hard Way: Adolescence in the 1980s.* Testimony prepared for the Crisis Intervention Task Force, House Select Committee on Children, Youth, and Families.

Lockwood, A.L. (1993). A letter to character educators. *Educational Leadership, 51*(3), 72–75.

Manning, M.L. (1993). Cultural and gender differences in young adolescents. *Middle School Journal, 25*(1), 13–17.

Milgram, J. (1985). The ninth grader: A profile. In J.H. Johnston (Ed.), *How Fares the Ninth Grade?* (pp. 5–9). Reston, VA: National Association of Secondary School Principals.

Milgram, J. (1992). A portrait of diversity: The middle level student. In J.L. Irvin (Ed.), *Transforming Middle Level Education: Perspectives and Possibilities* (pp. 16–27). Boston: Allyn and Bacon.

Modell, J. & Goodman, M. (1990). Historical perspectives. In S.S. Feldman & G.R. Elliott (Eds.), *At the Threshold: The Developing Adolescent* (pp. 93–122). Cambridge, MA: Harvard University Press.

National Association of Secondary School Principals (1984). *The Mood of American Youth.* Reston, VA: Author.

Offer, D., Ostrov, E., & Howard, K.I. (1989). Adolescence: What is normal? *American Journal of Diseases of Children, 143,* 731–736.

Ogbu, J.G. (1992). Understanding cultural diversity and learning. *Educational Researcher, 21*(8), 5–14.

Phinney, J.S. (1989). Stages of ethnic identity development in minority group adolescents. *Journal of Early Adolescence, 9,* 34–49.

Rice, F.P. (1990). *The Adolescent: Development, Relationships, and Culture,* (6th ed.). Boston: Allyn and Bacon.

Rutter, M. (1980). *Changing Youth in a Changing Society.* Cambridge, MA: Harvard University Press.

Savin-Williams, R.C. & Berndt, T.J. (1990). Friendship and peer relations. In S.S. Feldman & G.R. Elliott (Eds.), *At the Threshold: The Developing Adolescent* (pp. 277–307). Cambridge, MA: Harvard University Press.

Scales, P.C. (1991). *A Portrait of Young Adolescents in the 1990s: Implications for Promoting Healthy Growth and Development.* Carrboro, NC: Center for Early Adolescence.

Simmons, R.G. & Blyth, D.A. (1987). *Moving into Adolescence: The Impact of Pubertal Change and School Context.* Hawthorne, NY: Aldine De Gruyter.

Simmons, R.G., Blyth, D.A., & McKinney, K.L. (1983). The social psychological effects of puberty on white females. In J. Brooks-Gunn & A.C. Peterson (Eds.), *Girls at Puberty: Biological and Psychosocial Perspectives* (pp. 229–272). New York: Plenum.

Simpson, M.K. (1986). A teacher's gift: Oral reading and the reading response journal. *Journal of Reading, 30,* 45–51.

Spencer, M.B. & Dornbusch, S.M. (1990). Challenges in studying minority youth. In S.S. Feldman & G.R. Elliott (Eds.) *At the Threshold: The Developing Adolescent* (pp. 123–146). Cambridge, MA: Harvard University Press.

Steinberg, L. (1990). Autonomy, conflict, and harmony in the family relationship. In S.S. Feldman & G.R. Elliott (Eds.), *At the Threshold: The Developing Adolescent* (pp. 255–276). Cambridge, MA: Harvard University Press.

Strahan, D. & Toepfer, C.J. (1984). The impact of brain research on education: Agents of change. In M. Frank (Ed.), *A Child's Brain.* New York: Haworth Press.

Weisner, T.S. & Garnier, H. (1992). Nonconventional family life-styles and school achievement: A 12-year longitudinal study. *American Educational Research Journal, 29*(3), 605–632.

Wigfield, A. & Eccles, J.S. (1994). Children's competence, beliefs, achievement values, and general self-esteem: Change across elementary and middle school. *Journal of Early Adolescence, 14*(2),102–106.

Youth: Transition to Adulthood. (1974). Report of the panel on Youth of the President's Science Advisory Committee. Chicago: University of Chicago Press.

Chapter 3

Literacy Learning and the Curriculum

Change, growth, flexibility, and understanding are words that describe middle level schools and the people in them. In the midst of physical, social and emotional, and cognitive change, students must adjust to a new school environment. The ability to read expository text successfully can greatly improve a student's chance for academic success in a middle grades school.

Teachers concerned with literacy learning have experienced a monumental shift in philosophy over the last two decades. The reader, the text, and the context for reading and writing are important in developing strategic learners. In addition, integrating the language arts and integrating the curriculum as a whole have challenged middle level teachers to think differently about the role of literacy in understanding content. This chapter will discuss the problem of adjusting to a middle level school, explain interactive reading and learning, make reading and writing connections, and present a move to a more integrated curriculum.

The Problem of Adjustment

Profound changes occur within students during the middle school years. Growth spurts, social awareness, mood swings, and a new capacity for thought are changes to which the young adolescent must adjust. While struggling with internal changes, changing schools often brings anxiety, especially for girls (Simmons & Blyth, 1987). "Contextual factors like the kinds of school environments children encounter can be a major influence on children's competence beliefs for and valuing of different academic tasks" (Wigfield & Eccles, 1994, p. 130). The organization of the school, the mode of instruction, the number of independent activities, the attitudes of teachers, and the nature of reading materials change as students move into this new environment.

Changes in School Structure

During the past thirty years, middle level schools have moved from primarily 7-8-9 junior high school grade configurations to 6-7-8 or 7-8 middle school grade configurations (Valentine, Clark, Irvin, Keefe, & Melton, 1993). With this change in grade configuration also came restructuring in school organization (such as interdisciplinary team organization) and changes in programs (such as advisory). Elementary schools are generally self-contained through fifth grade whereas middle level schools are more or less departmentalized. Although efforts to break down the dominance of departments are impressive, gone for most young adolescents is the security of one teacher looking out for one group of students.

Changes in Instruction

Most middle level teachers were trained in secondary education with an emphasis in a content area but with little emphasis on the strategies necessary to teach the content. Each content requires its own specialized vocabulary and organizational skills: map reading in social studies, scientific inquiry in science, literary criticism in language arts. Most secondary-trained teachers, however, have little or no formal preparation in reading and writing instruction. These teachers acknowledge that reading competence is important, but are simply not comfortable teaching the strategies students need to read and write successfully, even when these literacy abilities are necessary to learn content.

Changes in Expectations of Learning

A substantiative and growing body of literature supports the belief that middle level schools are more performance focused and less task focused than are elementary schools (Ames, 1990; Epstein, 1989; Midgley, Anderman, & Hicks, 1995). "When task goals are salient, students perceive that what is valued is effort, improvement, mastery, and understanding. When performance goals are salient, students perceive that what is valued is the demonstration of ability, and how they stand in comparison to peers is the measure of their success" (Midgley, Anderman, & Hicks, 1995, p. 91). The emphasis on teacher control, few opportunities for student decision making, and the assignment to classes based on ability makes the developmental tasks of autonomy and socialization and the development of an identity especially difficult for young adolescents.

Changes in Reading Material

Textbooks are more difficult in the middle grades; also, there are more of them and students are expected to understand them with less assistance from the teacher. Studies by Armbruster and Anderson (1984) have shown that many of the texts students are given to read are poorly written and "inconsiderate." In other words, they are written in such a way that the text is not easily understood or remembered, even by a proficient reader.

In contrast, elementary students most often read from basal readers, which are generally written in narrative style. Narrative text is usually recognized by an identifiable plot, setting, group of characters, and sequence and the vocabulary in these texts is sometimes controlled.

Expository text, which is frequently found in content area texts, is more factual and usually contains a hierarchical pattern of main ideas and details. Teachers, however, do not spend much time teaching students to read from this kind of book. In fact, after almost three hundred hours of classroom observation, Durkin (1978–1979) found that *no* time was spent teaching students to comprehend expository text in social studies lessons. Teachers taught only content and facts. With the exception of literature class, middle grades students are expected to read almost exclusively expository text as found in their science and social studies textbooks. But who takes the responsibility to teach students to read these texts?

Most often the responsibility for teaching reading in the middle grades falls on the language arts teacher. After a review of practices and perceptions among content area teachers, Witte and Otto (1981) concluded that few secondary trained English teachers "express any concern for . . . [having students read] . . . the expository materials of social studies, sciences, and other content areas" (p. 154). Muth (1987) pointed out that, "the pictures of story scenes typically found in narrative text are replaced by tables, graphs, diagrams, and flowcharts" (p. 6); therefore, although middle level students are expected to read more expository text, no one, it seems, teaches them how to understand this type of text.

Attaining independence in reading the basal reader in elementary grades does not prepare students to read the expository material in their science, social studies, or arithmetic texts independently. Students must learn to adapt their reading ability to a variety of reading material. Ideally, students should receive a gradual introduction to reading expository text beginning in the elementary grades. "At each grade level, in each subject area, teachers must help students learn to read to learn at a level of sophistication consistent with the concepts and resources being studied" (Herber & Nelson-Herber, 1987, p. 586). Becoming an independent learner is a lifelong process. For this reason, continued and systematic reading instruction during the middle grades is imperative.

Interactive Reading and Learning

Past educators viewed the act of reading as a simple task of decoding words. They placed emphasis on sounding out words, recognizing words by "sight" and in isolation, and reproducing what was in the text by answering comprehension questions. Research in cognitive psychology, linguistics, and education has led to a new conceptualization of the reading and learning process—one that recognizes that reading is a complex process.

In this new view, readers construct meaning from text using strategies and their prior knowledge. "Meaning is something that is actively created rather than passively received" (Buehl, 1995, p. 8). As shown in Figure 3.1, the three conditions that affect comprehension and the use of strategies are the readers, the text, and the context for reading and writing. These conditions are recursive and interactive rather than linear. It is helpful for educators at all levels of schooling to understand how cognitive processes interact as a reader constructs meaning from text.

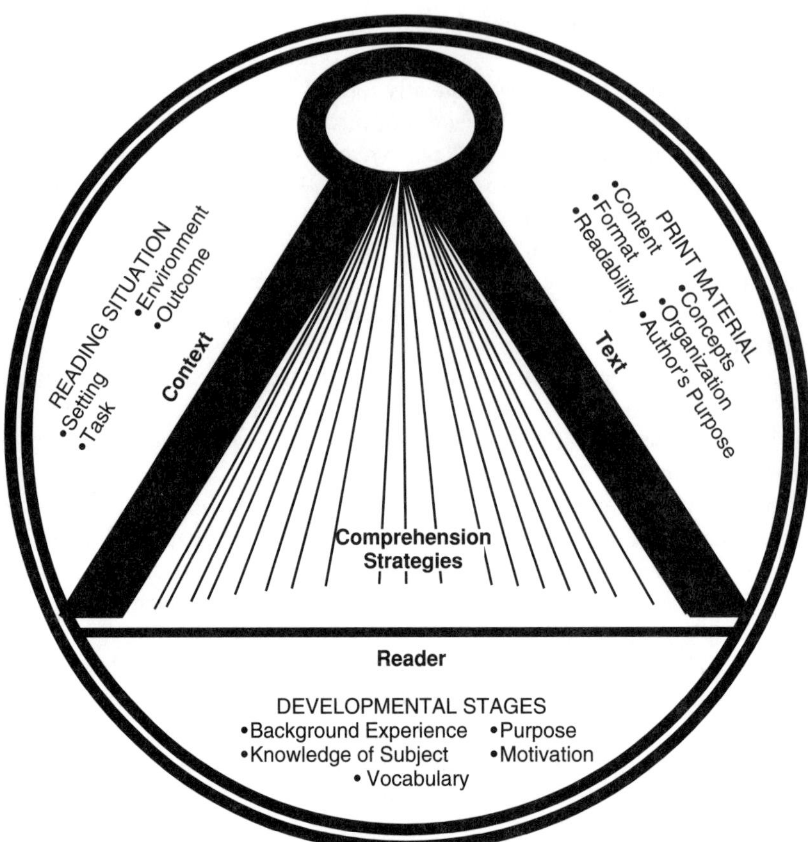

FIGURE 3.1 Wisconsin model for reading comprehension

Reprinted with permission from Cook, Doris M. *Strategic Learning in the Content Areas.* Wisconsin Department of Public Instruction, 125 South Webster Street, Madison, WI 53702; (800)243–8782.

The Reader

Former models of reading focused on whether students had acquired specific skills. Newer models of reading recognize that students come to a learning context full of information on particular topics, with an attitude about reading, writing, and school in general, motivation to learn (or not), and with particular purposes for reading and learning. It is the interaction of *what is in the head* with *what is on the page* within a particular context that causes students to *comprehend* what they read.

The Text

Imagine going to the mailbox and getting two letters addressed to you—one from a friend, one from a lawyer you do not know. These two letters look different even before you open them. You set yourself to read these two letters differently. Likewise, poetry is read differently than an insurance policy and a story is read differently than a science passage.

An entire chapter is devoted to the demands of text (Chapter 6) and how to develop student sensitivity in approaching different forms of text. The content, format, concepts presented, and organization are factors that make the text easy or difficult to understand. In addition, flexibility and sensitivity to different forms of text can enhance comprehension.

The Context

The context often sets the purpose for reading. Just as readers approach different types of text differently, they vary their reading according to their purpose. For example, if you encounter a difficult word in a novel you are reading for fun, you may guess at the meaning and then skip it and continue reading. An unknown word in a science textbook, however, could be an important concept that you need to understand before continuing. You may need to look it up in a glossary or ask someone. Purpose for reading also dictates how attentive readers are to details or how much work they put into remembering what they read. Where and when the selection is read are additional factors that affect the reading process.

Reading and Writing Connections

Reading and writing, in the majority of schools, have long been taught separately. Although teachers have observed the many similarities between the two processes, until recently, few have capitalized on these similarities by regularly integrating writing and reading instruction. One problem in teaching reading and writing as separate subjects is that students rarely apply what they learn in reading, vocabulary, spelling, and writing to each other. "Another major problem is that, while children may have mastered isolated subskills, they often experience difficulty reading and writing whole texts" (Noyce & Christie, 1989, p. 2). For too long, educators have treated reading and writing as separate subjects; instead, Shanahan (1990) suggested that educators should teach "reading for learning and writing for communication" (p. 10) rather than as an end in themselves.

Most students "read a text once without pausing to reflect, rarely refer to any other sources for relevant information, and rarely consider what they already know as they develop plans for dealing with the subject matter addressed in a text" (Pearson & Tierney, 1984, p. 11). Numerous research studies and theoretical assertions in the 1980s and 1990s have led most educators to believe in the "mirror metaphor"—that both reading and writing are acts of composing meaning. The reader begins with *text* and uses *language* to create *meaning*. A writer begins with *meaning* and uses *language* to create *text* (Birnbaum & Emig, 1983). This perceived connection underlies much of the current language arts curriculum development (Tierney & Shanahan, 1991).

Research has indicated that good writers are often (but not always) good readers. Similarly, good readers are often good writers (Stotsky, 1983). Knowledge of one process appears to reinforce knowledge of the other and students "derive learning benefits across reading and writing when they understand that connections exist" (Shanahan, 1990, p. 4).

In addition, McGinley and Tierney (1988) found that "writing emerged as a powerful means to foster students' subject matter learning" (p. 9). Based on research and current theory, Shanahan (1988) presented seven instructional principles enhancing the reading and writing relationship.

1. Teach both reading and writing because they are similar processes, but not the same.
2. Introduce reading and writing from the earliest grades.
3. Instruction should reflect the developmental nature of the reading process.
4. Make the reading and writing connection explicit.
5. Instruction should emphasize content and process relations.
6. Emphasize communications.
7. Teach reading and writing in meaningful contexts.

Understanding these relationships is especially important to the middle level educator, because the language development of the young adolescent—much like physical and social development—is in a transitional stage. During these years, educators have an opportunity to help students improve their language abilities by integrating the instruction of all language areas.

Integrated Learning

Middle level schools have always supported a cohesive, student-centered curriculum. Until recently, however, innovative practices focused on organizational aspects of schooling such as teaming or programs such as advisory or student activities. When Beane (1990) published *A Middle School Curriculum: From Rhetoric to Reality,* many middle level educators were well poised to challenge the sacred cow of subject matter. In the last few years, numerous articles and books have been written on the integrated curriculum and many schools have seriously attempted to design a student-centered, meaningful curriculum for young adolescents. The theories, the research, and the stories provide direction for those who understand the urgency of long lasting and penetrating curricular reform.

What is the role of literacy learning in the formation of a new curriculum for young adolescents? To help answer this question, some basic understandings are necessary: (1) an appreciation for the cognitive activities, or thinking abilities, that facilitate new learning, (2) language strategies and how they work together (sometimes known as the "integrated language arts"), and (3) current thinking on the integrated curriculum, including all subject areas, as it is implemented in middle level schools.

Thinking Abilities

Understanding the concepts of schema and metacognition helps "each of us make sense of our world by synthesizing new experiences into what we have previously come to understand" (Brooks & Brooks, 1993, p. 4). Learning is recursive. Students continue to revisit earlier thoughts until they understand and assimilate new information (Jones, Tinzmann, Friedman & Walker, 1987). Metacognition is the process that allows this assimilation by evaluating new learning and contrasting it with what is already known.

Current research on the brain clearly informs educators how to support meaningful learning with more effective instructional practices such as ensuring that cognitive activities are coupled with an emotional component. Sylwester (1995) presented a convincing argument that the activation of emotions is necessary for learning.

> *"Schools should focus more on metacognitive activities that encourage students to talk about their emotions, to listen to the feelings of classmates, and to think about the motivations of people who enter into their curricular world. For example, the simple use of WHY in a question focuses the discussion toward motivations and emotions, and away from mere rational facts.* Why did the pioneers settle where the two rivers came together? *is a much more emotionally loaded question than* Where did the pioneers settle?*" (p. 76).*

The emotions involved in an experience are necessary to remember it. Memory is contextual; that is, the context and surrounding emotions trigger the remembering and assimilation of the learning experience. Reading a story or discussing an historical event will not help students maintain memory networks of it unless they become emotionally involved. Role playing, cooperative learning, discussion, debate, and other activities that engage student emotions and cognition facilitate the assimilation of new learning experiences.

Besides using emotion to trigger memory, the brain searches for patterns and organization in its constant attempt to construct meaning. Brain-based learning has supported the move toward integration and student-based curriculum, instruction, and assessment. The curriculum is being transformed daily by courageous and creative teachers who see the benefit for students in crossing the subject area boundaries. Caine and Caine (1991) presented three reasons why interdisciplinary instruction is important:

1. The brain searches for common patterns and connections.
2. Every experience actually contains within it the seeds of many, and possibly all, disciplines.
3. One of the keys to understanding is redundancy or packaging the same message in different ways (pp. 119–120).

Gone are the days (hopefully) when teachers passively accept the curriculum guide and robotically "teach" one topic and then another. "Not only must middle grades teachers know about the curriculum of the middle school, they must also play a major role in creating that curriculum" (Erb, 1991, p. 26). Language arts and reading teachers have led this challenge to the subject areas partly out of necessity ("The kids can't read my textbook") and partly out of seizing the opportunity to use the powerful tool of literature to support content teaching.

Integrating the Language Arts

For too long, reading and writing have been taught as "subjects." They are not subjects like history, geography, or physical science; they are processes, strategies, or tools. "The lack of clarity about the crucial relationship between content and process in curriculum development is symptomatic of our isolation from the mainstream . . . content and process are inextricably bound" (Arnold, 1991, p. 8). We read and write about *something;* it is impossible to learn or use these language strategies separately from content.

It took years to move toward teaching phonics and word identification within the teaching of reading and it took years to move the teaching of grammar and spelling within the teaching of writing. Middle school language arts teachers are moving toward *whole language* instruction—teaching reading, writing, speaking, listening, and thinking together. A "good, coherent program can be sequenced around themes, literary works, composing processes and skills, and even the nature of language itself" (Tchudi, 1995, p. 40). Atwell's (1987) Reading/Writing Workshop certainly helped many language arts teachers provide structure to a literature-based and meaningful writing curriculum.

Many teachers, however, understood the potential of supporting other subject areas in language across the curriculum programs, showing other teachers in all disciplines that "language is a common denominator of instruction and that attending to language is a matter of attending to the quality of learning" (Tchudi, 1995, p. 41). The term *whole learning* has emerged as synonymous with whole language, although some authors (Pace, 1995; Beane, 1990; Siu-Runyan & Faircloth, 1995) feel that whole learning goes beyond the language arts curriculum to encompass the entire knowledge base found in all subject areas.

Integrating the Curriculum

Unfortunately, school administrators cannot shut their doors until they design a new curriculum. Teachers, students, parents, and administrators must change the curriculum as they deliver it. We have attempted to meet various student educational needs such as Chapter 1 or At Risk by instituting special programs (Lounsbury, 1991). This is a Band-Aid approach and Lounsbury argued for a "fresh start for the middle school curriculum" (p. 3). In addition, teachers attempting to provide more curricular connections in an already existing curriculum sometimes create artificial and contrived student activities.

Beane (1991; 1995) argued that the existing curriculum is like working a jigsaw puzzle without a picture and presented two crucial aspects for curriculum integration:

1. Integration implies wholeness and unity rather than separation and fragmentation.
2. Real curriculum integration occurs when young people confront personally meaningful questions and engage in experiences related to those questions (1991, p. 9).

Designing an integrated curriculum in middle level schools today presents numerous obstacles such as scheduling larger blocks of time for instruction and overcoming teachers' loyalty to subject matter. The integrative curriculum "dissolves and transcends subject area lines, though it does not abandon all of the knowledge and skill that have traditionally been defined within disciplines of knowledge" (Beane, 1993, p. 18). This new curriculum is more rigorous and cohesive because students can naturally apply such seldom taught processes as problem solving, critical analysis, ethics, valuing, and question posing to inherently interesting questions and problems. In addition, the true value of reading, writing, speaking, and listening are learned and used for their intended purpose—communication.

"The integrated curriculum fosters high-order thinking by involving students in learning, requiring them to think globally and to dissolve discipline lines by pulling together thoughts and ideas from various sources" (Brazee, 1995, p. 11). Young adolescents are just developing the capacity for abstract thought; it would be a shame to deny them the opportunity to learn and use these new abilities.

Summary

Students moving from the elementary to the middle school must adjust to an increasingly departmentalized and content-focused school system. Many middle level teachers forsake reading and writing instruction for content. Yet, the young adolescent years represent a productive opportunity to help students make the transition from the narrative-based reading of the elementary school to the almost exclusively expository-based reading of the high school.

To make this transition, students must learn to become strategic and independent readers. They must learn the strategies that good readers use before, during, and after reading. An effective writing program also contributes much to reading, and vice versa. By integrating the curriculum and supporting subject area learning, students have an opportunity to learn and use reading and writing strategies for their intended purpose, which is meaningful communication.

ReferencesReferences

Ames, C. (1990, April). *The Relationship of Achievement Goals to Student Motivation in Classroom Settings.* Paper presented at the annual meeting of the American Educational Research Association, Boston.

Armbruster, B. & Anderson, T. (1984). *Producing "Considerate" Expository Text: Or Easy Reading Is Damned Hard Writing* (Technical Report No. 46). Champaign, IL: Center for the Study of Reading.

Arnold, J. (1991). Toward a middle level curriculum rich in meaning. *Middle School Journal, 23*(2), 8–12.

Atwell, N. (1987). *In the Middle: Writing, Reading, and Learning with Adolescents.* Upper Montclair, NJ: Boynton/Cook.

Beane, J.A. (1990). *A Middle School Curriculum: From Rhetoric to Reality.* Columbus, OH: National Middle School Association.

Beane, J.A. (1991). The middle school: The natural home of integrated curriculum. *Educational Leadership, 49*(2), 9–13.

Beane, J.A. (1993). Problems and possibilities for an integrative curriculum. *Middle School Journal, 25*(1), 18–23.

Beane, J.A. (1995). *Toward a Coherent Curriculum.* Alexandria, VA: Association for Supervision and Curriculum Development.

Birnbaum, J. & Emig, J. (1983). Creating minds, created texts: Writing and reading. In R.P. Parker & F.A. Davis (Eds.), *Developing Literacy: Young Children's Use of Language* (pp. 87–104). Newark, DE: International Reading Association.

Brazee, E. (1995). An integrated curriculum supports young adolescent development. In Y. Siu-Runyan and C.V. Faircloth (Eds.), *Beyond Separate Subjects: Integrative Learning at the Middle Level* (pp. 5–24). Norwood, MA: Christopher-Gordon Publishers.

Brooks, J.G. & Brooks, M.G. (1993). *In Search of Understanding: The Case for Constructivist Classrooms.* Alexandria, VA: Association for Supervision and Curriculum Development.

Buehl, D. (1995). *Classroom Strategies for Interactive Learning.* Schofield, WI: Wisconsin State Reading Association.

Caine, R.N. & Caine, G. (1991). *Making Connections: Teaching and the Human Brain.* Alexandria, VA: Association for Supervision and Curriculum Development.

Durkin, D. (1978–1979). What classroom observations reveal about comprehension instruction. *Reading Research Quarterly, 14*(4), 481–533.

Epstein, J.L. (1989). Family influence and student motivation. In R.E. Ames & C. Ames (Eds.), *Research on Motivation in Education* (vol. 3) (pp. 259–295). New York: Academic Press.

Erb, T.O. (1991). Preparing prospective middle grades teachers to understand the curriculum. *Middle School Journal, 23*(2), 24–28.

Herber, H.L. & Nelson-Herber, J. (1987). Developing independent learners. *Journal of Reading, 7,* 584–589.

Jones, B.F., Tinzmann, M.B., Friedman, L.B., & Walker, B.B. (1987). *Teaching Thinking Skills: English/Language Arts.* Washington, DC: National Education Association.

Lounsbury, J.H. (1991). A fresh start for the middle school curriculum. *Middle School Journal, 23*(2), 3–7.

McGinley, W. & Tierney, R.J. (1988). *Reading and Writing as Ways of Knowing and Learning* (Technical Report No. 423). Champaign, IL: Center for the Study of Reading.

Midgley, C., Anderman, E., & Hicks, L. (1995). Differences between elementary and middle school teachers and students: A goal theory approach. *Journal of Early Adolescence, 15*(1), 90–113.

Muth, K.D. (1987). Teachers' connection questions: Prompting students to organize text ideas. *Journal of Reading, 31*(3), 254–259.

Noyce, R.M. & Christie, J.F. (1989). *Integrating Reading and Writing Instruction in Grades K–8.* Boston: Allyn and Bacon.

Pace, G. (Ed.) (1995). *Whole Learning in the Middle School: Evolution and Transition.* Norwood, MA: Christopher-Gordon Publishers.

Pearson, P.D. & Tierney, R.J. (1984). *On Becoming a Thoughtful Reader: Learning to Read Like a Writer* (Technical Report No. 50). Champaign, IL: Center for the Study of Reading.

Shanahan, T. (1988). The reading-writing relationship: Seven instructional principles. *Journal of Reading, 4*(7), 636–647.

Shanahan, T. (1990). Reading and writing together: What does it really mean? In T. Shanahan (Ed.), *Reading and Writing Together: New Perspectives for the Classroom* (pp. 1–18). Norwood, MA: Christopher-Gordon Publishers.

Simmons, R.G. & Blyth, D.A. (1987). *Moving into Adolescence: The Impact of Pubertal Change and School Context.* Hawthorne, NY: Aldine De Gruyter.

Siu-Runyan, Y. and Faircloth, C.V. (1995). *Beyond Separate Subjects: Integrative Learning in the Middle School.* Norwood, MA: Christopher-Gordon Publishers.

Stotsky, S. (1983). Research on reading/writing relationships: A synthesis and suggested directions. *Language Arts, 60*(5), 627–642.

Sylwester, R. (1995). *A Celebration of Neurons: An Educators' Guide to the Human Brain.* Alexandria, VA: Association for Supervision and Curriculum Development.

Tchudi, S. (1995). It must have a name: Coherence in and through the English and Language Arts. In J.A. Beane (Ed.), *Toward a Coherent Curriculum* (pp. 34–43). Alexandria, VA: Association for Supervision and Curriculum Development.

Tierney, R.J. & Shanahan, T. (1991). Research on the reading-writing relationship: Interactions, transactions, and outcomes. In R. Barr, M.L. Kamil, P.B. Mosenthal, & P.D. Pearson (Eds.), *Handbook of Reading Research* (vol. 2) (pp. 246–280). New York: Longman.

Valentine, J.W., Clark, D.C., Irvin, J.L., Keefe, J.W., & Melton, G. (1993). *Leadership in Middle Level Education: Volume I: A National Survey of Middle Level Leaders and Schools.* Reston, VA: National Association of Secondary School Principals.

Wigfield, A. & Eccles, J.S. (1994). Children's competence, beliefs, achievement values, and general self-esteem change across elementary and middle school. *Journal of Early Adolescence, 14*(2), 107–138.

Witte, P.L. & Otto, W. (1981). Reading instruction at the postelementary level: Review and comments. *Journal of Educational Research, 74*(3), 148–158.

Chapter 4

Learning Environments That Motivate Students

The American public seems to hold the perception that students today perform less well than their counterparts in other countries and less well than students in previous generations. Certainly, national "report cards" (often republished in local newspapers) cause alarm when they blast that "at least 30 percent at each grade level (4th, 8th, 12th) fail to reach even *basic* levels" of reading proficiency (National Assessment of Educational Progress, 1994, p. 7). It is certainly true that educators face numerous challenges in literacy learning and that many students leave middle level schools unable to perform basic literacy tasks. But the problem of underachievement in reading and writing is complex and grows more complex as students progress through the middle grades and on into high school. Cultural pressures, student attitudes about themselves as learners and about school in general, an increased demand for sophisticated literacy abilities in the middle grades, and the changing nature of the curriculum are factors that influence success or failure in learning to read and write proficiently.

New research on underachievement and motivation points to environmental factors within school and classroom learning environments, as well as at home and within the student, having an impact on learning. Cooperative strategies such as classroom discussions and paired retellings also hold promise for motivating young adolescents. This chapter will discuss the status of reading proficiency and the nature of underachievement in reading and writing and present new research on motivation. Discussion will conclude with numerous strategies for motivating young adolescents and working with disabled readers.

The Status of Reading Proficiency

Popular belief holds that students today read less well than students in previous generations. However, "data available for contrasting past and present reading abilities display no downward spiral of reading test scores; indeed, those data warrant the conclusion that the reading proficiency of today's students meets or exceeds that of students from any other era" (Kibby, 1993, p. 28). Then and Now studies (the same test administered to a large sample of students decades apart) reveal that there is "no evidence to support a conclusion of declining reading abilities in the United States" (p. 31).

Another data source for comparison is the restandardization of nationally normed tests. These tests show no significant decrease in reading achievement for students in grades 1 through 8 after 1950. For grades 9 through 12, the data are mixed—some show increases and others show decreases. One can only hypothesize that the effort to keep students in school longer may have influenced this apparent decline in reading achievement for high school students. National Assessment of Educational Progress (NAEP) provided data through reading assessments from 1971 that substantiate continual and significant increases in reading proficiency from 1970 to 1990.

Although it is comforting to note that students have increased their reading achievement in the past one hundred fifty years, expectations for reading and writing performance are more demanding than in generations past. Literacy tasks students face today require processing and synthesis of information from multiple sources and in varied formats while many students still struggle with even the simple tasks. An understanding of the contributing factors to underachievement in all areas may help educators understand how to help students construct more productive attitudes and acquire strategies for meeting the complex literacy demands they will surely face in their future.

Underachievement

Despite the efforts of teachers, administrators, At Risk program coordinators, and intervention specialists, some students do not learn to read and write. Family and societal conditions often contribute to students' lack of achievement in school; however, educators continue to attempt to overcome these powerfully influential factors.

The condition of young adolescents living with poverty, poor housing (if any), violence, and unsupportive families seems overwhelming to educators. Samuel Woodward (Griffin, 1988), however, investigated why children succeed despite overwhelming adversity. Looking at underachievement from the perspective of "those who make it" revealed these five factors:

1. Children who do well academically under adverse conditions tended to score well above the median on self-acceptance and self-respect measures.
2. Despite deprivation, these students saw their families as worthwhile and valuable.
3. These students did not see their difficult personal situation as a determinant of what they could become; they did not dwell on their victimization. They believed that *they,* not their situations, were in charge of their lives. These students had the attitude that whatever good or bad happened to them depended on their own behavior. They did not wait for fate or miracles to improve their lot in life.
4. From the earliest years, these children were expected to meet high standards and were rewarded for doing so within their families.
5. They were loved by someone (pp. 2–5).

Working with severely underachieving students, Griffin (1988) concluded that "there is the possibility of teaching what it takes to achieve academically to students who do not possess these qualities" (pp. 2–3). Some students seemed to catch these good qualities from the important people in their lives and internalize them. Applying sports psychology to his work with underachievers, Griffin taught students to seek and accept constructive criticism and ask for further clarification much in the way athletes take advantage of feedback from their coaches. Learning from failure rather than becoming defeated by it seems to be a key for helping underachievers become achievers.

Motivating Young Adolescents

One frustrating aspect about working with young adolescents is their apparent lack of interest in academic tasks. Developmental factors such as (1) changing beliefs about their ability, (2) an increasing need for control and autonomy, (3) an evolving self-concept, and (4) fears of failure, especially in front of peers, contribute to the decline in motivation during this time. The general climate of a middle level school, which is quite different from the elementary school, often exacerbates declines in motivation.

Young children generally believe that "ability can be increased through effort, and high effort signifies high ability. During early adolescence, however, students often develop the notion of ability as a capacity, and begin to think of effort and ability as being inversely related. Therefore, they are capable of understanding that high effort, without success, is a sign of low ability" (Urdan, Midgley, & Wood, 1995, p. 15). When students come to believe that ability is a fixed trait, then they become less likely to risk failure on a challenging task. In their thinking, if you try and fail at a task, you must be "dumb." Being perceived this way by peers is too much of a deterrent; it is safer to not try in the first place. The learning environment plays a critical role in determining how students view their own ability.

Eccles and Midgley (1989) argued that developmentally appropriate schools and classrooms provide a climate that is safe and intellectually challenging. Particularly harmful for young adolescents are schools that emphasize competition, social comparison, and ability self-assessment. Particularly beneficial are schools that encourage student decision making, provide for opportunities to demonstrate autonomy, and focus on task-focused goals where effort is valued rather than ability.

How students view their own intelligence largely affects their willingness to try more difficult tasks. Students with a *fixed* view of intelligence attribute their success (or failure) to factors outside of their control such as their intelligence. When told they did well on a test, they respond, "I was lucky." Students with an *incremental* view of intelligence attribute their success (or failure) to factors within themselves such as effort. When told they did well on a test, they respond, "I studied hard." Numerous studies document that students who hold an incremental view of their own intelligence achieve more in all academic tasks (Henderson & Dweck, 1990; Midgley, Anderman, & Hicks, 1995; Urdan, Midgley, & Wood, 1995; Wigfield & Eccles, 1995).

In working with underachieving high school students, Ignoffo (1988) tried to help students overcome the "inner critic" by using journals to help students confront failure, set goals, and gain confidence. Educators have been successful in developing isolated methods of motivating students to read and write by connecting with their interests and empowering them to make decisions, but these efforts may easily be undermined if "the school as a whole emphasizes grades, competition, and rewards. . . . Rather than focusing primarily on the designated problems of some, it may be profitable and more practical to identify contexts that are optimally beneficial to most" (Anderman & Maehr, 1994, p. 298).

Changing the culture of an entire school can be an overwhelming task and often not within the control of a classroom teacher. Teachers who understand developmental and cultural factors that influence student motivation, however, can change their environment and their way of interacting with students. Declining motivation for academic endeavors is a result of developmental factors of the students and cultural factors of middle level schools. Some courageous and innovative educators are attempting to avert declining motivation by changing the nature of teacher-student interactions, restructuring the curriculum to be more relevant to young adolescents, rethinking reward systems in their schools, reducing the number of comparisons based on ability between students, and creating a safe environment for students to learn from failure.

Rethinking (Dis)Ability

When an able student fails to complete a task successfully, most teachers assume the task was too difficult or confusing; when a reader fails, a search into "what is wrong with the student" often ensues. Instruction and "assessment must move away from the search for pathology and toward the specification of the conditions under which a child can and will learn" (Wixson & Lipson, 1984, p. 137). Focusing on student weaknesses often results in the recycling of students through word recognition and literal comprehension skills instead of focusing on their more immediate needs.

The nature of reading tasks changes in complexity when students move into the middle grades; expository reading begins to dominate. Students must shift from "learning to read" to "reading to learn" and master the strategies that accompany this emerging emphasis. Teachers of "social studies, natural sciences, social science, and mathematics must take responsibility for teaching their students the critical reading skills needed to learn from texts used in those content areas—subject area teachers must not assume that a child who can comprehend stories has sufficient reading skill to learn independently from expository textbooks" (Kibby, 1993, p. 38). Subject area teachers can do a great deal to enhance their students' reading success within a content area by (1) providing conceptual support for comprehension, (2) helping students understand text structure, and (3) teaching learning strategies that assist students in activating prior knowledge, interacting with text as they read, and organizing information after they read.

Sometimes students who are reading well below grade level are placed in a remedial reading class. Frequently, however, there is a "lack of congruence between regular class and remedial reading class . . . often the teachers do not talk to each other" (Johnston, Allington, & Afflerbach, 1985, p. 474). Young adolescents are notorious for their lack of ability to make great conceptual leaps of logic. When they read stories and learn to find the main idea during remedial reading class, they simply cannot make the application later that day (or that week) to an on-grade level, content area textbook. Teaching students strategies for understanding expository text that help them become more successful with their science, social studies, and narrative strategies for completing their literature assignments successfully is a more direct application.

A subtle, yet potent, cause for reading dysfunction is that often students are assigned reading material that is simply not meaningful or relevant to them. Students have little choice (and little interest) in what they read. The entire curriculum including what teachers ask students to read must be reconsidered to enhance student ability and motivation to learn.

I recently had a conversation with Jason, a seventh-grade student, who had a bit of a chip on his shoulder about school. The discussion centered around the kinds of books that he had read. Jason loved mysteries and adventure and had read the *Lord of the Rings* trilogy (Tolkien, 1937). After a lively dialogue about Frodo and his adventures, I asked him why his teachers complained that he did not and would not read at school. The twinkle left his eye and he replied, "I don't like to read the stuff they give us in school." Jason's lack of motivation to read "school stuff" can be attributed to three factors: attitude, interest, and self-concept.

First, Jason did not have a good attitude about reading expository text, and perhaps generally, about anything that was assigned by a teacher. Men and women who spend hours in a weight room have an attitude about working out. This attitude motivates them to endure pain and continue working out. A positive attitude toward reading can motivate a student to keep going and to try different types of reading challenges.

Second, Jason's interests were in mystery and fantasy. Why is it then that he could not become interested in studying ancient civilizations? Why is it that he could not become interested in reading about the discovery of King Tut's tomb? I suspect that his teacher did not know about his interests and that the connection between his reading interests in mysteries and the mysteries of the real world was not made.

Jason is a happy, well-adjusted young man at home. He gets along well with his family and they discuss favorite books. His self-esteem about himself as a learner at school, however, is poor. He does not see himself as one who can succeed in school work. This lack of confidence manifests itself in his resistance to assignments and in his "I don't care" attitude.

Reading is a highly valued skill in our society; it is especially valued in school. According to Quandt and Selznick (1984), children who believe they are not competent at performing a task that society has determined as important often develop a negative self-concept. They suggested that, as well as building an accepting classroom environment, teachers can use student interests as a powerful way to help students with a low self-concept. The teacher's challenge is to help the student achieve success by tapping the student's own interests and strengths.

Effective and Ineffective Reading Behaviors

Much of the research conducted in the last fifteen years has focused on how the behavior and experiences of effective readers differ from the behavior and experiences of ineffective readers. This work has direct implications not only for the instruction of poor readers but also for the instruction of *all* students. For example, poor readers report doing less independent reading than good readers. In fact, "poor readers report that their teachers use a narrower range of approaches than are used with better readers. The approaches that are used with poor readers are less likely to emphasize comprehension and critical thinking, and more likely to focus on decoding strategies" (Applebee, Langer, & Mullis, 1988, p. 6). The following is a listing of effective and ineffective reading behaviors before, during, and after reading.

Effective Reading Behaviors	***Ineffective Reading Behaviors***
Before Reading	
—**Preview** text (look at title, pictures, print)	
—**Build** background knowledge on the subject before reading	—Start reading without thinking about the subject
—**Think** about key words or phrases	—Do not preview text for key vocabulary
—**Set** purpose for reading	—Do not know purpose for reading
—**Focus** complete attention on reading	—Mind often wanders
During Reading	
—**Adjust** reading for different purpose	—Read different texts and for different tasks all the same
—**Monitor** understanding of text and use strategies to understand difficult parts	—Do not monitor comprehension —Seldom use any strategies for understanding difficult parts
—**Integrate** new information with existing knowledge	
After Reading	
—**Decide** if goal for reading has been achieved	—Do not know content or purpose of reading
—**Evaluate** comprehension of what was read and ideas in text	
—**Summarize** the major ideas in a graphic organizer or by retelling	—Read passage only once and believe to be finished
—**Apply** information to a new situation	—Express readiness for a test without studying.

If teachers understand what strategies effective readers use while reading, perhaps those students identified as ineffective readers can be taught to use those strategies. New thinking about what is effective and what is ineffective has helped redirect teachers' thinking and students' attitudes and behaviors, and has provided new directions for literacy programs in middle level schools.

Strategies for Disabled Readers

Successful readers engage in more teacher led activities before and after reading than their lower-performing classmates, and

> *thus, may have more opportunities to use the knowledge and experiences they already possess to enrich their reading experiences. They were also more likely to be asked to engage in thought-stretching activities after they have finished their reading of the text. In contrast, their lower-performing classmates seemed to report receiving more assistance in getting through the text. While this help is useful, it may be unnecessarily limiting—keeping students from also beginning to practice the very kinds of reading skills and strategies that are used by their higher-performing classmates (Applebee, Langer, & Mullis, 1988, p. 18).*

Low-achieving students have not been ignored; their instruction, however, often emphasizes decoding and skills at the expense of comprehension and strategies (Garcia & Pearson, 1990). Comprehension is often not viewed as the goal of reading because disabled readers struggle with decoding and experience vocabulary difficulties. For disabled readers to become proficient readers, their attitude about the goal of reading must change. Recent methods of working with severely disabled readers hold some promise.

Reading Rescue

Reading Rescue (Lee & Neal, 1992–1993) is a method adapted for older students from Marie Clay's reading recovery model designed for emergent readers. Reading Rescue includes (1) reading familiar material, (2) reading aloud, (3) taking a running record of oral reading, (4) working with words and letters as they arise naturally in text, (5) writing through language experience, and (6) reading material.

Another reading recovery type method was developed by Anderson and Roit (1993) for severely disabled six- through tenth-grade students. Working in a small group with a teacher who was familiar with strategy instruction, students worked on making strategies for reading expository text explicit. In the students' own words, ten strategies can be applied to text:

- Recognizing a problem
- Making things real
- Knowing what matters
- Making sense
- Agreeing and disagreeing
- Having reasons

- Getting ready for what comes next
- Getting back on track
- Explaining
- Wrapping up experiences (p. 126)

Teachers were engaged in reading sessions that resembled natural conversations about text, rather than teacher-determined lessons. The following "content-free" questions helped students access and use their prior knowledge and apply strategies for figuring out difficult text.

For assessing text content:

What is this about?
What are the most important ideas?
What is most interesting?
What did you find out that you did not know before?
What surprised you?

For accessing world knowledge:

What do you already know about this?
What would you like to find out about this?
Of what does this remind you?

For accessing strategic knowledge:

What problem are you trying to solve?
How are you trying to solve the problem?
How did your attempt work out?
What else might solve the problem?
What do you think and why do you think so?

For accessing knowledge about reading in general:

What did you learn about reading?
How can you use what you learned to read other things?
How did this help your reading? (pp. 134–135).

Typical sessions included students selecting a text (usually expository) and discussing what they already know about the topic. Students then skim the text to get an idea about potential problems and discuss difficult aspects about the text. Students volunteer to read the text aloud and periodic discussion of strategies for understanding text intervenes. After reading, students return to the ideas they expressed before reading and discuss what they learned from the text and what they learned about the reading process.

It has become clear that work on isolated skills does not help disabled readers become more proficient. They need to focus their attention on comprehension and learn strategies for understanding text. Initial efforts to work with small groups of young adolescents on strategy instruction are promising.

Using Classroom Discussion to Motivate Students

The positive benefits of conducting classroom discussions have been noted by researchers for years. Sternberg (1987) stated that because "our ability to think originates outside ourselves, we must view class discussion as more than just a peripheral part of a thinking-skills program. Discussion is essential" (p. 459). This interchange of ideas facilitates the maturation of the young adolescent from total egocentrism to a more balanced world view.

Alvermann, Dillon, and O'Brien (1987) stated that "discussion is an integral part of the comprehension process" (p. 13) and the use of "recitation and lecture . . . cannot compete with discussion in offering opportunities for students to communicate their views to other students with different views" (p. 9). Guthrie, Schafer, Wang, and Afflerbach (1993) documented many benefits of classroom discussion such as increased time reading about related topics and a better understanding of science concepts. Furthermore, reading is placed in a social context; that is, discussion reduces the isolation that students sometimes feel when they are left alone to interact with text.

Discussion often helps students to communicate, refine, and enrich their understandings of the assigned reading. Gallagher and Pearson (1989) pointed out that the typical practice in content area classrooms of reading a paragraph or section aloud and then discussing it as a class produced better understanding than students only reading by themselves. This practice not only "substantially enhances students' knowledge acquisition, when encountering novel content. . . . Further, the effectiveness of the instruction extends to students' independent reading of material about content related to that of the original instruction" (p. 37). Even more effective are integrated discussions that highlight relationships between important concepts that precede the reading of the text.

Alvermann, Dillon, and O'Brien (1987) maintained that discussion has the following "three criteria: (1) discussants should put forth multiple points of view and stand ready to change their minds about the matter under discussion, (2) students should interact with one another as well as with the teacher, and (3) the interaction should exceed the typical two or three word phrase units common to recitation lessons" (p. 7). Recitation might be visualized as a telephone switchboard operator—all lines run from the teacher to and from individual students; interaction between students is minimal. According to the preceding definition, recitation is not considered to be a discussion.

Three types of classroom discussions are considered to be basic to the classroom environment: (1) *Subject mastery discussions,* which extend student learning through talk about a topic. Activating prior knowledge and building background information is necessary in facilitating comprehension of any new topic of study (Chapter 9 contains a full discussion of using prior knowledge to comprehend text.). (2) *Issue-oriented discussions,* which may depend on student needs and interests. (3) *Problem-solving discussions,* which may grow out of a textbook assignment, lecture, or previous discussion or assignment.

To have a successful classroom discussion, it is necessary to have the proper setting and climate. Students must feel free to express their opinions and see that what they say will be accepted. A physical arrangement that is conducive to discussion is one in which the chairs are arranged in a circle or horseshoe shape. The teacher must be an effective listener who instills respect for the opinions of others. Teachers should clarify, reflect feelings, resolve different points of view, interpose summaries, and redirect questions to students.

Discussions should be limited. The teacher should announce the length of the discussion ahead of time, along with the purpose. The teacher should also maintain the focus of the discussion and should respect the privacy of individual students by not insisting on direct participation.

Think-Pair-Share

One way to get full participation from the entire class without putting any individual on the spot is through a strategy called "think-pair-share" (McTighe & Lyman, 1988). A question, usually requiring some bit of abstract thought, is posed. Students think and jot down an answer. Then students pair; that is, they talk about their answer with a partner. Then, as a class, they share answers. This strategy allows every student an opportunity to answer, at least to a partner, and also allows students time to think, respond, and try to make connections with the world they understand. In Chapter 2, it was suggested that "latent abstract thinkers" need time to consider their response and can then perhaps respond at a higher level of thinking. The think-pair-share strategy allows such time for thought and reaction, and provides for a fuller, richer, and more thoughtful discussion.

Directed Listening-Language Experience Approach

Gold (1981) used the Directed Listening-Language Experience Approach (DL-LEA) method successfully with middle grades students who could not read the assigned text. The strategy was designed to help students learn the content and improve their reading and writing ability. The steps of the DL-LEA are as follows:

1. **Motivate discussion and set purposes for listening.** Choose a strategy that will stimulate discussion and establish the purposes for listening.
2. **Present the information by reading aloud.** Direct students to listen for the purposes established. Be sure to exclude sentences or paragraphs irrelevant to the topic.
3. **Guide discussion and summarize.** Discuss the information with students in light of the purposes set forth. Have students summarize the most important points and put them in an appropriate sequence. The sentences are recorded by the teacher as the language experience story.

This strategy can be modified to meet the needs of students by having them map information before writing a summary or producing a class map and by having students read and write their summaries. Teaching content material to low or nonreaders is problematic; the DL-LEA addresses both content knowledge and reading and writing improvement.

Discussions can improve oral communication, and allow students to verbalize their opinions and consider the viewpoints of peers. Discussion can help students to (1) build on and activate what they know about a particular topic of study, (2) clarify their thoughts during post reading, and (3) thus promote reading comprehension.

Using Cooperative Strategies to Motivate Students

Reading and writing occur within a social context; notes are left on refrigerators, magazines and newspapers are read to discuss with others, and information is gathered to share with colleagues at meetings. The concept of *oral rehearsal* has convinced numerous educators that cooperative learning is a viable and motivating method of delivering instruction.

Interaction with peers is a powerful motivator for young adolescents. Developmentally, students are learning social skills that will serve them throughout their adult life and these new social abilities will enhance their cognitive and emotional development as well. It is prudent to capitalize on students' natural inclination toward social interaction to help them become better readers and writers. The following methods have been used successfully to motivate middle grades students to read and write and have increased the likelihood that disabled readers can and will participate in instruction and discussion.

1. *Paired Retellings.* In groups of two or three, students read a short section and retell it to their partner or group. Sometimes students can listen to a piece of text and retell a summary or the main points to the partner or group. Graphic organizers or maps have been used to help students organize their thoughts for retelling. Retelling can be used with stories or with content material. Paired retellings are effective because students have the advantage of working with a partner or group to help them with text, thereby reducing the amount of text students deal with at a particular time, and helping them organize their thoughts by capturing the important points.
2. *Read aloud.* Students of all ages love reading aloud. They will often become interested in reading a particular book because one by the same author has been read to them. Students also gain much in the way of vocabulary knowledge and thinking abilities by having others read to them. Chapter 7 offers suggestions in full detail about the best books and the best ways to read aloud to students.
3. *See the movie—read the book.* So many popular movies such as *The Outsiders* are available in both movie and written form. Already knowing the story line and characters helps students have more success with such books. Natural breaks in videos may coincide with book chapters, and discussions of how the book differed from the movie often spark young adolescents to become critics of both movies and books.
4. *Display evidence of book reading.* Alvermann (1987) suggested using a systematic way for students to share their evaluations of the books they have read. As a student finishes reading a book, one assignment could be for the student to fill out a simple card listing the name and author of the book and one or two lines about why the student liked or disliked the book. These cards can then be made available to other students as they select their own reading material. Teachers can suggest books that are written by the same author or that are conceptually related. The power of using trade books to build motivation and enhance reading and writing ability has been affirmed by both research and teacher testimonial.
5. *Develop an advertising campaign.* After students finished reading a book, one teacher sent two students to the library to be interviewed and videotaped. The interviewer had a set list of questions to ask, although deviation from the list was encouraged. Every

few weeks, the videotapes were shown to the whole class. This teacher found that shortly after the viewing, many students wanted to check out the books read by those students who were interviewed. Students also can make commercials, dress up in costumes like the characters and explain the book, or make posters about books.

6. *Comic books.* Students will often read comic books when they will not read something else. Students also can write new stories using the pictures. Comic strips from the newspaper can be used in much the same way.
7. *Reading to younger children.* Reading to younger children is an excellent excuse to have low-achieving students read materials that are below their grade level; it also provides an opportunity for older students to be in a position of authority and respect. Books should be selected with guidance from the teacher and rehearsed ahead of time.
8. *Language experience.* Language experience is a way to use students' language to improve their reading ability. Students dictate a story to someone who transcribes their language. Students then read their own language.

   Language experience enables low-ability readers to experience success through the use and extension of the language they already possess and through involvement with topics of their own interests. Usually the listening vocabulary of these students is larger than their reading or writing vocabularies. In other words, students know and can use more words orally than they are able to read or write. Thus, language experience enables students to use their larger oral vocabulary to build on their written vocabulary. Students are also likely to identify with their own writing or dictated ideas. The basic procedures in adapting the language experience approach to a content classroom follow:

   - The students are asked to interpret, explain, or describe, in their own words, an event, problem, or issue related to the content being studied. The subject should be something meaningful to the student. For example, if a social studies class is studying Native Americans, a student might look at several pictures of them, then tell a story about the life of a 12-year-old Native American.
   - The teacher then tapes the unrehearsed accounts and enters them into the computer.
   - The students then read their stories or accounts orally.
   - The teacher discusses with the students the meaning of the story and how they might change the story to improve it. If students have difficulty reading some of the words they dictated, these words should be marked and activities developed to use these words in a different context. For example, if a student had trouble with "culture," "elk," and "tribal," using these words in a new short story would help to reinforce learning of these words.

   The language experience approach requires time on the part of the teacher, but it clearly can be a valuable tool in providing many disabled readers with successful reading experiences. Teachers may be able to secure some help in word processing student stories from teachers' aides, volunteers, computer classes, and even older students. Some teachers have taught entire units using language experience activities. Collections of students' stories can be displayed and read by other students.
9. **Incorporating newspapers into classroom instruction.** Ammann and Mittelsteadt (1987) found that newspapers provide a natural vehicle for students to recognize and

practice paraphrasing and summarizing. Criscuolo and Gallagher (1989) suggested that the newspaper can answer some real-life questions such as how to find an apartment or job as well as provoke discussion about real-life heroes or heroines. Newspapers are interdisciplinary; current events, sports, comics, and editorials connect well to integrated themes of study. Additionally, the controversial issues so commonly found in newspapers can be used to motivate students to read further (Lunstrum, 1981).

10. **Using music and art to build motivation.** Contemporary music and lyrics can be used to motivate students and enable them to relate the content they are studying to their experiences. Smith (1981) suggested that "lyrics of many songs provide excellent sources for teaching vocabulary development at both literal and higher levels of comprehension" (p. 32).

Using music to evoke emotion, to instill nationalistic pride, and to develop a feeling of unity can be an interesting subject of study, and one that is directly related to historical movements. For substantiation of this claim, a person need only point to the impact of "We Shall Overcome" on the civil rights movement. More recently, "Hands Across America" was a song that literally united, if only for a time, the nation from coast to coast, and "We Are the World" is a song that children and adults sing with equal pride. Music is a powerful force in society and it is one in which students are intensely interested.

If students have an interest in drawing, art has also been used effectively in the content classroom to improve students' motivation to read. Students can be encouraged to create original cartoons of historical problems and events. Captions for these cartoons can be written and shared with others.

Using Technology to Improve Reading and Writing

With the advantage of hindsight, technologies such as the printing press and the ballpoint pen that have revolutionized our conceptions of literacy seem part of the natural evolution of creative intelligence. Looking ahead into a post-typographic world, though, is not as easy. It is difficult to ignore the pace at which the world is moving away from print: libraries provide books and journals on CD-ROM, debit cards eliminate the necessity of writing a check, and, for some people, E-mail has completely substituted the writing of letters. Literacy educators, for the first time, are questioning the centrality of books in teaching reading and writing.

Reinking (1994) argued that "the differences between printed and electronic texts are substantial enough to alter current conceptions of literacy" (p. 9). He delineated five ways in which printed and electronic texts are different.

1. *Interactivity and malleability.* Electronic texts can respond to individual readers as they manipulate text to meet their personal needs and these texts "can be programmed to monitor what a reader is doing or not doing while reading a particular text and to adjust the text presentation accordingly" (p. 10). Technology certainly brings new meaning to the byword, *Reading is an interactive process.*

2. *The ascendancy of nonverbal elements.* Nonverbal elements of electronic text such as pictures, icons, movies, animations, and sound are available and can be integrated with student writing. Literacy has traditionally included print and illustrations only; these nonverbal elements of electronic text raise the question "What is print?"
3. *New textual structures.* Hypertexts facilitate reading and writing in a nonlinear fashion and allow interaction with other readers and writers. Some teachers are responding to this new format by requiring students to write a synthesis of information gathered instead of "gather the information and write down the main points from an outline" type of report.
4. *Expanding the boundaries of freedom and control.* Teachers can control readers' access to text and monitor their strategic actions while reading a text. In addition, readers and writers now have choices and a certain degree of control over their literacy learning.
5. *The pragmatics and conventions of literate activity.* A letter neatly written on a piece of stationery conveys a message just as using capital letters in an E-mail message "shouts." New writing conventions are being formed as users participate in electronic discussions on bulletin boards. Teaching the conventions of print has been standard practice; new technology is challenging even the most dearly held traditions.

The use of technology is promising in teaching reading and writing. Software as "tutor" is giving way to software as "tool." Digitized voice synthesis, when readily used, has the potential to revolutionize learning to read and write for those disabled readers who previously did not have access to the computer. Through this medium, language experience can occur more naturally between a student and a computer without the intervention of a teacher. Interactive multimedia materials bring new meaning to comprehension and composition.

Computers have changed dramatically the teaching of the writing process. The linear way of approaching writing has been replaced with a more recursive mode of inserting, editing, and revising text. New technology has caused educators to question firmly held beliefs about literacy, but the potential inherent in such technology cannot be ignored.

Summary

New research on the status of literacy and new thinking on underachievement in general and reading and writing disability in particular have caused educators to rethink the literacy environment provided for students. Motivation research has substantiated the value of task-focused classrooms and schools and helped teachers rethink student attitudes about their own intelligence.

Strategies for helping teach and motivate disabled readers and their more able classmates include cooperative strategies and classroom discussion. New technologies certainly hold great promise for helping students learn to read and write, but also challenge some of our existing beliefs about literacy.

References

Alvermann, D.E. (1987). Developing lifetime readers. In D.E. Alvermann, D.W. Moore, & M.W. Conley (Eds.), *Research within Reach: Secondary School Reading* (pp. 38–51). Newark, DE: International Reading Association.

Alvermann, D.E., Dillon, D.R., & O'Brien, D.G. (1987). *Using Discussion to Promote Reading Comprehension.* Newark, DE: International Reading Association.

Ammann, R. & Mittelsteadt, S. (1987). Turning on turned off students: Using newspapers with senior high remedial readers. *Journal of Reading, 30*(8), 708.

Anderman, E.M. & Maehr, M.L. (1994). Motivation and schooling in the middle grades. *Review of Educational Research, 64*(2), 287–309.

Anderson, V. & Roit, M. (1993). Planning and implementing collaborative strategy instruction for delayed readers in grades 6–10. *The Elementary School Journal, 94*(3), 121–138.

Applebee, A.N., Langer, J.A., & Mullis, I.V.S. (1988). *Who Reads Best?: Factors Related to Reading Achievement in Grades 3, 7, and 11.* Princeton, NJ: Educational Testing Service.

Criscuolo, N.P. & Gallagher, S.A. (1989). Using the newspaper with disruptive students. *Journal of Reading, 32*(5), 440–443.

Eccles, J.S. & Midgley, C. (1989). State-environment fit: Developmentally appropriate classrooms for young adolescents. In C. Ames & R. Ames (Eds.), *Research on Motivation in Education* (vol. 3) (pp. 139–186). San Diego, CA: Academic Press.

Gallagher, M. & Pearson, P.D. (1989). *Discussion, Comprehension, and Knowledge Acquisition in Content Area Classrooms* (Technical Report No. 480). Champaign, IL: Center for the Study of Reading.

Garcia, G.E. & Pearson, P.D. (1990). *Modifying Reading Instruction to Maximize Its Effectiveness for All Students* (Technical Report No. 489). Champaign, IL: Center for the Study of Reading.

Gold, P.C. (1981). Two strategies for reinforcing sight vocabulary of language experience. *The Reading Teacher, 35*(2), 141–143.

Griffin, R.S. (1988). *Underachievers in Secondary School: Education Off the Mark.* Hillsdale, NJ: Lawrence Erlbaum Associates.

Guthrie, J.T., Schafer, W.D., Wang, Y.Y., & Afflerbach, P. (1993). *Influences of Instruction of Amount of Reading: An Empirical Exploration of Social, Cognitive, and Instructional Indicators* (Reading Research Report No. 3). College Park, MD: National Reading Research Center.

Henderson, V. & Dweck, C.S. (1990). Motivation and achievement. In S.S. Feldman & G.R. Elliott (Eds.), *At the Threshold: The Developing Adolescent* (pp. 308–329). Cambridge, MA: Harvard University Press.

Ignoffo, M. (1988). Improve reading by overcoming the "inner critic." *Journal of Reading, 31*(8), 704–707.

Johnston, P., Allington, R., & Afflerbach, P. (1985). The congruence of classroom and remedial reading instruction. *The Elementary School Journal, 85*(4), 465–477.

Kibby, M.W. (1993). What reading teachers should know about reading proficiency in the United States. *Journal of Reading, 37*(1), 28–41.

Lee, N.G. & Neal, J.C. (1992–1993). Reading rescue: Intervention for a student "at promise." *Journal of Reading, 36*(4), 276–283.

Lunstrum, J.P. (1981). Building motivation through the use of controversy. *Journal of Reading, 24*(8), 687–691.

McTighe, J. & Lyman, F.T., Jr. (1988). Cueing thinking in the classroom: The promise of theory-embedded tools. *Educational Leadership, 45*(7), 18–24.

Midgley, C., Anderman, E., & Hicks, L. (1995). Differences between elementary and middle school teachers and students: A goal theory approach. *Journal of Early Adolescence, 15*(1), 90–113.

National Assessment of Educational Progress. (1994). *Reading: A First Look.* Washington, DC: Author.

Quandt, I. & Selznick, R. (1984). *Self-Concept and Reading.* Newark, DE: International Reading Association.

Reinking, D. (1994, December). *Reading and Writing with Computers: Literacy Research in a Post-Typographic World.* San Diego, CA: Paper presented at the National Reading Conference.

Smith, C.F., Jr. (1981). Motivating the reluctant reader through the top twenty. In A.J. Ciani (Ed.), *Motivating Reluctant Readers* (pp. 26–34). Newark, DE: International Reading Association.

Sternberg, R.J. (1987). Most vocabulary is learned from context. In M.G. McKeown & M.E. Curtis (Eds.), *The Nature of Vocabulary Acquisition* (pp. 457–465). Hillsdale, NJ: Lawrence Erlbaum Associates.

Tolkien, J.R.R. (1937). *The Lord of the Rings.* NY: Ballantine Books.

Urdan, T., Midgley, C., & Wood, S. (1995). Special issues in reforming middle level schools. In A. Wigfield & J.S. Eccles (Eds.), *Middle Grades Schooling and Early Adolescent Development: Part II: Interventions, Practices, Beliefs, and Contexts* (pp. 9–37). Thousand Oaks, CA: Sage Periodicals Press.

Wigfield, A. & Eccles, J.S. (1995). Middle grades schooling and early adolescent development: Part II: Interventions, practices, beliefs, and contexts. In A. Wigfield & J.S. Eccles (Eds.), *Middle Grades Schooling and Early Adolescent Development: Part II: Interventions, Practices, Beliefs, and Contexts* (pp. 5–8). Thousand Oaks, CA: Sage Periodicals Press.

Wixson, K.K. & Lipson, M.Y. (1984). Reading (Dis)Ability: An interactionist perspective. In T. Raphael (Ed.), *The Contexts of School-Based Literacy* (pp. 131–148). New York: Random House.

Chapter 5

The Environment of the New Assessment

LORRAINE GERHART
The University of Wisconsin—Oshkosh

Middle school students and teachers react strongly to the word "test." To the swarming young people who fill the halls, the test causes an alarmed buzzing. "When is the test? What's it about? What should I study? Is it long? Does it count? What should I do?" To the teachers who have remained to clean up and regroup after the teaching day, the test also raises concerns. "Did I include enough questions? Is the test fair? What if they haven't really learned this material? What will I do? I wonder if they will study? I'm not sure that they are prepared. Maybe I should reteach. . . ." The environment of the new assessment represents an effort to change from a negative event where knowledge and people are measured to a positive event where knowledge is applied and people are valued.

Middle school students avoid tests whenever possible even if it means "being sick." Tests measure what they know and students are reluctant to be measured and ranked against their peers. The whole idea of testing conflicts with their social goals and their desire for approval. Tests measure what students know, and what if that is not enough? The philosophical shift from "test" to "assessment" seems more consistent with what educators know about the nature and needs of young adolescents.

Let's drop in on some conversations Sal has with a parent. *We took a big test today. You know, one of those standardized things where no one can talk and you have to finish in thirty minutes. No, I don't really know what it was about because there were a lot of questions on different things. Oh, you mean was it reading? Well, you had to read but mainly, you had to answer questions and you didn't have to write anything. I don't know how I did because I worked so fast that it all blurred together. Some things I never even heard of.*

Let's listen in several weeks later when Sal reported a class assessment. *Today we had to use the graph that we made in our discussion group. We wrote speeches about* Fallen Angels. *We were supposed to persuade the rest of the class that Perry was against war. I think my speech was good because our group had good information on the graph. Besides, I really liked that book and I understood it, too. Why would I make mistakes? I picked out the facts that proved my point and we've talked in front of the class hundreds of times. Here's my speech, want to read it?*

Several months later, Sal's mother received a copy of the standardized test scores. Sal reacted, *Well, I suppose it proves I can read because the score seems to be sort of average. You know, Mom, I guessed on some of the questions. But I suppose it doesn't matter. It doesn't count in our grade or anything.*

Why should educators change their view of testing? The reason is that education happens when meaning is created on a personal level; the meaning that Sal created for the assessment on *Fallen Angels* stands as an example of education over the mindless routine of the standardized test.

The new assessment has changed the environment of testing and learning. The environment is positive and has instructional purpose. It is both student friendly and teacher friendly. The new assessment leads to reflective instruction that helps learners to develop meaning. Discussion in this chapter will focus on the atmosphere and philosophy of assessment, the background of authentic assessment, how to use performance assessment, how to measure metacognitive progress and how to incorporate portfolios. The goal of the new assessment is to reach the level where learning is in the "heart(s) of our students" (Price, 1996).

Atmosphere and Philosophy of Assessment

The philosophy of assessment revolves around the question "Why are we testing?" The general public would answer that testing makes teachers and students accountable. The accountability question is difficult to answer unless the assessor can use a score or rank—a number that is precise and definitive. The score or the number becomes the purpose of testing because it is easy to report and no one can argue about the relative place of a number. When the goal of assessment centers more on sitting beside and helping (Wiggins, 1989), the answer to "Why are we testing?" changes. The goal of assessment should be to help meet the purposes of school and learning. Real life demands that people have skills and understandings of the world in which they live. Assessment is needed to let teachers and students know what skills and understandings they already have and what they still need to learn.

Standardized Tests

Standardized instruments have a role in the educational marketplace. They are prepared tests that have been normed by giving the test to a sample population from various geographical locations to set scoring standards or norm references. When the norming process is completed, the test is sold commercially and given to other students whose scores are compared with the original norming population. This comparative process appears to be a reliable method of measuring how much students are learning.

Although these tests can be used to compare students on broad content areas and as a rough screening device, the important questions about the purposes and effectiveness of standardized tests center around the following ideas.

- The assumption that the content of the tests is necessary and desirable for a student to know is in question.
- Standardized tests are generally not aligned with curriculum and have little impact on the instruction that takes place in the classroom on a daily basis.
- Although the tests are easy to machine score, they are not cost effective when considering cost of scoring, distribution of information costs, time lost before feedback, and lost instruction time.
- Renorming is not understood and comparisons to former groups of students are not valid.
- Learning that includes generating solutions, higher order thinking, leadership ability, and creativity cannot be measured in standardized tests.
- These tests cannot truly measure the ability to read and write but rather, measure isolated skills that may be a part of literacy.

Does a standardized test truly measure reading and writing ability? A standardized test can measure the ability to recognize definitions, find literal details, recognize a main idea, identify grammar, usage, and mechanics conventions, and choose a conclusion from a number of options. A neat score is provided, but is it valid?

Current understanding is that reading is a process that involves a number of factors interacting with each other. A valid reading test measures interactive reading including the context, prior knowledge, choosing and applying appropriate strategies, asking and answering questions, making predictions based on the text, generating solutions to problems, and synthesizing and applying knowledge. Reading is interactive, complex, and constantly changing with the interaction between writer and reader. A standardized test is not capable of reflecting those higher order thinking skills and the interactive process (Jett-Simpson, 1990).

Authentic Assessment

In the middle school reading/language arts program, the question "Why are we testing?" can be answered simply: teachers want to know how well students are reading and writing so that they can make sound instructional decisions. The assessment must look beyond the right and wrong answer to how learning and understanding are constructed by the student: knowledge is constructed individually. Meaning does not reside in the text alone but in what the learner brings to the text (Commodore & Telfer, 1996). To be useful, an assessment instrument must be able to reflect the diversity of student thinking.

The middle school movement has changed how teachers view students, which has caused schools to reorganize their entire focus. Physical, cognitive, emotional, social, and moral developmental tasks (described in Chapter 2) have become an important part of any educational planning for middle level students. These changes have brought new life to instruction and learning, which is more student centered and has more "real-life" problem solving. Assessment has also changed to reflect the learning process, needs and characteristics of young adolescents, the interdisciplinary nature of middle school organization, and the expectations of middle level curriculum. Complex, holistic activities have demonstrated these important changes in assessment.

> *"The trend today in middle school assessment is toward authentic types of measurement that focus less on recall of information than on processing of information. Product, portfolio, and performance tools and techniques, for example, reflect the mission of the middle school and its philosophy and components better than do their traditional counterparts of criterion and norm-referenced tests" (Lounsbury, 1995, p. 331).*

Authentic assessment means that if educators want to find out how students are reading and writing, then students must be observed in action. Fragments of the task will not yield valid conclusions; for example, a student reading several sentences and choosing a response from multiple choices is using minimal skill. A student reading a long passage is required to understand the context and social situation in which the piece was written, reflect on prior knowledge, and synthesize the ideas. The goals of instruction and assessment require students to gain new information and skills in a context that can be easily translated and applied to the world outside the classroom. The following comparison highlights the differences between standardized testing and authentic assessment.

Norm-Referenced Testing	***Authentic Assessment***
Selected response of discrete items	Complex, holistic activities
Compares students easily with average score	Compares students with significant effort
End result important	Learning process important
Passive recall or recognition	Active application of knowledge
Cannot study for . . .	Study definitely helps
Limited focus	Comprehensive view of what kids can do
Reliable results	Reliability varies
Usable for large comparisons	Usable for instructional decisions
Ranking or sorting	Finding strengths and weaknesses
Measures acquisition of facts	Measures using knowledge meaningfully, extending and refining
Involves lower-order thinking only	Involves higher order thinking
Passive student involvement	Active student involvement
No self-assessment	Includes self-assessment
Not a "real-world" activity	Involves "real-world" activity

The public and the educational community often have difficulty accepting assessment changes when evidence of reading and writing seems elusive. If students are observed reading longer passages, comprehension is more difficult to evaluate. If a student has written a piece, the quality of the writing is difficult to ascertain. This evidence cannot be summed up with a "neat" score. Conclusions, however, can be drawn using rubrics and other methods of quantifying results. Students, parents, and teachers have found the results more significant in conveying what has actually been learned. Assessment procedures have to communicate on several levels—to the public, to parents, to other concerned educators in the students' lives, to the teacher, and to the students themselves. The following questions may guide the decisions about assessment procedures.

- Why are we testing or assessing?
- What information are we gathering?
- What is it we want students to be able to do?
- Why should they be expected to know and use this knowledge? When and under what conditions?
- How will this evidence direct instruction?
- How will this evidence influence students to make decisions about their learning?
- How can we communicate the evidence and the instructional decisions to the stakeholders?

The Atmosphere of Authentic Assessment

Picture students arriving at class excited about learning. They have prepared a poster that demonstrates their knowledge about vocabulary words, their roots and origins. The students had control over which words were chosen and what images they would use to portray the knowledge. The teacher had control over the product, which was to be a poster, and what specific information about each word that was to be included. Both teacher and students had established the standards of success in the rubric. The kids were sharing their posters before class. Let me see what you have. *Oh, that's neat! I used a basketball player on mine.* The class started with a hushed expectancy because this was going to be a good day.

Students had taken an active part in the learning event and they had some choices in the assessment process. Students had helped choose materials and had contributed to the decisions about the lessons on vocabulary. They knew that vocabulary meaning resides in context and their posters would provide a context. They had learned new ideas, practiced the skills necessary to feel comfortable, participated in discussions about the words and the literature pieces using the words, introduced new words from the books they were reading, and were able to explain how a good reader uses this knowledge. The students knew that their poster would communicate their knowledge. They would have a brief time to give an explanation to the class and to answer questions. They would be able to share any problems or significant ideas. The atmosphere is positive, one of seeing what the students have learned, discussing ideas, involvement, and creativity.

The atmosphere of authentic assessment is not of sorting who is able and who is disabled, or how well a student can or cannot read and write, but rather, the atmosphere is one of what students can do. The assessment leads to instructional decisions naturally and automatically. The next step is visible. The assessment leads students to make learning decisions or to make further suggestions to the teacher. It is an atmosphere of collaboration, of inquiry, of process, and of pride in achievement. The direction and focus are clear and do not emphasize isolated facts or mini-bites of information. This environment is positive for all learners and allows students of all abilities to demonstrate what they have accomplished.

Background of Authentic Assessment

Authentic assessment involves several different forms or alternatives. Observations, interviews, conferences, "think-alouds," learning logs, response journals, metacognitive techniques that require students to understand their knowledge of process, and self-assessment are all authentic ways of assessing student ability. The three most well-known alternatives are product assessment, performance assessment, and portfolios. *Product assessment* requires a concrete result such as a videotape, learning package, experiment, script, production, manual, or exhibit. *Performance assessment* has been used since the 1930s in studio arts, athletics, vocational education, and performing arts. Performance assessment is concerned with the processes used rather than the final product. *Portfolios* are meaningful collections of student work that exhibit overall effort, progress, and achievement. Middle school reading-language arts teachers often combine product and performance assessments. They are concerned with the processes of reading and writing that culminate in a finished product. In the assessment, criteria are used to evaluate both the product and the process. Performance assessment, therefore, generally includes product assessment in the reading/language arts classroom.

Performance assessment is used to demonstrate knowledge of process, interactive reading, complex thinking in tasks that are typical classroom tasks, or tasks especially designed for that purpose. Performances simulate real-life, problem-solving situations. Students in one middle school classroom were asked to show how one of the characters in *The Wave* by Todd Strasser (1981) demonstrated original thinking and defended personal beliefs. The students met in small groups to decide on which character, what passages had proof of that idea, and whether the character's subsequent actions supported that independent thinking.

After the groups had discussed their choices and made decisions, they divided into pairs. Each pair of students prepared a transparency that included the three elements. Students were judged by their peers who determined how they met the criteria and whether they communicated the ideas clearly and concisely. Many groups selected Laurie Saunders who was the most obvious choice. But others chose Mrs. Saunders, David, and even Amy. The groups had valid reasons for their choices, had passages to support their thinking, and cited subsequent actions. This assessment was fairly informal. It reflected understanding of the characters and their actions, and demonstrated students' ability to read and interpret what they had read. The teacher was interested in how students would apply higher order thinking skills and if students would demonstrate originality. This task was engaging to even the normally unenthusiastic students who now supported their choices aggressively.

The next step was to apply that same kind of thinking to their own classroom and school. Students made connections from the book characters to people in their own lives. The teacher's anecdotal records reflected growth in social attitudes among her students. The language that was used in this assessment became language that was used by students to give feedback to one another. The teacher directed the class to write an entry in their journals describing what they had gained from this assessment. The students made direct applications to their own lives. Several students commented on how surprised they were to find out that books could teach you about real life.

Performance assessment is more than a product and more than a knowledge of specific facts. A multiple choice test would not have been as rich nor would it have caused students to use higher order thinking or apply the learnings to their own lives. The instruction and the performance assessment were integrated into a meaningful classroom activity.

How to Complete Performance Assessment

Performance assessment involves documenting student behaviors on a real-world task. The emphasis can be on performance or product. Using performance assessment for reading and writing processes is an ideal match. This literacy event is an opportunity for students to show knowledge and expertise by recitals, demonstrations, speeches, dramas, and explanations. Although people are rarely called on in real life to recognize the right answer in a field of wrong answers, paper and pencil tests can be performances if they are real-life applications.

Creating a performance assessment has five steps. Literacy performances almost always involve process over product and involve meaningful tasks that are interesting and enticing.

Step One involves thinking about what process or thinking skill students are expected to be able to demonstrate. The teacher considers what content or concept will be used as a vehicle for the process or skill and completes this step by formulating a plan.

The actual performance task is the focus of **Step Two.** The teacher writes a complete description of the task that includes the required resources and clear, specific directions that are consistent with the desired performance. Students may be invited to participate in the editing of the task description. Completion of the editing on a transparency using the overhead projector with the class can be useful and motivating. The teacher uses the students's questions as a means of checking the clarity of the task. **Step Three** involves the interpretation of the performance and the development of criteria and a scoring procedure. An analytic rubric that awards points to each element of the performance may be used, or a holistic rubric with criteria that evaluate the overall performance might be preferred. Perhaps a checklist or rating scale might be used instead. The choice should be meaningful to the students and motivate them to demonstrate their abilities.

Final editing and a trial run are part of **Step Four.** When the performance assessment has been tried, misconceptions, lack of clarity, and other problems can be edited and changed.

Teachers sometimes skip Step Four and proceed directly to **Step Five** due to time constraints. The performance is used with the students and incongruities are noted and allowances made during the scoring and interpretation. The performance will allow students to show how well they can use the process of reading or writing. After the scoring and self-assessment, the results will be happily reported by students and teachers.

The following examples are taken from students at Elmbrook Middle School, Brookfield, Wisconsin. Performance assessments are used extensively during instruction and as an overall view of how well students have grasped the processes of reading and writing. Examples are divided into literary appreciation, wide reading, strategic interactive reading, and application to life.

Literary Appreciation

The performance assessment used in Figure 5.1 was written by teachers, given several trials, and revised. It was part of a series of lessons using key words, discovering character, and appreciating literature. Students were enthusiastic and referred to this literacy event at different times during the year. Students also suggested repeating this assessment with other pieces of literature. This performance was more formal in its design and still maintained interest and motivation. It provided evidence that students understood and appreciated the Irving selections and understood how characters developed.

Another performance assessment was informal and spontaneous in nature. A middle school class was learning how to use more active verbs and more colorful adjectives in writing. The class was reading *Where the Red Fern Grows* by Wilson Rawls. The teacher created a quick, informal assessment to determine if students were understanding the book and its characters and to note how the students were using verbs and adjectives in speaking and writing. Each student created a character wheel for the character of their choice. They found examples in the novel that contained strong, active verbs and colorful adjectives to enter on the wheel. Tired words such as "gives," "goes," "got," "nice," "good," and "friendly" were discouraged. After sharing with one another, students prepared a short, spontaneous talk using the word wheel as their guide. Examples are included in Figure 5.2.

The time to prepare was limited and the objective of the talk was to communicate about the character while introducing some of the colorful language. Students were rated on a scale of 1 to 3 (three representing very good) on three questions.

- Did your classmates understand the story?
- Did your classmates use colorful verbs and adjectives?
- Did they communicate the ideas about the character?

The teacher discovered that the students were ready for the next step, which was to write about one of the characters, using colorful language. This assessment was quick and easy, with fairly consistent results, and gave feedback for subsequent instruction.

Wide Reading

Encouraging wide reading can be done in a variety of formats. Book shares, read-alouds, posters, recommendations, and finding the next book for your classmate to read are a few ideas. Students like to put together book lists of favorites, some annotated and some not.

Literary Selections from Washington Irving for Literary Appreciation

Instructional Objectives:
The student will be able to:

- Understand and appreciate literary selections by Washington Irving.
- Edit a selection and divide the prose for interpretive reading within a reader's theater.
- As an audience member, take notes using key words on the main character presented in each reader's theater to explain what the character says, does, and what others say about him.
- As an audience member, assess peers' reader's theater presentations.

Student Performance Description:

After a brief teacher introduction is made for each Irving excerpt, students form their literature circles by selecting the piece that interests them. The first task of each newly created literature circle is to read the selection. Groups must then decide what to cut and what to keep in order to share that excerpt with the class as a reader's theater presentation. Parts must be divided equitably between members. The first narrator must introduce the selection and the readers to the audience. Reader's theater presentations should involve as much dialogue as possible to provide for dramatic oral reading and to maintain audience interest.

Students in the audience will record information regarding what the main character says and does, and what other characters say about him in the form of key-worded notes in chart form. Later, students will formulate a significant statement from their notes.

Performance Based Assessment:

The audience will assess each reader's theater presentation; peer assessment is appropriate for a performance done for the entire group.

Prior Instruction:

- Appreciating literature
- Understanding characters
- Modeling of reader's theater
- Comparing reader's theater, plays, musicals, skits in chart form based on examples of each
- Keywording series of lessons for notetaking and comprehension
- Applying key words as a notetaking device
- Experience with literature circles
- Experience with peer assessment and self-assessment

Excerpts from Washington Irving:

"Rip Van Winkle"
"Legend of Sleepy Hollow"
"Knickerbocker's History of New York"

FIGURE 5.1 Sample assessment

Sample Listening Guide

Your name____

As you listen to other group presentations, identify the main character. Use key words to make notes about what the main character says, does, and what others say. From these notes, you will be able to write a significant statement about the main character.

Group leader, excerpt	Main character	What the character acts like	What the character does	What others say about the character
Jim *Rip Wan Winkle*	*Dame Van Winkle*	*shiftless man* *lazy*	*hits with broom* *nags*	*scolds sharp tongue*

Significant Statement:

The neighbors say that Dame Van Winkle has a sharp tongue because she nags Rip, hits him with a broom, and calls him shiftless.

Name__________________________ Date__________________

Washington Irving Literature Circles
Peer Assessment Sheet

Directions:

1. Before the presentation begins, record the title of their selection and the names of the group members below. This will help you focus on your job as assessor. Remember, you want to be attentive, thoughtful, and fair. When the audience is ready, the group will begin.
2. Read over the standards for performance and the criteria for assessment so that you know what is expected of each group.
3. During the presentation, listen thoughtfully and record your key word notes about the main character.
4. After the presentation take a few minutes to give a "+" to any standard that was met to your satisfaction.
5. Now think of the overall performance, the standards, and check the criteria description that most closely fits the performance you have just seen.

Title of Selection: ____

Group Members: ____

____

FIGURE 5.1 *Continued*

Standards for Performance:

(A "+" mark indicates an area that was done well.)

_____ Lines were delivered with adequate volume and clarity.

_____ People spoke with appropriate conviction and emotion.

_____ The presentation showed that group members read and practiced their parts.

_____ Group members read their lines on cue.

_____ When group members were not speaking, they were supportive to the other group members.

_____ The presentation helped to explain the main character by telling what he said, did, or what others said about him.

_____ The presentation included enough passages of description and narration to explain the scene's setting, action, and characters to the audience.

Criteria for Assessment:

______ An *exemplary* reader's theater presents the selection with as much dialogue as possible to show what the main character said and did, and what other characters said about him. Furthermore, because everyone read on cue with much conviction and emotion, the presentation was both entertaining and informative. Enough description and narration were included to help the audience understand the action of the scene, get a "taste" of the author's style, and "see" the scene in their mind's eye. Finally, all group members were involved in producing this effective presentation. They obviously put much time and effort into preparation, both as a group and individually.

______A *competent* reader's theater presents the selection with as much dialogue as possible to show what the main character said and did, and what other characters said about him. Furthermore, because everyone read on cue, the audience could follow the dialogue easily; however, members did not read with adequate conviction and emotion to make the presentation entertaining. Some description and narration helped the audience understand the action of the scene, get a taste of the author's style and imagine this scene in their minds eye. Finally, some group members were not as well prepared as they should have been, and this lessened the impact of the reader's theater on the audience.

______A *minimally* competent reader's theater presents the selection with as much dialogue as possible to show what the main character said and did, and what other characters said about him. Unfortunately, not everyone read on cue, and this made the presentation hard to follow. Members did not read with adequate conviction and emotion. Even with some description and narration to help the audience understand the action of the scene, lack of effective oral reading and poor cuing made it impossible for the audience to get a true taste of the author's style or see the scene in their mind's eye. The group needed much more practice.

FIGURE 5.1 *Continued*

(Audience, you may want to write some words of praise or a constructive suggestion for improvement for group members.)

____

____

____

How did understanding the main character help you to appreciate the excerpt?

____

____

____

FIGURE 5.1 *Continued*

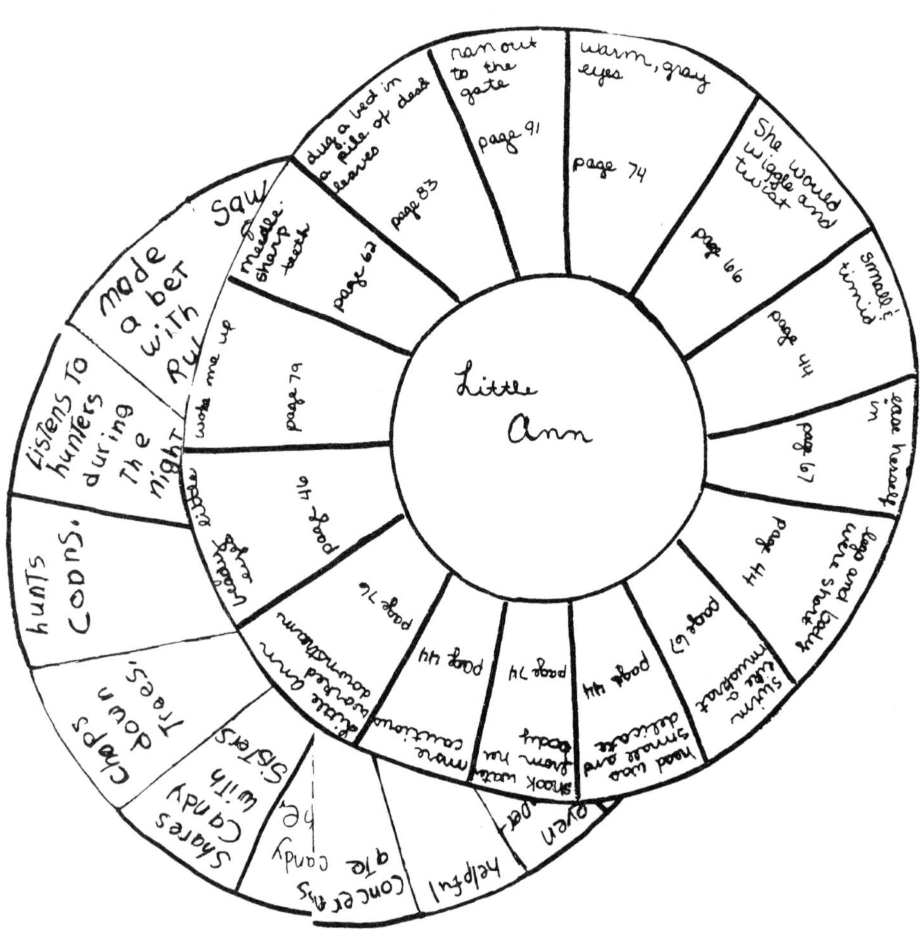

FIGURE 5.2 Word wheel

Students are able to develop their own rating scale to determine if the books are widely read and if they have a good sampling of books and literature. Figure 5.3 presents a student's recommendations in paragraph form written so that readers would know more about the book choices.

Students were encouraged to choose their own books and to reach out and sample new kinds of books. They shared the books by preparing something to bring to class such as what was outstanding or important to the reader, a special moment, or insights for everyone. The sharing session was the basis for a self-assessment. Students were asked to rate the book in two ways: (1) On a scale of 1 to 10, was this a good book? and (2) On a continuum, was this book like many other books you have read or was this book in different categories from other books you have read? Figure 5.4 illustrates the sharing and self-assessment of one student.

Dr. Larina Vassitchenko (1992), professor from the University of Estonia, shared an idea at the First Russian Reading Conference in Moscow that she called "Wide Reading—Picture It!" She developed a spider web grid, as shown in Figure 5.5A, where each supporting thread represented a different category. If students read a book in a particular category, a small dot was placed on the supporting thread. At specific times, students would connect the dots and a picture of their reading would emerge as in Figure 5.5B. If students had sampled many books and were well read, the picture would be a round ball. Naturally, few students had a perfect sphere. The idea led to a lively discussion and students decided to add a book category called "junk," which was for jokes, Book of Lists, and similar types. This interesting idea became an informal assessment that students requested at the beginning, middle, and the end of the year. They also included a list of titles that were on the picture web and added color to the pictures. Students did not want to be rated but they did want to share ideas and were willing to make comments about how their reading choices had changed over the year.

Strategic Interactive Reading

When thinking about the interactive reading process, several factors are to be considered before, during, and after reading. Students often use the following varied strategies to construct meaning from print.

The Reading Process

Before Reading	*During Reading*	*After Reading*
Building background	Interactive reading	Reviewing the facts
Preview or survey	Self-monitoring	Responding to what you have read
Activating prior knowledge	Metacognitive thinking	Applying the knowledge
Vocabulary (recognizing and knowing)	Selecting	Reshaping the knowledge
Providing a mental set (focusing attention)	Organizing	Reorganizing or manipulating the ideas
Setting the purpose	Recognizing structure	Integrating what you have read
	Interpreting	
	Applying strategies	

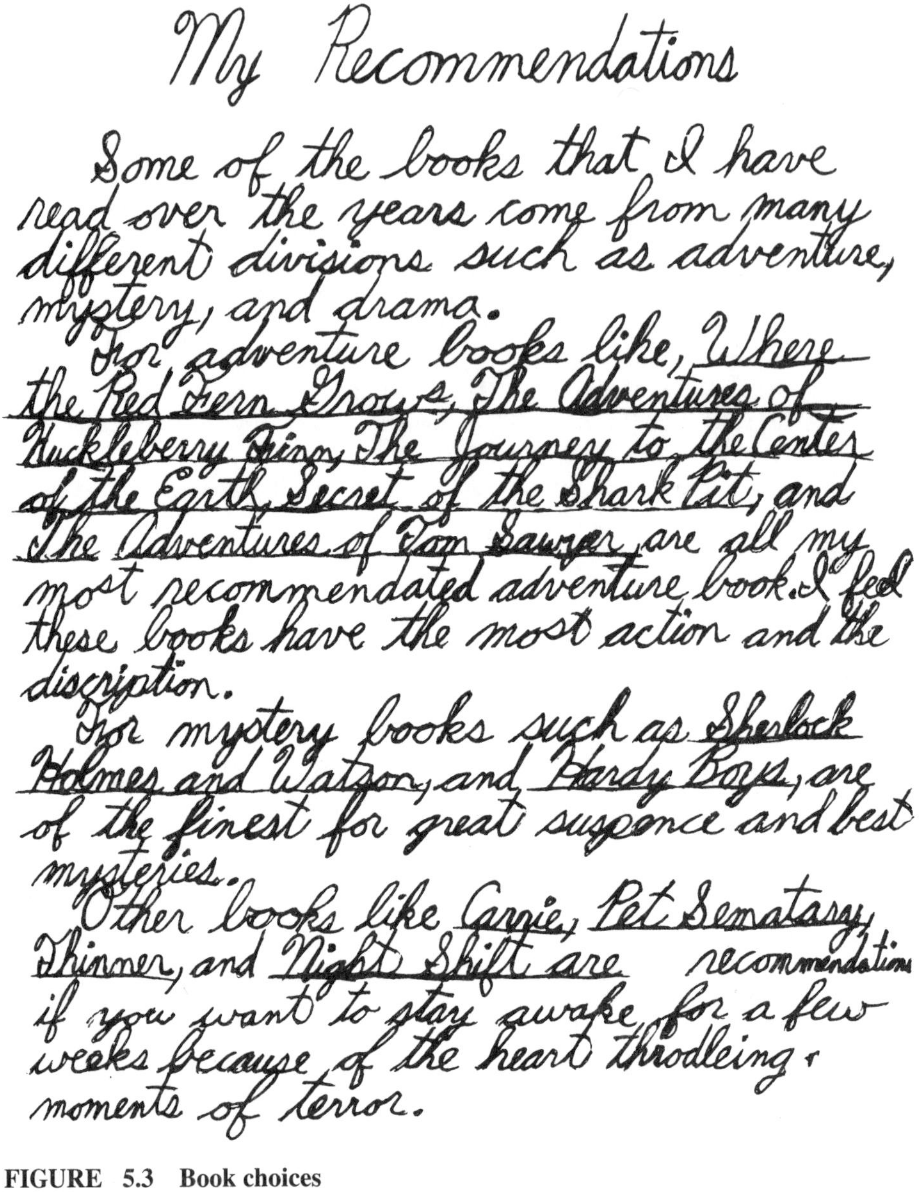

My Recommendations

Some of the books that I have read over the years come from many different divisions such as adventure, mystery, and drama.

For adventure books like, *Where the Red Fern Grows*, *The Adventures of Huckleberry Finn*, *The Journey to the Center of the Earth*, *Secret of the Shark Pit*, and *The Adventures of Tom Sawyer* are all my most recommendated adventure book. I feel these books have the most action and the discription.

For mystery books such as *Sherlock Holmes and Watson*, and *Hardy Boys*, are of the finest for great suspence and best mysteries.

Other books like *Carrie*, *Pet Sematary*, *Thinner*, and *Night Shift* are recommendations if you want to stay awake for a few weeks because of the heart throdleing moments of terror.

FIGURE 5.3 Book choices

A distinct advantage exists for students who monitor their own comprehension and possess metacognitive skill. In a language arts classroom, students will use strategies for successful reading such as for unknown words, for understanding literature, for understanding text structure, for activating prior knowledge. If students are aware of strategies and know how to use them, this knowledge can help them become more effective readers. Results of self-reporting through interviews, questionnaires, checklists, and discussions can signal to teachers when instruction is needed. Sometimes a series of explanations by the

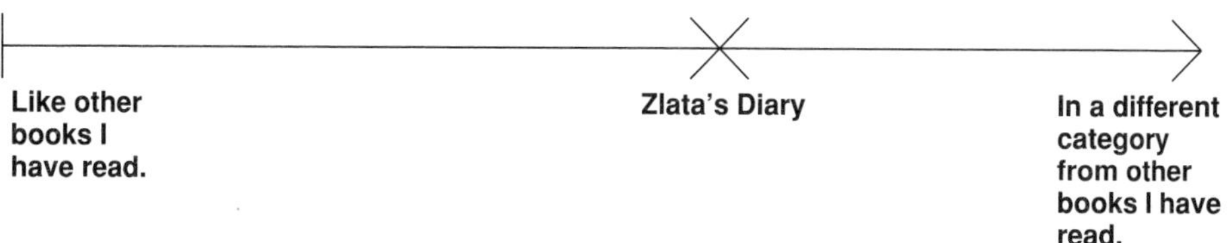

One student decided to place diverse categories as points on the continuum. Mysteries were placed on the left because they were read most often. Science fiction was placed on the far right because the student had never read a book from that category.

FIGURE 5.4 Zlata's Diary: rating 10

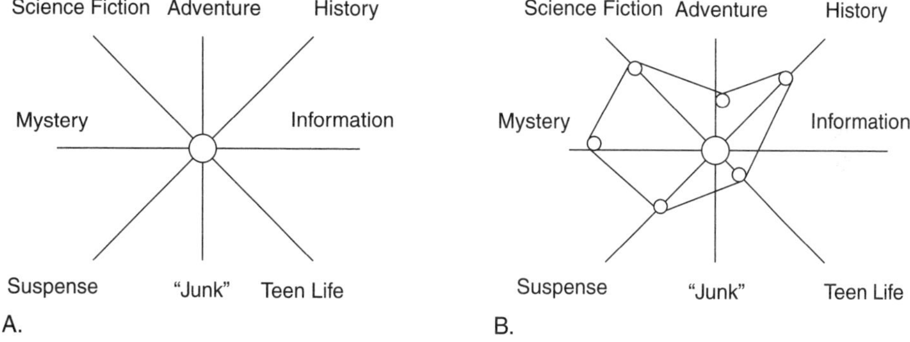

FIGURE 5.5 Wide reading—picture it!

students heightens awareness, provides the basis for discussion, and provides feedback to the teacher. In Figure 5.6, students answered the question "Are you a good reader?" The teacher discovered that the students were not aware of strategies they might use to help them and that they had not considered study reading at all. These responses were the basis for further instruction and metacognitive development for the students. The teacher devised a simple checklist for the class to monitor student awareness with this sample and subsequent samples. As students developed more self-awareness and a knowledge of strategies, their writing revealed these developments. Figure 5.7 includes ideas about improving vocabulary.

Learning about reading and understanding how to use strategies help to create a literate environment where the students read freely, interact with one another, discuss strategies to use, and participate in instruction. Misconceptions can be addressed. Self-assessment can be developed through self-reporting when students are asked to explain the purpose, to state what worked and what did not, to give suggestions to others, and to use a new strategy when it is needed. Figure 5.8 on page 80 demonstrates one student's struggle.

The examples presented in this section represent the metacognitive levels of the students based on their view of a good reader, how they developed vocabulary, and how their learning had progressed. The responses sometimes showed confusion and misconceptions or revealed the limits of the students' knowledge. The teacher assigned ratings that were used to make inferences about the instruction that would most benefit these students.

Are You a Good Reader?

Yes, I think I'm a good reader because I love read. I do understand almost all that I am reading. I usually read adults or young adults books. I usually read about 20-30 minutes a night. I like to read novels, mysteries, and serious stories. I do consider myself a good reader.

Are you a good reader?
I think I am a good reader because I can picture and understand the story. Although I read quite slowly it helps me to get more absorbed in a b-

I really enjoy reading. (honest!) More proof you say? Hmmm... I have read 900 pages over the past 4 days. That's all.

FIGURE 5.6 Are you a good reader?

Although the ratings were not shared, the conclusions about instruction were shared with the students so that they might give feedback. The following is a sample of the teacher's observation and rating sheet.

Metacognitive Progress

3 = very good

	Views reading as understanding	*Knows and uses reading strategies*	*Understands vocabulary strategies*	*Aware of progress in learning*
Kevin	3	1	1	3
Joe	2	1	3	2
Debbie	3	1	2	3
Kathy	1	1	3	2

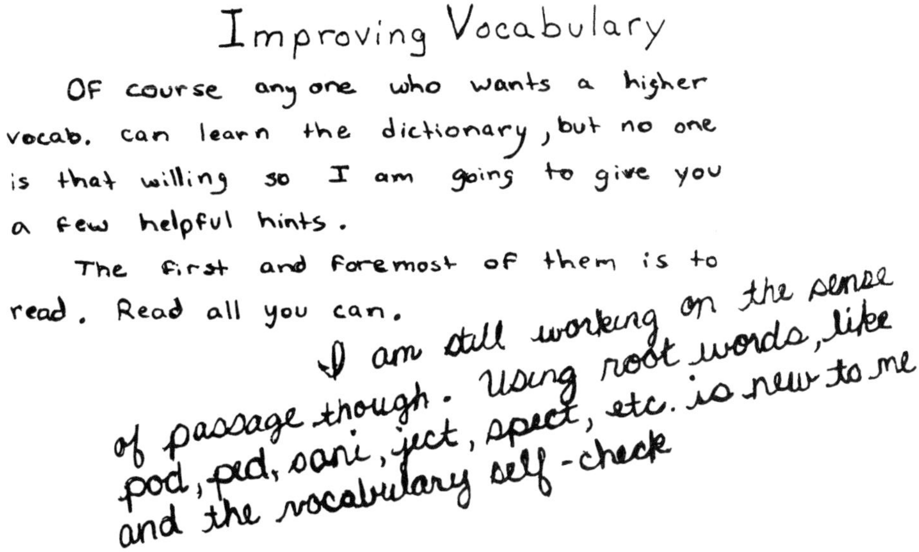

Improving Vocabulary

Of course any one who wants a higher vocab. can learn the dictionary, but no one is that willing so I am going to give you a few helpful hints.

The first and foremost of them is to read. Read all you can.

I am still working on the sense of passage though. Using root words, like pod, ped, sani, ject, spect, etc. is new to me and the vocabulary self-check

FIGURE 5.7 Improving vocabulary (The teacher concluded that students were knowledgeable about vocabulary but could benefit from comprehension strategies. Students agreed.)

One of the most important things students can do is monitor their own understanding. Students need to make sense of what they are reading. If students cannot construct meaning, they should stop and use a fix-up strategy of some sort. At the very least, students should reread. Teachers can help students to be aware of what they know and what they do not know. To be effective readers, students need to be alert to what is confusing, to be aware of reasons for reading, and to have purposeful interactions. Two techniques can be used to train students metacognitively or to assess their understanding: think-alouds and metacognitive interviews.

Think-Alouds

Think-alouds give students the opportunity to talk the book through while they are reading. A teacher might give students sentences to which they can respond and explain. The teacher should select a piece of text, hard enough and long enough but not discouraging. The text can be taped during the think-aloud, then students can listen and make notes. The teacher does not give extensive directions because too much conversation will direct the students' thinking and control the content of the think-aloud. The teacher might begin by saying, "I am interested in what you think about as you read. So I'd like you to read a sentence and then say out loud what you are thinking as you work at understanding the text."

Metacognitive Interviews

The second technique is metacognitive interviews, which can be small group discussions or individual interviews. The interview might even take the form of a written dialogue. Possible questions to use in an interview are suggested on page 80.

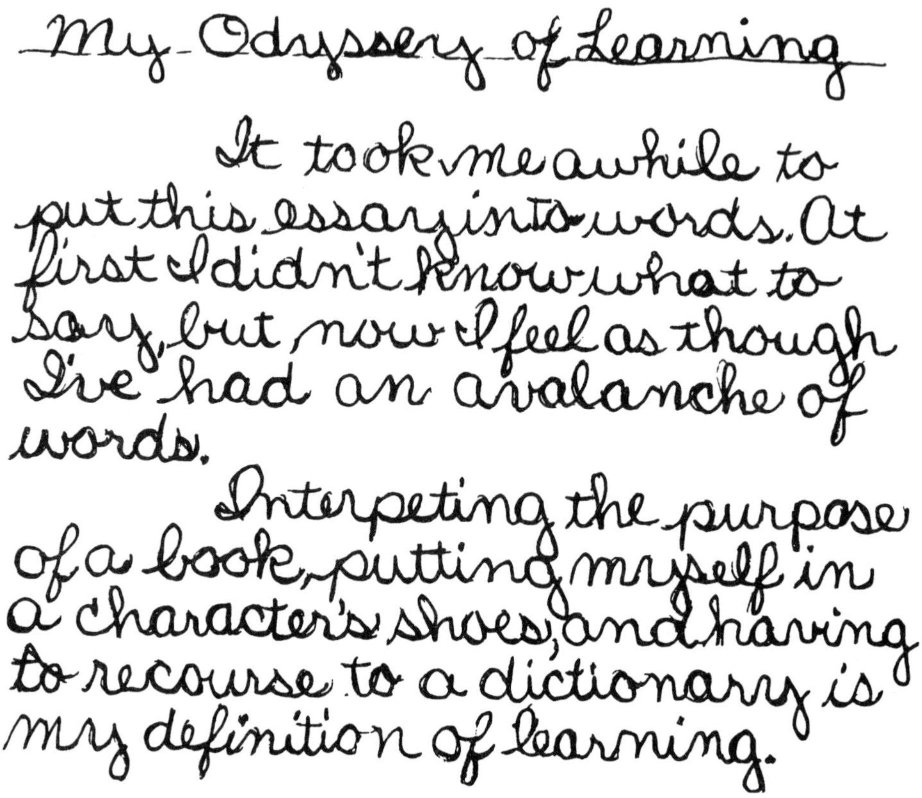

My Odyssey of Learning

It took me awhile to put this essay into words. At first I didn't know what to say, but now I feel as though I've had an avalanche of words.

Interpeting the purpose of a book, putting myself in a character's shoes, and having to recourse to a dictionary is my definition of learning.

FIGURE 5.8 Self assessment

Possible Questions for a Metacognitive Interview

- What is the first thing you do when you begin reading?
- Do you look for anything special when you read?
- Which portion of the reading is more important to you—beginning, middle, or end?
- How can you tell which sentences are the most important?

Planning

- Before you read, do you do anything special?
- If you were in a hurry and could only read one part, which part would you read?
- What could you do while you are reading that would help you remember better?
- What do you notice about a selection before you begin reading?

Monitoring your comprehension

- Do you ever go back and read a part over again?
- What do you do if you come to a word that you do not know?

- When do you skip a part of the reading?
- How do you adjust your speed when reading?
- What do you do if you find that you do not understand what you are reading?

Think alouds and metacognitive interviews are both techniques that are good methods to assess comprehension and yield significant information about the strategic behavior of students. The teacher has an illustration of the readers' process thinking and is able to use the information as a guide to plan instruction. These two informal assessment techniques slow the reader down, encourage thinking, and highlight text that is confusing. How others think as they read is revealed to the peer group, which advances their comprehension.

Application to Life

A consistent message in this chapter has been the tie of assessment to real-world learning. The first example is shown in Figure 5.9 on page 82 and details a cooperative discussion in which students relate to their own lives what they have learned by reading *The Wave* by Todd Strasser. The feedback provided by the discussion involves a new understanding of the book and information about the quality of the discussion.

The second example is a formal assessment for an issues unit. Students studied an issue of their choice such as war, abuse, or price of success. They formulated significant questions and were assigned to frame an opinion based on facts and examples. Students gained information from magazines, nonfiction books, television shows, interviews and discussions, and novels written with their issue as a central theme. Each student was assigned an advisory group who would discuss and question the opinions framed by group members. Figure 5.10 on page 84 describes the task, and shows a preparation guide for writing and the rubric used to judge the opinion paper.

Portfolios

Portfolio assessment has become increasingly popular in the educational arena. Students, teachers, and parents like to peruse collections of students' work. The collection, which is personal and inviting, allows an inner view. The portfolio demonstrates students' knowledge about learning and their approaches used to accomplish a task. Portfolios show engagement and self-reflection and provide a snapshot of students' personalities.

Portfolios are not meant to be wild collections of every piece of work that a student has done. To be effective, the collection of work must be selective and demonstrate the care and reflection that the student used to put it together. The portfolio becomes a series of pictures of the student's performance. The decision making, the thought given to how the entry fits in and what it shows about the effort and progress of the individual, the evidence of personal goals and interests, the testimony to growth and change are all part of a learning process for the student.

Planning portfolio assessment should be carefully completed. The stakeholders will be cooperative and enthusiastic if they have had a chance to be part of the planning and

A cooperative discussion on *The Wave* by Todd Strasser

The Big Question: What kinds of control or pressure are placed on people? What can you do about this pressure?

Task: Answer the big question using the examples from *The Wave* and from your own life.

Expected Behavior:
You will be able to:
1. Answer the question with examples from *The Wave* and from your own life.
2. Stay with your group and participate.
3. Sign the recorded notes to show that you agree that this is what was said.

Roles:

SUMMARIZER:	Retell or restate each point given.
RECORDER:	Record participation by recording notes during the discussion.
FACILITATOR:	Keep the discussion going. Ask clarifying questions. Encourage everyone to make contributions. Collect participation chips.

(The object is to give up all ten of your chips when you contribute so that you have none at the end of the discussion.)

Goals:
- All participate
- All accountable, able to answer the question orally or on paper
- Socially, encourage each other (no putdowns)

Process:
- List three things that went well and one area to be improved.

From the First Round:
1. Did everyone participate? How did you know?
2. Was everyone able to answer the big question?
3. Was there an opportunity to encourage each other?
4. Which job was the hardest to do?
5. How did the practice session help?
6. What could be improved?

FIGURE 5.9 A cooperative discussion

become engaged and committed to the activity. Students and adults are motivated by an activity that centers on themselves and their interests. The only thing that could go wrong is poor planning, which would create a scenario where all parties become overwhelmed and discouraged. Beginning on a smaller scale with a limited portfolio that is well planned is a beneficial approach. Johns (1993) used three questions to provide an organizing structure for the planning.

1. What do I want to find out?
2. How will I collect the data?
3. What do I do with it when I have it collected?

The team, a school committee, or a working group of representative stakeholders, might serve as a focus group to discuss the questions and to contribute to decision making.

Portfolios can represent some formal planning when the information included also serves the interests of teachers, parents, or the school district. They may be used all year for parent and student conferences, for planning the next steps of instruction, and as evidence that students are developing literacy skills. Sharing the portfolio may be done student to student, student to teacher, student to parent, parent to teacher, teacher to teacher, or teacher to supervisor. How the portfolios will be used has an impact on the decisions about what to include. Some formal use of portfolios have included rubrics or standards of performance, self-evaluation, and a collection that passes to the next level of schooling.

A personal bias is toward using the portfolio in a more informal, spontaneous manner. Other kinds of assessments are used that meet the needs of formal evidence. Picture a classroom scene where a spontaneous, informal portfolio is used. To introduce the idea of a portfolio, the teacher can assemble a display that has a chart as the centerpiece. Many examples, pictures of portfolios, and types of portfolios surround the chart. What might be included on the chart to answer the question "What are portfolios?"

What are Portfolios?

A series of pictures of your performance

The answer to the question "How well am I doing?"

A range of examples

A portrait of you and your work

A reflection of your growth

Samples of your capabilities

Demonstrations of the unique you

Reflections of you in the process of learning

Larger than a report card but smaller than a suitcase

Contains artifacts or pictures

Looks like a folder or accordion folder

Issues Unit Opinion Paper

Your task is to write an opinion paper that shares what you have learned about the issue on which you were working. You have studied the issue by reading widely and gathering information from a variety of sources. Some information was gathered from interviews and discussions just as it is done in daily life. A preparation sheet is provided for you to use as prewriting thinking in planning your opinion paper. Your advisory group will help you clarify your opinion and review the standards of performance that are expected.

Organize your paper using the following plan:

Paragraph 1: Restate the question as a statement. The second sentence should contain your opinion followed by a transition sentence.

Paragraphs 2–5: Support your position with evidence and information from your sources.

Concluding paragraph: Summary and clincher.

When you have completed the rough draft, meet with your peer editing group to help you make revisions and corrections. Make a final draft to submit to your teacher.

Preparation Guide for Your Opinion Paper

What book(s) did you read?

What is the big question that concerns your issue?

What is your opinion about the issue? Your opinion may answer the question directly or it may relate to the question.

FIGURE 5.10 Issues unit opinion paper

What sources of support do you have for your opinion? Cite the source and a key phrase that explains the support.

1.
2.
3.
4.
5.
6.

What did the people you interviewed say about it? Include who said it and state briefly what they said.

1.
2.
3.

What did your advisory group say?

1.
2.
3.

List at least five examples from the novel(s) that support your opinion.

Issues Unit Opinion Paper Assessment

Standards for Performance:
(A check mark indicates an area that needs improvement.)

_____ The issue statement is in the introduction.
_____ The thesis or opinion sentence is clearly stated in the introduction.
_____ An effective transition is written between the introduction and the first paragraph.
_____ Each paragraph presents a distinctive support for your position.
_____ Convincing evidence for each support is given in the body.
_____ Transitions are supplied to weave evidence together throughout the body.
_____ The last paragraph provides an accurate summary of the most important ideas.

FIGURE 5.10 *Continued*

_____ The last paragraph ends with an effective clincher sentence.
_____ Correct spelling, capitalization, punctuation, and grammar are used throughout.
_____ Final copy format is used (ink, cursive, lined paper, one side only).
_____ Writing is neat with a minimum of crossouts.

Criteria for Assessment:

_____An *exemplary* opinion paper clearly states the issue and the author's opinion in the introduction. Through a skillful transition, the reader is drawn to the body of the essay where each paragraph supplies convincing support. This support is backed with well-documented evidence from a variety of sources. Thorough research and careful prewriting obviously are the basis of this comprehensive document. The concluding paragraph offers an accurate summary of the author's main supports and a satisfying clincher sentence to restate the opinion. The quality of the prose, the grammatical correctness of the written message, and the appearance of the final copy attest to the considerable time and effort put forth by the author.

_____A *competent* opinion paper clearly states the issue and thesis in the introduction. A transition is provided to the first paragraph of the body. Convincing support is provided in each body paragraph; this information is provided by evidence from several sources. It is apparent, however, that further reading and documentation of evidence could have been done. Although the concluding paragraph accurately summarizes the main support, a satisfying clincher sentence is not provided. Furthermore, some errors in word choice, grammar, or the final copy appearance undermine the author's message. Adequate time and effort certainly went into this essay.

_____A *minimally* competent opinion paper clearly states the issue and thesis in the introduction. No effective transition is provided to the body. Support is given in each body paragraph, but because the evidence is inadequate, the support is not convincing to the reader. Further reading and documentation should have been done. Either a concluding paragraph is missing, or it does not completely summarize the main support nor restate the thesis. Finally, errors in word choice, grammar, and final copy appearance make it obvious that much more time and effort should have been put into this essay.

FIGURE 5.10 *Continued*

The teacher's portfolio is shared and put on display. After some discussion about portfolios and why such an activity is beneficial, the teacher and students brainstorm. They try to suggest as many pieces of evidence as possible to answer the question "How can you show that you are a good reader?" Brainstorming sets the stage for building the portfolio as a final literacy activity for the middle school experience.

The product of the brainstorming and description of the activity are provided in Figure 5.11. The results exceeded everyone's expectations. The eighth graders decided they wanted to participate so other teachers became involved. Students and parents were enthusiastic. Reflections contained important insights. Sharing sessions were happy events reflecting a true middle school "hum." The portfolios became a synthesis of the students' literacy learning in middle school.

Grade Eight Reading Portfolio

A portfolio is a way to present your work to others. Photographers, artists, models, and business people use this tool to show their competencies. The portfolio of samples helps to answer the question "What are you capable of doing?"

In putting together a reading portfolio, we are trying to answer the question, "How can you show that you are a good reader?"

Assignment:

Create a portfolio for yourself that illustrates your capability as a reader. Your portfolio will have different sections according to your choices. Once you begin working on this idea, you will probably think of some unique items to include.

1. Books
   - List of books that you have read
   - A copy of one or two of your best reading logs
   - A summary of a book read this year
   - A book report
   - Sample lists to show the variety of books read
   - Description of a favorite book
   - List of books that you have read at home and a list for those read at school
   - Brief description of the five latest books read
   - List and/or descriptions of favorite authors

2. Personal Data
   - Grades for middle school
   - Grades for reading class
   - Create an application for high school and complete it
   - Short data sheet
   - Description of you (picture?)

3. Background
   - History of parents, relatives, or others who have read a great deal
   - Statement of how others influenced your reading
   - Discussion of your ability as a reader
   - Description of your experiences with reading
   - Plans for your future occupation and/or college
   - Things from the past such as projects, essays, etc

4. Testimonials
   - Letters of recommendation from people who know your reading habits
   - A page of teacher comments
   - Suggested books for others (celebrity list)
   - An interview with someone you think is a good reader

FIGURE 5.11 Grade eight reading portfolio

Continued

5. Factual Material
    - A copy of a newspaper or magazine article that you think is important
    - Your reaction and opinions on the topic from a magazine article
    - A short bibliography for a problem that you think is especially important

6. Special Options
    - Advertisements or commercials for reading
    - Presentations you have made
    - Certificates of recognition
    - Self-recognition
    - Taped reading of you at your best
    - A chart to show speed of reading, perhaps on the books you have read
    - Special vocabulary list related to a problem area or a favorite topic

7. Unique Ideas
    - Your own special thoughts or creations

8. Strategies Used in Reading
    - Proving answers to questions
    - Comprehension model
    - Ways to monitor comprehension
    - SQ3R using the question/answer columns
    - Key wording
    - Semantic map
    - A description of techniques that you use when reading
    - Event/reaction chart

9. Writing
    - A short story that you have written
    - Writing a characterization for one of the books read
    - Poems that you have read or written
    - An essay question concerning your literacy
    - A copy of your writing assessment (if possible)
    - Critiques of pieces of writing

Please organize your portfolio in sections and include a table of contents. Put your portfolio in a colored pocket folder or accordion folder. Decorate the cover appropriately and in a way that represents you and your special interests. For example, someone who is interested in soccer might decorate the cover with soccer balls. On the label, include your name, year, and high school that you will attend.

FIGURE 5.11 *Continued*

Summary

Standardized testing has a role in education as a means of ranking students and appears to hold students and teachers accountable. The new assessment, however, has changed the environment of testing and learning to one of positive accomplishment with instructional purpose. Authentic assessment means that if educators want to find out how students are reading and writing, then students must be observed in action. Performance assessment requires students to demonstrate their understanding of the process of reading and writing as well as their ability to read and write effectively. Performance assessment gives evidence of literary appreciation, wide reading, strategic interactive reading, and application to life. Portfolios are useful collections of student work that show evidence of effort, progress, personal goals, interests, and growth of a student. The most important aspect of the new assessment is the tie to instruction because it indicates to the teacher what new learning should be initiated or what learning needs reinforcement. Self-assessment is powerful because it involves students in their own learning. Teachers no longer dispense knowledge and students receive it. The environment of the new assessment creates a positive collaboration between teacher and student as a learning team.

References

Commodore, C. & Telfer, V. (1996, January). The pluses and minuses of the elimination of the WSAS performance assessment for the 1995 budget. *Highlighter: Focusing on Assessment.* Sturgeon Bay, WI: Wisconsin Association for Supervision and Curriculum Development.

Jett-Simpson, M. (1990). *Toward an Ecological Assessment of Reading Progress.* Schofield, WI: Wisconsin State Reading Association.

Johns, J. (1993, February). *Portfolios and How to Use Them.* Paper presented at Waukesha County Reading Council, Pewaukee, WI.

Lounsbury, J. (Ed.) (1995). *Teaching at the Middle Level: A Professional's Handbook.* Lexington, MA: D.C. Heath.

Myers, W. (1988). *Fallen Angels.* New York: Scholastic.

Price, J. (1996). Learning in the heart: A different view of assessment. *Highlighter: Focusing on Assessment.* Sturgeon Bay, WI: Wisconsin Association for Supervision and Curriculum Development.

Rawls, W. (1986). *Where the Red Fern Grows.* Garden City, NY: Doubleday.

Strasser, T. (1981). *The Wave.* New York: Dell.

Wiggins, G. (1989). A true test: Toward more authentic and equitable assessment. *Phi Delta Kappan 70*(8), 703–713.

Recommended for Further Reading

Anderson, Cris. (1994). Literacy portfolios in eighth grade language arts. *The Delta Kappa Gamma Bulletin, 60*(3), 31–35.

Graves, D. & Sunstein, B. (Eds.) (1992). *Portfolio Portraits.* Portsmouth, NH: Heinemann Educational Books.

Guskey, T. (Ed.) (1996). *ASCD Yearbook 1996: Communicating Student Learning.* Alexandria, VA: Association for Supervision and Curriculum Development.

Herman, J., Aschbacher, P., & Winters, L. (1992). *A Practical Guide to Alternative Assessment.* Alexandria, VA: Association for Supervision and Curriculum Development.

Hill, B. & Ruptic, C. (1994). *Practical Aspects of Authentic Assessment: Putting the Pieces Together.* Norwood, MA: Christopher-Gordon Publishers.

Jett-Simpson, M. (1994). *Ecological Assessment under Construction.* Schofield, WI: Wisconsin State Reading Association.

Marzano, R., Pickering, D., & McTighe, J. (1993). *Assessing Student Outcomes: Performance Assessment Using the Dimensions of Learning Model.* Alexandria, VA: Association for Supervision and Curriculum Development.

Perrone, V. (Ed.) (1991). *Expanding Student Assessment.* Alexandria, VA: Association for Supervision and Curriculum Development.

Rhodes, L. & Shanklin, N. (1993). *Windows into Literacy: Assessing Learners K–8.* Portsmouth, NH: Heinemann.

Sharp, Q. (1989). *Evaluation: Whole Language Checklists for Evaluating Your Children.* New York: Scholastic.

Smith, Carl (Ed.) (1990, August). *Alternative Assessment of Performance in the Language Arts: Proceedings.* Paper presented at the Phi Delta Kappa and ERIC/RCS national symposium, Bloomington, IN.

Valencia, S., Hiebert, E., & Afflerback, P. (Eds.) (1992). *Authentic Reading Assessment: Practices and Possibilities.* Newark, DE: International Reading Association.

Valencia, S., McGinley, W., & Pearson, P.D. (1990). *Assessing Reading and Writing: Building a More Complete Picture for Middle School Assessment.* (Technical Report No. 500). Champaign, IL: Center for the Study of Reading.

Valencia, S. & Pearson, P.D. (1987). Reading assessment: Time for a change. *Reading Teacher, 40*(8), 726–732.

Chapter 6

The Demands of Text

Young adolescents read a variety of text—advertisements for blue jeans, movie schedules, yearbooks, and CD covers. "School reading" generally addresses only two kinds of text—narrative and expository. Young children first learn to read stories. Young adolescents continue their enjoyment of reading and listening to stories through the middle school years as their understanding of plot, characterization, and setting matures. A different source of reading, however, is prevalent in middle grades classrooms—the content area textbook. Awareness of how expository textbooks are structured begins later than for narratives and develops as students acquire more abstract levels of thinking. A major task for middle level educators is to assist students in developing a schema for expository text so that they can read, use, and understand textbooks successfully.

In this chapter, the two main types of text (narrative and expository) are compared and suggestions are given for helping students to become more sensitive to these text structures. Factors that make expository text "considerate," and ways of helping students overcome the obstacles of "inconsiderate" text are presented. Difficulties that students have with content area textbooks are also explained in this chapter, and the use and evaluation of textbooks are discussed.

Kinds of Text

Young children think in terms of stories that grow out of their everyday lives. Stories comprise their literary exposure and their thinking until about the third grade when textbooks are introduced. Scholars have acknowledged the close connections that exist between student experiences, thinking, and text structure (Goodman, 1986; Meyer, 1984; Smith, 1982). *Stories* rely on "linking causal or sequential events, [whereas] *description* evokes visual-spatial thinking and *exposition* involves abstract logical processes to accomplish such tasks as comparison and classification" (Sinatra, 1991, p. 425). As students progress through the grades, they must become more sensitive to a variety of text structures and adapt their thinking accordingly.

When students can use text structure, they tend to remember what they read better and over a longer period of time (Taylor, 1982); however, teachers often fail to devote much time to helping students become aware of text structure. Awareness of text structure is an important metacognitive skill that should be made a part of learning to read and write. Although adults are generally proficient with a variety of text structures such as persuasion, advertising, and technical reading, two types of text are most commonly found in school settings, which, as stated, are narrative text and expository text.

Narrative Text

This type of text is usually encountered in stories such as those commonly found in basal readers and literature anthologies. Narrative text usually has the following elements: setting, sequence, characterization, and plot. Middle level students generally have less trouble with this type of text because it usually has a clearly defined structure. A reader can expect meeting characters, a time period and a setting, a series of events, and some type of resolution. *Story grammars* have been developed to heighten student awareness of the structure of stories. Story grammars facilitate the identification of the different predictable aspects of a story. One way to help students understand the structure of a story is to show students a story grammar before the reading. Then, as stories are read aloud, students fill in the boxes and blanks. Presumably, their understanding of the story and the structure is better as a result of this exercise. Figure 6.1 illustrates is a typical story grammar.

This diagram may be modified to fit different purposes. Students can fill in the different parts of the diagram as a teacher reads a story to them. This diagram may then be used as a springboard for discussion. Students may be asked to read the story first and then fill in the story structure.

Story frames can help students understand either the structure of stories through writing or the relationships between people and events. The story frame shown in Figure 6.2 and the relationships chart in Figure 6.3 can be used in a variety of ways such as a story starter or a summary for an existing story.

Because middle grades students are more familiar with the structure of narrative text, they tend to have less difficulty reading it than they do reading content area textbooks. During the middle years, students are moving from "learning to read" to "reading to learn." Using narrative texts in content areas (as discussed in Chapter 7) addresses this "transitional stage in reading maturation when adolescents are acquiring knowledge" (Chall, 1983). Additionally, using narrative texts to learn content area material increases the likelihood of information transfer (Lynch-Brown, 1990).

Expository Text

Social studies and science textbooks offer more complex reading than stories and are written in a variety of structures. These books require more abstract thinking for such tasks as compare-contrast and cause-effect. Expository text provides an explanation of facts and concepts; a reader can usually identify a hierarchy of ideas in this type of text. Research in the area of expository text has helped educators understand the ways in which these types of books are organized. The three categories of informational text are *description*

The setting/main characters
Statement of the problem
Event 1
Event 2
Event 3
Event 4
Event 5
Event 6
Event 7
Statement of the solution
Story theme (What is this story *really* about?)
Values brought out in the story

FIGURE 6.1 Story grammar

From James M. Macon, Diane Bewell, & MaryEllen Vogt (Eds.), *Responses to Literature: Grades K–8.* Copyright © 1991 by the International Reading Association. Reprinted with permission of the International Reading Association. All rights reserved.

(simple listing, definition with examples); *compare-contrast;* and *explanation* (temporal sequence, cause-effect, problem-solution) (Armstrong & Armbruster, 1991).

Text Structure Activity

Taylor (1982) found that students who are sensitive to text structure remember more of what they read. The three-step text structure activity was designed by Readence, Bean, and Baldwin (1985) to help students recognize and use different types of textual organization. For these activities, teachers should choose well-organized text that has a well-defined structural type.

Story Frame

The story takes place ______________________________

______________________________ .

______________________________ is a character in the story who

____

______________________________ is another

character in the story who ______________________________ .

A problem occurs when ______________________________

______________________________ .

After that, ______________________________

____

and ______________________________ .

The problem is solved when ______________________________

______________________________ .

The story ends with ______________________________

______________________________ .

FIGURE 6.2 Story frame

From James M. Macon, Diane Bewell, & Mary Ellen Vogt, *Responses to Literature: Grades K–8.* Copyright © 1991 by the International Reading Association, Inc. Reprinted with permission of the International Reading Association.

Step One: The teacher *models* the thinking process used in determining the text structure. In essence, teachers are thinking aloud about how and why a text is organized the way it is. The teacher should point out connectors or signal words that provide cues to the structure of the text; for example, a section in a social studies textbook may be organized around a cause-and-effect structure. The teacher would point out that signal words such as "because," "since," "therefore," "consequently," and "if . . . then" are generally found in the cause-and-effect organization.

Step Two: Students are asked to *recognize* certain text structures. If the text is difficult to read, this part of the activity may be done at the listening level. Passages need not be long. To continue with the social studies example, the teacher would provide students

Pilot Relationships Chart

Somebody	Wanted	But	So

FIGURE 6.3

From James M. Macon, Diane Bewell, & Mary Ellen Vogt, *Responses to Literature: Grades K-8.* Copyright © 1991 by the International Reading Association, Inc. Reprinted with permission of the International Reading Association.

with paragraphs organized in a cause-and-effect structure. Students would be asked to identify the signal words that alert the reader to this type of organization.

Step Three: Students *produce* the same text structure recognized earlier. Through writing, students can reinforce their learning about how text is organized. After discussing a cause-and-effect relationship in a social studies class, one student wrote the following paragraph.

> *Americans rebelled against England because they wanted to be independent. They realized that if they fought, then they would pay a price in lives and resources. Since they felt strongly about their freedom, they joined hands and began the rebellion.*

Taylor and Beach (1984) demonstrated that the comprehension of middle school students can be improved by teaching them to understand text structure. Because this task involves abstract thinking, the ability to capitalize fully on expository text structures is probably a late developing skill (Baker & Brown, 1984).

Just as skill instruction in isolation is not recommended to teach comprehension, text structure instruction should not occur out of context. Students learn reading strategies best when such strategies are related to the content they are expected to learn. Students can be given many opportunities to learn text structure in relation to the texts they read. Students who are taught this skill in isolation and expected to apply it later may never take the next step.

Difficulty with Content Area Textbooks

Middle grades students often read stories or entire novels with little difficulty. When they turn to their social studies or science book, however, they have a harder time understanding what they have read. In fact, this negative experience can sour students' interest in disciplines such as history, anthropology, or physical science. Content area textbooks are different from and usually more challenging to read than basal readers, stories, or novels.

The purpose of reading a content area textbook is to acquire new information. Students may have difficulty reading expository text for the following reasons: (1) they lack the content or strategic knowledge to understand the text; (2) they are confronted with inconsiderate text; (3) they have varied classroom experiences with reading in the content areas (Armbruster, 1988); and/or (4) they do not comprehend the task to be performed.

Content and Strategic Knowledge

Any reader at any age has difficulty understanding text about an unfamiliar topic. To learn anything new, this information must be connected in some way with existing prior knowledge. Developing and activating students' background knowledge are imperative before attempting to read a content area textbook. Students who have difficulty with textbooks may (1) lack prior knowledge; (2) have the knowledge, but fail to access it; or (3) have knowledge or beliefs that interfere with acquiring new information. When teaching students how to comprehend expository text or during remediation, it is best to use highly familiar passages as a starting point (Winograd & Newell, 1985).

One reason students have difficulty with content area textbooks is that they are "unfamiliar with exposition as a discourse type" (Armbruster, 1988, p. 2). What elementary students read in their basal readers is mostly narrative and contains few expository pieces. In addition, the selections contained in basal readers are not much like their content area textbooks. Flood (1986) maintained that elementary "children need to make the transition from narrative to expository texts through direct instruction from the teacher during reading lessons with basal readers and during subject matter lessons with subject matter textbooks" (p. 786). When students enter a middle level school not knowing how to read a content area textbook, it must be taught. Content teachers often deal only with the learning of facts, concepts, and generalizations rather than help students develop strategies for acquiring new knowledge from a textbook.

"Structure strategies" (Meyer, Brandt, & Bluth, 1980), or the ability to use the structure of text to comprehend, correlates highly with recall of information and comprehension scores; that is, "students who have processed the text strategically using their knowledge of expository text structures will recall the text better" (Richgels, McGee, Lomax, & Sheard, 1987, p. 179). Sensitivity to text structure is an "important component in text comprehension and memory, perhaps because readers who are sensitive to text structure are better able to form macrostructures for the text they read" (Armbruster, Anderson, & Ostertag, 1987, pp. 333–334).

Developing and activating content knowledge and teaching students to use strategies to learn from textbooks are keys to helping students become more successful. Prereading and prewriting strategies (see Chapter 9) help students access, evaluate, and use their prior knowledge during reading. Using text structures to comprehend text takes a certain degree of abstract thinking. Given the developing nature of cognition during early adolescence, the middle grades are an opportune time to deliver instruction in text structure. Obviously, the more active the students are in constructing maps, frames, or graphic organizers, the better they will comprehend and the more they will learn about the structure of text.

Inconsiderate Text

Armbruster, Anderson, Bruning, and Meyer (1984) analyzed middle school American history textbooks in terms of organization and the types of questions contained. They concluded their study by saying:

> *We are struck by the complex world of middle grade social studies text structures, question types, the background knowledge required, and the sheer amount of information that students and teachers face . . . each of these factors come to bear on the complicated task of teaching students to read in the content areas (p. 65).*

Textbooks are often difficult to understand because they are inconsiderate; that is, the way they are written may lack structure, unity, and coherence. Yet, students are expected to read, often independently, these poorly written textbooks. *Structure* refers to the plan for how the ideas are arranged and connected to each other. *Unity of purpose* helps readers understand main ideas because only relevant information is included. *Coherence* refers to the clarity of relationships between ideas. Inconsiderate textbooks can "bore and bewilder even sophisticated adult readers. For children who are not only novice readers but also novices in the content areas, the problem can be overwhelming" (Armbruster, 1988, p. 3).

Classroom Experiences with Textbooks

Unlike basal readers, content area textbooks are used inconsistently in all levels of schooling. Some teachers use them only as a reference or ask students to read only short selections. Other teachers depend heavily on textbooks, but rely on round-robin reading. In addition, textbook reading is usually fragmented by teacher questioning or activities. Middle level students are rarely taught how to detect text structures or the hierarchy of ideas in content area textbooks. If teachers gave more time and attention to helping students become successful readers of expository text, perhaps students would be able to apply this lifelong skill to new texts.

Many students are not aware that texts are to be read at different rates for different purposes. Novels are read rather quickly to maintain the story line. Textbooks are often read more slowly to gain new information. Reading to write a report requires a different type of reading and notetaking than reading to answer questions on a test. These study skills and more will be discussed in depth in Chapter 11.

Helping Students Deal with Inconsiderate Text

Teachers must learn to recognize poorly written textbooks and try to avoid them; however, that is not always possible. Moore, Moore, Cunningham and Cunningham (1986, pp. 165–166) developed the following set of guidelines for teachers who are obliged to use inconsiderate texts.

1. **Hold students responsible for only part of a text.** Students do not need to read every page of every chapter in the textbook. Chances are, they will not remember most of it anyway. The teacher should make the decision as to what parts of the text are most important, most interesting, and most comprehensible.
2. **Help students to prepare for reading and to set a clear purpose for reading.** Activities that activate prior knowledge or build background information are necessary for students to get the maximum benefit from their reading. The more students understand the purpose for their reading, the more likely they are to understand what they read.
3. **Use difficult but important material in a listening comprehension lesson.** Listening comprehension is the same process as reading comprehension except that students listen rather than read material. Because listening and speaking vocabularies are usually larger than reading and writing vocabularies, students can learn the information through this approach and improve their listening comprehension at the same time.
4. **Make extensive use of visual aids.** Pictures, charts, maps, diagrams, and other visual aids provide and clarify information. Students may often may guess what the text will say based on the visual information.

Helping Students Understand Text Structure

Recognizing inconsiderate text and helping students make sense of it is a coping strategy. When students understand and use text structure to comprehend text, they can reap the long-term benefits of such understanding. Students who fail to demonstrate sensitivity to text structure generally remember less of what they have read than students who demonstrate this sensitivity (Taylor, 1982). Presenting students with information and activities about how text is constructed helps them recall more of what they read and helps them comprehend the material better. Two methods for helping students understand and use text structure are paragraph frames, which help students to recognize and maximize the use of signal words, and text structure frames, which help them to summarize important information learned from text.

Paragraph Pattern	*Structure Words*
Simple listing	for example, for instance, specifically, another, besides, also, in addition, moreover, furthermore, in particular
Cause-effect	consequently, therefore, thus, as a result, however, hence
Contrast-compare	on the other hand, but, by contrast, yet
Time order	another, additionally, next, first, second (etc.), then, and, furthermore, also

FIGURE 6.4 Structure words

Source: M.W. Olson and B. Longnion, "Pattern Guides: A Workable Alternative for Content Teachers," *Journal of Reading, 25* (May 1982). Reprinted with permission of M.W. Olson and the International Reading Association.

At the end of _______what happened was that ______________________________

_________________________. Previous to this ______________________________

____.

Before this ____.

The entire chain of events had begun for a number of reasons including ____________

____.

Some prominent incidents which helped to trigger the conflict were _______________

____.

FIGURE 6.5 Time order

Source: J.N. Nichols, "Using Paragraph Frames to Help Remedial High School Students with Written Assignments," *Journal of Reading, 23* (December 1980). Reprinted with permission of J.N. Nichols and the International Reading Association.

Paragraph Frames

Signal words do just as the name implies. They signal relationships between words and ideas. A common list of signal words (or structure words) is presented in Figure 6.4. One way to encourage students to recognize signal words while reading and use signal words in writing is through the use of *paragraph frames.* These frames are an excellent way to teach students how to use signal words and text structure to understand content reading material. Nichols (1980, p. 229) designed the examples shown in Figures 6.5 and 6.6.

TOURO COLLEGE LIBRARY

__________ are different from __________________________

__________ in several ways. First of all ________________________

______________ while __________________________________

____.

Secondly, ____

while ____.

In addition, ____

while ____.

So it should be evident that _______________________________

____.

FIGURE 6.6 Compare-contrast

Source: J.N. Nichols, "Using Paragraph Frames to Help Remedial High School Students with Written Assignments," *Journal of Reading, 23* (December 1980). Reprinted with permission of J.N. Nichols and the International Reading Association.

Text Structure Frames

The three most common text structures found in textbooks are description, compare-contrast, and explanation. Figures 6.7, 6.8, and 6.9 illustrate how a *text structure frame* can organize information learned for later recall.

The last decade has yielded much research on text structure and how students can make use of this structure to comprehend text better and longer. Publishers have taken advantage of this research and thinking to produce textbooks that are more considerate than those available for previous generations. In the next section, guidelines for evaluating textbooks are presented.

Using and Evaluating Textbooks

Textbooks have a powerful influence on American education (Armbruster & Ostertag, 1989). Goodlad (1976; 1984) concluded that the "textbook predominated throughout as a medium of instruction" (p. 14). Some researchers found that students spend 75 percent of their classroom time and 90 percent of their homework time using textbooks and that, in fact, the textbook has become the curriculum (Tyson-Bernstein, 1988).

Despite the predominance of textbooks in classrooms, their use varies greatly and the amount of actual reading of the textbook is questionable. Textbooks are read

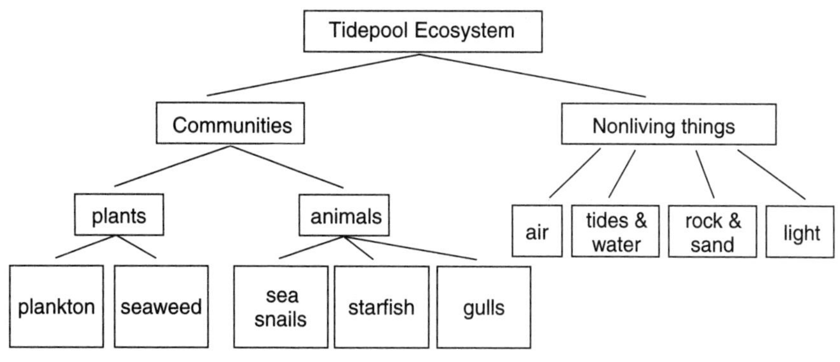

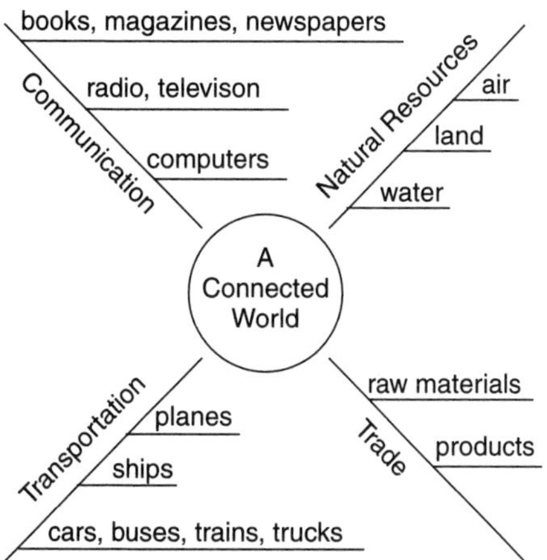

The Netherlands

Land	Water	Agriculture	Commerce & Industry
sand dunes lowlands	North Sea canal system 3 large rivers	garden plants dairy products	international trade oil refineries natural gas

FIGURE 6.7 Description (branching tree, wheel, table)

Source: B.B. Armbruster, "Using Graphic Organizers in Social Studies," *Ginn Occasional Papers* (No.22). Lexington, MA: Ginn.

	Nile River	Amazon River
Location	Africa; flows through desert	South America; flows through rain forest
Length	the world's longest river	the world's second longest river
Uses	water for crops; water power for electricity	materials

FIGURE 6.8 Compare-contrast (matrix)

Source: B.B. Armbruster, "Using Graphic Organizers in Social Studies," *Ginn Occasional Papers* (No.22). Lexington, MA: Ginn.

silently, orally, or often only "looked at" (such as graphs, maps, or pictures). Crismore (1989) found that

> *the number of pages assigned or covered in a textbook (at one time) ranged from 1 page to 16 pages and the amount of time given for a textbook reading task ranged from [five] minutes to [forty-five] minutes. Surprisingly, the number of interruptions during silent reading in classrooms sometimes equaled the number of minutes given for the task. It was not unusual to find an interruption of some sort every minute or two (p. 2).*

Many teachers depend heavily on round-robin reading especially when students have difficulty reading the text. This type of reading is frequently interrupted by teacher questions and discussion. Students tend to depend on the teachers, however, and not the textbook as the primary source of information (Armbruster, Anderson, Armstrong, Wise, Janisch, & Meyer, 1990; Ratekin, Simpson, Alvermann, & Dishner, 1985). The textbook seems to provide the impetus for questions and discussion in most content area classrooms. (Chapters 9, 10, and 11 present numerous strategies for reading and using the textbook meaningfully.)

Students spend much time answering questions related to the text. Armbruster, Anderson, Bruning, and Meyer (1984) advised that it is "important for students to learn to analyze what questions are asking" (p. 65). Most questions originating from the textbook focus on "names, definitions, and other facts that can be assessed 'objectively,' and not meaningful learning of 'big ideas,' or higher order, critical thinking, or the ability to write extended answers (Armbruster & Ostertag, 1989, p. 9). Well-designed questions follow the structure of the text (description, compare-contrast, explanation) and focus on the important points of the selection.

Teacher-designed questions that highlight the text structure assist students in becoming more sensitive to the structure and to understand the relationships of the important ideas presented. Muth (1987) suggested two types of questions: (1) questions that focus on the *internal connections* between the ideas in the text and following its structure, and (2) questions that focus on the *external connections* between the ideas presented in the text and the students prior knowledge or experience.

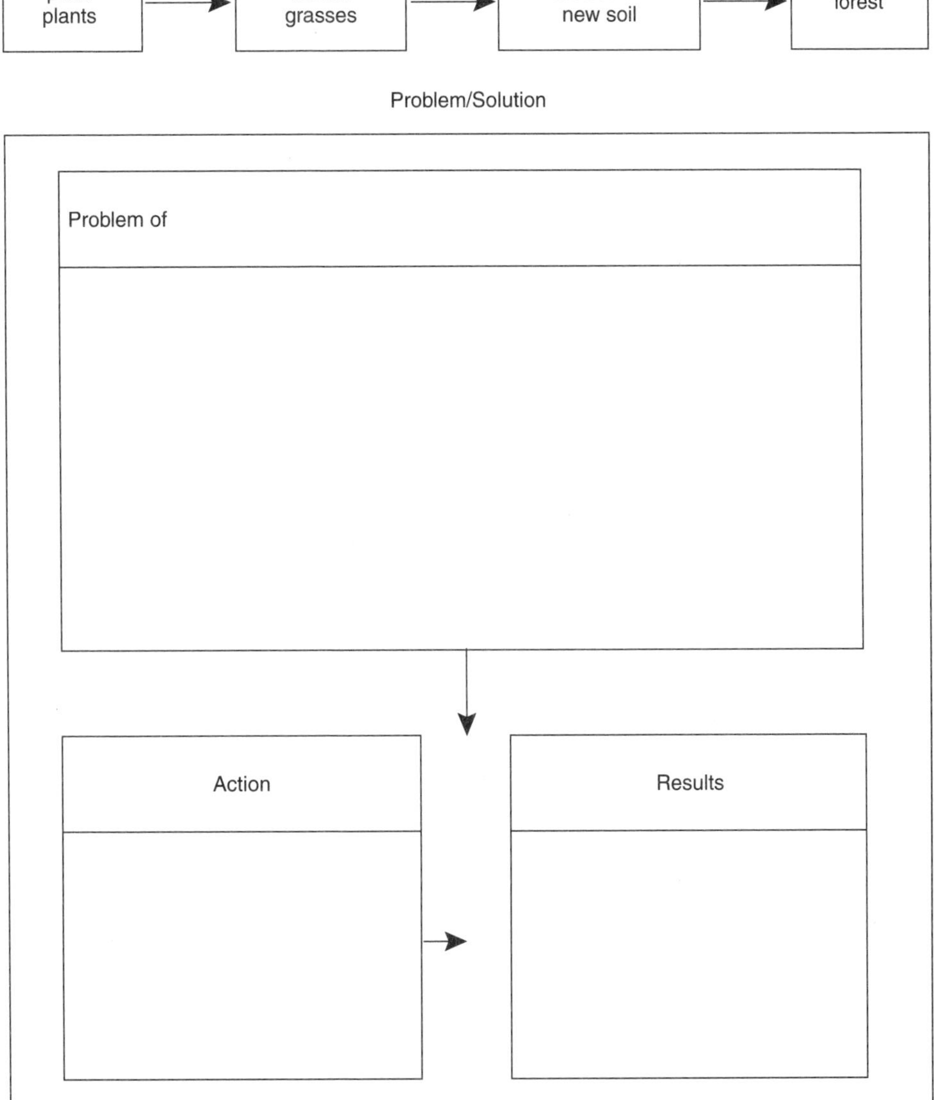

Problem = something bad; a situation that people would like to change
Action = what people do to *try* to solve the problem
Results = what happens as a result of the action; the effect or outcome of trying to solve the problem

FIGURE 6.9 Explanation (chain, problem/solution chart)

Source: B.B. Armbruster, "Using Graphic Organizers in Social Studies," *Ginn Occasional Papers (*No. 22). Lexington, MA: Ginn.

If students are having difficulty reading a textbook, the reason may be that they have not yet acquired proficiency in reading, or, that the textbook is inconsiderate or just plain difficult to read. Science textbooks, in particular, often contain an overabundance of unfamiliar words that are specialized or technical (Tyson & Woodward, 1989). The teacher, then, must determine how textbooks are chosen and how they are used. Clewell and Cliffton (1983) suggested the following questions to ask about a text's comprehensibility.

- Does the book contain an ample amount of *textual aids* such as illustrations, headings, and so forth that are intended to serve as a guide to the reader?
- Is the *content* appropriate to the target audience? Is information accurate and explicit?
- Is the text *coherent?* Are ideas clearly related and organized? Are transitions clearly indicated? Are references clear?
- Is the *style* of the text appropriate and interesting?
- Is *language* clear; are terms defined as they are used? Does sentence structure and length lend to clarity?
- Is the *structure* of the text obvious and consistent?

Advances in technology will soon change dramatically the nature of expository reading for middle grades students. Certainly gathering information from a CD-ROM requires a set of abilities not previously taught in school such as skimming and scanning, and making decisions about narrowing down a topic. Synthesizing important data becomes vital. The ability to determine importance (discussed in depth in Chapter 10) will, however, remain critical. In the meantime, students must be taught to read, understand, and use content area textbooks effectively.

Summary

Narrative and expository text were discussed and strategies for helping students become more sensitive to their structure were presented. A clear text structure (description, compare-contrast, and explanation) and questions that reflect that structure make a textbook considerate. Reasons why students often have difficulty with content area textbooks and ways to help them read, use, and understand them were also discussed. Finally, teachers must assume the responsibility of evaluating and choosing textbooks that facilitate rather than impede student learning.

References

Armbruster, B.B. (1988). *Why Some Children Have Trouble Reading Content Area Textbooks.* (Technical Report No. 432). Champaign, IL: Center for the Study of Reading.

Armbruster, B.B., Anderson, T.H., Armstrong, J.O., Wise, M.A., Janisch, C., & Meyer, L.A. (1990). *Reading and Questioning in Content Area Lessons.* (Technical Report No. 502). Champaign, IL: Center for the Study of Reading.

Armbruster, B.B., Anderson, T.H., Bruning, R.H., & Meyer, L.A. (1984). *What Did You Mean by That Question?: A Taxonomy of American History Questions.* (Technical Report No. 308). Champaign, IL: Center for the Study of Reading.

Armbruster, B.B., Anderson, T., & Ostertag, J. (1987). Does text structure/summarization instruction facilitate learning from expository text? *Reading Research Quarterly, 22*(3), 331–346.

Armbruster, B.B., & Ostertag, J. (1989). *Questions in Elementary Science and Social Studies Textbooks.* (Technical Report No. 463). Champaign, IL: Center for the Study of Reading.

Armstrong, J.O. & Armbruster, B.B. (1991). *Making Frames for Learning from Informational Text.* (Technical Report No. 542). Champaign, IL: Center for the Study of Reading.

Baker, L. & Brown, A.L. (1984). Cognitive monitoring in reading. In J. Flood (Ed.), *Understanding Reading Comprehension: Cognition, Language, and the Structure of Prose* (pp. 21–44). Newark, DE: International Reading Association.

Chall, J.S. (1983). *Stages of Reading Development.* New York: McGraw-Hill.

Clewell, S.F. & Cliffton, A.M. (1983). Examining your textbook for comprehensibility. *Journal of Reading, 27*(3), 219–224.

Crismore, A. (1989). *Rhetorical Form, Selection, and Use of Textbooks.* (Technical Report No. 454). Champaign, IL: Center for the Study of Reading.

Flood, J. (1986). The text, the student, and the teacher: Learning from exposition in middle schools. *The Reading Teacher, 39*(8), 784–791.

Goodlad, J.I. (1976). *Facing the Future: Issues in Education and Schooling.* New York: McGraw-Hill.

Goodlad, J.I. (1984). *A Place Called School.* New York: McGraw-Hill.

Goodman, K. (1986). *What's Whole in Whole Language?* Portsmouth, NH: Heinemann.

Lynch-Brown, C. (1990). Using literature across the curriculum. In J.L. Irvin (Ed.), *Reading and the Middle School Student: Strategies to Enhance Literacy* (pp. 154–171). Boston: Allyn and Bacon.

Meyer, B.F. (1984). Organizational aspects of text: Effects on reading comprehension and applications for the classroom. In J. Flood (Ed.), *Promoting Reading Comprehension* (pp. 113–138). Newark, DE: International Reading Association.

Meyer, B.J.F., Brandt, D.M., & Bluth, G.J. (1980). Use of top-level structure in text: Key for reading comprehension of ninth-grade students. *Reading Research Quarterly, 16*(1), 72–103.

Moore, D.W., Moore, S., Cunningham, P.M., & Cunningham, J.W. (1986). *Developing Readers and Writers in the Content Areas: K-12.* New York: Longman.

Muth, K.D. (1987). Teachers' connection questions: Prompting students to organize text ideas. *Journal of Reading, 31*(3), 254–259.

Nichols, J.N. (1980). Using paragraph frames to help remedial high school students with written assignments. *Journal of Reading, 24*(3), 228.

Ratekin, N., Simpson, M.L., Alvermann, D.E. & Dishner, E.K. (1985). Why content teachers resist reading instruction. *Journal of Reading, 28*(5), 432–437.

Readence, J.E., Bean, T.W., & Baldwin, R.S. (1985). *Content Area Reading: An Integrated Approach.* Dubuque, IA: Kendall/Hunt.

Richgels, D.J., McGee, L.M., Lomax, R.G., & Sheard, C. (1987). Awareness of four text structures: Effects on recall of expository text. *Reading Research Quarterly, 22*(2), 177–196.

Sinatra, R. (1991). Integrating whole language with the learning of text structure. *Journal of Reading, 34*(6), 424–433.

Smith, F. (1982). *Understanding: A Psycholinguistic Analysis of Reading and Learning to Read.* New York: Holt, Rinehart, and Winston.

Taylor, B.M. (1982). Text structure and children's comprehension and memory for expository material. *Journal of Educational Psychology, 74*(3), 323–340.

Taylor, B. & Beach, R.W. (1984). The effects of text structure instruction on middle grade students' comprehension and production of expository text. *Reading Research Quarterly, 19*(2), 134–146.

Tyson, H. & Woodward, A. (1989). Why students aren't learning very much from textbooks. *Educational Leadership, 47*(3), 14–17.

Tyson-Bernstein, H. (1988). *A Conspiracy of Good Intentions: America's Textbook Fiasco.* Washington, DC: The Council for Basic Education.

Winograd, P. & Newell, G. (1985). *The Effects of Topic Familiarity on Good and Poor Readers' Sensitivity Text.* (Technical Report No. 337). Champaign, IL: Center for the Study of Reading.

Chapter 7

Literature across the Curriculum

CAROL LYNCH-BROWN
Florida State University

Literature, a component of our cultural heritage, can enrich the lives of students in middle grades, can encourage critical and imaginative thinking, can educate while it entertains, and can lay a foundation for literary experiences later in life. As students begin the process of deciding their own futures, experiences with literature provide young people with an opportunity to explore other worlds and other lives, those very different from their own as well as those similar to their own.

Reading literature also serves other educational purposes: it can enhance the study of content areas; it can foster vocabulary development and reading comprehension; and it is inherently enjoyable. Because literature is usually written in a more interesting manner than textbooks, it can be a valuable resource for teaching content area courses. Textbooks, for the most part, contain passages of information that omit the narrative aspects of the events; that is, the stories of the people who made the events happen.

Trade books—books published for the general trade market—are generally sold in single copies or only a few copies to libraries or through bookstores. By both design and content, trade books are primarily for the purposes of entertainment and information. Trade books in the form of fiction and biography can therefore breathe life into the dates, places, and events of content area textbooks. Works of historical fiction and biography can motivate young adolescents to learn about the period of history described. For example, when studying the Second World War, Naziism, and the attempted genocide of the Jewish people, a work of fiction such as *Friedrich* by Richter (1970) can help young adolescents understand the anguish of a 13-year-old Jewish boy suffering injustice and humiliation.

(Other books written by international authors on this topic can be found in Lynch-Brown & Tomlinson, 1986; Tomlinson & Lynch-Brown, 1996).

Reading ability is also promoted through the wide reading of literature, which especially fosters vocabulary development and reading comprehension. Most reading selections assigned to students, whether drawn from content area textbooks, basal readers, or literary readers, share a common trait of relative brevity. Only through reading longer, more fully developed works of literature, will students have opportunities to study a single topic in depth, to follow complex plots, to know characters fully depicted as real human beings, and to appreciate places and worlds different from their own.

Of the many reasons that literature should have a central role in the middle school curriculum, the most powerful reason is that literature is enjoyable. By discovering the joy of reading, students will become lifelong readers. Literature offers students another form of recreation—recreation of the mind, a chance to stretch the mind by encountering new ideas. And literature provides recreation for the heart—a chance to experience empathy for others.

Literature serves three main purposes in the middle school curriculum: (1) the study of literature itself is an important curricular area; (2) literature can serve as a vehicle to enhance the learning of other subject areas; and (3) the enjoyment of literature can help to develop a lifelong habit of reading. In this chapter, the study and use of literature to fulfill these three purposes will be discussed under two headings: literature for intensive reading and literature for extensive reading. In addition, a starter list of annotated titles and a list of book selection aids are included to help teachers locate titles. For the purposes of this chapter, "literature" is defined as *good quality trade books, of prose and poetry, of fiction and nonfiction.*

Literature for Intensive Reading

Literature can enhance instruction in language arts, social studies, science, health, mathematics, home economics, and the fine arts. Intensive reading of literature is used when the teacher wishes to make the literary work the focus of study. Teachers in some content areas, however, seldom receive advice on how to use literature in their instruction. Using literature in content area classrooms calls for shared literary experiences for the students and teacher. A single book or other work of literature, or a group of literary works involving a similar theme or topic will comprise a shared literary experience. These book experiences can be the focus of study and can expand and enrich concepts from textbooks. Books selected for intensive reading of literature will be challenging ones, often needing teacher explication for full understanding. These books should help children to grow in their thinking abilities within a "zone of proximal development," an area in which students are pushed to stretch their abilities, but not too far, according to Vygotsky's (1962) theories of cognitive development. Books chosen for intensive reading must be ones that stretch students' minds and imaginations, promoting their cognitive and affective development.

Suggestions for integrating literature and textbook instruction are provided for teachers in this section. The four steps to shared literary experiences are: (l) to brainstorm ideas, topics, themes related to a unit of study in the content area, (2) to identify titles and to locate books, (3) to provide shared literary experiences and to dwell on these experiences, and (4) to consider alternate ways to share books and to extend the book experience.

Step One: Brainstorm ideas, topics, or themes related to a unit of study in the content area. Textbooks in most subject areas (science, health, social studies, home economics, and mathematics) are generally arranged by units of varying length that usually take three to nine weeks. For example, a health education teacher might select a unit on nutrition and exercise. At first glance, such a topic may seem to require a nonfiction treatment. Information books on foods, exercising, and sports naturally come to mind. But what about incorporating fiction and other narrative texts? Brainstorming may bring to mind the idea that nutrition and exercise are studied to maintain good mental and physical health, to avoid abuses such as anorexia, bulimia, and obesity, and to encourage balance in life through attention to and care of one's body. A biography of a sports figure or a story of a young person struggling to overcome anorexia may make these topics more relevant to students.

The *webbing technique* has been found useful by teachers for brainstorming the related concepts and for finding books on particular topics. A web is a means of generating ideas and linking them to a central focus. Webbing can center on concepts, topics, or themes; the focal point of a web can also be a book or group of books (Huck, Hepler, Hickman, & Kiefer, 1997, p. 646). Two webs are presented here: one presents a topic at the center; the other, a work of literature.

The first web centers on the theme of survival. This theme may be slanted to lend itself to a unit in health (bodily needs, emotional consequences of loneliness), science (natural foods, plant and animal study), social studies (survival in nature versus city survival, qualities needed to be a survivor, interdependence of human beings, effects of isolation), or language arts (ways to communicate while in isolation, comparison of various types of literary stories that focus on survival). One set of ideas brainstormed on the topic of survival is presented in Figure 7.1.

The second web, which is in Figure 7.2, was developed after reading a modern retelling of the Pied Piper legend, *What Happened in Hamelin,* by Skurzynski (1979) who researched the historical background of this medieval legend. A traveling musician, Gast, convinces the baker's apprentice, Geist, to bake treats for the town's children. Afterward Gast lures the children away.

Step Two: Identify titles and locate books. Once you have brainstormed the topics and themes that may be explored relative to the upcoming unit, they will need to identify actual titles and locate the books. Begin the search for books close to home; perhaps the collection of books in the classroom will have a few appropriate titles. Ask the school media specialist to help locate books on the topics that have been identified through brainstorming. Media specialists have access to reference guides that can aid a content area teacher in this search, or they know the books in the school library so well that, with a few minutes of browsing, they can identify a dozen or more books.

Because these books will be the focus of study in class it is incumbent on the teacher to select the best books available. Recommended sources such as major U.S. and international book award lists, children's book review journals, annual lists of recommended new books from professional associations such as the International Reading Association and

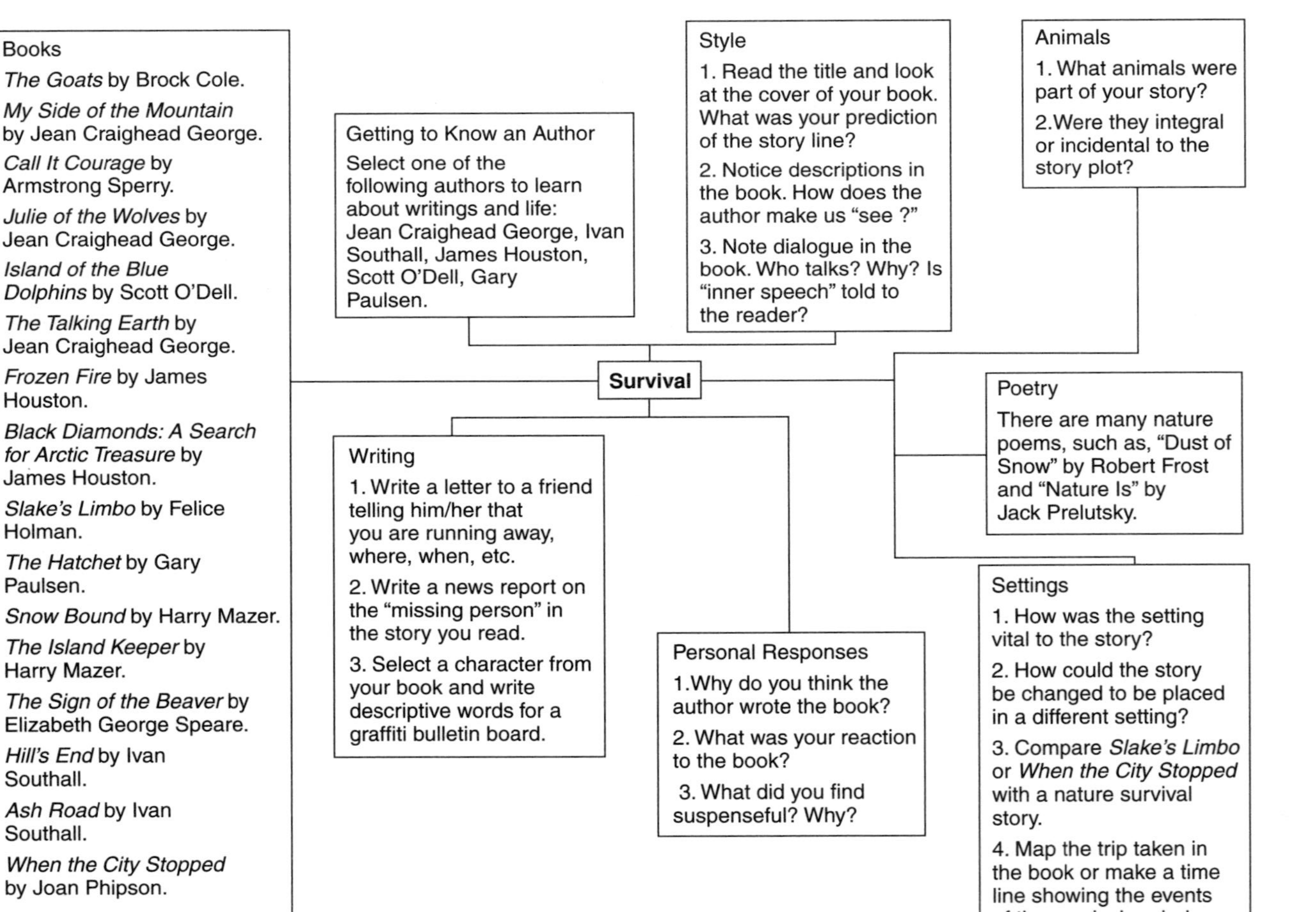

FIGURE 7.1 Brainstorming ideas by topic

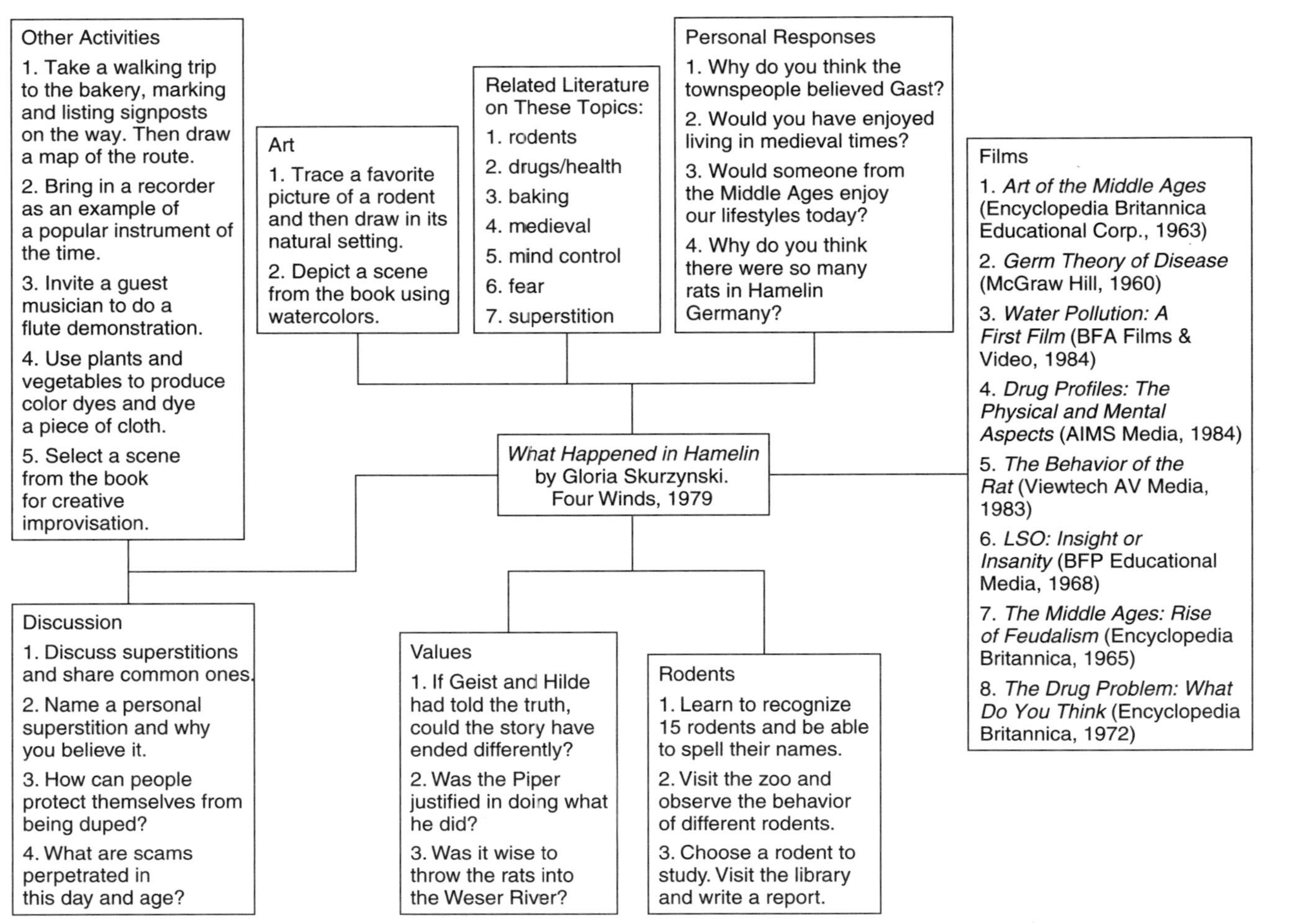

FIGURE 7.2 Brainstorming ideas by book

the National Council for the Social Studies, and children's and adolescent literature textbooks are good starting places for location of good titles. Reading the books ahead of time to ensure the quality and appropriateness of the content for the students is necessary. At the end of this chapter, a list of book selection aids for identification of related titles may be particularly helpful, especially for those seeking less common topics and themes or if library support services are limited.

Most communities have public libraries with literature for young people. Determine the availability of books and the type of help the library may be willing to offer. Some librarians will do a search of titles on the themes or topics; others will set the books aside on a special shelf to help students when they come. Some libraries have cooperative lending programs that permit teachers to check out a set of books for use in their classrooms.

Perusing the paperbacks in nearby bookstores may result in the discovery of some books that students could purchase. A list of these books can be provided to students for them to purchase or to check out from the library. Once a list of suitable paperback books is developed, most local bookstores will gladly order these in sufficient quantity for students to purchase.

Eventually, teachers who wish to use literature to enhance their subject matter will want to strive for the purchase of excellent quality books on the themes and topics taught every year. These books can be kept in the classroom on shelves marked by specific topics such as ecology, space science, animals, and earth science. In this way the task of material selection and location becomes easier with time. Many parent-teacher organizations will provide funds for the purchase of such books. It will be incumbent upon the teacher to (l) locate the titles, authors, and ordering information; (2) write this information down; and (3) submit it with a cover letter requesting the purchase of the materials and the rationale for use of the books. This task, though time consuming, will be well rewarded when the books arrive.

Step Three: Provide shared literary experiences and dwell on the book experiences. Teachers have found many ways to provide a book experience that can be shared by all class members. Two ways that are most popular and successful are for the teacher to read aloud to the entire class and for the students to read books selected from a list of titles on the topic or theme.

Teachers Read Aloud

The first way to provide a shared literary experience is by reading a good book to an entire class. This activity can provide a joyful experience for both teacher and class, which can be used for future discussion of concepts from the unit of study. A trade book may be used as a schema and interest builder before reading the textbook or to elaborate and extend the content and concepts during and after the reading of the text (Brozo & Tomlinson, 1986). Techniques to consider for an enjoyable read-aloud experience can be found in Figure 7.3.

The trade book can be used to amplify and deepen the concepts and understandings being taught in the unit of study. This deeper understanding may be accomplished by asking the students how the facts or events being studied were presented in the trade book and how they were presented in the textbook, and identify which facts were treated in each source. For example, in studying the industries of Australia, students may be asked what

1. Select a book appropriate to the topic. Be sure the book has well-described characters that students can relate to, a fairly fast-moving plot, and strong emotional appeal. Read the book yourself before reading it aloud.You may encounter words that you need to practice for pronunciation and certain phrasings that need rehearsing. You will also want to know generally what to expect as you read the story aloud. Some books contain sensitive material that you will want to consider how to treat.

2. Minimize distractions by asking students to put papers, books, and pens aside and to remain quiet and seated. Be sure students are comfortable and relaxed. External distractions might be lowered by posting a sign on the classroom announcing reading time.

3. Give a brief introduction to the book before beginning the reading. Include the title, author, and some hint at the topic of the story to gain attention and build interest in the story. It often helps to permit students to see how the book may relate to their lives or connect with their prior knowledge. For example, a teacher may say, "I will be reading the book, *The Fire in the Stone,* by Colin Thiele, for the next few weeks. This story is set in Australia and is about a 14-year-old boy who makes friends with a boy of a different race. . . . What do you know about Australia? To what do you think the title refers? Now let's see what happens in this book."

4. Read fluently with lots of expression in your voice. Your voice is an effective tool for conveying the meanings, feeling, and drama of the story. You can vary your voice by using a low to high pitch, soft to loud volume, and slow to fast pace. I usually begin a story with a soft, steady voice, which permits me to change volume, pace, and pitch for dramatic effects.

5. Maintain eye contact with class while reading aloud. This provides greater closeness between the reader and the class.

6. Break at a natural stopping point, usually a chapter ending. Permit students to share their reactions to the story. It is not necessary, and often not desirable, to ask comprehension questions after reading. Explanations of parts of the story, however, can be made if the teacher senses that the students are having difficulty understanding.

FIGURE 7.3 Read-aloud techniques for teachers

types of industries were pursued in central Australia where the book, *The Fire in the Stone* by Thiele (1974), took place.

After a read-aloud session, it is worthwhile to elicit students' responses to the book to keep them actively involved in the story. Some topics for discussion may include: What kind of story is this? What do you think of Ernie? his father? his best friend? What do you think will happen tomorrow? Of what does this story remind you? Students may also record their responses in written form. Some teachers encourage students to keep a response journal in which they record their reactions to the reading.

Students Read from a List

The second way to provide a shared literary experience is for individual students to read books selected from a list of related titles. When using this approach the teacher develops a list of titles and authors with an indication of where each book can be obtained (school or class library, public library, bookstore). A brief annotation helps students to know something about each book so that they can select books of interest to them. The list may have four to eight titles so that students have a choice. Then, after the books are read, students are placed in groups according to the book read.

On a designated day, students bring the books they have selected to class. A few minutes of class time may be used for students to share first impressions of the book, which are gleaned from the cover, from the book jacket, or by scanning the book. The remaining twenty or so minutes of class time are best devoted to reading the books to help students get a good start. Students will then find it easier to continue the reading on their own outside of class. Students should be encouraged to carry the book with them so that any extra time in other classes can be spent on reading.

Next, the teacher sets a date by which the books should be completely read. On this date students bring their books to class. The students will meet in book groups to share reactions to their books and to connect their books to their topic of study. These groups might be established by the type of books read; for example, all books placed in urban Australia will be discussed in one group, rural Australia in another, stories with Aborigines separated into another group. When using this strategy, students reading the same book or books by the same author may be placed in the same book discussion group. Groups may also be composed of students who have all read a novel of the same genre with three or four different genres available for selection by students. In these groups the actual titles may be different, but the genre will be the same.

The size of the groups may vary. More mature and socially cooperative classes may be grouped into fewer, larger groups of as many as seven or eight students. Less mature students seem to work better in groups of three or four. As students become more familiar with book discussion groups, they also become more adept at and capable of working together.

A chart that helps students identify aspects of the book that relate to the topic of study is often helpful. Students may address certain points in relation to the topic of study. A sample follows in Figure 7.4. Another chart compares concepts treated in the trade books with those presented in the textbook. An example from social studies follows in Figure 7.5.

Step Four: Consider alternate ways to share books and extend the book experience. The class discussions and book groups previously described are two ways teachers can help students relate a trade book to the unit of study and encourage their responses to the literary experience. Traditional book reports have often been assigned as a means to encourage response to a book. Students, however, perceive this practice as "checking up" on them and as such, it seldom has the desired effect. In fact, many students comment that they dread reading the books because they know the inevitable book reports will follow. A list of ten book-related projects in Figure 7.6 offers additional ideas for extending the students' experiences with the book and enriching the unit of study. Activities involving cooperative learning are especially appropriate with young adolescents who are naturally peer oriented. Many of the activities can be completed in pairs or groups.

Book: *Fire in the Stone*
Topic of Study: Australia
Author: Colin Thiele (1974)

	General Relationship to Unit of Study	Specific Incidents from Tradebook
Setting Place Time	Australia—modern times	Central Australia in a mining town; distances between places not specified
Characters Homes Families Schooling Occupations Relationships	mixed races—white and Aborigines	occupations—unskilled labor, mining of opals, no school
Themes or values	judge people by their acts, not their color or race	Ernie develops a true friendship with an Aborigine boy

FIGURE 7.4 Identifying aspects of a book

Providing a shared literary experience to enhance the teaching of specific content areas can (1) develop renewed interest in the content being studied, (2) deepen students' understandings of the people under study and their lives, and (3) help students develop critical thinking abilities as they weigh and compare information from different sources. In addition, using trade books in content area classrooms is one way to start students reading more widely. Once students become involved in either a good book read-aloud by a skilled reader or a book they enjoyed reading individually, they are ready to read other books.

Literature for Extensive Reading

Extensive reading of literature for enjoyment has many benefits. Students develop automaticity in their reading skills through this practice. They also can read more fluently and rapidly, develop the habit of reading, and increase their reading vocabularies and comprehension abilities.

One approach to encourage extensive reading of literature that has enjoyed success in middle schools across the country is the sustained silent reading (SSR) program. These programs are often implemented school-wide but can be instituted by individual teachers or teams of teachers. Sustained silent reading is a period of time, usually ten to thirty minutes daily, set aside for the purpose of free choice reading by students, teachers, administrators, and other school personnel. Adults who read during this time serve as positive role models—as examples of people who enjoy reading.

	Textbook	Tradebook
Economy Natural resources Occupations Industries Transportation Money		
Political System Government Capitol Political divisions (states, territories)		
History Early Modern		
Social Institutions Families Schools Homes Hospitals Prisons Religion Sports Culture: art, theater, dance, music		

FIGURE 7.5 Comparing concepts in textbooks and tradebooks

Students are assured of an uninterrupted period of time when they may read materials of their own choosing without any requirement to report on what they have read—no homework, no book report, no "what is the name of the main character"—only reading for enjoyment. A wide range of materials, varied in type and difficulty, needs to be available for student selection. Information books, picture books, novels, poetry collections, and magazines on a wide range of topics should be included. Providing students with time in the school media center on a regular basis for selection of reading matter is important for establishing a lifelong habit of reading and is another way to make materials available. A field trip to the public library will encourage students to use this wonderful free resource. If such trips are not an option, parents can be encouraged to establish a routine of regular library visits with their children.

Sustained silent reading programs evolved in the 1960s. Fader and McNeil (1968) in *Hooked on Books* received considerable recognition for the success they had with such a program in a school for delinquent boys. Sustained silent reading programs probably arose out of a new societal need for practice in reading. Until the 1950s, students read widely at

1. Prepare a brief biography of the author and present it orally or in writing.
2. Develop a TV script based on one exciting scene from the book. Groups could select, plan, write, and present different scenes to the class.
3. Describe the setting of the book and explain how the setting was important to the events.
4. Select one character from the book to discuss in detail—physical appearance; emotional, mental, and physical attributes; kinds of friends and family; and so forth.
5. Tell what kind of people would enjoy this book and why.
6. Discuss why you think the author wrote the book and what the author thought readers would get from the book.
7. Write a first-person description of an event in the story, told as though the writer was an onlooker (such as a new character, a pet, or an inanimate object).
8. As a group, plan and write a sequel to the story. Compare sequels written by different groups.
9. Develop a list of new words and their meanings. This activity can be fun when related to a book set in a foreign country. Foreign words and phrases can be explored.
10. Compare the facts found in the tradebook with those found in the textbook. Look for agreement and contradictions. Seek additional sources to determine authenticity.

FIGURE 7.6 Ten book-related projects

home; the need to practice their reading skills was provided by the natural desire for recreation through books. After television became a readily available form of recreation, however, schools found that students were not reading as widely as before. Wide reading continues to be important to the development of good reading ability and, therefore, time must be provided in school for silent reading. Suggestions for beginning and maintaining a successful SSR program are presented here.

Starting a Sustained Silent Reading Program

In beginning a school-wide SSR program, all staff (including teachers, librarians, administrators, office personnel, custodial and food service personnel) not only need to be informed of the philosophy and purposes of the program but also need to participate in its implementation. A school-wide meeting is an appropriate way to accomplish this goal. Practical issues that can be resolved in such a meeting are (1) when and how long the SSR period should be, (2) how a sufficient variety of reading materials will be acquired and displayed, (3) how each adult can become a "reader role model" and the importance of such a role, and (4) how to encourage and motivate reluctant readers. One middle school decided to motivate students by a kickoff program in which local luminaries such as the nearby university football coach, ministers, and business owners came for a ceremony to honor the students for their posters advertising the new program and to announce the winner of a contest for the best name for the new program. These preliminary activities helped involve, inform, and motivate the students in readiness for the new program.

In middle level schools, SSR programs generally start out with ten minutes daily, at the same time each day. Later, as students are accustomed to reading, the time may be lengthened. In one middle school, the teachers agreed to shorten each class period by two minutes, providing fourteen minutes after third period for silent reading. School bells were rung as for any other period. Students are encouraged to select and bring their own reading materials. These materials may be books, magazines, or comics. Although many students will come prepared with reading materials, a table or shelf with other materials displayed will assist students who have forgotten a book or have just finished what they were reading. Reading time is not "earned" by good behavior or by "finishing your work"; rather, the time is allocated to an important and enjoyable activity—reading.

With books available in the classroom some teachers do a "book talk"—show a book and briefly tell the title, author and something about the story. For example, while showing the book, the teacher says, "I just finished this book that some of you might enjoy. The title is *The Hatchet* by Gary Paulsen and it's the story of a boy who survives fifty-four days in the Canadian wilderness after the plane taking him to visit his father crashes. It has an exciting beginning and it held my interest all the way through. I read it because it was a 1988 Newbery Honor Book; I try to keep up with the award winners."

Providing a few minutes at other times of the day for students to share reactions to their selections can aid all students in locating new materials to read. Permitting students to meet in small groups of four or five to discuss what they are reading can be an activity that motivates students to read. Activities within the groups can be highly structured or open ended. Students introduce their books with a standard "book talk." They show their books first. The book talk will include author, title, and a brief retelling of the story without telling the ending. (Six to eight sentences is a good rule of thumb for most books.) Personal reactions to the book are included in the book talk. In fact, most students start with personal reactions and follow with the story summary. After a book talk, group members are encouraged to ask questions of the reader or offer their personal thoughts on the book.

Students will usually need help locating materials of interest to them. Teachers can share some techniques such as finding books in a series (science fiction series, modern fantasy series, Nancy Drew/Hardy Boys series), books by the same author, award-winning book lists, and books on the same topic (mystery, romance, adventure). Friends can also recommend good books for reading enjoyment.

Maintaining a Successful Sustained Silent Reading Program

Evaluating a program periodically and correcting any problems is an important part of maintaining a successful SSR program. The following teacher checklist in Figure 7.7 has proven useful in evaluating different facets of the SSR program in the classroom.

Periodically, administrators need to consider ways to encourage the continued success of the SSR program school-wide. A workshop in which teachers share ideas they

1. Is SSR held at the same time each day?
2. Are students "staying put" during SSR?
3. Are you reading silently while students are reading?
4. Are others in the room (aides, parents, volunteers) reading silently while the students are reading?
5. Is there a reading corner in your room with books displayed and available for students?
6. Do you rotate (freshen) the books periodically (once a month)?
7. Do you read aloud to your class and then place those books in the reading corner?
8. Do you do "book talks"—tell the class a little about some of the books in the reading corner to whet their interest in them?
9. Do you occasionally share with the class what you are reading?
10. Do students have the opportunity to go to the media center weekly to select new books?
11. Are all materials and work that may distract students put away?
12. Do you post signs of this reading time to prevent others from disrupting your class and to mark the importance of reading time to the students?
13. Are students permitted free choice of reading matter?
14. Are you consistent in *not* requiring written book reports and so forth from students on their SSR?
15. Do your students know how to locate materials of interest to them?

FIGURE 7.7 Evaluation of the sustained silent reading period: Teacher checklist

have used to encourage attentive reading has been successful in some schools. New materials can be provided and teachers can be encouraged to trade materials a few times a year. Regular monthly rotation of classroom book collections is essential to maintain student interest.

Visitors and "guest readers" can be invited to share a silent reading period and then tell students what they enjoy reading. The principal, guidance counselors, coaches, and community members might serve as guest readers. These and other techniques can help ensure a successful SSR program.

Extensive reading of literature can benefit students by increasing their reading pace, by enhancing their reading comprehension and vocabulary, and by improving their attitudes toward reading. Educators often enthusiastically attest to the fact that SSR programs have worked successfully in their middle level schools.

Summary

Literature is an important aspect of the middle level school curriculum and can readily be integrated into all content area classrooms. Sustained silent reading programs may help students develop the habit of wide reading. Literature may enliven and enrich the teaching of content area classes by telling the stories of the people who made the events of social studies and science happen. Strategies for using literature across the curriculum are included in this chapter.

At the end of this chapter, two lists are provided to assist teachers in their selection of good books to supplement the content area curricula. The "Starter List of Literature for Shared Literary Experiences" suggests titles arranged by content areas. Each title is briefly annotated to indicate the topics of the books. Many outstanding books have not been mentioned for lack of space and many fine new titles are published each year. Books on any of the lists may be considered by a teacher in selecting literary texts. A second list provides titles of professional resources for the teacher who wishes to seek additional titles for specific topics and ideas for teaching with the use of trade books. These resources are listed in the "Book Selection Aids" section.

References

Brozo, W.G. & Tomlinson, C.M. (1986). Literature: The key to lively content courses. *The Reading Teacher, 40*(3), 288–293.

Fader, D.N. & McNeil, E.B. (1968). *Hooked on Books: Program and Proof.* New York: Berkley.

Huck, C.S., Hepler, S., Hickman, J., & Kiefer, B. (1997). *Children's Literature in the Elementary School.* Madison, WI: Brown & Benchmark.

Lynch-Brown, C. & Tomlinson, C.M. (1986). Batchelder books: International read alouds. *Top of the News, 42,* 260–266.

Paulsen, G. (1987). *The Hatchet.* New York: Bradbury.

Richter, H.P. (1970). *Friedrich.* New York: Holt, Rinehart, and Winston.

Skurzynski, G. (1979). *What Happened in Hamelin?* New York: Four Winds.

Thiele, C. (1974). *Fire in the Stone.* New York: Harper.

Tomlinson, C. & Lynch-Brown, C. (1996). *Essentials of Children's Literature,* (2nd ed.). Boston: Allyn and Bacon.

Vygotsky, L.S. (1962). *Thought and Language.* Cambridge, MA: MIT Press.

Starter List of Literature for Shared Literary Experiences by Content Area

Code: NF=nonfiction, F=fiction, Biog=biography, IL=international, PI=picture book

Language Arts

Aliki. *The Gods and Goddesses of Olympus.* HarperCollins, 1994. (F, traditional tales)

Anderson, Rachel. *The Bus People.* Holt, 1992. (F, short character portrayals, different disabilities)

Avi. *Nothing But the Truth.* Orchard, 1991. (F, story told through documents and various perspectives)

Bodker, Cecil. *The Leopard.* Atheneum, 1975. (F/IL, set in Ethiopia, exciting plot)

Bridgers, Sue Ellen. *All Together Now.* Knopf, 1979. (F, mental retardation, love)

Carlson, Lori M., and Cynthia L. Ventura, Eds. *Where Angels Glide at Dawn: New Stories from Latin America.* Illustrated by Jose Ortega. Lippincott, 1990. (F/IL)

Cleary, Beverly. *Strider.* Morrow, 1991. (F, letter and journal writing)

Cleaver, Vera and Bill. *Where the Lilies Bloom.* Lippincott, 1979. (F, integral setting, Appalachian mountain region)

Creech, Sharon. *Walk Two Moons.* Harper Collins, 1995. (F, complex plot structure, characterization)

Doherty, Berlie. *Dear Nobody.* Hamish Hamilton, 1991. (F/IL, teen pregnancy)

Hamilton, Virginia. *In the Beginning: Creation Stories from Around the World.* Illustrated by Barry Moser. Harcourt, 1988. (F, traditional tales)

_____. *Sweet Whispers, Brother Rush.* Putnam, Philomel, 1982. (F, first person narrative)

Hooks, William H. *The Ballad of Belle Dorcas.* Illustrated by Brian Pinkney. Knopf, 1990. (F/PI, Gullah folktale, South Carolina)

Janeczko, Paul B. *The Place My Words Are Looking For: What Poets Say About and Through Their Work.* Bradbury, 1990. (Poetry and poets)

Lewis, C.S. *The Lion, the Witch and the Wardrobe.* Macmillan, 1961. (F, struggle between good and evil, first in the Narnia quest series)

Lowry, Lois. *Rabble Starkey.* Houghton, 1987. (F, theme of home, love, and security)

Lyons, Mary E. *Sorrow's Kitchen: The Life and Folklore of Zora Neale Hurston.* Scribner's, 1990. (Biog, African American, twentieth-century author)

Marsden, John. *Letters from the Inside.* Houghton, 1994. (F/IL, two teenage girls are penpals, abuse, prison)

_____. *So Much to Tell You.* Joy Street, 1989. (F/IL, Australian school setting, journal writing)

Mazer, Norma Fox. *I, Trissy.* Delacorte, 1971. (F, first person, letter)

McKinley, Robin. *A Knot in the Grain and Other Stories.* Morrow, 1994. (F, fantasy quest short stories)

McKissack, Patricia C. *The Dark-Thirty: Southern Tales of the Supernatural.* Illustrated by Brian Pinkney. Knopf, 1992. (F, short stories, African American)

O'Brien, Robert. *Z for Zachariah.* Atheneum, 1975. (F, diary format)

O'Dell, Scott. *Island of the Blue Dolphins.* Houghton, 1960. (F, Native American girl survives alone on an island in the Pacific)

Ottley, Reginald. *Boy Alone.* Harcourt, 1966. (F/IL, Australian outback setting)

Ross, Stewart. *Shakespeare and MacBeth: The Story Behind the Play.* Illustrated by Tony Karpinski. Viking, 1994. (NF/PI)

Salisbury, Graham. *Blue Skin of the Sea.* Delacorte, 1992. (F, short stories about Hawaii)

San Souci, Robert D. *Cut from the Same Cloth: American Women of Myth, Legend, and Tall Tale.* Illustrated by Brian Pinkney. Philomel, 1993. (F, traditional tales)

Singer, Isaac. *When Shlemiel Went to Warsaw and Other Stories.* Farrar, 1968. (F/IL, folk tales)

Soto, Gary. *Baseball in April and Other Stories.* Harcourt, 1990. (F, Latino short stories)

Stanley, Diane, and Peter Vennema. *Bard of Avon: The Story of William Shakespeare.* Illustrated by Diane Stanley. Morrow, 1992. (Biog/PI)

_____. *Charles Dickens: The Man Who Had Great Expectations.* Illustrated by Diane Stanley. Morrow, 1993. (Biog/PI)

Thiele, Colin. *Fire in the Stone.* Harper, 1974. (F/IL, opal mining town in Australian setting, exciting plot, strong character development)

Tolan, Stephanie S. *Save Halloween!* Morrow, 1993. (F, censorship)

Wolf, Virginia Euwer. *Make Lemonade.* Holt, 1993. (F, teen parent)

_____. *Probably Still Nick Swansen.* Holt, 1988. (F, learning disability)

Wrightson, Patricia. *The Ice Is Coming.* Atheneum, 1977. (F/IL, first in Australian fantasy trilogy, based on Aboriginal myths)

Social Studies

Ancona, George. *Powwow.* Harcourt, 1993. (NF, modern-day celebration of Native Americans, with photos)

Atkin, S. Beth. *Voices from the Fields: Children of Migrant Farmworkers Tell Their Stories.* Little, Brown, 1993. (NF)

Auel, Jean. *The Clan of the Cave Bear.* Bantam, 1980. (F, cave men)

Chang, Ina. *A Separate Battle: Women and the Civil War.* Lodestar, 1991. (NF)

Collier, James, and Christopher Collier. *My Brother Sam Is Dead.* Scholastic, 1974. (F, Revolutionary War)

Curtis, Christopher Paul. *The Watson's Go to Birmingham—1963.* Delacorte, 1995. (F, humor and history)

Cushman, Karen. *Catherine, Called Birdy.* Clarion, 1994. (F, medieval life depicted accurately and humorously, journal)

_____. *The Midwife's Apprentice.* Clarion, 1995. (F, medieval life)

Filipovic, Zlata. *Zlata's Diary: A Child's Life in Sarajevo.* Viking, 1994. (Biog, ethnic wars and their effects)

Fleischman, Paul. *Bull Run.* HarperCollins, 1993. (F, Civil War story told through the eyes of characters from both the North and the South)

Fox, Paula. *The Slave Dancer.* Bradbury, 1973. (F, Pre-Civil War)

Freedman, Russell. *Eleanor Roosevelt: A Life of Discovery.* Clarion, 1993. (Photobiography)

_____. *An Indian Winter.* Illustrated by Karl Bodmer. Holiday, 1992. (NF, photoessay)

_____. *Kids at Work: Lewis Hines and the Crusade Against Child Labor.* Photos by Lewis Hine. Clarion, 1994. (NF, PI)

_____. *Lincoln: A Photobiography.* Houghton, 1987. (Biog, a photoessay about Abraham Lincoln)

Gallaz, Christophe, and Roberto Innocenti. *Rose Blanche.* Illustrated by Roberto Innocenti. Creative Education, 1985. (F/PI, concentration camp, World War II)

Greenfield, Howard. *The Hidden Children.* Ticknor & Fields, 1993. (NF, people who saved Jewish childen from the Nazis)

Hamanaka, Sheila. *The Journey: Japanese Americans, Racism, and Renewal.* Orchard, 1990. (NF/PI)

Hamilton, Virginia. *Many Thousand Gone: African Americans from Slavery to Freedom.* Illustrated by Leo and Diane Dillon. Knopf, 1993. (NF, historical accounts)

Holman, Felice. *Slake's Limbo.* Scribner's, 1974. (F, survival in New York subway system)

Hunt, Irene. *Across Five Aprils.* Follett, 1964. (F, Civil War)

Konigsburg, E.L. *A Proud Taste for Scarlet and Miniver.* Atheneum, 1973. (F, Eleanor of Aquitane)

Kullman, Harry. *The Battle Horse.* Bradbury, 1981. (F/IL, Stockholm in 1930s)

Lowry, Lois. *The Giver.* Houghton, 1993. (F, futuristic novel portrays a thought-provoking society)

Lyons, Mary E. *Letters from a Slave Girl: The Story of Harriet Jacobs.* Scribner's, 1992. (Biog, fictionalized story of a slave in North Carolina)

Maartens, Maretha. *Paper Bird: A Novel of South Africa.* Translated by Madeleine van Biljon. Clarion, 1991. (F/IL)

Magorian, Michelle. *Good Night, Mr. Tom.* Harper, 1982. (F, World War II)

Maruki, Toshi. *Hiroshima No Pika.* Lothrop, 1980. (NF/PI, effects of nuclear warfare)

McKinley, Robin. *Beauty: A Retelling of the Story of Beauty and the Beast.* Harper, 1978. (F, Middle Ages based on folktale)

Meltzer, Milton. *Columbus and the World Around Him.* Watts, 1990. (NF, Columbus, the events, and views of his time)

_____. *Lincoln: In His Own Words.* Illustrated by Stephen Alcorn. Harcourt, 1993. (NF, an authentic, but different presentation of Lincoln)

Myers, Walter Dean. *Malcolm X: By Any Means Necessary.* Scholastic, 1993. (Biog, objective account of the life of this controversial figure)

Orlev, Uri. *The Island on Bird Street.* Houghton Mifflin, 1984. (F/IL, boy struggling for survival in a Polish ghetto during World War II)

Paterson, Katherine. *Jacob Have I Loved.* Harper, 1980. (F, isolated island setting off Maine during World War II)

Peck, Robert Newton. *A Day No Pigs Would Die.* Knopf, 1972; Dell, 1978. (F, 1920s in rural Vermont, a Shaker family)

Phipson, Joan. *When the City Stopped.* Harcourt, 1978. (F/IL, Sydney, Australia closes down, havoc ensues)

Richter, Hans. *Friedrich.* Holt, 1970. (F/IL, World War II, Germany, persecution of Jews)

Skurzynski, Gloria. *What Happened in Hamelin.* Four Winds, 1979. (F, Middle Ages)

Stanley, Jerry. *Children of the Dust Bowl: The True Story of the School at Weedpatch.* Crown, 1992. (NF, migrant workers, Depression era)

Staples, Suzanne Fisher. *Haveli: A Young Woman's Courageous Struggle for Freedom in Present-Day Pakistan.* Knopf, 1993. (F, nomadic tribe)

_____. *Shabanu: Daughter of the Wind.* Knopf, 1989. (F, modern-day desert nomads, Pakistan)

Sutcliff, Rosemary. *The Road to Camlaan.* Dutton, 1982. (F, Middle Ages, King Arthur)

Taylor, Mildred. *Roll of Thunder, Hear My Cry* and sequels including *Let the Circle Be Unbroken.* Dial, 1976; 1981. (F, 1930s in rural Mississippi, an African American family)

Temple, Frances. *A Taste of Salt: A Story of Modern Haiti.* Orchard, 1992. (F)

Thiele, Colin. *The Fire in the Stone.* Harper, 1974. (F/IL, Australia, opal mines)

Toll, Nelly S. *Behind the Secret Window: A Memoir of a Hidden Childhood During World War II.* Dial, 1993. (Biog)

Uchida, Yoshiko. *Journey to Topaz.* Scribner's, 1971. (F, internment of Japanese Americans during World War II)

van der Rol, Ruud, and Rian Verhoeven. *Anne Frank: Beyond the Diary: A Photographic Remembrance.* Translated by Tony Langham and Plym Peters. Viking, 1993. (NF, excellent companion to *The Diary of Anne Frank*)

Yep, Laurence. *Dragonwings.* Harper & Row, 1975. (F, Chinese immigration to California)

Science

Baker, Jeanne. *Window.* Julia McRae, 1991. (PI/IL, the effects of development on the environment seen through a window)

_____. *Where the Forest Meets the Sea.* Greenwillow, 1987. (IL/PI, tropical forest, environmental issue)

Bond, Nancy. *The Voyage Begun.* Atheneum, 1981. (F, depletion of energy supply)

Brandenburg, Jim. Edited by Joann Bren Guernsey. *To the Top of the World: Adventures with Arctic Wolves.* Walker, 1993. (NF)

Brooks, Bruce. *Nature by Design.* Farrar, 1991. (NF, architecture of animal habitats)

_____. *Predator!* Farrar, 1991. (NF)

Engdahl, Sylvia. *The Far Side of Evil.* Atheneum, 1971. (F, misuse of nuclear power)

Farmer, Penelope. *The Ear, the Eye, and the Arm.* Orchard, 1994. (F, future world set in Zimbabwe, genetic mutations, humor)

Flackham, Margery. *And Then There Was One: The Mysteries of Extinction.* Illustrated by Pamela Johnson. Little, Brown, 1990. (NF/PI)

Freedman, Russell. *The Wright Brothers: How They Invented the Airplane.* Holiday, 1991. (NF, a photoessay)

George, Jean Craighead. *The Cry of the Crow.* Harper, 1980. (F, communication between a girl and a crow)

_____. *Julie.* HarperCollins, 1994. (F, sequel to Julie of the Wolves)

_____. *Julie of the Wolves.* Harper & Row, 1972. (F, natural science, wolves on the tundra)

Hesse, Karen. *Phoenix Rising.* Holt, 1994. (F, effects of nuclear contamination)

Hoover, H.M. *This Time of Darkness.* Viking, 1980. (F, future world in which people live underground safe from outside air and sun)

_____. *Traces of Life: The Origins of Humankind.* Illustratead by Whitney Powell. Morrow, 1990. (NF/PI)

Lauber, Patricia. *Fur, Feathers, and Flippers: How Animals Live Where They Do.* Scholastic, 1994. (NF/photoessay)

Lasky, Kathryn. *Surtsey: The Newest Place on Earth.* Photos by Christopher G. Knight. Hyperion, 1992. (NF/photoessay, formation of a new island)

LeGuin, Ursula. *A Wizard of Earthsea.* Houghton, 1968. (F, magician and evil powers)

L'Engle, Madeleine. *A Wrinkle in Time.* Farrar, 1962. (F, extraterrestrials in outer space)

Mowat, Farley. *Never Cry Wolf.* Brown, 1963. Bantam, 1979. (F, scientist's adventure in the Arctic)

O'Brien, Robert C. *Mrs. Frisby and the Rats of NIMH.* Atheneum, 1971. (F, animal experiments) Also, see sequels by Jane Conly, *Racso and the Rats of NIMH; R.T., Margaret, and the Rats of NIMH.*

Paulsen, Gary. *Dogsong.* Bradbury. 1985. (F, Eskimo life, survival story)

_____. *Hatchet.* Bradbury, 1987. (F, survival in Canadian wilderness)

Pringle, Laurence. *Global Warming: Assessing the Greenhouse Threat.* Arcade, 1990. (NF)

Sleator, William. *House of Stairs.* Dutton, 1974. (F, psychological experiments on humans)

Health and Physical Education

Blume, Judy. *Deenie.* Bradbury, 1973. (F, curvature of the spine)

_____. *Then Again, Maybe I Won't.* Bradbury, 1971. (F, developing sexuality, 13-year-old boy)

Byars, Betsy. *Cracker Jackson.* Viking, 1985. (F, spouse abuse)

_____. *Summer of the Swans.* Viking, 1970. (F, mental retardation)

Childress, Alice. *A Hero Ain't Nothin' but a Sandwich.* Putnam, 1973. (F, heroin addiction)

Coman, Carolyn. *What Jamie Saw.* Front Street, 1995. (F, abuse)

Conly, Jane Leslie. *Crazy Lady!* HarperCollins, 1993. (F, mental retardation)

Crutcher, Chris. *Athletic Shorts: Six Short Stories.* Greenwillow, 1991. (F)

Donovan, John. *I'll Get There, It Better Be Worth the Trip.* Harper, 1969. (F, brief homosexual encounter between two boys, alcoholism)

Fine, Anne. *Flour Babies.* Hamish Hamilton, 1992. (F, novel about a teen's reaction to a school assignment to care for a "child")

Harris, Robie H. *It's Perfectly Normal: A Book About Changing Bodies, Growing Up, Sex, and Sexual Health.* Illustrated by Michael Emberley. Candlewick, 1994. (NF/PI)

Krementz, Jill. *How It Feels to Live with a Physical Disability.* Simon & Shuster, 1992. (collective biographies of teens with disabilities, heavily illustrated)

Kuklin, Susan. *Speaking Out: Teenagers Take on Sex, Race, and Identity.* Putnam, 1993. (NF)

_____. *What Do I Do Now?: Talking about Teenage Pregnancy.* Putnam, 1991. (NF)

Littlefield, Bill. *Champions: Stories of Ten Remarkable Athletes.* Illustrated by Bernie Fuchs. Little, Brown, 1993. (Biog, inspirational)

Lipsyte, Robert. *The Contender.* Harper, 1967. (F, Harlem setting, drug abuse)

Macy, Sue. *A Whole New Ball Game: The Story of the All-American Girls Professional Baseball League.* Holt, 1993. (NF)

Mazer, Norma Fox. *After the Rain.* Morrow, 1987. (F, aging and death)

Nelson, Theresa. *Earthshine.* Watts, 1994. (F, parent with AIDS)

Oneal, Zibby. *The Language of Goldfish.* Viking, 1980. (F, 13-year-old girl's depression, suicide attempt, and recovery)

Rylant, Cynthia. *Missing May.* Orchard, 1992. (F, dealing with death)

Slepian, Jan. *The Alfred Summer.* Macmillan, 1980. (F, cerebral palsy)

Voigt, Cynthia. *Dicey's Song* and *Homecoming.* Scribner's, 1982; Atheneum, 1981. (F, mental illness)

Art

Cummings, Pat, Ed. *Talking with Artists.* Illustrated by various artists. Bradbury, 1992. (NF)

Davidson, Rosemary. *Take a Look: An Introduction to the Experience of Art. Viking,* 1994. (NF)

Greenberg, Jan, and Sandra Jordan. *The Painter's Eye: Learning to Look at Contemporary American Art.* Delacorte, 1991. (NF)

Muhlberger, Richard. *What Makes a Van Gogh a Van Gogh?* The Metropolitan Museum of Art/Viking, 1993. (NF/others in this series, such as Bruegel, Degas, Raphael)

Welton, Jude. *Drawing: A Young Artist's Guide.* Dorling Kindersley, 1994. (NF)

Zhensun, Zheng, and Alice Low. *A Young Painter: The Life and Paintings of Wang Yani—China's Extraordinary Young Artist.* Scholastic, 1991. (Biog/PI)

Book Selection Aids

1. General annotated subject guides are helpful for locating books on particular topics.

a. *The Children's Catalog,* (16th ed.). New York: H.W. Wilson Co., 1991, with annual supplements. Includes 5000 recent books, grade levels, and summaries, a selective list of best books in fiction and nonfiction.

b. *High Interest—Easy Reading: A Booklist for Junior and Senior High Students, (6th ed.).* W.G. McBridge, Ed. Urbana, IL: NCTE, 1990. Includes topics and lively book annotations.

c. *The Bookfinder: A Guide to Children's Literature about the Needs and Problems of Youth.* Circle Pines, MN: American Guidance Service, 1977, 1981, 1985, 1989. Includes cross-indexing by subject, author, and title. Books selected are annotated and focus on emotions, problems, and relationships.

d. *The Elementary School Library Collection, (19th ed.).* L. Lee, Ed. Williamsport, PA: Bro-Dart Foundation, 1994. A bibliography of print and nonprint materials for elementary school media collections. This basic list includes annotations, bibliographic information, and author, title, and subject indexes.

e. *Your Reading: A Booklist for Junior High and Middle School Students, (9th ed.).* Urbana, IL: National Council of Teachers of English, 1993. An annotated list of books for grades 5–9, arranged in broad subject categories.

2. In addition, booklists for separate content areas and for specific needs can also be helpful:

a. *Portraying Persons with Disabilities: An Annotated Bibliography of Fiction for Children and Teenagers.* D. Robertson. New Providence, NJ: R.R. Bowker, 1992. Books are annotated with plot descriptions and analyses of works.

b. *Historical Figures in Fiction.* D.K. Hartman and G. Sapp. Phoenix: Oryx Press, 1994. This reference is designed to locate fictional biographies of famous and not-so-famous individuals from history.

c. *Re-creating the Past: A Guide to American and World Historical Fiction for Children and Young Adults.* L.G. Adamson. New York: Greenwood Press, 1994. Includes plot summaries of well-written historical fiction, reading and interest levels are also included.

d. *Reading for Young People Series.* Chicago, IL: American Library Association, 1979–1985. Eight volumes, by region, of annotated bibliographies of fiction and nonfiction for elementary through tenth grade of books on the life and history of various American regions.

e. *Science and Technology in Fact and Fiction: A Guide to Children's Books.* DayAnn M. Kennedy, Stella S. Spangler, and Mary Ann Vanderwerf. New York: R.R. Bowker, 1990. An annotated bibliography of science tradebooks of good quality.

f. *E for Environment: An Annotated Bibliography of Children's Books with Environmental Themes.* Patti Sinclair. New York: R.R. Bowker, 1992. Annotates 500 books that focus on endangered species, pollution, and other environmental topics.

g. *Careers in Fact and Fiction.* June Klein Bienstock and Ruth Bienstock Anolick. Chicago, IL: American Library Association, 1985. An annotated list of fiction and nonfiction, including biographies, which discuss careers.

h. *Read Any Good Math Lately? Children's Books for Mathematical Learning, K–6.* David J. Whitin and Sandra Wilde. Portsmouth, NH: Heinemann, 1992.
It's the Story that Counts: More Children's Books for Mathematical Learning, K–6. David J. Whitin and Sandra Wilde. Portsmouth, NH: 1995. Both books have annotated lists of children's books that present mathematical concepts and ideas for use of the books with children.

i. *Against Borders: Promoting Books for a Multicultural World.* Hazel Rochman. Chicago: American Library Association, 1993. Essays in Part One are followed by recommendations and annotations of books for junior and senior high school students in Part Two. Apartheid, the Holocaust, and various ethnic groups are included as topics.

3. Two books recommend titles especially enjoyable for reading aloud.

a. *The Read Aloud Handbook.* Jim Trelease. New York: Penguin Books, 1995. Lengthy annotations in which appropriateness for different age levels are included.

b. *For Reading Outloud: A Guide to Sharing Books with Children.* M.M. Kimmel and

E. Segel. Dell, 1988. Full annotations with appropriate listening levels indicated and also has a chapter cross-listing the books by settings—regions of United States and other countries.

4. Finally, textbooks on children's literature and adolescent literature include books for the middle school level student. The adolescent literature books focus on high school literature but also provide many titles appropriate for early adolescents. There are sections in these textbooks in which different genres of literature and types of books within them are discussed. For example, a science teacher might read the sections on science fiction, realistic animal stories, biographies of famous scientists in selecting related literature for the seventh-grade science curriculum.

a. *Children's Literature in the Elementary School, (6th ed.).* Charlotte S. Huck, Susan Hepler, Janet Hickman, and Barbara Kiefer. Madison, WI: Brown & Benchmark, 1997.
b. *Essentials of Children's Literature, (2nd ed.).* Carl M. Tomlinson and Carol Lynch-Brown. Needham Heights, MA: Allyn & Bacon, 1996.
c. *Literature and the Child, (3rd ed.)* by Bernice Cullinan and Lee Galda. Fort Worth, TX: Harcourt Brace, 1994.
d. *Literature for Today's Young Adults, (5th ed.). Aileen Pace Nilsen and Kenneth L. Donelson. Glenview, IL: Scott Foresman, 1997.*
e. *Reaching Adolescents: The Young Adult Book and the School.* Arthea J.S. Reed. New York: Holt, 1985.

Chapter 8

Vocabulary Knowledge

Educators have long recognized the strong relationship between vocabulary knowledge and the ability to read and write proficiently. In fact, most educators intuitively know that "people who do not know the meanings of many words are probably poor readers" (Anderson & Freebody, 1983, p. 244).

Although the vocabulary students need for reading predominates the literature and most instructional strategies, people in general have four types of vocabulary: listening, speaking, reading, and writing. The *listening* vocabulary is, of course, the earliest to develop and the largest. This vocabulary is composed of all the words people hear and understand and serves as the foundation for learning other vocabularies. The second vocabulary to develop, the *speaking* vocabulary, includes all the words a person uses appropriately in everyday speech. The *reading* vocabulary consists of the words a person recognizes or can figure out in print and the *writing* vocabulary encompasses those words a person can use appropriately during written communication. Listening and reading vocabularies are receptive; speaking and writing vocabularies are expressive. Although a normal sequence exists for the development of these vocabularies, they are recursive and one sequence naturally builds on the other. For example, words learned during reading are reinforced by speaking, writing, and listening. New words encountered during listening can be added to speaking, writing, and reading vocabularies.

When children begin the process of learning to read, they understand the meanings of many words (listening vocabulary), but can recognize only a few in print. The focus of emergent reading instruction is to assist children to connect the written symbol to the words they already use in listening and speaking. By about third or fourth grade, however, students "begin to encounter an increasing number of words whose printed forms they cannot recognize immediately and whose meanings are unknown" (Harris & Sipay, 1990, p. 511). The learning task shifts from word recognition to word identification (Nagy, 1988b).

Recommendations for vocabulary instruction have improved in the last decade because educators now view vocabulary acquisition within the broader context of language and concept learning. They understand that vocabulary development is more than looking up words in a dictionary and writing sentences; rather, it involves the complex process of relating words to ideas or concepts.

"Vocabulary" and "concept" are difficult words to define because new understandings of learning have made the lines between them increasingly fuzzy. People are considered to have an extensive vocabulary when they know the meanings of and fine distinctions between many words. Vocabulary knowledge also means using a vast array of prior knowledge to understand concepts and relate them to each other. Vocabulary knowledge also encompasses the application of many subtleties of our language and culture to "get" jokes and idioms. For the purposes of this book, the term "vocabulary knowledge" will be used in the broadest sense to include conceptual knowledge.

After a discussion of the importance of vocabulary knowledge, the various factors in vocabulary acquisition identified by researchers in the last decade are presented in this chapter. A discussion of the issues related to vocabulary instruction and a presentation of guidelines for increasing vocabulary knowledge using researched and field-tested learning strategies are described in the context of a unit of study.

The Importance of Vocabulary Knowledge

A wealth of research documents the strong relationship between vocabulary knowledge and academic achievement, specifically reading and listening comprehension. Anderson and Freebody (1981) hypothesized that vocabulary knowledge is strongly related to comprehension because (1) understanding words enables readers to understand passages, (2) verbal aptitude underlies both word and passage comprehension, and (3) vocabulary knowledge may be related to a person's store of background information. Stahl (1990) demonstrated that the "truth" of each of these hypotheses depends on "the particular contexts in which a word is found, the way the task of comprehension is defined, and the amount and types of knowledge a person has about a word" (p. 18). Whatever the reason, educators know that the proportion of difficult words in text is the single most powerful predictor of text difficulty, and a reader's general vocabulary knowledge is the single best predictor of how well that reader can understand text.

Nagy and Herman (1984) estimated that for students in fourth through twelfth grade, a 4,500 to 5,400 word gap existed between low versus high achieving students. Other researchers (Graves & Slater, 1987; Graves & Prenn, 1986) found huge individual differences between high and low ability students. The findings are clear: high achieving students know more words than low achieving students.

Until about 1950, the focus of vocabulary research was directed in four areas: (1) vocabulary size at various ages, (2) the relationship between vocabulary and intelligence, (3) identifying the most useful words to know, and (4) identifying a core of words that make text more understandable. In summary, most early research in vocabulary centered on choice of words to teach beginning readers and implementation of readability formulas in the attempt to control text difficulty.

The last few decades have yielded much high-quality research in language comprehension and production. It is only within the context of this research base that researchers and practitioners can understand vocabulary acquisition and make viable recommendations for effective instructional practices. Beck and McKeown (1990) contended that those interested in vocabulary acquisition must first understand the relationship between words and ideas, the role of inference, and the organization of information. Most likely, previous attempts to study vocabulary acquisition were fruitless until researchers were able to reach at least some level of understanding of the complexities of the mental processes involved in relating words to ideas.

Factors in Vocabulary Acquisition

Chall (1987) estimated that typical first graders understand and use about six thousand different words. Most primary students understand thousands more words than they recognize in print; nearly all of these words represent concrete rather than abstract concepts. A shift in children's language takes place around age 10. The words they meet with increasing frequency after age 10 are often abstract rather than concrete, as they encounter concepts in social studies texts, inferences in stories, and specialized content words in science.

Between grades 3 and 12, a typical student will learn approximately three thousand words per year, perhaps more (Nagy & Herman, 1987; White, Power, & White, 1989). Only a small fraction of these words can be attributed to direct instruction of particular words (Jenkins & Dixon, 1983; Nagy & Anderson, 1984). The logical assumption, and one supported by research, is that students learn most words from using context and morphology (word parts) while reading and listening.

The research of the last two decades has helped to illuminate the complexity of the role of vocabulary learning. Prior knowledge (especially topical prior knowledge), students' use of context and morphology, and metacognitive abilities work together to facilitate the development of an extensive vocabulary. Based on this new information, the first step in making decisions about effective and efficient vocabulary instruction is an understanding of various factors in vocabulary acquisition. These factors include (1) what it means to "know" a word, (2) the role of morphology and context in incidental word learning, (3) the usefulness of definitions, and (4) the size and growth of vocabulary as a student matures.

Knowing Words

Beck, McKeown, McCaslin, and Burkes (1979) identified three levels of word knowledge: unknown, acquainted, and established. Suppose you ask a young child about different ways of measuring things in your home. You mention a "gauge" which she does not recognize (unknown). She recognizes "yardstick" as something to do with measuring, but would not be able to hand you one (acquainted). She has used a "ruler" in the past to measure her foot (established). Nagy (1985) contended that it takes more than a simple, superficial knowledge of words to make a difference in reading comprehension. In other words, readers do not need to know all words in text at the established level to comprehend what they are reading; but, for instruction of specific words to make an impact on reading comprehension, the understanding must be beyond a superficial level.

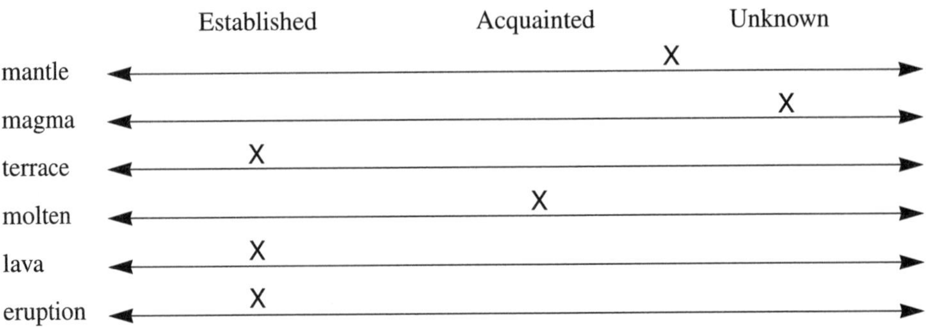

FIGURE 8.1 Knowledge rating of words about volcanoes

Blachowicz (1986) suggested the use of knowledge rating before reading, as in Figure 8.1, to help students analyze their level of word knowledge. Before students read, the teacher presents a list of words related to the topic of study by placing a check mark along the continuum that reflects their level of knowledge of the word. The students analyze what they know about each word individually and then discuss which words are known or unknown and share information with each other. This activity leads naturally to the preteaching of vocabulary to be used later in the reading.

A related issue to knowing words is knowing the importance of words in the text. Students seemingly do not need to know all words in a text to understand it, especially with narrative text. Freebody and Anderson (1983) found that replacing one word in six with a difficult synonym did not reliably decrease sixth graders' comprehension of text. Students generally encounter text with 3 to 6 percent unfamiliar words. For example, when reading the sentence, "Her mauve skirt fluttered in the wind as she fell over the precipice," a student may not know "mauve" and "precipice"—one is important to comprehend, the other is not. In summary, if the unfamiliar words are not important to the understanding of the text, students can tolerate a fairly large number of unknown words (about 15 percent) and still read with comprehension.

Morphology

Morphology is the "ability to gain information about the meaning, pronunciation, and part of speech of new words from their prefixes, roots, and suffixes" (Nagy, Diakidoy, & Anderson, 1991). Students increase their vocabularies by some twenty thousand words from grades 3 to 7—the "combination of context clues and morphological analysis is the only plausible explanation for this increase in word knowledge" (Anderson & Freebody, 1979; Ryder, 1986). White, Power, and White (1989) speculated that "seventh-grade students may analyze successfully at least [three thousand] and as many as [nine thousand] prefixed words a year" (p. 301).

Clearly, when students learn to "chunk" letters in a long word into meaningful morphemes, this ability facilitates the processing of new words. Much of the instruction in what is normally called "structural analysis" is often random and not connected with the context of text or the student's prior knowledge. When students learn to use morphology, context, and strategies for activating prior knowledge, they possess a powerful tool for expanding their vocabularies.

Context

Few educators would dispute the value of students learning to use context to understand text and improve vocabulary growth. New research, however, has challenged some of the limited approaches of teaching context clues used extensively in the past. In naturally occurring text (such as a novel as opposed to materials produced for use in school), context is relatively uninformative (Deighton, 1959; Schatz & Baldwin, 1986). Most recent approaches to context clues encourage students to use their prior knowledge, their knowledge of syntax (how words are put together in a sentence), their knowledge of morphology and phonics if applicable, and their use of semantics (what makes sense in the context). It is this attention to semantics, especially the larger context of the story or passage that facilitates students' abilities to make accurate inferences about word meanings.

Deriving meaning of an unfamiliar word from context and learning the meaning of a word are at two different levels of comprehension. A single encounter with an unknown word may be enough to help a reader understand the text at hand, but not enough for a thorough understanding of the word. The word remains at the acquainted level of understanding until another more in-depth encounter may move it to an established level.

Nagy (1985) calculated that the probability of learning a word from a single encounter (in context) was between 5 and 11 percent with seventh and eighth graders. Herman, Anderson, Pearson, and Nagy (1987) found that learning from context was facilitated by higher reading ability and by explicit text. The authors of these and other studies concluded that some learning from context occurs, but the effect is not at all powerful. Most word learning occurs incrementally, over time, and with repeated exposures to words.

Even considering these limitations, experts in vocabulary acquisition contend that using strategies to maximize the use of context, even if the context is lacking richness, is still helpful instructional practice, especially when its usage is paired with other strategies such as definitions. Nagy (1988b) proposed that a combination of definitional and contextual approaches is more effective than either approach in isolation.

Definitions

Used by itself, looking up words in a dictionary or committing definitions to memory does not lead to improved comprehension. This activity—a daily occurrence in hundreds of classrooms—leads to only a superficial understanding and rapid forgetting of a word. Two problems with definitions as a way to learn new words are that (1) often a person must know a word to understand the definition, and (2) definitions do not always contain enough information to understand and be able to use a word. For example, a student finding "trade" as a definition for the word "commerce" is likely to write a sentence such as "I will commerce my baseball for your goalie shirt." This sentence hardly captures the true meaning of "commerce." Miller and Gildea (1987) examined the types of errors students commonly make when asked to write a sentence from the definition of a new vocabulary word. They found that this "substitution error" based on partial understanding of a word was common. They concluded that looking words up in the dictionary and writing sentences was "pedagogically useless." Perhaps technology will be developed that can give students more "context-specific definitions without requiring readers to employ reference skills such as the ability to locate words alphabetically and to determine which of several meanings apply to a given context" (Reinking & Salmon-Rickman, 1990, p. 396).

Reading comprehension depends on a deep understanding of the intent of the text, not merely on the definitional knowledge of the words contained therein. It appears, then, that the dictionary or glossary can best be used as a verification of meaning; that is, after the reader has a hunch as to the meaning of a word. Students need to learn how to combine the use of context, prior knowledge, and definitions to infer the meanings of unknown words.

Learning a word involves more than lifting its meaning from context or reading its meaning in a dictionary. Word knowledge involves a complex process of integrating new words with ideas that exist in the schema of the reader. Dictionaries are, of course, powerful aids to understanding. Scott and Nagy (1991) concluded that "current instruction appears to deal largely with the mechanics of dictionaries—alphabetization, keywords, and pronunciation keys . . . it is clear that some type of instruction is needed that focuses on the central problem of dictionary use—translating the cryptic and conventionalized content of definitions into usable word knowledge" (p. 13).

Size and Growth of Vocabulary

This subject has been a topic of long-standing debate. The number of words a person knows at any particular age depends on what an investigator counts as a word, with or without derivatives, and at what level a word is known. Nagy and Herman (1987) estimated that students learn approximately 2,700 to 3,000 new words annually.

A related factor to the size and growth of vocabulary involves the number of words available for exposure. Nagy and Herman (1987) analyzed the stock of words in school-printed material in grades 3 through 9. They found that materials available for those grade levels contained approximately 88,500 words with approximately one hundred thousand distinct meanings. Anderson and Freebody (1983) indicated that average fifth graders would likely encounter almost ten thousand new words a year while completing their normal school reading assignments.

Researchers have helped educators understand that most children are capable of learning large numbers of new words per year. The question to raise is: Where and how do students learn these words? Durkin (1978–1979) spent almost three hundred hours observing fourth- through sixth-grade students and found that only nineteen minutes of the instructional time was spent in direct vocabulary instruction. Nagy, Herman, and Anderson (1985) also analyzed the number of words suggested in basal and content area textbook teacher's guides. They determined that only 290–460 of the 3,000 words that students learn each year can be attributed to direct instruction. Nagy and Herman (1987) concluded that "teaching children specific words will not in itself contribute substantially to the overall size of their vocabulary" (p. 23).

Although the belief is not held universally, Nagy and Herman (1987) contended "that incidental learning of words from context while reading is, or can be, the major mode of vocabulary growth once children have really begun to read" (p. 24). Their belief is based on previous studies (Herman, Anderson, Pearson, & Nagy, 1987; Nagy & Herman, 1987) that indicated that reading grade-level texts produces a small but statistically reliable increase in word knowledge in grades 3, 5, 7, and 8 that were tested. The chance of learning a word from one exposure in text is somewhere around 1 in 20. Nagy and Herman (1987) concluded, however, that "if students were to spend [twenty-five] minutes a day reading at a rate of [two hundred] words per minute for [two hundred] days out of the year, they would read a million words of text annually" (p. 26). With this amount of reading, children would encounter between 15,000 and 30,000 unfamiliar words and if 1 in 20 of these words is learned, the yearly gain in vocabulary will be between 750 and 1,500 words.

Nagy (1988a) explained that few people have experienced systematic, intensive, and prolonged vocabulary instruction; yet many adults have acquired an extensive reading vocabulary. People learn words from a number of sources, but "after third grade, for those children who do read a reasonable amount, reading may be the single largest source of vocabulary growth" (p. 30).

Understanding these factors helps educators made decisions about which words to choose for direct instruction, how much time to spend on them, and the most effective instructional approaches. In the remaining pages of this chapter, these important instruction considerations will be discussed.

Choosing Words for Instruction

Given that it is unlikely that students will learn a large number of words from direct instruction and given that instruction must be rich and extended, the particular words teachers choose for instruction are important. Graves and Prenn (1986) classified words into three types—known concepts, synonyms and antonyms, and unknown concepts—each in succession requiring a higher investment of teacher and learner instructional time.

Known Concepts

The first type of word is one that may be in the student's oral vocabulary. Students merely need to identify the written symbol for this word. These words are generally mastered by the third or fourth grade, but poor readers continue to have problems with them. These types of words also may be for concepts the students understand but have never connected with the written symbol. For example, "aglet" may be an unfamiliar word, but when told that it is "what you call the plastic tip on the end of a shoelace," a typical response might be "Oh! is that what you call it?" No further explanation is necessary. Kibby (1995) developed a hierarchy of "things and words that signify them" that is extremely useful when designing instruction (p. 208).

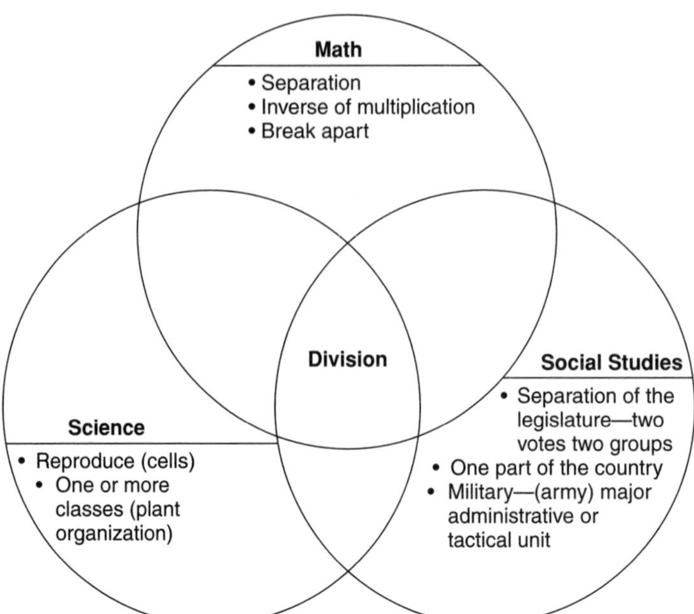

FIGURE 8.2 Interdisciplinary reinforcement of polysemous words

Synonyms and Antonyms—Multiple Meaning Words

A second type of word is in neither the oral nor the reading vocabulary of the student, but can be easily defined through the use of more familiar synonyms or antonyms. For example, although a student may not know the meaning of the word "altercation," this word can easily be defined by the words "argument" or "quarrel." Antonyms often help students understand a word by explaining what it is *not* (Powell, 1986).

Another type of word that fits into this category is a multiple-meaning word such as "bank," "run," or "bay." A student may know one meaning of a word but need a new or second meaning explained. It is estimated that one-third of commonly used words have multiple meanings. These multiple-meaning words are called *polysemous*. Teams of teachers can reinforce different meanings of concepts across disciplines by using the simple configuration presented in Figure 8.2. Words such as "negative," "distance," "function," "age," "product," "relation," "time," "solution," "process," "space," "element," and "positive" are polysemous words that lend themselves to this type of word meaning expansion.

Polysemous words may be historically related; for example, students may know that the word "coach" means someone who guides a team. They may not know that a coach is also a vehicle. The new meaning can be traced to what people in medieval England called the person who drove the team of horses pulling the coach. The term was later applied to tutors in college, leaders of crew teams, and even later to anyone who guided a team as hard to handle as eight spirited horses. Polysemous words may also have a specific meaning in a content area; for example, all students know the word "change" as it relates to money. In social studies, however, "change" has a specific meaning somewhat different from the everyday sense of the word, which may have to do with "changing societies" or "environmental change."

Unknown Concept

The third type of word is one for which the student has acquired no concept. This type of word is encountered frequently in the content areas. The teacher must take the time to develop the concept through instruction before the student can understand the word. Words such as "scarcity" or "acculturation" are difficult concepts that are more readily understood after examples are given. It is for these words that are difficult to teach and are commonly found in the content areas that rich, direct instruction is most helpful.

Words that are already in the student's listening vocabulary may be taught through language experience activities or other writing experiences; however, multiple-meaning words and words embodying unfamiliar concepts need more direct instruction. Words chosen for instruction should be considered to be important to the understanding of a particular content area or to enhance general background knowledge.

Guidelines for Instruction

The average fifth grader reads about one million words of text in a year. Of the 10,000 "new" words this student might encounter, 4,000 are derivatives of more frequent words, 1300 are inflections of more frequent words, 2,200 fall into a variety of categories such as capitalizations, numbers, and deliberate misspellings, and 1,000 are truly new words not directly related to more familiar words (Nagy, Winsor, Osborn, & O'Flahavan, 1994). "Skilled readers depend not [only] on knowing a large number of words, but also on being able to deal effectively with new ones" (p. 46). Readers derive the meanings of unknown words by using three sources of information: (1) context to infer a word's meaning, (2) phonics to determine a word's pronunciation, and (3) structural analysis or knowledge of word parts to determine both a word's meaning and pronunciation.

The English language is composed of a small number of words that occur frequently and a large number of words that occur infrequently (Nagy, Winsor, Osborn, & O'Flahavan, 1994, p. 45). Students must use the strategies they have learned to derive new word meanings, but more importantly, they must access their prior knowledge and engage their metacognitive thinking abilities to infer the meaning of the word or even decide if it is important enough to stop and think about. Sometimes the most useful strategy is to make a general guess at the word's meaning and move ahead with the reading. Knowing a large number of words is good, making expedient decisions about new words is better. Some general guidelines for vocabulary instruction are presented in the following section.

Help Students Become Independent Word Learners

If wide reading is the most effective vehicle for large-scale vocabulary growth, then helping students make the most of learning words independently is imperative. Carr and Wixson (1986) related this independence to the concept of strategic readers suggesting that readers should (1) be responsible for learning a variety of methods to acquire word meanings (such as using context, structural analysis, and activating prior knowledge), (2) have the ability to monitor a student's understanding of new vocabulary, and (3) gain the capacity to change or modify strategies for understanding in the event of comprehension failure. Teachers and other students sharing how they derived a meaning of a new word can help other students. The more opportunities students have to use strategies to guess at the meanings of unknown words, the better they will become at that ability.

Encourage Active Involvement and Deep Processing of Words

What students do with newly learned words is more important than the number of words presented. Teachers can help students associate new words with what they already know through meaningful content or known synonyms. Students can learn how to make associations on their own to relate new words to their existing knowledge. Nagy (1988b) advocated "meaningful use" of words. "Effective vocabulary instruction requires students to process words meaningfully—that is, make inferences based on their meanings—and will include tasks that are at least in some ways parallel to normal speaking, reading, and writing" (p. 13).

Provide Multiple Opportunities to Use Words

The likelihood of a student acquiring an adult understanding of a word from one exposure in a natural context is quite low (Nagy, Herman, & Anderson, 1985). Many encounters with a new word are necessary if vocabulary instruction is to have a measurable effect on comprehension (McKeown, Beck, Omanson, & Pople, 1985; Stahl & Fairbanks, 1986). If words are to be retained, they must be used in meaningful ways in future reading and writing assignments. In addition, story read-alouds to students are a significant source of vocabulary acquisition and when teachers explain words as they are read, additional benefits are reaped (Elley, 1989).

It seems logical that the introduction and use of new words should occur within a content area where reinforcement can naturally occur. Nelson-Herber (1986) explained that "extensive reading can increase vocabulary knowledge, but direct instruction that engages students in construction of word meaning, using context and prior knowledge, is effective for learning specific vocabulary and for improving comprehension of related materials" (p. 627). An obvious cause-and-effect relationship is at work here: the more students are exposed to a word that occurs in a meaningful context, the higher the chance of students using and understanding that word.

Help Students Develop a Good Attitude about Learning Words Outside of the Classroom

Activities and gimmicks that help students identify, say, hear, or see words studied in class offer students repeated exposures in a meaningful context. Additionally, these application exercises help students develop the attitude that developing their vocabulary is a lifelong process.

One strategy that teachers have found helpful is when a teacher develops a list of three to five words for the week. These words are written down and taped to the corner of the teacher's desk for her referral. She attempts to use each word five times during the week and tallies each time she uses one. Eventually, she tells the students what she is doing and why. ("I am trying to increase my vocabulary.") Soon the students model her behavior, copy her list, and try to use the words also. Some students make up their own lists. Other teachers have mystery words for the day or week. Richek (1988) suggested that for students to become alert to words in their environment, attention to the meanings of first names, automobile names, food words, or sports headlines can be helpful. However the details of these types of activities work out, the clear message is that learning new words is a lifelong process.

Foster Extensive Reading Outside of Class

Wide reading facilitates large-scale vocabulary growth as discussed repeatedly throughout this chapter. Teachers should encourage students to read outside of class. Sustained silent reading times, giving students lists of books, and using the media center are good ways of encouraging wide reading beyond the classroom walls.

Evaluating vocabulary knowledge returns to the notion of how well students know words and for what purposes they will use them. White, Slater, and Graves (1989) documented that simply asking students if they know a word (yes or no) was a fairly reliable indicator of word knowledge. Many teachers have found asking students to evaluate a particular word as unknown, acquainted, or established helpful in both assessing word knowledge and as a basis for learning and remembering a word (Chase & Duffelmeyer, 1990). Personal interviews are likely the most accurate form of word knowledge assessment, but also the most time consuming. The type of assessment a teacher chooses depends on the breadth and depth of word knowledge and the purposes of the evaluation.

A Sample Unit: The Ancient Chinese

The major thrust of this chapter thus far has been on vocabulary knowledge in its broadest sense. The two approaches to increasing vocabulary knowledge are (1) instruction in the individual meanings of words which adds specific words to an individual's store of knowledge and (2) instruction in deriving meanings of words which enhances a student's ability to learn new words independently. Both approaches "hold potential for adding significantly to students' vocabulary . . . [and] combining both techniques may be more effective than relying exclusively on either strategy" (Jenkins, Matlock, & Slocum, 1989, p. 234). This chapter concludes with a sample unit illustrating specific word instruction and instruction in deriving meaning to illustrate many of the concepts presented in this chapter.

Suppose a social studies teacher is about to begin a unit on China. The new unit words suggested in the textbook for instruction are: "dynasty," "pictographs," "character," "mandarin," "Mandate of Heaven," "jade," "civil service," and "porcelain." After reading the particular selection, the teacher determines that the following additional words might be unfamiliar to students: "chariot," "nomad," and "millet."

The major concepts to be learned in this selection are that (1) dynasties were predominant among early civilizations and (2) early Chinese writing, based on symbols called pictographs, eliminated all but the wealthy and educated people from positions of power, because writing was a prerequisite for rulers.

Earlier in this chapter, two important points were made that can help a teacher decide which words merit extensive treatment and which should be treated lightly or ignored. The first point is that some words are more important than others for students to understand the text. The second point is that the extent of student prior knowledge must be considered when making decisions about vocabulary instruction as explained with the three types of words (known concepts, synonyms and antonyms, and unknown concepts). Next is an example of the decisions made relative to the unit on the ancient Chinese.

a. "Dynasty" is an important concept and necessary for understanding of the text; needs preteaching.
b. "Character" is a high utility word and also polysemous. Other meanings for the word "character" should be explored first to help students make the connection.
c. "Mandate of Heaven" and "civil servant" are important concepts to the understanding of the selection and need some preteaching.
d. "Jade," "porcelain," "chariot," "nomad," "millet," "mandarin," and "pictograph" are words that are incidental to understanding of the text; meanings should be reinforced in postreading activity.

The activities to be presented are samples of ways to develop vocabulary that are related to a particular reading or topic. Most likely, a teacher would choose among these activities depending on the prior knowledge of students and the teaching objectives.

The learning strategies presented are used widely in classrooms and are flexible enough to fit a variety of content. These particular strategies were chosen because they help students become independent word learners; encourage active involvement by having students relate new words to previously learned concepts; provide multiple opportunities to use new words through reading, writing, speaking, and listening activities; and encourage students to use words in new contexts outside the classroom.

List-Group-Label

Taba (1967) first developed the list-group-label strategy as part of her concept formation model. This strategy can also be used as a diagnostic instrument to find what students know about a subject and as an organizational tool to facilitate higher level thinking. Because the strategy involves the categorization and labeling of words, list-group-label also makes an excellent prereading strategy for a vocabulary development lesson.

Step One: The teacher elicits from students a list of as many words as possible related to a particular subject. A variety of stimuli may be used: the teacher may show a picture, read a story, show a film, give a lecture, or display artifacts or objects. Pictures

❂ *rickshaw*	✪ *chopstick*	✢✻ *kings*
❂ *bicycle*	● *kimono*	✻ *very polite*
✻ *farmers*	✢ *dynasty*	✻ *sons*
✻ *poor*	✢ ✻ *rulers*	❍ *paddies*
● *pointed hats*	❑ *Buddha*	▼ *books*
✪ ❍ *rice*	▼ *porcelain*	❑ *Confucius*
✪ ❍ *tea*	▼ *silk*	▼ *vases*

FIGURE 8.3

❂ *transportation*	❍ *farming*	✪ *food/mealtime*
✻ *people*	❑ *religion*	✢ *rulers*
● *clothing*	▼ *things they made*	

FIGURE 8.4

of China from the textbook or other sources may evoke responses such as farmer, rice, pagoda, people, very old, rickshaw, bicycle, chop suey, great wall, gun powder and so forth. Words may also be elicited by simply asking students to brainstorm what they know about a particular topic. A sample list shown here was gathered by showing students pictures of China.

rickshaw	chopsticks	kings
bicycle	kimono	very polite
farmers	dynasty	sons
poor	rulers	paddies
pointed hats	Buddha	books
rice	porcelain	Confucius
tea	silk	vases

Step Two: The teacher helps students group related items by asking students which words may go together to form a group. Students may note that items may belong to more than one group. After students determine appropriate categories, they group words accordingly. One type of marking system is shown in Figure 8.3 above.

Step Three: The teacher helps students give a label to each group. After students have grouped related items, the teacher asks them to label each group of related words. The list in Figure 8.4 above shows the marking system used to identify the labels or concepts.

Taba's model extends this initial phase of categorizing into interpretation of data. To encourage students to think at higher levels, they would be asked to compare observations of ancient Chinese civilization with what they know about life in China today. They may then be asked to identify similarities and differences. Further, the students would be asked to make generalizations concerning the similarities and differences noted. In the third

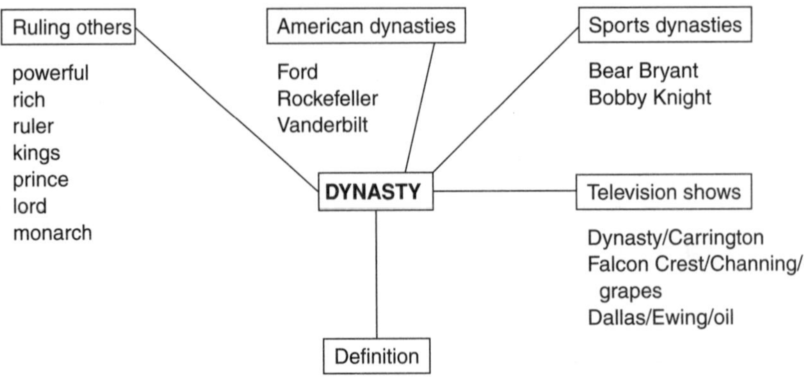

FIGURE 8.5 Word map

phase, application of generalization, students would apply the generalization to a new situation and examine what would happen if the generalization were applied. To continue the example, after the list-group-label activity about China, the students may form the generalization that "China is radically different today due to a change in government." The students then may be asked to apply this same statement to a new situation by considering the question, "What changes will occur in the next hundred years?"

Educators have used the Taba model as a means of promoting concept development, higher level thinking, and developing vocabulary knowledge in students for four decades. This activity provides motivation through opportunity for success. All students can participate by sharing with the class their perceptions of a picture. Students can then develop in higher order thinking through categorizing, interpreting, and making generalizations. In addition, students learn words by grouping them logically and in a way that makes sense to them. By considering examples of a concept and grouping them, students learn new vocabulary as they are exposed to the labels other students apply.

Word Maps

Although students may know little about dynasties, they are familiar with the television show "Dynasty." They also know some things about rulers, kingdoms, monarchs, and presidents. Word maps can take many forms. An example of one word map for "dynasty" is shown in Figure 8.5. Teachers can add as much or as little structure as the students need to build background for a particular concept.

Word maps can be open ended; for example, if a student (or class or group) constructed a word map of "character," the polysemous (multiple meaning) nature of the word would soon become evident. For students to have a deeper meaning of the word, the relationship between the Chinese "character" and the person "character" would add a richer meaning to both words.

Word maps can be used during the prereading phase, the reading phase, and the postreading phase to teach and reinforce vocabulary learning. Some teachers ask students to map a word (usually a larger concept such as arthropods or landforms) individually, then share with a group while adding other thoughts to their map, and then add to their map as they read and discuss the concept (Wood, 1987).

Capsule Vocabulary

The unique feature of capsule vocabulary is that it incorporates the four language areas, (listening, speaking, reading, and writing) into the process of building vocabulary. This strategy was originally developed by Crist (1975) to improve the vocabulary skills of college students in a language lab; however, it has been successfully adapted for use in middle and secondary school classrooms. Some teachers choose to use review words from previous units to give students an opportunity to read, write, speak, and listen to the capsule words. The steps comprising this strategy are illustrated by using the topic "dynasties."

Step One: The teacher prepares the capsule. A group of words related to a particular topic is identified. These words can come from a previously studied chapter or a new topic. The list of words is handed to the students. For "dynasty," the following words were chosen:

dynasty	kingdom
monarch	authority
colleague	potentate
ruler	dominion
family	generation
noble	emperor

Step Two: The teacher introduces capsule words. Teacher and students engage in a ten- to twenty-minute discussion on the topic using as many of the capsule words as possible. The students try to identify these words. As each word is identified, it is checked off on their list of words and defined, if necessary. If the students or teacher are uncomfortable with the discussion format, a written format may be used as suggested by Cunningham, Cunningham, and Arthur (1981). This format consists of a paragraph containing the words. The students underline the capsule words found within the paragraph.

Step Three: Students practice using the words as part of their speaking/listening vocabularies. Students are placed into small groups where they have their own discussion. They are instructed to use as many of the new words in a conversation as possible and record when they use each word with a tally system.

Step Four: Students practice using the words in writing. The final step is to have the students write. Students can write themes, dialogues, or stories about the topic, again using as many new words as possible. The writing may be done by individual students or in cooperative writing groups.

Many educators agree that using the four language systems reinforces learning. This strategy provides students with an opportunity to speak new words, read new words, listen to others use the new words, and finally write those new words in a meaningful context.

One young woman in Crist's (1975) original pilot group summarized the experience by saying: "It's cool—or I should say, 'gratifying'—to be verbose" (p. 149).

Contextual Redefinition

One important aspect of assisting students in becoming independent vocabulary learners is helping them to use context effectively. The use of context allows readers to make predictions about unknown words and then to verify those predictions using syntactic and semantic clues. Contextual redefinition (Cunningham, Cunningham, & Arthur, 1981) is a strategy that introduces new vocabulary in rich contexts. These contexts help students to define words and facilitate the retention of these words.

Step One: The teacher selects words that may be unfamiliar to students. These are words that may be troublesome to students but are important for their understanding of the passage.

Step Two: The teacher presents the words in isolation. The teacher asks the students to provide a definition for each unfamiliar word. Some guesses may be funny or highly unusual, but these guesses should be accepted in the spirit of guessing. Students may, for example, guess that "Mandate of Heaven" means finally getting a date with the person of their dreams; or, "civil service" may mean a wedding in which everyone is polite. After the guessing, students are asked to reach consensus about the meaning of the word.

Step Three: The teacher presents a sentence that illustrates the meaning of the unknown word. If such a sentence exists in the text, that sentence should be used. Different types of context clues such as contrast or synonym should be used to accustom students to making use of such clues. Following are sentences that could be helpful to students attempting to determine the meanings of "Mandate of Heaven" and "civil service":

> *The Chinese people supported each new ruler because of what they called the "Mandate of Heaven." They believed that the king or emperor who gained power had been selected by heaven to rule.*
>
> *T'ang emperors developed an examination system for government officials that was used for centuries. This system established "civil service." In the civil service system, government officials were selected based on their qualifications rather than on noble birth.*

Using these contextually rich sentences, the teacher then asks the students to offer guesses as to the meanings of the new words. Students should be asked to provide a rationale for their guesses, which is important because it is helpful for students to hear the thought processes of others.

Step Four: Students use the dictionary to verify guesses. A student is asked to look the word up in the dictionary or glossary to confirm the guesses of the class.

Contextual redefinition not only provides an opportunity for students to learn new words but it also assists them in becoming independent word learners through the use of context clues. After this activity, students will in all likelihood realize that trying to guess at a word's meaning in isolation is frustrating and often futile. As mentioned earlier, students also benefit from being actively involved in predicting and confirming word meanings. Finally, the proper role of the dictionary or glossary is emphasized throughout this activity—that of verifying guesses as to word meaning.

Assessing Vocabulary

After the reading, the meanings of some less important words may be reinforced. Here is an example of a postreading activity.

1. Which of these would you _________?

a. read	1. millet
b. ride	2. jade
c. eat with	3. chariot
d. wear	4. pictograph
e. eat	5. porcelain

2. Could a *nomad* be a *mandarin?* Why or why not?

These words may be reinforced by asking students to use them in a writing activity or by asking students to find the words in speaking, listening, reading, or writing experiences outside the classroom. This type of activity helps students to use words in a meaningful context and leads them to a more sophisticated understanding of words.

Summary

The important role of vocabulary and conceptual knowledge in comprehending text has been recognized by educators for years. Researchers in the last decade have pointed the way to more effective instruction in this area. Recent investigations in the richness of context in natural text, the usefulness of text, the level to which a person knows a word, and the size and growth of vocabulary and concepts helped educators understand that the acquisition of a full, rich, and functional vocabulary involves the complex process of relating words to ideas.

Experts in the field of language development agree that the main vehicle for instruction should be encouraging students to read widely. Selected words, however, should be chosen for extended, rich instruction. This instruction should also focus on helping students become independent learners, encouraging students to become actively involved in the processing of selected words, providing multiple opportunities to use words, and guiding students to develop a good attitude about learning words outside the classroom. Research-based and field-tested learning strategies such as list-group-label, contextual redefinition, and mapping are available for teachers' use at any level. With wide reading, these strategies help students learn unfamiliar words by associating words to be learned with ideas and words they know.

References

Anderson, R.C. & Freebody, P. (1979). *Vocabulary Knowledge and Reading.* (Technical Report No. 11). Champaign, IL: Center for the Study of Reading.

Anderson, R.C. & Freebody, P. (1981). Vocabulary knowledge. In J.T. Guthrie (Ed.), *Comprehension and Teaching: Research Reviews* (pp. 77–117). Newark, DE: International Reading Association.

Anderson, R.C. & Freebody, P. (1983). Reading comprehension and the assessment and acquisition of word knowledge. In B. Hutton (Ed.), *Reading/Language Research: A Research Annual* (pp. 231–256). Greenwich, CT: JAI Press.

Beck, I.L. & McKeown, M.G. (1990). The acquisition of vocabulary. In P.D. Pearson (Ed.), *Handbook of Reading Research,* (2nd ed.) (pp. 789–814). White Plains, NY: Longman.

Beck, I.L., McKeown, M.G., McCaslin, E.S., & Burkes, A.M. (1979). *Instructional Dimensions That May Affect Reading Comprehension: Examples from Two Commercial Reading Programs.* Pittsburgh: University of Pittsburgh, Learning Research and Development Center.

Blachowicz, C.L. (1986). Making connections: Alternatives to the vocabulary notebook. *Journal of Reading, 29*(7), 643–649.

Carr, E. & Wixson, K.K. (1986). Guidelines for evaluating vocabulary instruction. *Journal of Reading, 29*(7), 588–595.

Chall, J.S. (1987). Two vocabularies for reading: Recognition and meaning. In M.G. McKeown & M.E. Curtis (Eds.), *The Nature of Vocabulary Acquisition* (pp. 7–18). Hillsdale, NJ: Erlbaum.

Chase, A.C. & Duffelmeyer, F.A. (1990). VOCAB-LIT: Integrating vocabulary study and literature study. *Journal of Reading, 34*(3), 188–193.

Crist, B.I. (1975). One capsule a week: A painless remedy for vocabulary ills. *Journal of Reading, 19*(2), 147–149.

Cunningham, J.W., Cunningham, P.M., & Arthur, S.V. (1981). *Middle and Secondary School Reading.* New York: Longman.

Deighton, L.C. (1959). *Vocabulary Development in the Classroom.* New York: Teachers College Press.

Durkin, D. (1978–1979). What classroom observations reveal about reading comprehension instruction. *Reading Research Quarterly, 14*(4), 481–533.

Elley, W.B. (1989). Vocabulary acquisition from listening to stories. *Reading Research Quarterly, 24*(2), 174–187.

Freebody, P. & Anderson, R.C. (1983). Effects on text comprehension on different proportions and locations of difficult vocabulary. *Journal of Reading Behavior, 15*(3), 19–39.

Graves, M.F. & Slater, W.H. (1987, April). The development of reading vocabularies in children from three social, economic, and linguistic settings: A preliminary report. Paper presented at the American Educational Research Association Annual Meeting, Washington, DC.

Graves, M.F. & Prenn, M.C. (1986). Costs and benefits of various methods of teaching vocabulary. *Journal of Reading, 29*(7), 596–602.

Harris, A.J., & Sipay, E.R. (1990). *How to Increase Reading Ability: A Guide to Developmental and Remedial Methods,* (9th ed.). New York: Longman.

Herman, P.A., Anderson, R.C., Pearson, P.D., & Nagy, W. (1987). Incidental acquisition of word meaning from expositions with varied text features. *Reading Research Quarterly, 22*(3), 263–284.

Jenkins, J.R., & Dixon, R. (1983). Vocabulary learning. *Contemporary Educational Psychology, 8*(3), 237–260.

Jenkins, J.R., Matlock, B., & Slocum, T.A. (1989). Two approaches to vocabulary instruction: The teaching of individual word meanings and practice in deriving word meaning from context. *Reading Research Quarterly, 24*(2), 215–235.

Kibby, M.W. (1995). The organization and teaching of things and the words that signify them. *Journal of Adolescent and Adult Literacy, 39*(3), 208–224.

McKeown, M., Beck, I., Omanson, R., & Pople, M. (1985). Some effects of the nature and frequency of vocabulary instruction on the knowledge and use of words. *Reading Research Quarterly, 20*(5), 222–235.

Miller, G.A. & Gildea, P.M. (1987). How children learn words. *Scientific American, 257*(3), 94–99.

Nagy, W.E. (1985, November). *Vocabulary Instruction: Implications of the New Research.* Paper presented at the meeting of the National Council of the Teachers of English, Philadelphia.

Nagy, W.E. (1988a). *Teaching Vocabulary to Improve Reading Comprehension.* Newark, DE: International Reading Association.

Nagy, W.E. (1988b). *Vocabulary Instruction and Reading Comprehension.* (Technical Report No. 431). Champaign, IL: Center for the Study of Reading.

Nagy, W.E. & Anderson, R.C. (1984). How many words are there in printed school English? *Reading Research Quarterly, 19*(3), 304–330.

Nagy, W., Diakidoy, I.N., & Anderson, R.C. (1991). *The Development of Knowledge of Derivational Suffixes.* (Technical Report No. 536). Champaign, IL: Center for the Study of Reading.

Nagy, W.E. & Herman, P.A. (1984). *Limitations of Vocabulary Instruction.* (Technical Report No. 326). ED 248 498. Urbana, IL: Center for the Study of Reading.

Nagy, W. & Herman, P.A. (1987). Breadth and depth of vocabulary knowledge: Implications for acquisition and instruction. In M.G. McKeown, & M.E. Curtis (Eds.), *The Nature of Vocabulary Acquisition* (pp. 19–36). Hillsdale, NJ: Erlbaum.

Nagy, W.E., Herman, P.A., & Anderson, R.C. (1985). Learning words from context. *Reading Research Quarterly, 20*(2), 233–253.

Nagy, W.E., Winsor, P., Osborn, J., & O'Flahavan, J. (1994). Structural analysis: Some guidelines for instruction. In F. Lehr & J. Osborn (Eds.), *Reading, Language, and Literacy* (pp. 45–58). Hillsdale, NJ: Erlbaum.

Nelson-Herber, J. (1986). Expanding and refining vocabulary in content areas. *Journal of Reading, 29*(7), 626–633.

Powell, W.R. (1986). Teaching vocabulary through opposition. *Journal of Reading, 29*(7), 617–621.

Reinking, D. & Salmon-Rickman, S.S. (1990). The effects of computer-mediated texts on the vocabulary learning and comprehension of intermediate-grade readers. *Journal of Reading Behavior, 22*(4), 395–412.

Richek, M.A. (1988). Relating vocabulary learning to world knowledge. *Journal of Reading, 32*(3), 262–269.

Ryder, R.J. (1986). Teaching vocabulary through external context clues. *Journal of Reading, 30*(1), 61–65.

Schatz, E.K. & Baldwin, R.S. (1986). Context clues are unreliable predictors of word meanings. *Reading Research Quarterly, 21*(4), 439–453.

Scott, J.A. & Nagy, W.E. (1991). *Understanding Definitions.* (Technical Report No. 528). Champaign, IL: Center for the Study of Reading.

Stahl, S.A. (1990). *Beyond the Instrumentalist Hypothesis: Some Relationships Between Word Meanings And Comprehension.* (Technical Report No. 505). Champaign, IL: Center for the Study of Reading.

Stahl, S. & Fairbanks, M.M. (1986). The effects of vocabulary instruction: A model-based meta-analysis. *Review of Educational Research, 56*(1), 72–110.

Taba, H. (1967). *Teacher's Handbook for Elementary Social Studies.* Reading, MA: Addison-Wesley.

White, T.G., Power, M.A., & White S. (1989). Morphological analysis: Implications for teaching and understanding vocabulary growth. *Reading Research Quarterly, 24*(3), 283–304.

White, T.G., Slater, W.H., & Graves, M.F. (1989). Yes/No method of vocabulary assessment: Valid for whom and useful for what? In S. McCormick & J. Zutell (Eds.), *Cognitive and Social Perspectives for Literacy Research and Instruction,* (pp. 391–397). Thirty-eighth Yearbook of the National Reading. Rochester, NY: National Reading Conference.

Wood, K.D. (1987). Teaching vocabulary in subject areas. *Middle School Journal, 19*(1), 11–13.

Chapter 9

Prior Knowledge

Anyone who has worked with computers knows that some computer manuals are written better than others. Some manuals are written in a user-friendly fashion and some are not. Surprisingly enough, however, a number of people can make sense of even the most poorly written manuals. They are usually the people who know computers well already; that is, their prior knowledge of the subject is great, which enables them to make up for the deficiencies of the text. Prior knowledge is an important ingredient of comprehension. Johnston (1983) went so far as to say that a test of prior knowledge may be an effective predictor of reading comprehension.

Johnston described the reading process as a "slot-filling" activity; that is, if a person already knows something about a topic, that person needs only to add more specific information—or to fill in the slots. The more a person knows about a topic, the easier the "slots" can be filled; thus a smaller amount of visual information from the page is needed. Conversely, the reader who knows little about a topic tends to rely more heavily on the text, using word recognition to build meaning, sentence by sentence.

This over reliance on text generally inhibits efficient reading (Spiro & Taylor, 1980); but, if readers rely too heavily on what they know without attending closely enough to the text, they make reckless predictions about the meaning of what they read. A balanced interaction between the mind of the reader and the cues in the text seems to lead to a more efficient understanding of the printed message.

Pace, Marshall, Lipson, Horowitz, and Lucido (1989) proposed that proficient readers (1) have schema available to them, (2) can access their schema readily, (3) are able to maintain their schema while reading, and (4) integrate new knowledge into their existing schema. The more students know about the world or about text structure, or the more they understand a large number of concepts, the more schema they have *available* to them. However, unless learners can *access* their knowledge and apply it to new learning, it is useless. Some readers have difficulty seeing the relationships between facts and concepts, which leaves new learning isolated from existing schema. For schema to be available and accessible during reading, it must be *maintained* much like keeping a computer file open so that it can be accessed when needed. Finally, to add to or modify existing schemata, readers must *integrate* new learning into what they already know.

Strategies presented in this chapter and in Chapters 10 and 11 are designed to assist students in their maximum use and extension of existing schema. Prior knowledge will be discussed and then strategies for accessing and extending prior knowledge will be presented in the remainder of this chapter.

Activating Prior Knowledge

Reading educators have recognized the value of background experience for many years; research on prior knowledge, however, is relatively recent. As reading educators study the relationship between what readers know and how well they understand print, more precise terms have appeared. *Prior knowledge* is all the information and all the experience a reader has in memory. *Topical knowledge,* however, relates to the information a reader has on a particular topic; but readers must activate much more than what they know about a topic to have a successful reading experience. Knowledge about *social interaction* helps readers understand characters and actions. Knowledge of *text structure* helps readers predict what will happen next and confirms their understandings. The *metacognitive skill* of monitoring comprehension discussed in Chapter 6 is another important aspect of reading to comprehend. These types of knowledge and skill come into play during reading. All learning seems to revolve around the condition that new information must be, in some way, associated with what is already known.

Activating prior knowledge is one role of the teacher; another is to diagnose what students know and do not know or to determine what misconceptions they may hold. The prereading strategies suggested in this chapter can serve this diagnostic function and instruction may then be adjusted accordingly. For reading to be successful, a teacher may decide to spend more time in preparation to read, building the necessary background information.

The act of reading may be likened to a trip to an art museum. People with a limited appreciation for art may wander throughout the museum, glancing at paintings. For the artistically misinformed, the museum experience may serve to give them an overview of the great works of art or the trip may serve only to reinforce misconceptions about art works. An art student, however, may spend a good deal of time studying and analyzing a painting because prior knowledge compels the student to view the painting in more depth. The breadth and depth of prior knowledge on a particular topic partially determine the significance of an encounter with print or any other medium. The extent and quality of prior knowledge will then determine how new or dissimilar information is assimilated.

Langer and Nicolich (1981) suggested that students should be helped to become aware of relevant prior knowledge and that teachers should judge whether that knowledge is sufficient for comprehension of the text. In some instances, teachers need to build background where little exists. The authors of *Becoming a Nation of Readers* (Anderson, Hiebert, Scott, & Wilkinson, 1985) stated:

> *Systematic classroom observation reveals that preparation for reading is the phase of the . . . lesson that is most often slighted, or even skipped altogether . . . little focused attention is given to developing a background knowledge that will be required to understand the day's story (pp. 49–50).*

Research suggests that children are not particularly good at drawing on their prior knowledge, especially in school settings (Owings & Peterson, 1980). Students may possess relevant information about the topic to be studied but not realize that what they know can be applied to what they are to learn. Teachers must therefore spend time to help students activate this prior knowledge. Vaughn and Estes (1986) argued that one-half of instructional time should be spent helping students connect new information to old. Time invested before reading will reduce the amount of time required to explain to students what they did not understand after reading.

In the past, teachers have provided students with learning activities that follow a reading assignment. Teachers have also provided certain types of study guides to aid students during reading. *Prereading strategies* include any activity that prepares the student before a passage is read: these are activities that help to bridge the gap between what readers already know and what they will learn while reading. Previously, the term "reading readiness" has been used to refer to the time spent for educators to prepare children to read print. As reading theorists continue to define the acquisition of reading ability as a natural and on-going process, readiness has come to be associated with preparing for any reading task at any age. In this sense, prereading strategies can be considered "readiness" activities that prepare students for the reading task at hand. A good part of this preparation includes activating and building on students' prior knowledge.

Prereading strategies are designed to stimulate cognitive functioning. The affective dimension, however, should not be ignored (Frager, 1993). Students must feel confident "that they have prior knowledge about a subject, a feeling too frequently lacking" (p. 617). Classroom discussions are often a part of prereading strategies and too many students choose not to participate. Teachers need to recognize that a certain element of risk is involved whenever a student volunteers what they know or do not know about a particular topic. Teachers can also create a climate of acceptance and safety for this risk taking. Interest is also an important affective dimension. Prereading activities often create student interest by asking students to predict or otherwise become involved in the material to be read. As interest in a subject increases, so does motivation and confidence for the reading task.

Assessing the Knowledge Base of Students

How does a teacher determine how much students know? Most of the time, this assessment takes place during instruction, often times during the prereading phase. For example, the first step of the prereading plan (PReP) activity is to have students brainstorm a particular topic. After the initial brainstorming session, the teacher may determine that the students lack the prior knowledge and vocabulary required to comprehend the text.

Misconceptions

Not all prior knowledge is helpful, however. "Students come to classrooms with extensive prior knowledge about scientific phenomena, but often that knowledge consists of naive conceptions or misconceptions" (Dole & Smith, 1989, p. 345). These misconceptions can hinder the learning of new information. Anderson and Smith (1984) found that students' "comprehension of science instruction is often affected by their prior beliefs or preconceptions" (p. 200). These researchers found that many children were strongly committed to their preconceptions even though these ideas about the world were not consistent with scientific thinking. Students hold these beliefs despite instruction and information in their textbooks to the contrary, because they seem logical based on their previous experience.

Researchers investigating which strategies are most useful to correct misconceptions, generally concluded that teacher-mediated discussions help to correct student thinking such as the discussion web designed by Alvermann and Hynd (1989). These more successful strategies usually involve a graphic, so that students can be an active part of the reconstruction of knowledge. One important factor in this discussion is, of course, the content knowledge of the teacher (Dole & Smith, 1989).

A person's schema—their collection of knowledge, attitudes, and beliefs—acts as a filter for new information always asking the question "Does this make sense?" Learning consists of modifying, extending, and integrating information into existing schema. Prereading strategies are essential because they assist in the formation of a student's schema.

Prereading Strategies

Prereading strategies help students activate what they know about a topic and anticipate what they will read or hear. Students need to understand the purpose for learning strategies and how to use them on their own. Such strategies also direct students' attention to the major points in the reading or lecture. Teachers can also use prereading strategies to point out how a text or lecture is organized, to teach unfamiliar vocabulary or concepts, and to provide the student with a purpose for reading or listening.

"Comprehension of narrative texts seems to be less dependent on prior knowledge than comprehension of expository texts" (Valencia & Stallman, 1989, p. 434). Middle grades students are generally familiar with story structure and can readily identify with characters, setting, and plot. Expository text, on the other hand, does not always have such a clearly identified structure and the topic may be unfamiliar to students. For this reason, the use of prereading strategies is imperative, especially in the content areas.

Knowledge of the structure of the text or discussion can help students recognize and record the most important information. For example, if students are to read a social studies text that compares two ancient civilizations, they may be directed to look for likenesses and differences with respect to certain characteristics such as religion, politics, economics, and so on. The teacher may help students further by pointing out that students may want to look for signal words such as "conversely," "on the contrary," or "like" to help them compare and contrast the two civilizations.

The prereading strategies described in the remainder of the chapter are separated into three categories: (1) building background when students know little about a subject,

(2) activating prior knowledge when students know something about a subject, and (3) organizing information when students know a great deal about a subject.

Building Background Information When Students Know Little about a Subject

Educators would agree that background experiences and information are important in the learning process. A student raised in a rural town has a difficult time understanding the subway system in New York. Kindergarten teachers in a small rural town in northern Florida plan a trip to a mall in a nearby city so that the children can ride the elevators and escalators; their small town has no two-story buildings. Experiences, of course, are best for facilitating learning, but reading can provide vicarious experiences for students.

Students must, however, have some prior knowledge to assimilate new information; otherwise, the reading is meaningless. If teachers perceive that students know little or nothing about a topic to be studied, then prereading strategies become even more important in building the necessary information to relate to the unknown topic. Pearson and Spiro (1982) suggested beginning with a positive attitude about what a student may know and then using analogies and numerous examples to tie new information to existing prior knowledge. It seems obvious, then, when teaching a young adolescent to read that instruction should begin with familiar topics (Winograd & Newell, 1985). The following three strategies can be used when students know little about a topic: (1) a predicting and confirming activity, (2) reciprocal questioning (ReQuest), and (3) a visual reading guide.

Predicting and Confirming Activity

Based on Beyer's (1971) inquiry model, the predicting and confirming activity (PACA), like most prereading strategies, uses student predictions to set a purpose for reading. This process is what most good readers do naturally. The PACA strategy allows students to make predictions about a topic based on some initial information provided by the teacher, even if they have little prior knowledge. Given additional information, students can revise their predictions (or hypotheses) and pose them as questions for further reading.

Suppose that a teacher wishes to teach a lesson about the Hausa people of Nigeria and surmises that students will probably have little prior knowledge of the culture or geographical location of the Hausa. The teacher gives a short explanation that the Hausa people live in Nigeria and shows students where Nigeria is located within Africa.

Step One: The teacher poses a general question. One such question may be, "What are the Hausa people like?"

Step Two: The teacher provides initial information. The teacher places the students into small groups for discussion and provides them with a list of Hausa words and again poses the general question, "Based on the words commonly used by the Hausa, what are the Hausa people like?" Word lists similar to the following can generally be found at the end of a chapter in content area textbooks.

cotton	goat	Sabbath	God
rainy season	trader	desert	yams
prohibition	merchant	ghost	farm
witchcraft	grandmother	aunt	umbrella
Koran	debtor	servant	slavery
walled town	tent	tax collector	son
blacksmith	camel	dry season	clay oven
mosque	mountain	sheep	mother
prophet	devil	gold	bargain

Step Three: Students and the teacher write predictions. After small group discussions, the teacher again poses the question "What are the Hausa people like?" to elicit predictions from the students. The teacher then writes these statements on the chalkboard and should remember to ask students to cite the word or words that caused them to make such a prediction. The teacher may also record group responses using categories such as religion, politics, economics, history, and technology. Here are some typical responses:

—The Hausa people are Moslem.

—They have a low level of technology.

—The Hausa people are nomadic.

—They have a structured society.

Step Four: The teacher presents new information. The teacher presents new information at this time. Pictures that are normally found in content textbooks are a good resource, but this additional information may be a film or story.

Step Five: Students and teacher revise or modify statements. Based on the visual information, students, assisted by the teacher, revise their predictions by confirming or rejecting their original hypotheses. For example, a picture of three Hausa people on motorcycles, wearing sunglasses, would help students understand the need to modify some of their original predictions. This picture may also elicit a new prediction relating to the extent to which the Hausa people engage in trade with other countries. A picture of a walled city may encourage students to reject the notion that they are a nomadic people. A picture of a mosque, however, may confirm students' earlier prediction that the Hausa people are Moslem.

Step Six: Students then read the selection in the textbook using their predictions as a purpose for reading. The teacher encourages students to keep their predictions in mind while reading. Writing predictions on the chalkboard for easy reference is often helpful.

Step Seven: The teacher helps students to revise their predictions based on the reading. Suppose, for example, students made a prediction based on the word list that the Hausa people had a low level of technology, and the textbook described advanced techniques of farming used by the Hausa. The teacher would then help students revise these statements to reflect the new information. These statements, thus revised, may be used for further research or as an impetus for writing.

Although the Hausa people is a topic about which students may have little information, they have an extensive knowledge base about cultures. The purpose of PACA is to start with a familiar knowledge base while building background about a particular topic. Students can then use this new information to extend their understanding of culture in general.

The predicting and confirming activity may be used with a variety of topics for which teachers need to build background information. Teachers have found this strategy to be a good way to help students relate to the vocabulary and concepts in a text before asking them to use this information. In addition, making and revising predictions based on a limited amount of information is an excellent way to introduce students to formal reasoning, in a gradual way. Accepting the premise that knowledge is tentative and can be revised based on new information is a first step for students toward more abstract reasoning.

Reciprocal Questioning

Reciprocal questioning, or ReQuest, was developed by Manzo (1969). This procedure was designed to help students develop an inquisitive attitude about what is to be read and to have students formulate questions. Students then use the questions to set their own purpose for reading.

This ReQuest strategy is dependent on the teacher being a model of "good" questioning behavior. The teacher answers the questions of students and asks thought-provoking questions in return. The students and teacher then read a predetermined section of text silently. After the reading, they take turns asking each other questions. The teacher models good questioning behavior by asking questions that promote higher level thinking and the making of predictions.

Suppose, as part of a unit on space, a science teacher wishes to have students read about the geological features of the moon. Judging that students will have much folklore but little technical information about the moon, the teacher chooses the ReQuest procedure to stimulate thinking about the reading.

Step One: Both teacher and students read the first sentence in the first paragraph of a selection.

"The moon is the earth's nearest neighbor."

Step Two: The teacher closes the book; the students keep their books open. The students may ask the teacher any question they wish that relates to the first sentence. The teacher must answer as accurately and completely as possible. When pertinent, the teacher gives feedback to the students on the quality of the types of questions being asked. For example, questions that require analysis or synthesis can be praised. Questions such as the following may represent possible student responses: "Is the moon a planet?" "What are our other neighbors?" "How far away is the moon?"

Step Three: The students then close their books and the teacher asks another set of questions. These questions may include some that will help the students realize what knowledge they have relative to the topic, or they may be questions that students emulate when their turn comes again. Students attempt to answer these questions as accurately as possible; for example, the following paragraph may elicit questions such as "What is the moon like?" or "How do we know about the moon's surface?" or "What does it mean to have no atmosphere?"

> *The moon is the earth's nearest neighbor in space. Telescopes on the earth can easily make out the main features of the moon's surface. Rugged mountain ranges, wide level plains, and hundreds of large and small craters can be clearly seen. These features stand out because there is no atmosphere to mask them. But it was not until the astronauts landed on the moon that the actual conditions on earth's closest neighbor became known. (From Ramsey, W.L., Gabriel, L.A., McGuirk, J.F., Phillips, C.R., & Watenpaugh, F.M. [1979].* General Science. *New York: Holt, Rinehart and Winston, p. 412.)*

Step Four: Students and teacher begin reading paragraphs using the same reciprocal questioning technique. Students then read the next paragraph or two about the moon and its geological makeup, asking and answering questions as they go. Students will soon be able to project answers to such questions as "What do you think you will find out in the rest of the selection?"

Content area teachers who fear that teaching reading will take time away from their content like this strategy because it focuses on content while it facilitates effective reading abilities and questioning strategies. Eventually, students should be able to engage in self-questioning, and thus improve their comprehension ability.

Visual Reading Guide

Visual information such as charts, tables, graphs, and pictures is found abundantly in content area textbooks and often ignored or used only casually by students and teachers. In addition, "development of visual literacy typically receives limited attention in basals and content area texts" (Rakes, Rakes, & Smith, 1995, p. 46). Experienced teachers use this visual information by providing strong cuing strategies and directing attention to visual information. Stein (1978) suggested that discussion and interpretation of visual information can serve as a way to build background information about a topic in which students have little prior exposure.

A teacher may wish to take a more or less structured approach to building background information using this visual data. For example, the teacher may direct students' attention to the picture of Hannibal and his army and ask students to speculate about what role elephants had in Roman history and why the Romans were clothed as they were. The answers to these questions may serve the students as a study guide while they read. Or the teacher may wish to use visual information to facilitate students' predictions about the content of the chapter. These predictions may serve to set a purpose for reading and be checked for accuracy after the reading is completed.

A visual reading guide is a vehicle for students organizing their thoughts before reading or studying a topic. Especially for students who lack the necessary prior knowledge about a topic, study questions can help them see the important aspects of the content before reading. Later, in reading, discussion, and assignments, students can use this acquired information to begin to formulate generalizations about the content being studied.

Activating Prior Knowledge When Students Know Something about a Subject

Students often know something about a topic, and reading will be more meaningful if that prior knowledge is activated before they read. As mentioned, misconceptions about a topic can hinder students' understanding of a selection. When teachers perceive that students know something about a topic, the following strategies can be used to help students share information and activate what they already know before reading: (1) an anticipation guide, (2) a prereading plan, and (3) a scavenger hunt.

Anticipation Guide

The purpose of the anticipation guide is to create a mismatch between what students may know and believe and what is presented in the text. Shablak and Castallo (1977) referred to this mismatch as "conceptual conflict" and suggested that this conflict plays a role in stimulating curiosity and motivation to learn. The anticipation guide was first developed by Herber (1978) who suggested that comprehension may be enhanced if students make predictions about concepts covered in the text.

The steps involved in this strategy are listed and illustrated by using an example from a story in which a dress is stolen in a locker room during physical education.

Step One: The teacher identifies the major concepts and supporting details in the reading selection, lecture, or film. In this story the major concept is "stealing."

Step Two: The teacher elicits the students' experiences and beliefs that relate to the major concept(s) previously identified. The teacher could ask students to write down all the words that they associate with the concept of "stealing."

Step Three: The teacher creates statements reflecting personal beliefs concerning a topic that may contradict or modify the beliefs of the students. The teacher should also include some statements that are consistent with the students' experiential background and with the concepts presented in the material or lesson. Three to five statements are usually adequate. In this example, students would be asked to place a check mark next to those statements with which they agree.

_____ a. Stealing is always wrong.
_____ b. Sometimes stealing is justified.
_____ c. Persons who steal should be punished.
_____ d. Honest people sometimes steal.
_____ e. Everyone steals sometime during his or her life.

Step Four: The teacher arranges the statements on a sheet of paper, overhead transparency, or the chalkboard. The students respond positively or negatively to each statement on an individual basis. Students should then record their justification for each response in writing, so they will have a reference point for discussion.

Step Five: The teacher engages students in a prereading discussion by asking for a hand count of responses to the five statements on stealing. Students can then share the justifications for their responses.

Step Six: Read the selection. In this example, the reading would be a story about someone who had a valued object stolen.

Step Seven: The teacher engages students in a postreading discussion comparing their reactions with the statements before and after the reading. This discussion may take place either in small groups or as a class activity.

Duffelmeyer (1994) maintained that effective statements (1) convey a sense of the major ideas students will encounter, (2) activate and draw on students' prior experiences, (3) are general rather than specific, and (4) challenge students' beliefs. The anticipation guide is an excellent method for promoting active reading, raising expectations about meaning, and helping students to modify erroneous beliefs. Middle school students particularly enjoy talking about value issues. As they move from the influence of their families to the influence of their peer groups, it is important for students to have a forum for stating their opinions and considering the opinions of others. Additionally, when students can identify with the value issues involved in a story or passage, they tend to comprehend better on literal as well as higher levels of understanding because the information is more meaningful to them (Lunstrum & Irvin, 1979).

A Prereading Plan

Langer (1981) developed a prereading plan (PReP) to help readers use what they know to understand new ideas. She also advocated using the PReP technique as an assessment tool to see how much students understand the topic to be studied or if they maintain any misconceptions.

Step One: The teacher asks students to make a list of words they associate with a topic. A social studies teacher may wish to discuss "crime." Students would then list words such as "steal," "hurt," "jail," or "murder."

Step Two: The teacher asks students to reflect on their reasons for making the associations. A question such as "What made you think of that?" may help elicit responses. Through this process, teachers can help students become aware of the network of associations available to them and how to make maximum educational use of these associations. Also, by discussing reasons that one word is associated with another, a teacher can help students to cluster and categorize their responses. If students associate "jail" with "crime," the students' rationale may be "because when people commit a crime, they are always punished." In Step Three, the teacher could explore this statement further by asking if criminals are always caught, or asking what is a crime.

Step Three: After some organizational patterns have developed, the teacher asks the students to elaborate on and clarify their initial responses. Students, either individually or as a class, may be asked to use these patterned associations to write statements or perhaps a paragraph about the topic. The value of this activity is to encourage students to think beyond their initial response, integrate their thoughts with the thoughts of others, and organize their information before reading about the topic.

A teacher may determine through this discussion that the students' prior knowledge of a topic is insufficient and thus that the reading may prove to be too difficult. In such a situation, an activity to build background information may be a more appropriate lesson at this time.

Scavenger Hunt

Designed by Cunningham, Crawley, and Mountain (1983), the intent of the scavenger hunt is to build an understanding of unfamiliar concepts before beginning a unit on a particular topic. This activity is not only enjoyable for both teachers and students, but it also serves to expose students to vocabulary associated with a subject before the subject is actually studied. The steps to this activity are as follows:

Step One: A few days before a new unit of study, the teacher announces the topic for that unit and dictates to the class some of the key vocabulary words and concepts. Units that may lend themselves well to such an activity are environment, democracy, and conflict.

Step Two: The teacher then divides the class into teams, and each team selects a captain or the teacher may select one.

Step Three: Each team is given an identical list of terms for the scavenger hunt. Teams are allowed a limited number of days to gather all the information they can about these concepts. They may complete this assignment in or out of school—perhaps as part of a homework assignment. Information may be obtained from books, by asking others, or perhaps by sneaking a peak at the chapter. Students should be told that they need to *understand* the word so that only looking up the word in the dictionary or glossary would not be enough.

Step Four: On the first day of the new unit, each team shares what they found in their hunt. This sharing allows every class member exposure to a wide range of sources of information. Students should be asked to use words in a sentence, explain their meaning by giving examples, and/or be able to answer questions by the teacher or other students.

Step Five: The teacher may wish to award points and/or credit for participation or successful completion of assigned tasks. The following are directions and a list from an American history class:

> ***Day 1:*** For fifteen to twenty minutes, look over the list of words. Discuss words and concepts without using the book. You may use other resources
>
> ***Day 2:*** Go over the list of words. You may use the book.
>
> ***Day 3:*** Competition: Each team shares what they found in the hunt. You will be asked to use words in a sentence, explain their meaning by giving examples, and/or still be

able to answer questions by the teacher or other students. Points will be awarded and a prize will be given to the winning team in each class.

emancipate	draft	Monitor
Gettysburg Address	inflation	George McClellan
Robert E. Lee	civilians	habeas corpus
Stonewall Jackson	Edwin Stanton	martial law
Confederacy	General Phillip Sheridan	Dorothea Dix
Fredericksburg	Chancellorsville	Bull Run
Union	Emancipation Proclamation	bounties
Ulysses S. Grant	General William Tecumseh Sherman	Merrimac
Clara Barton	copperheads	tax-in-kind

Most middle school students seem to enjoy mild competition and group work if the undertaking is of interest. As discussed earlier, teachers have found that cooperative learning activities heighten student interest and motivation to study a topic before a unit begins, and they provide students with necessary prior knowledge to begin that study.

Organizing Information When Students Know a Great Deal about a Subject

Teachers may wonder if precious class time is spent wisely on a prereading strategy if students already know a great deal about a topic. It is often helpful when dealing with a lot of information, such as a unit on the ocean, to organize the information for (or with) students before beginning that study. Some teachers use a blue marker to construct a graphic organizer or semantic map with students at the beginning of a unit. As they learn new things, they fill in the new information with red marker. Students and teacher are always gratified to see the organizer or map become more filled with red than blue. This practice is also a nice reminder that new information must be connected to what learners already know.

The graphic organizer and the semantic map can be used in all types of instructional settings and at all age levels. These two strategies can be used to strengthen vocabulary, as prereading or prewriting activities, to organize information during reading, or as a study guide after reading. In this section, these strategies will be discussed as prereading strategies with application, of course, during and after reading.

Graphic Organizers

The value of graphic organizers, also known as structured overviews or advanced organizers, has been recognized by educators since Ausubel (1968) first conducted his work on conceptual development. Using a graphic organizer can introduce concepts and illustrate the nature of the relationships among these concepts. To summarize, (1) the use of graphic organizers seems to have a moderate positive effect on vocabulary test scores, (2) more mature learners seem to obtain greater benefit from the use of graphic organizers, (3) students perform better when they produce a graphic organizer after reading

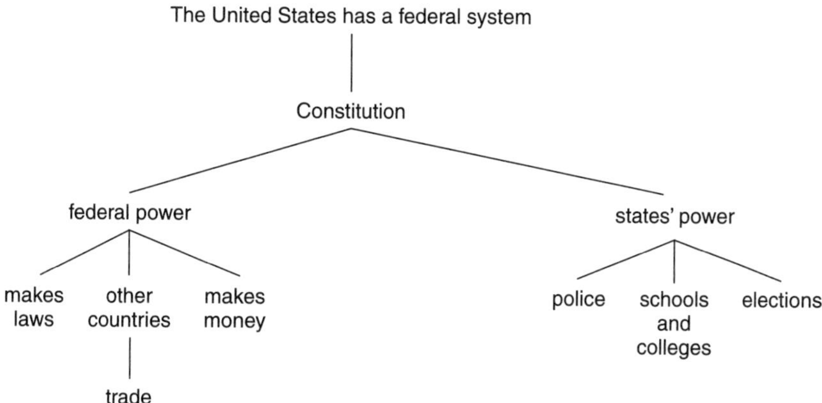

FIGURE 9.1 Simple listing

(instead of being presented with a complete organizer before reading), and (4) teachers report that they are more confident when using graphic organizers. The level of student involvement in the construction of the organizer also seems to be a significant factor (Moore & Readence, 1984).

More recent research (Groller, Kender, & Honeyman, 1991) on advanced organizers suggests that "students need to use metacognitive strategies in order to use advance organizers effectively" (p. 470). Students need to be taught how "to use, monitor, and evaluate their use of advance organizers in order to use these to their best advantage" (p. 473).

Alvermann (1986) presented the graphic organizer as a vehicle for "improving students' main idea comprehension ability . . . as a device for cuing the reader about the relation of superordinate (more important) to subordinate (less important) textual information" (p. 211). She suggested that there are four primary types of organizational structures in textbooks. These structures include simple listing, time ordering, compare-contrast, and cause-effect relationships. "A fundamental rule in constructing graphic representations is that the structure of the graphic should reflect the structure of the text it represents" (Jones, Pierce, & Hunter, 1988, p. 21). Graphic organizers have been used more extensively with expository text rather than narrative, story type material. Aulls (1978; 1986) maintained that there are major differences in identifying the main idea in these two types of text. Therefore, the following illustrations represent only expository text.

Simple Listing

A social studies teacher may assign a reading on the federal system of government. The simple listing shown in Figure 9.1, discussed before the reading, may provide students with an overview that will help them understand their reading.

Time Ordering

A timeline often helps students understand difficult concepts such as the relationship of events in time. The timeline shown in Figure 9.2 may help a student who is struggling with Russian history to understand the temporal relationship of important events.

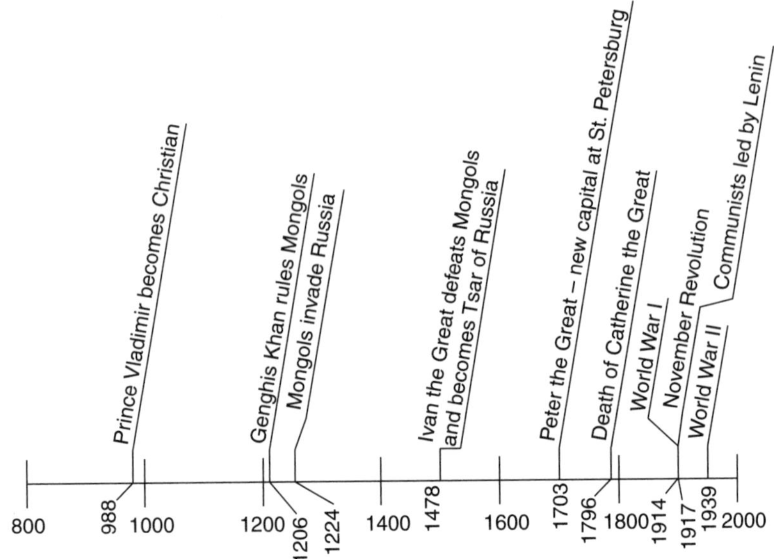

FIGURE 9.2 Time ordering

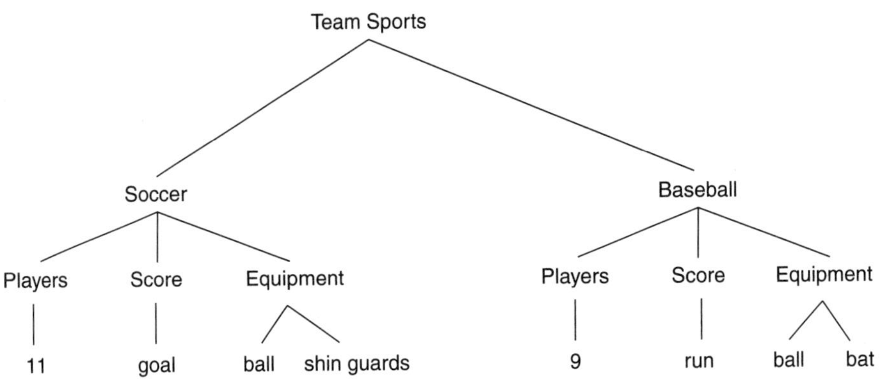

FIGURE 9.3 Compare-contrast

Compare-Contrast

As shown in Figure 9.3, a physical education teacher may wish to illustrate graphically the difference between two team sports.

Cause-Effect

Before asking students to read a section on the heart, a science teacher may share the graphic organizer in Figure 9.4 with her students so that they will understand the cause-effect relationships before they begin reading.

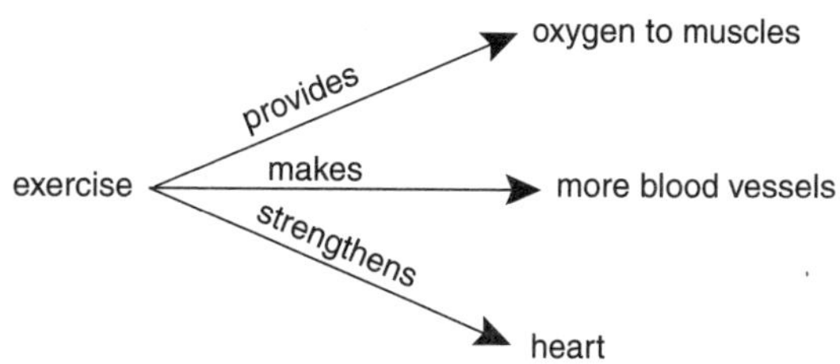

FIGURE 9.4 Cause-effect

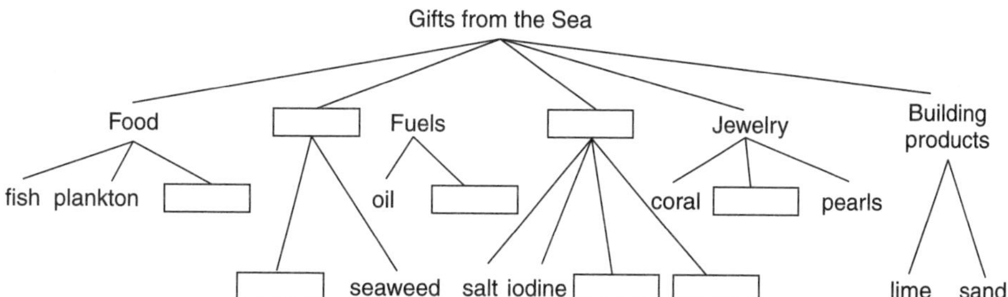

FIGURE 9.5 Cloze graphic organizer

Cloze Graphic Organizer

One advantage of graphic organizers is that they visually represent the structure of text. Readers are more likely to comprehend new material if they know how the information will be presented. Figure 9.5 shows a cloze graphic organizer, thus named because some of the information is intentionally left out. If students were assigned, for example, a section in their science textbook about the products of the ocean, the teacher could present this graphic organizer, discuss the organization of the text, and direct students to fill in the organizer either during reading or directly after reading. By using graphic organizers in this way, students become actively involved in reading and become more aware of the structure of text.

Semantic Mapping

Semantic maps are diagrams that help students see how words or ideas are related to one another. Circles and lines are used to show relationships between concepts. Hanf (1971) suggested mapping to help students learn how to think critically because to create a map, students must receive, organize, and evaluate information so that it makes sense to them. The map becomes a graphic display of main points, subcategories, and supporting details. *Semantic Mapping: Classroom Applications* (Heimlich & Pittleman, 1986) is an excellent publication that explains the many classroom applications of semantic mapping.

Figure 9.6 illustrates how one teacher used a map before reading to help students organize their ideas about the "hamburger" and provide an aid to writing. Although students

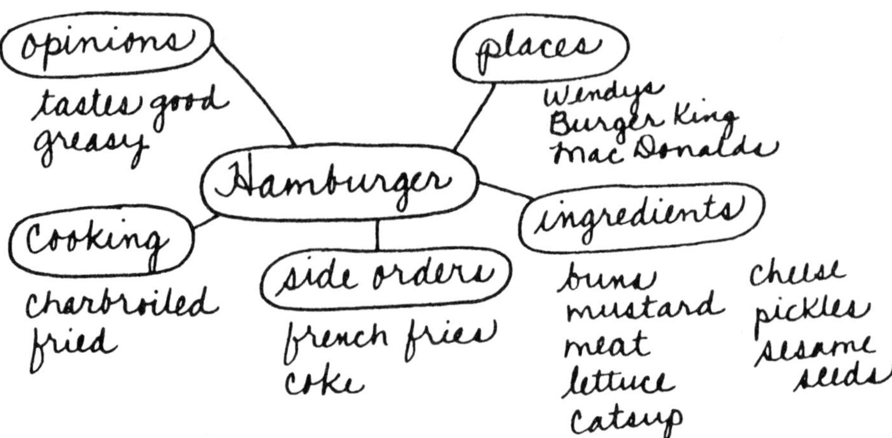

FIGURE 9.6 Semantic mapping

may not have historical information about hamburgers, the subject will certainly elicit some useful associations.

The teacher then asked students to read the following story about the history of the hamburger, using semantic mapping to summarize the information. Students were asked to compare their new map with the one they constructed before reading.

*The Hamburger**

Hundreds of years ago, the Romans got the idea of eating meat and other foods between pieces of bread. They called their invention an offula. The Romans gave us the offula.

Much later, around the year 1760, an Englishman named John Montague was in charge of the English Navy. He was also known as the Earl of Sandwich. The head of the Navy spent a lot of time playing cards. He did not like to stop just to eat, so he began to order meals placed between pieces of bread. That way, he could eat and play cards at the same time! Meat served between pieces of bread became known as "sandwiches!" The English gave us the sandwich.

For many years people in Northern Europe enjoyed eating raw shredded beef. The raw shredded meat was served on a plate without bread. It became especially popular in the city of Hamburg, Germany. For some reason, the dish became known as the hamburg steak. The city of Hamburg, Germany, gave us the hamburg steak.

During the late 1800s, thousands of Germans came to America. They started calling their shredded meat dish a hamburger steak. Later the name was shortened to hamburger . . . and then sometimes just to burger.

As the hamburg-steak's name was changing, so was its appearance. Few Americans would be attracted to raw beef on bread. In 1904, at the St. Louis World Fair, the cooked meat hamburger got a lot of attention. Almost overnight it was a sensation. By the 1960s hamburgers were as American as apple pie and

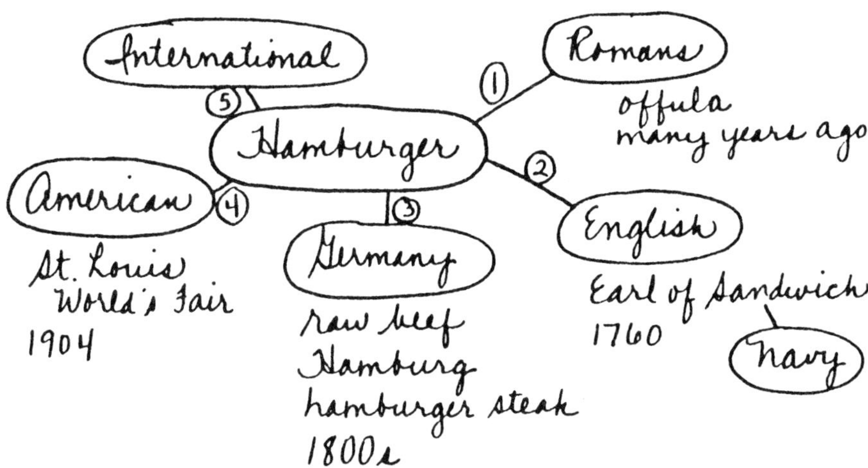

FIGURE 9.7 Semantic map of the history of the hamburger

corn on the cob. Americans were eating hamburgers by the millions. McDonald's Golden Arches swept across the nation. Closely behind McDonald's were Jack in the Box, Burger King, Wendy's, Hardee's and a host of other hamburger places. Even the famous Mariott Hotel Corporation got its start selling root beer and hamburgers in Washington, D.C.

The American love affair with the hamburger continues today. Every city or town in America can accommodate a visitor with a "burger all the way." The hamburger has even returned to Europe with the new, improved American hamburger sold in McDonald's restaurants and in many others. Our hamburger has gone international!

**[From Allen, R.F. & Irvin, J.L. (1986).* The Urban Reader. *St. Charles, IL: Educational Publishing Concepts, Inc.]*

A student constructed the map shown in Figure 9.7 after reading "The Hamburger." The teacher then used both maps as a springboard for writing. Students who usually had difficulty knowing what to write used the maps to provide the information for their essays. Even students with very low writing ability produced a paragraph or two using this method.

Semantic mapping has proven useful before, during, and after reading. As a prereading strategy, though, it serves to activate prior knowledge when used as a springboard for discussion or to organize a lot of information, as shown in Figure 9.8.

Summary

Prior knowledge is the sum of all experiences and information held in the mind of the reader. Reading is an interaction between the mind of the reader and the cues given in the text. Thus, to a large extent, the scope and depth of a reader's prior knowledge determine

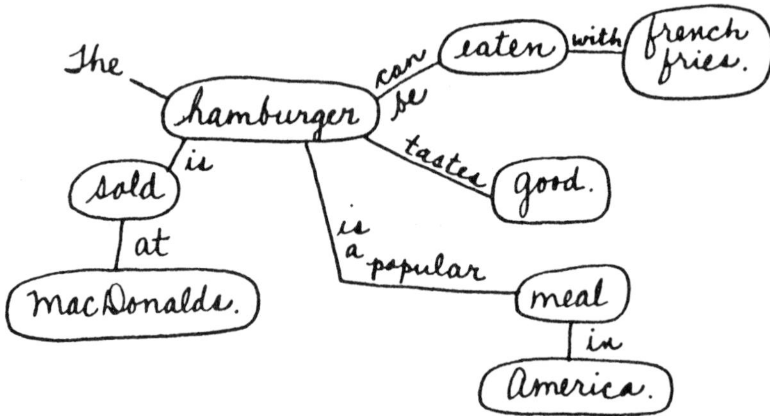

FIGURE 9.8 Semantic map of hamburgers organized into sentences

the quality of the reading experience. Activities involving prior knowledge can be grouped into three categories: (1) those that build knowledge related to a topic where little or none existed before, (2) those that activate and build on existing prior knowledge, and (3) those that help to organize large amounts of information. By building, activating, and organizing prior knowledge before reading, a teacher can enable students to bring the most to, and thus to get the most from, their reading experience.

References

Alvermann, D.E. (1986). Graphic organizers: Cuing devices for comprehending and remembering main ideas. In J.F. Baumann (Ed.), *Teaching Main Idea Comprehension* (pp. 210–226). Newark, DE: International Reading Association.

Alvermann, D. & Hynd, C. (1989). Study strategies for correcting misconceptions in physics: An intervention. In S. McCormick & J. Zutell (Eds.), *Cognitive and Social Perspectives for Literacy Research and Instruction* (pp. 353–361). Rochester, NY: The National Reading Conference, Inc.

Anderson, C.W. & Smith, E.L. (1984). Children's preconceptions and content-area textbooks. In G.G. Duffey, L.R. Roehler, & J. Mason (Eds.), *Comprehension Instruction: Perspectives and Suggestions* (pp. 187–201). New York: Longman.

Anderson, R.C., Hiebert, E.H., Scott, J.A., & Wilkinson, I.A.G. (1985). *Becoming a Nation of Readers: The Report of the Commission on Reading.* Champaign, IL: Center for the Study of Reading.

Aulls, M.W. (1978). *Developmental and Remedial Reading in the Middle Grades.* Boston, MA: Allyn & Bacon.

Aulls, M.W. (1986). Actively teaching main idea skills. In J.F. Baumann (Ed.), *Teaching Main Idea Comprehension* (96–132). Newark, DE: International Reading Association.

Ausubel, D.R. (1968). *Educational Psychology: A Cognitive View.* New York: Holt, Rinehart & Winston.

Beyer, B.K. (1971). *Inquiry in the Social Studies Classroom.* Columbus, OH: Charles E. Merrill Publishing Company.

Cunningham, P., Crawley, S.G., & Mountain, L. (1983). Vocabulary scavenger hunts: A scheme for schema development. *Reading Horizons, 24,* 45–50.

Dole, J.A. & Smith, E.L. (1989). Prior knowledge and learning from science text: An instructional study. In S. McCormick & J. Zutell (Eds.), *Cognitive and Social Perspectives for Literacy Research and Instruction* (pp. 345–352). Rochester, NY: The National Reading Conference, Inc.

Duffelmeyer, F.A. (1994). Effective anticipation guide statements for learning from expository prose. *Journal of Reading, 37*(6), 452–457.

Frager, A.M. (1993). Affective dimensions of content area reading. *Journal of Reading, 36*(8), 616–623.

Groller, K.L., Kender, J.P., & Honeyman, D.S. (1991). Does instruction on metacognitive strategies help high school students use advance organizers? *Journal of Reading, 34*(6), 470–475.

Hanf, M.B. (1971). Mapping: A technique for translating reading into thinking. *Journal of Reading, 14*(4), 225–230, 270.

Heimlich, E. & Pittleman, S.D. (1986). *Semantic Mapping: Classroom Applications.* Newark, DE: International Reading Association.

Herber, H.L. (1978). *Teaching Reading in Content Areas.* Englewood Cliffs, NJ: Prentice-Hall.

Johnston, P. (1983). *Prior Knowledge and Reading Comprehension Test Bias.* (Technical Report No. 289). Champaign, IL: Center for the Study of Reading.

Jones, B.F., Pierce, J., & Hunter, B. (1988). Teaching students to construct graphic representations. *Educational Leadership, 46*(4), 20–25.

Langer, J.A. (1981). From theory to practice: A prereading plan. *Journal of Reading, 25*(2), 152–157.

Langer, J.A. & Nicolich, M. (1981). Prior knowledge and its effect on comprehension. *Journal of Reading Behavior, 13*(4), 375–378.

Lunstrum, J.P. & Irvin, J.L. (1979). Improving reading comprehension through value analysis. *Selected Articles on the Teaching of Reading, 30.* New York: Barnell-Loft.

Manzo, A.V. (1969). Request procedure. *Journal of Reading, 13*(2), 123–126.

Moore, D.W. & Readence, J.E. (1984). A quantitative and qualitative review of graphic organizer research. *Journal of Educational Research, 78*(1), 11–17.

Owings, R.A. & Peterson, G.A. (1980). Spontaneous monitoring and regulation of learning: A comparison of successful and less successful fifth graders. *Journal of Educational Psychology, 72*(2), 250–256.

Pace, A.J., Marshall, N., Lipson, M.Y., Horowitz, R., & Lucido, P. (1989). When prior knowledge doesn't facilitate text comprehension: An examination of some of the issues. In S. McCormick & J. Zutell (Eds.), *Cognitive and Social Perspectives for Literacy Research and Instruction* (pp. 213–224). Rochester, NY: The National Reading Conference, Inc.

Pearson, P.D. & Spiro, R. (1982). The new buzz word in reading is schema. *Instructor,* 46–48.

Rakes, G.C., Rakes, T.A., & Smith, L.J. (1995). Using visuals to enhance secondary students' reading comprehension of expository texts. *Journal of Adolescent and Adult Literacy, 39*(1), 46–55.

Shablak, S. & Castallo, R. (1977). Curiosity arousal and motivation in the teaching/learning process. In H.L. Herber & R.T. Vacca (Eds.), *Research in Reading in the Content Areas: The Third Report.* Syracuse, NY: Syracuse University Reading and Language Arts Center.

Spiro, R.J. & Taylor, B.M. (1980). *On Investigating Children's Transition from Narrative to Expository Discourse.* Urbana, IL: Center for the Study of Reading. (ED 199 666)

Stein, H. (1978). The visual reading guide (VRG). *Social Education, 42*(6), 534–535.

Valencia, S.W. & Stallman, A.C. (1989). Multiple measures of prior knowledge: Comparative predictive validity. In S. McCormick & J. Zutell (Eds.), *Cognitive and Social Perspectives for Literacy Research and Instruction* (pp. 427–436). Rochester, NY: The National Reading Conference, Inc.

Vaughn, J.L. & Estes, T.H. (1986). *Reading and Reasoning Beyond the Primary Grades.* Boston, MA: Allyn & Bacon.

Winograd, P. & Newell, G. (1985). *The Effects Of Topic Familiarity On Good And Poor Readers' Sensitivity Text* (Technical Report No. 337). Champaign, IL: Center for the Study of Reading.

Chapter 10

Comprehending Text

A recent conversation with two reading teachers—one young and only three years out of college and the other a fifteen-year veteran—delightfully illustrated old and new attitudes toward reading. The veteran reminisced about how she used to teach reading the "old-fashioned way," teaching isolated skills, charting scores, and correcting workbooks. She told the younger teacher that teaching was much more fun now and the younger teacher responded that she could not imagine life any other way.

Reading instruction of two decades ago focused on skill development and was viewed as a collection of discrete subskills that could be learned and measured. Most teachers are familiar with activities that teach and assess students' ability to use such basic skills as finding the main idea, locating details, and detecting sequence; comprehension was viewed as a collection of these skills that could be tested and evaluated. Numerous lists of comprehension skills, which seem to grow with each revision, can be found in state departments and school districts. These lists have served as a basis for both curriculum and instruction.

After determining that a student lacked the ability to perform these tasks, a teacher could presumably improve comprehension by teaching the skills directly. The process of how a person went about performing these tasks (e.g., finding the main idea) was given less emphasis than the final product (e.g., an answer on a test).

More recently, skills have been woven into the larger context of strategy instruction. To provide an analogy, soccer players spend many hours developing their skill level in ball dribbling. That work pays off when a player dribbles past the opposing defenders, then strategically makes a nice cross to a teammate who is open at the far goalpost. Skill only takes a player so far unless that player has a strategy for making a goal. Literacy instruction today emphasizes learning strategies—those approaches that coordinate the various reading and writing skills and prior knowledge to make sense to the learner. Just as the soccer player must monitor the field for player position, time remaining, and a possible tackle, readers and writers must monitor their progress, understanding, and purpose for reading. This process is called *metacognition* and, because it involves abstract thinking, it is not generally fully developed until about age 15. The middle grades are critical for teaching students to use prior knowledge and monitor their comprehension while reading and writing. In this chapter, (1) research-based and classroom-tested comprehension strategies are discussed, (2) guidelines for instruction are presented, and (3) strategies for teaching comprehension are explained.

Strategic Reading

To say that students are generally not *involved* in their reading might be an understatement. They sometimes "read" the teacher-assigned selection with little thought of their purpose for reading and often do not retain much of the information for the later discussion, test, writing assignment, or other application exercise. Kletzien and Bednar (1988) proposed that for students to be strategically involved with their reading they must have knowledge and control of four variables: students must (1) know their strengths and weaknesses as learners (knowledge of themselves as readers, knowledge of other readers and the strategies they use, and awareness of the reading process); (2) set reasonable goals and keep them in mind (understanding the purpose for reading and assessing how well those goals are met after reading); (3) be able to size up learning tasks, knowing what makes them easy or difficult (knowing how to approach a task); and (4) know appropriate strategies to take to reach their goals (choosing appropriate strategies and monitoring their effectiveness).

For students to become independent and involved readers, they must orchestrate these four variables and control them simultaneously. "Showing students how a particular skill or strategy fits into the entire act of reading can be very difficult" (Englot-Mash, 1991, p. 150). To help students with this challenging process, Englot-Mash developed a flow chart, as in Figure 10.1, showing the thought processes of a skilled reader.

Just as the soccer player monitors action on the field, the reader must have knowledge of and control many variables while reading. Teaching students to be independent in their reading involves being aware of themselves as readers, understanding the reading process, setting their own purposes for reading, analyzing the task before them, and monitoring their comprehension. Rather than performance on a series of discrete skills, mastering these processes is the goal of reading instruction.

Comprehension Strategies

According to Weinstein (1987), "learning strategies include any thoughts or behaviors that help us to acquire new information in such a way that the new information is integrated with our existing knowledge. Learning strategies also help us retrieve stored information" (p. 590). These strategies may be as simple as underlining a main idea or as complex as organizing an entire chapter into a graphic organizer. For information to be learned and remembered, it must become relevant for the reader. Information generally becomes relevant when readers elaborate or do something with it (Weinstein, Ridley, & Weber, 1989).

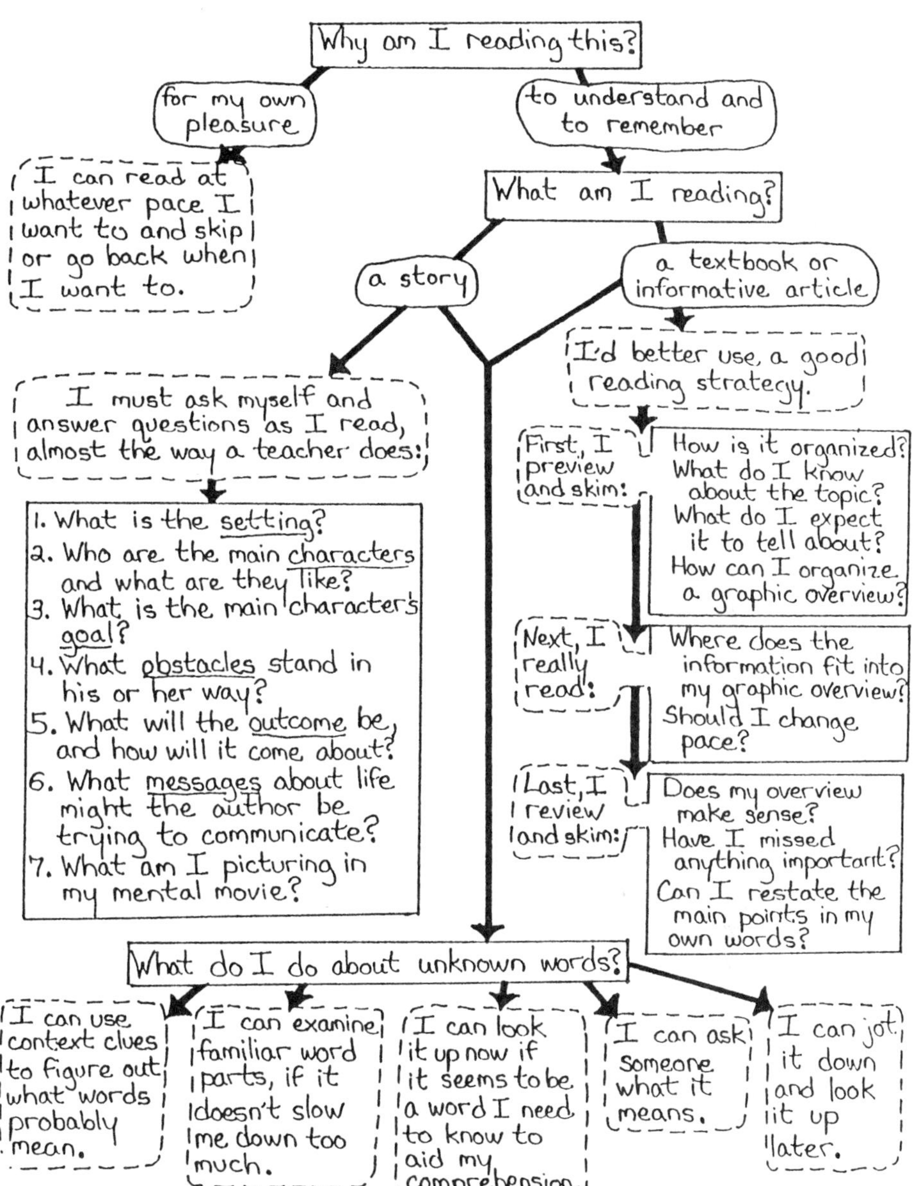

FIGURE 10.1 A skilled reader's possible "flow chart"

From Englot-Mash, Christine (1991, October). Tying together reading strategies. *Journal of Reading, 35*(2), 150–151. Reprinted with permission of Christine Englot-Mash and the International Reading Association. All rights reserved.

"Readers who monitor their comprehension by periodically pausing, asking themselves questions, paraphrasing, and looking forward and backward in the text understand materials in greater depth than readers who simply proceed through the text identifying or pronouncing words (Winograd & Paris, 1989). Johnston (1985) contended that "strategies not only make students more successful at learning tasks, but also that strategy use can help motivate students and make them feel more in control of their own learning" (p. 636). When students understand when and how to use strategies and with which body of content, they become more proficient readers. Obviously, becoming a strategic reader takes many years and experience with increasing difficult narrative and expository text. Applying strategies and monitoring their use is a metacognitive ability that involves abstract thinking and serves as a strong rationale for direct instruction in reading during the middle grades.

Dole, Duffy, Roehler, and Pearson (1991) identified five comprehension strategies that are consistent with a cognitive-based view of the reading process, that differentiate between skilled readers and novices, and that lend themselves to instruction. These strategies include determining importance, summarizing information, drawing inferences, generating questions, and monitoring comprehension and set the stage for the teacher-directed instructional strategies presented later in this chapter.

Determining Importance

Finding the main idea has traditionally been a focal point in comprehension instruction. Determining importance in text includes identifying main ideas, but, in a broader sense, involves determining what the author considered important when writing the text in the first place (Garcia & Pearson, 1990). Good readers use three sets of prior knowledge to determine importance: (1) general prior knowledge; (2) knowledge of author biases, intentions, and goals; and (3) knowledge of text structure (Baumann, 1986; Dole, Duffy, Roehler, & Pearson, 1991; Garcia & Pearson, 1990; Meyer, 1984; Johnston & Afflerbach, 1985).

Baumann (1986) rewrote inconsiderate expository text into more considerate pieces and found that middle grades students could compose significantly more main ideas when the text was written well. Hare, Rabinowitz, and Schieble (1989) found that students could often determine importance in texts such as basal readers but had more difficulty in science and social studies texts. These authors suggested that students would benefit from practice with identifying important ideas with naturally occurring text. Most researchers concur that determining importance in text is not only a vital strategy, but one that can be taught through direct instruction.

Summarizing Information

A summary is a collection of main ideas, but is broader in scope because summarizing involves integrating the ideas into a coherent whole. Summarization is discussed in more detail in Chapter 11 because this strategy is an essential component of learning to remember. Two components comprise summarizing: synthesizing information from reading (a comprehension task) and producing a summary for some purpose (a composing task).

The ability to summarize is closely aligned to developmental maturity. Young children can summarize simple narratives but need more experience with reading, writing, and text structure to complete more complex tasks. Direct instruction in summarization is an essential component of comprehension and study skill instruction at any age; the task and the text, however, must become longer and more complex to assist students with higher levels of synthesis.

Drawing Inferences

Drawing inferences while reading is so automatic that most people are not aware of this critical process. Prior knowledge and clues from text are constantly "filling in" information that is not provided in the text. Even the simplest of texts requires that readers draw inferences to comprehend. Making inferences while reading can be taught through methods such as the question-answer-relationship (presented in Chapter 11) because students recognize when they are making inferences from their prior knowledge and/or textual information. Sometimes students need permission to "guess" what is happening in a story or the meaning of a concept. Drawing inferences while reading is an essential reading and listening strategy.

Generating Questions

Teachers spend much of their time asking questions (Durkin, 1978–1979). These questions, however, are generally designed to check comprehension rather than teach comprehension. Teaching students to engage in self-questioning before, during, and after reading has been found to improve comprehension ability (Andre & Anderson, 1978–1979).

The reasons for this improved performance may be that students are forced to pause frequently, determine whether they understood the text, and decide what strategic action should be taken next. Proficient readers naturally perform these tasks when they monitor their comprehension.

Self-questioning leads the student to an active monitoring of the learning activity. It is critical that students be taught how to ask good questions. Teachers can model the process of asking good questions rather than simply using questions as an oral quiz. Students should be given the opportunity to practice and evaluate good questions as they read various content area paragraphs (Tei & Stewart, 1985). Self-questions can be "content oriented" or "process oriented." Content questions focus on the content of the reading such as "How do we get energy from fossil fuels?" whereas process questions encourage students to monitor and check their own comprehension such as "Am I understanding this reading?" or "What will the author explain next?" (Davey, 1985, p. 26). Following are examples of process questions before, during, and after reading.

Before reading, students may ask themselves:

—What is my purpose for reading?

—What task will I be asked to perform (test, paper, speech)?

—What do I know about the topic?

—Do I know enough to skim the material or should I read slowly and carefully, perhaps taking notes?

—What is the organization of the text?

—What signal words might help me understand the text?

—What might I learn about from this reading?

During reading, students may ask themselves:

—Do I understand what I am reading? Does it make sense to me?

—What did I just read (summary)?

—How are the ideas in one paragraph (section) related to another paragraph (section)?

—What will I learn about next?

After reading, students may ask themselves:

—What were the major ideas in what I just read?

—What did I learn that was new to me?

—What will I do with this information now?

Davey (1983) suggested that students can learn self-questioning behaviors by cognitive modeling; that is, the teacher must "think aloud" and give personal responses to questions. Self-questioning charts are helpful to remind students the kinds of questions that will help them to monitor comprehension. The process may be carried out with pairs of students to help less able readers adopt a more metacognitive approach to reading. Typically, less able readers are passive, and self-questioning helps them to become more involved and active while reading.

Another activity that seems to motivate students to ask good questions about content is to let them make up questions for the test. Teachers can share the kind of questions they might ask and then let students share their own questions. Having these questions in mind while reading helps students focus on the major ideas in the reading and thus helps them remember the content.

Monitoring Comprehension

Good readers are better than poor readers at monitoring their understanding and knowing what to do with comprehension failure. This strategy involves two components: monitoring comprehension, and knowing when and how to use "fix up" strategies. The process of monitoring comprehension has been discussed throughout this book and is intricately linked to a young adolescent's budding powers of abstract thinking. Even young children, though, should be encouraged to speak up when something does not make sense to them. Proficient readers generally know when to "speed up, slow down, look back, reread, skim, predict, generalize, or even resort to a dictionary" (Garcia & Pearson, 1990, p. 6).

Students need to be taught what to do when their reading does not make sense to them. Efficient readers do something about the misunderstanding. They reread the passage, they skip ahead for clues, they stop and ask themselves a question, or they review their prior knowledge to see if they can relate something known to this new information. The more that students know about the process of reading and how to cope with it, the better readers they will become. This means, of course, that teachers must understand the nature of reading and learning.

The application of these strategies depends on the purpose for reading. When reading for pleasure, for example, a reader may skip over a misunderstood passage; however, if studying for a test, the reader may consult a teacher for clarification. When students read to remember, they must have some awareness of their own understanding. They must be alert to "comprehension failure" and call on their repertoire of strategies to fix the misunderstanding.

Metacognitive skills usually do not fully develop in students until late adolescence, but much can be done to enhance this ability during the middle level years. Before students can use metacognitive skills, they must become aware of text, their own ability, how to interpret the demands of a task, and the best ways to interact with text to maximize learning. Metacognitive skills include (1) clarifying the purposes of reading, understanding both the explicit and implicit task demands; (2) identifying the important aspects of a message; (3) focusing attention on major content rather than trivia; (4) monitoring ongoing activities to determine whether comprehension is occurring; (5) engaging in self-questioning to determine whether goals are being achieved; and (6) taking corrective action when failures in comprehension are detected (Brown, 1982).

For middle grades students, therefore, metacognitive skills can be facilitated but not expected. One teacher asked students to write a short journal entry or response log after each class to help them become more aware of their own learning. Periodically, students were asked to write journal summaries to draw conclusions about their learning.

An inventory that may help make metacognitive strategies more explicit for students was developed by Miholic (1994). This inventory, which is shown in Figure 10.2, may serve as a vehicle for teachers to discuss effective and ineffective strategies with students. Central to these strategies is bringing prior knowledge, text structure, and the context for reading together to enable students to comprehend text more proficiently. Students with reading difficulties often become frustrated and give up when they do not understand. Learning strategies can be taught along with when and how to use them, thus giving students the essential tools to become independent readers.

Guidelines for Instruction

Educators have made great strides toward the development of a theory of reading in the last decade. Comprehension is now viewed as a "much more complex process involving knowledge, experience, thinking, and teaching" (Fielding & Pearson, 1994). Comprehension involves thinking and it can be taught (Tierney, 1982). The following guidelines for instruction may be helpful to middle level educators in designing instruction.

1. Focus on the process of comprehension and move toward independent learning. The goal of instruction should be to improve the students' abilities to comprehend text,

There is more than one way to cope when you run into difficulties in your reading. Which ways are best? Under each question here, put a checkmark beside *all* the responses you think are effective.

1. What do you do if you encounter a word and you don't know what it means?

+ a. Use the words around it to figure it out.
+ b. Use an outside source, such as a dictionary or expert.
+ c. Temporarily ignore it and wait for clarification.
– d. Sound it out.

2. What do you do if you don't know what an entire sentence means?

+ a. Read it again.
– b. Sound out all the difficult words.
+ c. Think about the other sentences in the paragraph.
– d. Disregard it completely.

3. If you are reading science or social studies material, what would you do to remember the important information you have read?

– a. Skip parts you do not understand.
+ b. Ask yourself questions about the important ideas.
+ c. Realize you need to remember one point rather than another.
+ d. Relate it to something you already know.

4. Before you start to read, what kind of plans do you make to help you read better?

– a. No specific plan is needed; just start reading toward completion of the assignment.
+ b. Think about what you know about the subject.
+ c. Think about why you are reading.
– d. Make sure the entire reading can be finished in as short a period of time as possible.

5. Why would you go back and read an entire passage over again?

+ a. You did not understand it.
– b. To clarify a specific or supporting idea.
+ c. It seemed important to remember.
+ d. To underline or summarize for study.

6. Knowing that you do not understand a particular sentence while reading involves understanding that

+ a. the reader may not have developed adequate links or associations for new words or concepts introduced in the sentence.
+ b. the writer may not have conveyed the ideas clearly.
+ c. two sentences may purposely contradict each other.
– d. finding meaning for the sentence needlessly slows the reader.

7. As you read a textbook, which of these do you do?

+ a. Adjust your pace depending on the difficulty of the material.
– b. Generally, read at a constant, steady pace.
– c. Skip the parts you do not understand.
+ d. Continually make predictions about what you are reading.

FIGURE 10.2 Metacognitive reading awareness inventory

8. While you read, which of these are important?
   + a. Know when you know and when you do not know key ideas.
   + b. Know what it is that you know in relation to what is being read.
   – c. Know that confusing text is common and usually can be ignored.
   + d. Know that different strategies can be used to aid understanding.
9. When you come across a part of the text that is confusing, what do you do?
   + a. Keep on reading until the text is clarified.
   + b. Read ahead and then look back if the text is still unclear.
   – c. Skip those sections completely; they are usually not important.
   + d. Check to see if the ideas expressed are consistent with one another.
10. Which sentences are the most important in the chapter?
   – a. Almost all of the sentences are important; otherwise, they would not be there.
   + b. The sentences that contain the important details or facts.
   + c. The sentences that are directly related to the main idea.
   – d. The ones that contain the most details.

(When you give this inventory to students, remember to remove the "+" and "–" marks.)

FIGURE 10.2 *Continued*

From Miholic, Vincent (1994, October). An inventory to pique students' metacognitive awareness of strategies. *Journal of Reading, 38*(2), 84–87. Reprinted with permission of Vincent Miholic and the International Reading Association. All rights reserved.

without the teacher's assistance. The emphasis during instruction should be on students acquiring the ability to use comprehension strategies on their own. All too often teachers are interested merely in the product, having students pass the test or exhibit the skill, rather than developing within students a true understanding of the process of comprehending.

This approach is often difficult for teachers because it means a transfer of control from the teacher to the student. After a thorough review of the literature on comprehension instruction, Pearson and Dole (1988) concluded that teachers should model what they want their students to do, then they should provide guided practice opportunities where teachers slowly and gradually turn the responsibility of completing the task over to students. Finally, students should apply what they learned by actually transferring their learning to new reading materials.

2. Provide ample amount of time for reading. Students typically spend more time completing worksheets than they do actually reading. Sustained silent reading programs (described in Chapters 7 and 14) are a vehicle during the busy and often fragmented middle school day that provide students with time to read. Silent reading provides students with practice in orchestrating skills and strategies with a variety of texts. Reading also results in the acquisition of new knowledge and thus helps students with future reading experiences (Fielding & Pearson, 1994).

Teachers can improve the chances that students increase their comprehension during silent reading by providing (1) materials that are optimally difficult, and (2) opportunities for choice of materials and time to share their responses to reading with peers and adults.

3. Provide opportunities to learn collaboratively and talk about reading. When students talk about their reading with each other, they learn about the strategies used by others to comprehend text. One student shared this statement with a small group: "When I come to a word I don't know, I skip it and see if the story still makes sense without it." Group members were able to learn a strategy because the teacher provided time for students to talk about reading. In addition, when students share their impressions, interpretations, and reactions to reading with others, the conversation elevates reading to an activity worthy of social interaction.

4. Facilitate comprehension instruction before, during, and after reading. The importance of building background information and activating prior knowledge *before* asking students to read was the focus of Chapter 9. Equally as important as comprehension before reading is teaching students ways of being actively involved *during* reading, which is the subject of this chapter. Students should also be shown how to organize information *after* they read, which is especially necessary when students are studying or organizing information for later retrieval. This is discussed in Chapter 11.

5. Think aloud. Many strategies can be illustrated and demonstrated by sharing your own reasoning processes with students (Davey, 1983). It is also helpful for students to share their own thought processes with teachers and other students; "think-alouds require a reader to stop periodically, reflect on how a text is being processed and understood, and relate orally to what reading strategies are being employed" (Baumann, Jones, & Seifert-Kessell, 1993, p. 3). Think-alouds may be beneficial for students with content material, literature, or newspaper articles especially when paired with prediction strategies and may occur while students are working in pairs or small groups.

6. Reinforce and develop reading abilities through writing. To express their thoughts clearly in writing, students must have the ability to organize and relate information in an understandable manner. Good reading, like effective writing, involves the creative cognitive processes by building relationships between the text and the schema of the reader. Learning to read with comprehension, then, uses the same generative skills as learning to write.

Students should be taught to "read like a writer" (Harris & Sipay, 1985). Studies (Squire, 1983; Stotsky, 1983) have shown that good writers are usually good readers, that they tend to read more, and that they produce more syntactically mature writing than poorer readers. Flood and Lapp (1986) contended that writing instruction can enhance reading development. By assigning writing tasks with reading tasks, teachers reinforce reading through writing and writing through reading.

7. Make assessment compatible with the kinds of learning encouraged. Chapter 5 is devoted to assessment techniques that are compatible with instruction. When the assessment of comprehension becomes a seamless activity with instruction, students can document their growth in reading comprehension across a variety of texts.

Comprehension Strategies

Neal and Langer (1992) constructed a framework of teaching options, shown in Figure 10.3, for content area instruction that may help teachers see the purposes of different learning strategies as they are applied during the comprehension process. The strategies presented in

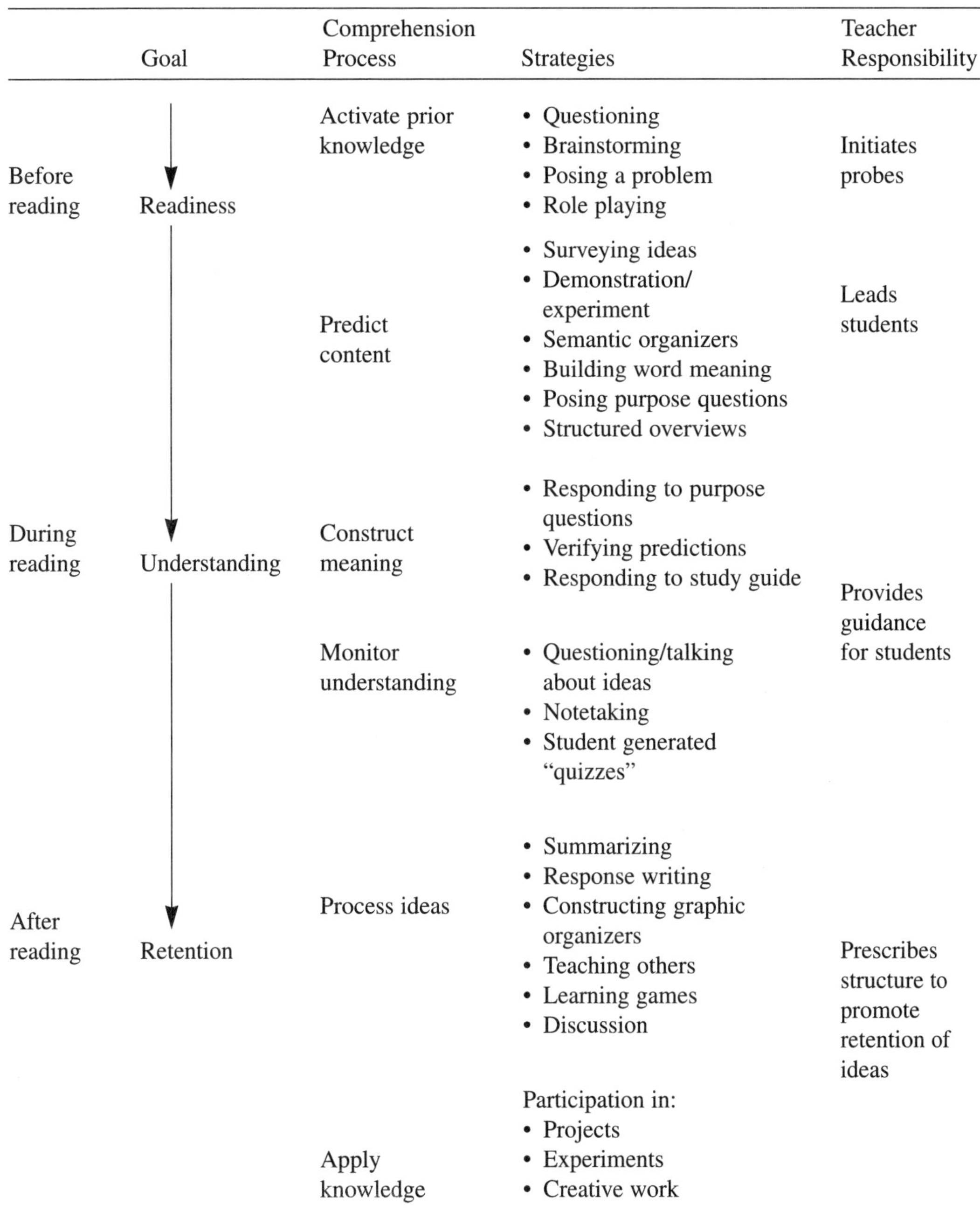

	Goal	Comprehension Process	Strategies	Teacher Responsibility
Before reading	Readiness	Activate prior knowledge	• Questioning • Brainstorming • Posing a problem • Role playing	Initiates probes
		Predict content	• Surveying ideas • Demonstration/ experiment • Semantic organizers • Building word meaning • Posing purpose questions • Structured overviews	Leads students
During reading	Understanding	Construct meaning	• Responding to purpose questions • Verifying predictions • Responding to study guide	Provides guidance for students
		Monitor understanding	• Questioning/talking about ideas • Notetaking • Student generated "quizzes"	
After reading	Retention	Process ideas	• Summarizing • Response writing • Constructing graphic organizers • Teaching others • Learning games • Discussion	Prescribes structure to promote retention of ideas
		Apply knowledge	Participation in: • Projects • Experiments • Creative work	

FIGURE 10.3 Mediated instruction of text: A framework of teaching options for content area instruction

From Neal, Judith C., & Langer, Margaret A. (1992, November). Open to Suggestion: A framework of teaching options for content area instruction: Mediated instruction of text. *Journal of Reading, 36*(3), 227–230. Reprinted with permission of Judith C. Neal and the International Reading Association. All rights reserved.

the remainder of this chapter are consistent with the guidelines for instruction presented here and have been reported to be successful with middle grades students. Strategies will be presented in three categories: (1) teacher-guided directed activities that facilitate comprehension before, during, and after reading; (2) comprehension monitoring activities; and (3) study guides.

Teacher-Guided Strategies

The following strategies provide teachers with the opportunity to model thinking processes and guide student thinking. All strategies have a before, during, and after reading component for facilitating comprehension.

Reciprocal Teaching

Every teacher understands the old saying that "to teach is to learn twice." Developed and validated by Palincsar and Brown (1984; 1986), reciprocal teaching "is an instructional procedure originally designed to teach poor comprehenders how to approach text the way successful readers do" (Palincsar, Ransom, & Derber, 1989, p. 37). Teachers and students take turns talking to one another about the meaning of text. Reciprocal teaching provides the opportunity for both teacher guidance and modeling and eventual student independence. With this strategy, the adult and the students take turns leading the dialogue.

Palincsar and Brown chose the four activities of this procedure—self-questioning, summarizing, clarifying, and predicting—because they aid in fostering and monitoring comprehension.

Step One: Students and teacher read a short section of text together. The reading should not be lengthy; one or two paragraphs is sufficient. Students who have difficulty reading the text alone can be paired with a more proficient reader.

Step Two: Students are given approximately three minutes to summarize the content, formulate questions, and predict the next passage. By including this step, all students in the class can respond to the steps in the strategy and become actively involved in the discussion.

Step Three: The teacher (student or adult) asks one or more "teacher-like" questions. This activity allows students to practice self-questioning and to determine important points that may be asked later on a test.

Step Four: The teacher (student or adult) summarizes the content. Other students may add comments from their summaries if they choose.

Step Five: The teacher (student or adult) asks for clarifying questions. At this point, students ask questions about areas they found difficult or want to have clarified. The teacher can ask questions and then entertain any from the class.

Step Six: The teacher (student or adult) makes a prediction about the future content. Students may add their predictions as well.

Step Seven: Another teacher is chosen and the procedure is repeated until all the assigned content is read.

Reciprocal teaching generally does not run smoothly the first time. Initially, teachers must spend time helping students formulate good questions, instructing them on how to

K (Know)	W (Want to Know)	L (Learned)
had ceremonies ate berries lived in America lived in teepees hunted made canoes		

FIGURE 10.4 K-W-L chart: K column

make predictions based on the text, and reminding them of such things as summaries are shortened versions of the text. As students become more and more proficient and comfortable in the steps, however, reciprocal teaching can be a powerful tool for helping students understand and internalize the comprehension process. This procedure can be used with individuals or groups of students.

This procedure has been the object of investigation (Brown & Palincsar, 1985; Palincsar, 1984); in which these researchers implemented the reciprocal teaching procedure in six middle school remedial reading classrooms. Those students learning reciprocal teaching improved their comprehension to a much greater degree than the control group. The technique was used in small and large heterogeneous groups (Palincsar & Brown, 1984). Teachers also reported that they experienced fewer behavior problems because students were actively involved in the lesson and enjoyed playing the role of the teacher.

The K-W-L Plus

Developed by Ogle (1986), the know-want to know-learn (K-W-L) strategy provides an organizational tool for students to list (1) what they know about a topic, (2) what they want to learn, and (3) what they learned about a topic. This simple, yet powerful procedure can be completed individually, in small groups, or with the entire class. Group discussions can help students generate ideas and foster interest in the subject, which is an effective learning strategy. The following steps illustrate how this strategy might be used with a topic such as American Indians.

Step One: The teacher provides a chart in which students fill in the *K* column—what they know about a topic, as shown in Figure 10.4. This step is, of course, designed to activate prior and topical knowledge and allow students to brainstorm ideas. After brainstorming as a class or small group, students fill in the "Know" column individually.

Step Two: Students categorize the information they have generated and anticipate categories of information they may find in the reading. These categories serve as an impetus for further information and anticipation about the topic, and as a structure for

K (Know)	W (Want to Know)	L (Learned)
had ceremonies ate berries lived in America lived in teepees hunted made canoes	Did Indians live in one place? Did they use stone tools? Did they domesticate the dog? Did they believe in spirits? How did they make pottery?	

Categories of information we expect to use:

A. LOCATION
B. FOOD
C. CUSTOMS
D. WAYS OF LIVING

FIGURE 10.5 K-W-L chart: K-W column

mapping and summarizing steps. Identifying categories that may emerge is helpful in providing a stimulus for beginning to organize information. These categories may be revised throughout the process. Categories about the American Indian may be location, food, customs, and ways of living.

Step Three: The teacher leads a discussion to help students pull together information and formulate questions for reading. The teacher may wish to write statements on the chalkboard; this way student knowledge is shared. Although most students know that some American Indians lived in teepees, some students may also know that other American Indians lived in huts. Statements may be revised as the discussion continues.

Step Four: As a result of sharing and discussion, students then fill in the *W* column of the chart. This step may be completed either individually or in a large group. One way to think about this column is to write down what you *think* you know about a topic. This tentative information helps students set a purpose for reading and focuses their attention while they are reading. A sample chart is shown in Figure 10.5.

Step Five: Students read the selection. The text should be divided into manageable units. Students should be encouraged to interrupt their reading after one or two paragraphs to see if any of their questions were answered or to make notes in the *L* column. As students have additional questions, they can add them to the *W* column.

K (Know)	W (Want to Know)	L (Learned)
had ceremonies	Did Indians live in one place?	many different tribes in America
ate berries	Did they use stone tools?	used many different kinds of tools
lived in America	Did they domesticate the dog?	rode horses, had dogs, cooked many dishes
lived in teepees	Did they believe in spirits?	lived off the land
hunted	How did they make pottery?	had sophisticated religion
made canoes		
LOCATION FOOD CUSTOMS WAYS OF LIVING		

FIGURE 10.6 K-W-L chart: K-W-L columns

Step Six: Students fill in the *L* column of the chart listing the things that they learned from the reading. A completed chart may look like Figure 10.6. The primary value of this part of the activity is that information is shared among the students. Thus, this strategy activates and builds on the prior and topical knowledge not only of the individual but also of the class as a whole. Students learn to view each other as sources of information, an experience that seems to foster the emotional well-being of the young adolescent.

The steps of mapping and summarizing were added to the K-W-L to form the K-W-L Plus strategy (Carr & Ogle, 1987). This extension aids students in organizing information and serves as a tool for writing.

Step Seven: Mapping: Students use the K-W-L worksheet to construct a semantic map. Semantic maps help students to understand relationships between ideas. The categories established before reading may be used as the major headings of the map and the information learned during reading may serve as supporting data for the map. A sample map of American Indians is presented in Figure 10.7.

Step Eight: Summarizing: Students use the map to produce a summary. Preparing a written summary has been shown to improve comprehension (Brown & Day,

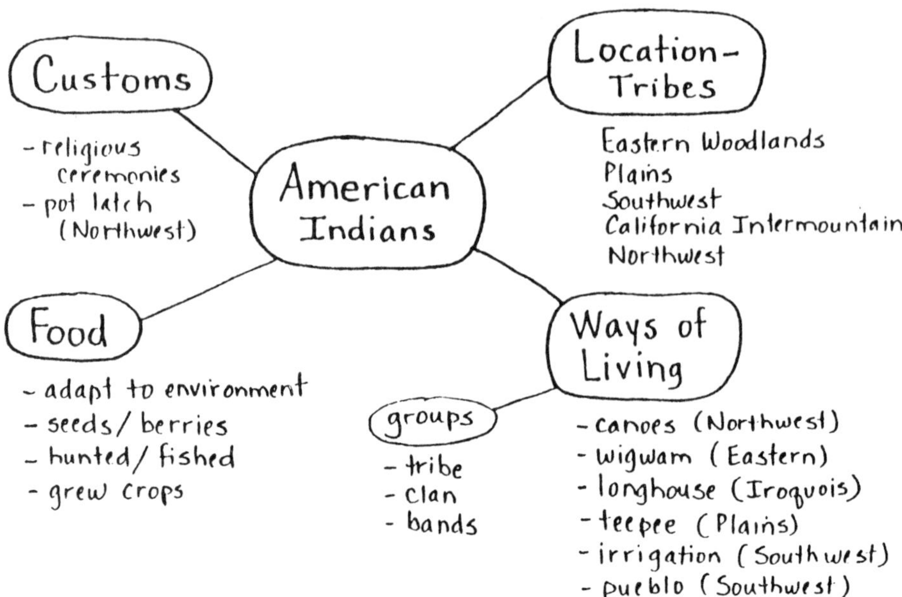

FIGURE 10.7 Semantic map from K-W-L

1983), because it helps students distinguish between important and unimportant ideas. The categories on the map may be numbered and serve as topic sentences.

A modification added by Sippola (1995) is to add a fourth column titled "What I still need to learn," which may serve as an impetus for further inquiry. The K-W-L Plus has been used successfully in middle school classrooms and has been found to improve comprehension monitoring, enhance student awareness of content and how it is structured, and provide opportunities for summarizing information (Carr & Ogle, 1987). K-W-L Plus is a procedure that involves students in the learning process before, during, and after reading a passage.

Guided Reading Procedure

The guided reading procedure (GRP) was developed by Manzo (1975). The purpose of this procedure is (1) to assist students in the recall of specific information, (2) to improve students' ability to generate their own questions as they read, (3) to improve students' abilities to organize information, and (4) to help students understand the process and importance of self-correction. The reading selection should be short enough to be completed in one brief sitting—approximately seven to ten minutes. The following example is used to illustrate the steps of the GRP. The example is based on "Feathered Friend" by Arthur C. Clarke (1958).

The story is about life on a space station. Sven, the main character, smuggles a canary to the space station. Claribel soon becomes everyone's pet. One morning, Sven, feeling drowsy and heavy with sleep, finds Claribel feet up and looking rather limp. Oxygen revives Claribel. Because of this incident, the crew discovers a leak in the oxygen system. Claribel saved the day.

Step One: The teacher prepares students for the reading assignment. The teacher should lead a discussion that motivates students to read the selection, activates prior knowledge, and helps them to identify expectations about the reading. For the story, "Feathered Friends," the teacher leads a discussion about what it would be like to live in a space station and what would be the assets and liabilities of having different animals as pets there.

Step Two: Students read the selection silently.

Step Three: The teacher asks students to recall information without looking at their books. They may recall central ideas or details. All ideas are listed on the chalkboard or overhead. The information for this story may look like the following:

— Claribel needed oxygen.

— Sven smuggled Claribel on board the space station.

— The alarm did not go off.

— Sven was a big man.

— Claribel could hang in the air.

— Everyone wakes up drowsy.

— Claribel appears dead.

— The crew tried to hide Claribel.

Step Four: Students return to the reading for additional facts. Students and the teacher add new information to the list.

Step Five: The teacher helps the students organize the recalled information into an outline or semantic map. The organization should illustrate the general idea and supporting details. The map of "Feathered Friends" in Figure 10.8 was difficult to construct because students had a difficult time finding the central theme of the story. Teachers should be sensitive to the fact that not all text has a main idea; therefore, students may need additional help in the construction of a map or outline.

Step Six: The teacher provides the students with a thought-provoking question. This question may help them associate this story with something read previously. For example, this section of the literature text dealt with plot. The teacher asked the students to compare the plot of "Feathered Friends" with the plot of two other previously read stories.

Step Seven: Students are tested on their knowledge of the information in the text. It makes no difference whether the test is essay or objective. The point is to see if students have committed the information to short-term memory.

Manzo (1975) cautioned that this activity should not be used more than once every two weeks. It is a fairly intense reading activity. Also, as shown in Figure 10.8, when using the GRP for narrative text, some stories do not lend themselves well to a central theme that can be easily mapped or outlined. The GRP works well with expository text.

The GRP has been field tested in seventh-grade classes. It seemed to enhance the short- and long-term comprehension of students using content material (Bean & Pardi, 1979). The researchers found that looking over the story before reading was important in activating prior knowledge and that collaborating in the construction of the map or outline helped students organize what they had read.

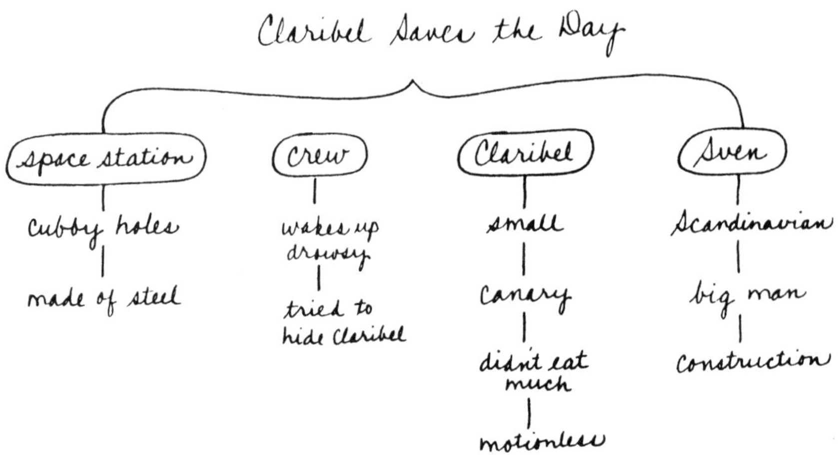

FIGURE 10.8 Map of "Feathered Friend"

Comprehension Monitoring Activities

For students to become independent learners, they must monitor their own comprehension. The following strategies are designed to help students become more proficient with metacognitive processes.

Paired Readings

Working under the assumption that two heads are better than one, Dansereau (1977) suggested paired readings as a means of helping students to learn and retain more of what they have learned.

Step One: Two students silently read a short segment of an assignment (about six hundred words). The student who finishes first can reread the material for the important points. After reading, both students put material out of sight.

Step Two: When both students are finished reading, the recaller orally retells what was read without referring back to the text. One student recalls (the recaller) the information in the text and the other student listens (the listener).

Step Three: During the retelling, the listener should only interrupt to obtain clarification.

Step Four: After the retelling, the listener should do two things: (1) point out and correct any ideas that were summarized incorrectly, and (2) add any ideas that were not included in retelling, but that the listener thinks should have been included. The two students work together to note as many ideas as possible.

Step Five: Students should alternate roles after each segment. Students tend to recall information better than if they worked alone. Students also seem to enjoy working with a partner.

Paired readings are particularly good for middle school students because they require student to make a social contract to work together. Students learn from each other's point of view and thinking strategies. To facilitate this learning, teachers should encourage students to share their reasoning strategies with each other. Students understand material better because they have read the information in short segments, and have spoken and listened to the information. One student may understand something that confuses the other. This activity strengthens students' metacognitive abilities while it provides them with an opportunity to work cooperatively with others.

Paired Questioning

Instead of conducting the ReQuest procedure (which is generally used with an entire class), Vaughn and Estes (1986) suggested that teachers assign pairs of students to proceed through the steps together in the paired questioning strategy. The steps in paired questioning are presented here.

Step One: Pairs of students read the title or subtitle of a manageable section of text together.

Step Two: Each student asks questions that come to mind about the title. The partner answers questions if possible.

Step Three: Each student reads the same section of the text silently.

Step Four: After completing the reading, reader A asks a question concerning the information and ideas in the text. Reader B answers, using the text if necessary.

Step Five: Reader B then asks questions of reader A. Reader A answers the questions, again using the text if necessary.

Step Six: Reader A identifies the important and unimportant ideas. Reader A must explain why the ideas are important or unimportant and the process for drawing these conclusions.

Step Seven: Reader B must either agree or disagree and offer reasons for agreement or disagreement. The following activities may be completed for extension activities.

Step Eight: Each student writes a paraphrase or summary of the reading. Semantic mapping could also be used during this stage of the activity.

Step Nine: Students read their paraphrases to each other and develop a synopsis on which they both agree. If students construct maps, they may combine their information to form a more complete diagram. Students may want to draw pictures to enhance their summaries.

Step Ten: Students proceed to the next segment, switching roles. The paired questioning technique serves the purpose of getting students to read thoughtfully, and to ask and answer questions about their reading. The notion that "two heads are better than one" applies here.

INSERT (An Interactive Notation System for Effective Reading and Thinking)

Vaughn and Estes (1986) developed INSERT, which is a simple procedure to help students become more involved in their reading and to help them make decisions as they read and clarify their own understanding. The strategy consists of a marking system illustrated in

✓ I agree
X I disagree/Ithought differently
+ New information
! Wow
? I wonder
?? Don't understand
• Important

FIGURE 10.9 Marking system for INSERT strategy

Figure 10.9 that records the students' reactions to what is being read. If marking in a book is a problem, supply students with strips of paper to place along the side of the text.

A person may wonder what information a sixth grader would assign a "!" while studying ancient civilizations. Perhaps teachers need to acknowledge what may be already suspected: students may find much of what they read boring or confusing. If teachers know which parts of the text elicit such a reaction, they can plan assignments more effectively. Students could note a *C* for confusing or a *B* for boring. Teachers can help students through such passages with added concept building. The entire INSERT marking system should be introduced gradually and may be simplified and changed when needed. For narrative text, teachers may wish to substitute notations that represent responses to reading. Regardless of which notation system is used, the INSERT method provides a guide for thinking about and reacting to reading, which serves to improve metacognitive abilities in students.

Study Guides

The purpose of a study guide is to lead students through a reading assignment and focus their attention on main points, thereby improving their metacognition. Study guides can motivate students by providing a structure for them, thus encouraging them to become active rather than passive readers. Group work seems to be especially effective when using study guides and is an activity young adolescents particularly enjoy.

The construction of study guides takes time and effort. Teachers should first focus on the major points to be learned and the reading abilities to be practiced. Overcrowded print may confuse students; thus the urge to overload students with information should be resisted. Teachers should try to make the study guide interesting. Students usually need to be talked through the study guide before they begin reading. As students become more and more proficient in using study guides, the teacher can make them less detailed, thus releasing some of the responsibility to students as they are able to handle it. Middle grades students also enjoy composing study guides for other students. The textbook activity guide provides an example of one type of study guide that middle school students enjoy.

Textbook Activity Guide

Textbook activity guide (TAG) facilitates the active involvement of students using content area materials. These guides are different from other guides in that they do not depend on hierarchical levels of comprehension and they are not dependent on clear organizational patterns in textbooks. Also, "TAGs emphasize active student involvement through cooperative learning and a self-monitoring component" (Davey, 1986, p. 490).

Students are quick to understand and use coding systems designed by teachers. Again, as with the study guides, TAGs take time to construct but students seem to benefit from that time. The steps in constructing a TAG include the selection of learning objectives, and the location of features in the text that best facilitate the mastery of those objectives. A sample TAG is presented in Figure 10.10.

Davey (1986) suggested that TAGs be used for only a limited period of time, starting with twenty minutes. She found that secondary students benefited from using the TAG because it facilitated their active involvement in textbook reading and assisted them in monitoring their comprehension of that reading. The teacher's role is to help students become independent learners. As students are more able to read expository text successfully and independently, the TAGs can be less structured. Some students have enjoyed making TAGs for other students.

Geography Affected Indian Ways

Names: ______________________________ Date initiated: ________________

____

Strategy codes:

DP = Read and discuss with your partner
PP = Predict with your partner
WR = Each partner writes response on separate paper
Map = Complete the semantic map
Skim = Read quickly for the purpose slated; discuss with your partner

Self-monitoring codes:

__+__ I understand the information.
__/__ I'm not sure if I fully understand this information.
__?__ I do not understand this information. I need to restudy.

---

1. **PP** pp. 21–25—title and headings
   What do you think you will learn from this section?
   List at least eight things.
2. **DP** p. 21—headings and first three paragraphs
   Explain the second sentence in this section, beginning "The type of shelter. . . ."
   What are some examples from the passage?
   What are some examples from today?

FIGURE 10.10 Sample TAG *Continued*

3. **WR** p. 21—right column, first and second paragraphs
   a. Why did the Haidas and the Iroquois need different kinds of boats?
   b. Using other resource books in the classroom, draw an Iroquois canoe and a Haida boat. Add them to your booklet on Indians.
4. **Skim** p. 21—last two paragraphs; p. 22—first paragraph
   Purpose: Find out about the shelter and food of the Plains Indians.
5. **DP** p. 22—second to sixth paragraph
   How did the climate of the Southwest affect:
   ______ the materials the Pueblo Indians used for their shelters?
   ______ the way they built their shelters?
   ______ the way they grew their food?
6. **Skim** p. 22—second to last paragraph of section
   Purpose: Find out about the features of homes of the Mayan Indians.
7. **WR** p. 22—last paragraph of section
   Give an example from the section to prove each of the following:
   ______ Geography influenced Indian homes.
   ______ Geography influenced Indian clothing.
   ______ Geography influenced Indian food.
8. **DP** Map pp. 24, 25
   Compare and contrast two types of Indian homes.

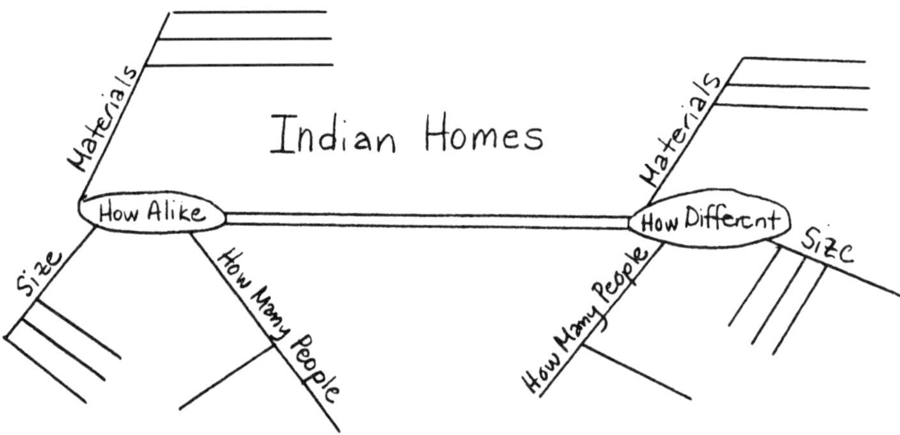

FIGURE 10.10 *Continued*

Summary

Traditionally, reading has been viewed as a collection of discrete subskills, each of which could be tested and taught. Many modern educational theorists, however, have come to view reading as a whole that is greater than the sum of its parts. Reading is comprehension, and only by emphasizing the process of comprehending will we help students to acquire a knowledge of what reading means.

Students must acquire a repertoire of learning strategies to help them deal effectively with problems in comprehension. Teachers can model, guide, and provide feedback, but students must learn how to apply these strategies to their own reading.

References

Andre, M.D.A. & Anderson, T.H. (1978–1979). The development and evaluation of a self-questioning study technique. *Reading Research Quarterly, 14*(4), 605–623.

Baumann, J.F. (1986). Effect of rewritten content textbook passages in middle grade students' comprehension of main ideas: Making the inconsiderate considerate. *Journal of Reading Behavior, 18*(1), 1–21.

Baumann, J.F., Jones, L.A., & Seifert-Kessell, N. (1993). *Monitoring Reading Comprehension by Thinking Aloud* (Instructional Resource No. 1). Athens, GA: National Reading Research Center.

Bean, T.W. & Pardi, R. (1979). A field test of a guided reading strategy. *Journal of Reading, 23*(2), 144–147.

Brown, A.L. (1982). Learning how to learn from reading. In J.L. Langer & M.T. Smith-Burke (Eds.), *Reader Meets Author/Bridging the Gap* (pp. 26–54). Newark, DE: International Reading Association.

Brown, A.L. & Day, J.D. (1983). Macrorules for summarizing texts: The development of expertise. *Journal of Verbal Learning, 22*(1), 1–4.

Brown, A.L. & Palincsar, A.S. (1985). *Reciprocal Teaching of Comprehension Strategies: A Natural History of One Program for Enhancing Learning.* (Technical Report No. 334). Champaign, IL: Center for the Study of Reading.

Carr, E. & Ogle, D. (1987). K-W-L Plus: A strategy for comprehension and summarization. *Journal of Reading, 30*(7), 626–631.

Clarke, A.C. (1958). Feathered Friend. In *The Other Side of the Sky.* New York: Scott Meredith Literary Agency.

Dansereau, D.F. (1977). How to create and maintain a crummy mood. In D.F. Dansereau (Ed.), *Instructional Packet: Techniques of College Learning.* Fort Worth, TX: Texas Christian University.

Davey, B. (1983). Think aloud: Modeling the cognitive processes of reading comprehension. *Journal of Reading, 27*(1), 44–47.

Davey, B. (1985). Helping readers think beyond print through self-questioning. *Middle School Journal, 17*(1), 26–27.

Davey, B. (1986). Using textbook activity guides to help students learn from textbooks. *Journal of Reading, 29*(6), 489–494.

Dole, J.A., Duffy, G.G., Roehler, L.R., & Pearson, P.D. (1991). Moving from the old to the new: Research on reading comprehension instruction. *Review of Educational Research, 1*(2), 239–264.

Durkin, D. (1978–1979). What classroom observations reveal about comprehension instruction. *Reading Research Quarterly, 14*(4), 481–533.

Englot-Mash, C. (1991). Tying together reading strategies. *Journal of Reading, 35*(2), 150–151.

Fielding, L.G. & Pearson, P.D. (1994). Reading comprehension: What works. *Educational Leadership, 51*(5), 62–67.

Flood, J. & Lapp, D. (1986). Getting the main idea of the main idea: A writing/reading process. In J.F. Baumann (Ed.), *Teaching Main Idea Comprehension* (pp. 227–238). Newark, DE: International Reading Association.

Garcia, G.E. & Pearson, P.D. (1990). *Modifying Reading Instruction to Maximize Its Effectiveness for All Students.* (Technical Report No. 489). Champaign, IL: Center for the Study of Reading.

Hare, V.C., Rabinowitz, M., & Schieble, K.M. (1989). Text effects on main idea comprehension. *Reading Research Quarterly, 24*(1), 72–88.

Harris, A.J. & Sipay, E.R. (1985). *How to Increase Reading Ability.* New York: Longman.

Johnston, P. (1985). Teaching students to apply strategies that improve reading comprehension. *The Elementary School Journal, 85*(5), 635–645.

Johnston, P. & Afflerbach, P. (1985). The process of constructing main ideas from text. *Cognition and Instruction, 2*(3–4), 207–232.

Kletzien, S.B. & Bednar, M.R. (1988). A framework for reader autonomy: An integrated perspective. *Journal of Reading, 32*(1), 30–33.

Manzo, A.V. (1975). Guided reading procedure. *Journal of Reading, 18*(4), 287–291.

Meyer, B.J.F. (1984). Organizational aspects of text: Effects on reading comprehension and applications for the classroom. In J. Flood (Ed.), *Promoting Reading Comprehension* (pp. 113–160). Newark, DE: International Reading Association.

Miholic, V. (1994). An inventory to pique students' metacognitive awareness of reading strategies. *Journal of Reading, 38*(2), 84–87.

Neal, J.C. & Langer, M.A. (1992). A framework of teaching options for content area instruction: Mediated instruction of text. *Journal of Reading, 36*(3), 227–230.

Ogle, D.M. (1986). KWL: A teaching model that develops active reading of expository text. *The Reading Teacher, 39*(6), 564–570.

Palincsar, A.S. (1984). The quest for meaning from expository text: A teacher guided journey. In G.G. Duffy, L.R. Roehler, & J. Mason (Eds.), *Comprehension Instruction: Perspectives and Suggestions* (pp. 251–264). New York: Longman.

Palincsar, A.S. & Brown, A.L. (1984). Reciprocal teaching of comprehension-fostering and comprehension-monitoring activities. *Cognition and Instruction, 1*(2), 117–175.

Palincsar, A.S. & Brown, A.L. (1986). Interactive teaching to promote independent learning from text. *The Reading Teacher, 39*(8), 771–777.

Palincsar, A.S., Ransom, K., & Derber, S. (1989). Collaborative research and development of reciprocal teaching. *Educational Leadership, 46*(4), 37–41.

Pearson, P.D. & Dole, J.A. (1988). *Explicit Comprehension Instruction: A Review of Research and a New Conceptualization of Instruction* (Technical Report No. 427). Champaign, IL: Center for the Study of Reading.

Sippola, A.E. (1995). K-W-L-S. *The Reading Teacher, 48*(6), 542–543.

Squire, J.R. (1983). Composing and comprehending: Two sides of the same basic process. *Language Arts, 60*(5), 581–589.

Stotsky, S. (1983). Research on reading/writing relationships: A synthesis and suggested directions. *Language Arts, 60*(5), 627–642.

Tei, E. & Stewart, O. (1985). Effective studying from text: Applying metacognitive strategies. *Forum for Reading, 16*(7), 46–55.

Tierney, R.J. (1982). Essential considerations for developing basic reading comprehension skills. *School Psychology Review, 11*(3), 299–305.

Vaughn, J.L. & Estes, T.H. (1986). *Reading and Reasoning Beyond the Primary Grades.* Neeham Heights, MA: Allyn & Bacon.

Weinstein, C.E. (1987). Fostering learning autonomy through the use of learning strategies. *Journal of Reading, 30*(7), 590–595.

Weinstein, C.E., Ridley, D.S.T., & Weber, E.S. (1989). Helping students develop strategies for effective learning. *Educational Leadership, 46*(4), 17–19.

Winograd, P. & Paris, S.G. (1989). A cognitive and motivational agenda for reading instruction. *Educational Leadership, 46*(4), 30–36.

Chapter 11

Learning and Remembering

Most students read not only for their own pleasure, but also to acquire information relevant to a test, a report, a project, or some other assignment. Reading for remembering—that is, studying—involves reading for meaning and much more. Readers who have in mind a specific academic goal must be able to choose among important ideas and organize these ideas so as to remember them clearly. In other words, they must know how to remember information and what information to remember. Study skills such as outlining, summarizing, underlining, and notetaking have been taught in middle schools for many years. Although research has failed to endorse any one of these strategies over another, what seems to make a strategy effective is (1) the level of processing involved while using the strategy (being actively involved in the learning), and (2) the knowledge of the criterion task or the task on which students will be asked to perform, such as a test or a report (Anderson & Armbruster, 1984). In this chapter, the following will be presented and discussed: (1) the importance of depth of processing and knowledge of the criterion task, (2) factors in successful study strategy instruction and programs, and (3) strategies for teaching study skills before, during, and after reading.

Depth of Processing

A student taking notes may merely copy the author's words or may synthesize and summarize ideas into a graphic organizer. The former is a fairly passive task whereas the latter indicates deep processing—an understanding of the major concepts presented in the text. Deep processing is facilitated by strategies such as chapter mapping that allow the reader to connect ideas in the text to each other and to their prior knowledge. Whether students take notes or underline the text is not as significant as how well they understand the relationship between ideas presented in the text and how well they choose "strategies that meet the goals and demands of the task at hand" (Tei & Stewart, 1985, p. 46).

Brown (1985) advised that for effective study "effort must be coupled with strategic ingenuity" (p. 5). Some teachers use learning logs or journals to assist students in the metacognitive awareness it takes to monitor understanding (Commander & Smith, 1996; Hoffman, 1983). These logs help students evaluate their study and performance on tests, make their strategies for organizing material more public, and give teachers a starting point for discussing effective strategies for studying.

Whatever the task, students must actively engage in learning the material by organizing information, remembering, and demonstrating learning at a later time. Teachers can help students identify the important ideas in text by "engaging students in a dialogue about how important ideas are selected and what relationship these ideas have to one another" (Schmidt, Barry, Maxworthy, & Huebsch, 1989, p. 430). Successful study occurs when students monitor their understanding of the important ideas in text and select a strategy that matches the criterion task.

Knowledge of the Criterion Task

The tasks for which students read to remember are familiar to students and teachers alike. These goals, such as multiple-choice or essay exams, research papers, book reports, or speeches, are called "criterion tasks." The degree of knowledge students have about the criterion task is the second important variable in the effectiveness of time spent studying. "When the criterion task is made explicit to the students before they read the text, students will learn more from studying than when the criterion task remains vague" (Anderson & Armbruster, 1984, p. 658). Students who are to study effectively and efficiently must have enough information about the task at hand so that they can adjust their studying accordingly.

Meyer (1934; 1935; 1936) found that when students anticipated essay and completion exams rather than multiple-choice and true-false tests, they performed better on all types of tests. When studying for objective tests (multiple-choice and true/false), students engaged in "random" notetaking and underlining. Meyer suggested that studying for an essay exam prompts students to focus on the understanding of major points. An understanding of the major concepts in the text and their relationship to each other seemed to aid students in their overall recall of the text. Clearly, "different study activities involve students in very different thinking patterns and also lead to different kinds of learning" (Langer, 1986, p. 406).

Factors in Successful Study Strategy Instruction

The purpose of instruction in study strategies is to foster independent learning. Content area teachers are the most capable of teaching study strategies because they can best explain the criterion task and help students adjust their studying accordingly. Content area teachers are best able to identify important concepts to be learned and can develop the necessary background information to help students see the relationship between concepts. Additionally, content teachers are most familiar with the text and its organization and can most effectively guide students through it.

Many factors, of course, affect learning and remembering and some of them are beyond the scope of the teacher's influence. Heredity and environment play important roles, as well as the student's self-concept, management of time, and particular style of learning. A deficit in many of these areas, however, can often be overcome by hard work, determination, and motivation to learn. "Many highly successful individuals have above-average but not extraordinary intelligence. Accomplishment in a particular activity is often more dependent upon hard work and self-discipline than on innate ability" (United States Department of Education, 1986, p. 16). Beyond this, however, Brown (1980) suggested two general classes of problems that can impede effective study: impoverished background knowledge and inefficient application of strategies.

Chapter 9 described the importance of activating prior knowledge before reading. Learning becomes an impossible task if the new information cannot be related in some way to what is already known. Good teachers tailor instruction to the students' level of understanding and continually help to focus students' attention on the main points. They also monitor students' degree of understanding during reading or during a lecture, and supply students with the knowledge they need to facilitate understanding. In summary, good teachers help students relate new knowledge to what they already know.

Good teachers also help their students realize that reading is an active process and that it is important to use "problem-solving . . . routines to enhance understanding" (Baker & Brown, 1984, p. 376). Having knowledge of strategic routines, however, does not seem to be adequate for effective study behavior (Brown, 1980). Students must be able to apply these strategies at the appropriate time.

Successful Study Strategy Program

Successful study skills training programs have three main components: (1) training and practice in the use of task-specific strategies (knowing *what* to apply), (2) instruction in the monitoring of these skills (knowing *when* and *how* to apply strategies), and (3) information concerning the significance and outcome of these activities and their range of utility (knowing *why* to apply strategies) (Paris, Newman, & McVey, 1983). "Students who receive only instruction in the skills often fail to use them intelligently and on their own volition because they do not appreciate the reasons why such activities are useful, nor do they grasp where and when to use them" (Baker & Brown, 1984). Elements of effective studying include:

1. Having specific purposes or goals for the study session.
2. Recognizing the inherent structure of the reading material.
3. Purposefully extracting information.
4. Assessing the knowledge gained (Tei & Stewart, 1985, pp. 48–49).

In summary, a middle school study strategy program should include both instruction in the strategies and instruction in the metacognitive skills that help students know when and how to apply these strategies. Middle school educators should help students develop these metacognitive abilities but cannot expect that students will make rapid progress as these abilities are late developing in most students. Middle school is a time of transition for students in their capacity for metacognitive thought; the development of such thought, however, is necessary for the effective use of study strategies.

Strategies That Facilitate Learning and Remembering

Studying is not an act that occurs only before a test. Studying involves getting organized, extracting and organizing information, and demonstrating that knowledge later (Irvin & Rose, 1995). The following strategies facilitate learning and remembering before, during, and after reading.

Before Reading

Survey Techniques

Survey techniques serve the purpose of helping to establish in the reader expectations about the content and the meaning of the text. Survey, question, read, recite, review (SQ3R) (Robinson, 1970) has been a popular survey technique for many years. Although many educators find such methods helpful, training in "cookbook methods often results in 'blind rule following' rather than self-awareness and learning to learn" (Brown, 1982, p. 48). Although such a formula may be appropriate for the reading of one text, it may be inappropriate for the reading of another. Tierney and Pearson (1981) stated that "teaching prescriptions for how to process a text that disregard the ever changing interplay of text, purpose, and reader should be disregarded" (p. 1).

Basically, SQ3R, or any other formula technique, has two major shortcomings: (1) the techniques do not train the student to learn how to learn and how to evaluate the success of the strategy used, and (2) the techniques require the learning of activities that are difficult for many students (Andre & Anderson, 1978–1979; Baker, 1979; Brown, Campione, & Day, 1981; Brown & Smiley, 1977). The reasons for this difficulty may be that students are often told to "just do it" rather than being taught how to formulate good questions, summarize a text, and select topic sentences.

Any study technique, including SQ3R, can be effective when it helps students to focus attention on understanding important ideas in a text (Anderson & Armbruster, 1984). Anderson (1979) maintained that students are rarely given instructions on what to look for as they preview a text. The steps and rationale of SQ3R are as follows:

1. Survey. Students become familiar with the general structure and content of the text. "The ability to utilize the text's top-level structure appears to be an important organizational strategy for remembering information in text" (Meyer, Brandt, & Bluth, 1980, p. 97). Understanding the structure of the text and activating prior knowledge about the content are the two main purposes of surveying the text.

Surveying the text naturally leads to self-questioning. Questions such as "How much do I know about this topic?" or "How do I feel about this information?" or "How can I best remember this information?" are process questions (see Chapter 10) that proficient readers naturally ask when surveying information. The next step involves questions related to content.

2. Question. Students are encouraged to turn subheadings into questions. Some teachers have modified the SQ3R by having students draw a line vertically down their paper and write the questions to the left of that line. This modification is sometimes called active SQ3R. These questions generally involve who, what, when, where, why.

3. Read. Students benefit most when they predict possible answers to the questions they pose before reading the text (Jacobowitz, 1988). Self-questioning with prediction "forces poor comprehenders to monitor the events in the passage more actively, not only in an attempt to seek out answers to their questions, but also to discover whether predictions will be confirmed" (Nolan, 1991, pp. 135–136). After making predictions, students read to confirm or revise their predictions. McCormick and Cooper (1991) found that students who are learning disabled performed better using the SQ3R if sections in the text were broken into shorter sections and interspersed with discussions.

4. Recite. One of the premises of cooperative learning is that "oral rehearsal" is a powerful learning and remembering method. To explain something to someone else is to process the material more deeply. Students can work in pairs to answer their questions or the questions of other students or they can "recite" by writing summaries or paraphrasing information for themselves.

5. Review. Graphic organizers or summaries help students organize information for more accurate recitation and review. In addition, these written records can be used to study or use the information at a later time. The better information is organized while learning, the easier it is to retrieve at a later date.

Whether students use SQ3R or another survey technique, information is learned and remembered more and better when these basic steps are followed. Dansereau (1977) suggested the following guidelines for previewing a book before reading.

1. Think about the title of the selection, asking yourself what you already know about this concept.
2. Read any questions or summaries that may appear at the end of the sections or chapters.
3. Notice how the chapter is divided into sections.
4. Examine the pictures and graphs in the chapter for ease of referral when they are mentioned in the text.
5. Make a few preliminary notes about what you expect to learn from the reading.
6. Think about the reading you are about to do in relation to the goals it will serve.
7. Place this reading in a specific schedule of work, established on the basis of the relative importance of all you have to do.
8. Put yourself in a proper mood for study.
9. It is sometimes helpful to turn subheadings into questions that you try to answer as you read.
10. Try to keep curiosities—those things about the selected topic that make you curious—in mind as you read.
11. Think about the kinds of questions you usually see on tests of related subjects.
12. Be sure you understand the study questions, if your teacher provides them for you to use in the reading assignment, before you begin reading.

Many students have found that survey techniques help them anticipate what they will study. Study is therefore made more meaningful because new information is connected to what is known (or anticipated).

During Reading

Active reading facilitates better understanding of text. Active reading involves self-questioning, prediction, and an understanding of the main ideas. Efficient readers make adjustments in their reading rate; therefore, a discussion of flexible reading will precede the presentation of strategies that facilitate active reading.

Flexible Reading

> *"I took a course in speed reading then read* War and Peace.
> *It was about Russia."*

The ability to read quickly pays off for college students and professionals. Reading text quickly without understanding is a waste of time; however, reading slowly and carefully is often inefficient as well. So how fast should a person read? The answer depends on the purpose for reading (including knowledge of the criterion task), the reader's prior knowledge, and the nature of the material. Reading speed also fluctuates with grade level (ability), although the relationship between reading speed and comprehension changes dramatically as children's reading abilities develop.

With primary students who struggle with word recognition, the correlation between their reading rate and their comprehension is quite high. As students progress in reading and become more proficient with word recognition, however, the correlation between reading rate and comprehension lowers. In other words, the faster students at this level read, the lower their comprehension of the material. This relationship typifies the "normal" progression of reading ability; however, it is also normal for students to display a wide variety of abilities in reading rate. Table 11.1 shows average reading rates of students in grades 4 through 8. Data are taken from several standardized test scores and represent the median number of words read per minute at each grade level (Harris & Sipay, 1990, p. 634).

Note that a difference of 50 to 79 words per minute is reported between the highest and lowest test at each grade level. While reading scores on a standardized test may not reflect reading rates in the classroom, such scores do indicate the wide variety in reading rates that a teacher may expect to find in grades 4 through 8. The reading rate of the average American high school student is 200 to 250 words per minute. The average eighth grader is close to that rate when entering high school.

Carver (1992) developed a theory of "rauding" which refers to "comprehension of complete thoughts in the sentences of textual material, whether presented visually or auditorily" (p. 84). The various rates of reading can be broken into the five types shown in Table 11.2. The actual rates are only approximate (Tonjes & Zintz, 1981, p. 111).

Efficient reading is flexible. Students should be able to adjust their rate according to their purpose for reading, their prior knowledge, and the nature of the material. For example, consider two students: Alesha and Emmelyn. The physical education teacher has given

TABLE 11.1 Median Rates of Reading for Different Grades as Determined by Several Standardized Reading Tests

	Grade 4	5	6	7	8
Highest test	170	195	230	246	267
Median test	155	177	206	215	237
Lowest test	120	145	171	176	188

Source: From *How to Increase Your Reading Ability: A Guide to Developmental and Remedial Methods.* Albert J.Harris and Edward R. Sipay, Copyright © 1940, 1947, 1956, 1961, 1970, 1975, 1980, and 1985. Longman Inc. All rights reserved.

TABLE 11.2 Reading Rates for Different Purposes

Slow/study rate	50–250
Average/normal rate	200–300
Rapid reading	300–800
Skimming	800–up
Scanning	1000–up

Source: From Marian J. Tonjes and Miles V. Zintz, *Teaching Reading/Thinking/Study Skills in Content Classrooms.* Copyright © 1981 Wm. C. Brown Publishers, Dubuque, Iowa. All rights reserved. Reprinted by permission.

them a small book on soccer and tells them that they will have a test on Friday that covers soccer rules. Alesha has been playing soccer on city teams since she was 6, and her father is a soccer coach. Therefore, the game is dinnertime conversation. Emmelyn, on the other hand, has taken violin lessons since age 6, her father is a chemist, and she has never played a game of soccer. Alesha needs only to skim the material, stopping periodically and checking to make sure her prior knowledge of the rules match the text. She reads the book rapidly and hurries off to the match. Emmelyn, on the other hand, spends hours with the book writing down the rules so that she can study them later and asking Alesha the meaning of terms such as "offsides" and "heading." Good readers decide how fast to read before beginning and adjust their rate while reading according to their comprehension.

A Self-Monitoring Approach to Reading and Thinking (SMART)

SMART is a strategy that helps students identify what they do and do not understand in their reading. Vaughn and Estes (1986) described the steps that comprise SMART. These steps are many but they are simple and easy to use.

Step One: Students place a "√" in the margin if they understand what they are reading, and place a "?" if they do not understand what they are reading. A paper folded three times lengthwise with page numbers at the top makes a handy substitute for marking in the margins of the book.

Step Two: After each section of the assignment, students paraphrase the facts and ideas they have understood. Students may look back at the text while they do this.

Step Three: Next, after each section, students examine those ideas that they did not understand and then do these things:

a. Read again the parts that were not understood and if they now understand something that was previously unclear, change the "?" to a "√."
b. If the idea remains unclear, try to specify what is causing the problem. Is it a word? A phrase? A relationship?
c. Try to think of something to help understand, (such as using the glossary, examining pictures or diagrams in the text, reviewing another part of the text), and try it out. Again, if the strategy works, change your "?" to a "√."
d. Finally, try to clarify those ideas that are still causing the misunderstanding.

Step Four: Have students study the entire assignment using these three steps. Students might find it useful to divide the assignment into sections. After studying the entire assignment, students should be instructed to do the following things:

a. Close the book and review the ideas that you do understand. Some people do this by talking out loud to themselves.
b. Look back at the book and refresh your memory for anything you left out.
c. Now, reexamine those ideas you still do not understand. Think about those ideas. What could they possibly mean? Is there anything else you could do to help you understand? Do not worry about what you do not understand. Ask someone later.
d. Close the book one last time and review what you do understand.

Students should be encouraged to think about rather than to memorize information. Students often ask for help without seeking a solution for themselves. By requiring them to specify what they do not understand (word, phrase, relationship) and to be able to explain what they did to try to understand it, this strategy encourages students to solve problems independently whenever possible. Thus, SMART enables students to develop their metacognitive abilities and to become more in control of their reading.

Underlining

Underlining, or highlighting, is the most popular aid used to study text. This study strategy requires that students know what is worth underlining or remembering, although underlining has not been shown to be any more effective than any other study technique. The major benefit of this study strategy, it seems, comes not from merely marking information but from rereading and from the decision of what to underline. This decision takes a certain amount of deep processing.

Have you ever seen a college textbook that was inundated with yellow highlighting? The reader apparently could not discriminate between important and unimportant information. Harris and Sipay (1990) suggested that students should be told not to underline until they have finished reading or surveying a headed section because waiting may reveal a summary statement. These authors also suggested at least a two-tiered system of underlining or highlighting to differentiate between important ideas. One two-tiered system of underlining consists of the full line side of the marker for major points and the half line side of the marker for less major points.

McAndrew (1983) made the following suggestions for using underlining:

1. Students should be given preunderlined material whenever possible.
2. Students should be given training in effective underlining, which is generally accomplished by copying short selections and having the teacher model good strategies for underlining and giving students feedback on their underlining.
3. Encourage students to underline superordinate general ideas.
4. Remind students that with underlining, less is more.
5. Students should use the time saved by underlining to study the material.
6. Students should know when to use some techniques other than underlining (p. 107).

Devine (1987) stated that "underlining is only one step from passivity" (p. 168) and suggested that making marginal comments and using personal coding systems (such as the INSERT method described in Chapter 10) facilitates the remembering of important points better than just underlining. With this caveat in mind, underlining is used widely and can be an effective study technique to record important ideas in text.

Taking Notes from Text

When students reach high school, teachers generally assume that they come there with the ability to take notes from text and during lecture. All too often, however, this skill is not taught explicitly by middle school teachers. The act of taking notes helps students learn and remember more information. Students who take notes recall up to 78 percent of the information they recorded, but only 5 to 34 percent of the information is retained when students did not record the information (Kiewra, 1984). Apparently, the act of taking notes facilitates a deeper processing of the information and greater attention is focused on the information recorded (Irvin & Rose, 1995). The two explanations generally offered for the effectiveness of notetaking are (1) the very act of taking notes heightens students' attention to information presented and engages them in active organization of this information, and (2) the storage function of notes aids in reviewing information before tests and other tasks (Davey & Bensky, 1989).

To take good notes, students must select what is worth recording. They must separate the major points from the minor ones and consider the relationship between ideas (Harris & Sipay, 1990). Students often merely copy the author's words, but to take good notes, they must be active readers.

Many middle school students have never been taught to take notes from a chapter. The best way to start teaching notetaking skills is to start simply and (1) model effective notetaking, (2) inform students how notetaking can help them and when to use it, and (3) give students time to practice and give feedback on their notes (Davey & Bensky, 1989). Some teachers insist that students take notes in a notebook reserved just for that class and have found it helpful to give out partial notes that require students to fill in the blanks. Over time, students are given more and more responsibility. Keep the following guidelines in mind when teaching notetaking.

1. Tell the students to examine the chapter first to get an idea of the overall structure.
2. Use a textbook with good subheadings.
3. Review notes from short sections before going on to longer ones.
4. Give students plenty of feedback and examples.
5. After taking notes from a textbook, students should be instructed to summarize the information using a summary, an outline, or a chapter map.
6. Most importantly, students should use the notes to study for a test.

Some schools have found it helpful to adopt a notetaking system that can be taught and reinforced in each class. One notetaking system that is the result of decades of research and is widely used is the divided page or Cornell notetaking method (Pauk, 1974). In this method, the paper is divided as shown in Figure 11.1. The important information is listed on the right side. In the left column a few key words are written that help students remember what is written on the right side. This example of notes was taken from a lecture on how the Cornell notetaking method works.

Taking Notes from Lecture

As with any other learning strategy, students who engage in self-questioning during the process use the strategy most efficiently. Spires and Stone (1989) encouraged students to ask the following kinds of questions before, during, and after the lecture.

Planning (before taking notes):

How interested am I in this topic?

If my interest is low, how do I plan to increase interest?

Do I feel motivated to pay attention?

What is my purpose for listening to this lecture?

How will I be assessed on this information?

Monitoring (while taking notes):

Am I maintaining a satisfactory level of concentration?

Am I taking advantage of the fact that thought is faster than speech?

Am I separating main concepts from supporting details?

What am I doing when comprehension fails?

What strategies am I using for comprehension failure?

Key Words	Notes
Preparing the system	1. Take a few minutes to review notes from previous lecture or text. 2. Use loose-leaf paper. 3. Use one side of paper only. 4. Draw a line ⅓ from the left side of the paper. 5. Write ideas and facts on the right side of the line. 6. Skip lines between major ideas.
Using the system	1. Record notes simply. 2. Do not make an outline. 3. Use abbreviation system. 4. Write neatly. 5. Leave space when daydreaming. 6. Strive for capturing the main ideas rather than details. 7. Record the lecturer's or text's examples that may clarify an abstract idea.
After the lecture or reading	1. Consolidate your notes. 2. Read through the notes. 3. Neaten the scribbles. 4. Reduce notes to concise topics. 5. Check or rethink key words. 6. Mark important ideas. 7. Box or underline assignments. 8. Reflect on your notes.
Review	1. Before class. 2. After class. 3. After study time. 4. On the run.
Review method	1. Cover right side of notes. 2. Using the key words in the column, recite aloud the facts and ideas of the lecture or reading in your own words.
Payoff	1. The procedure of reciting is the most powerful learning tool you can use. 2. Improved test scores. 3. Less time spent on study, better results.

FIGURE 11.1 The Cornell notetaking system

Source: Walter Pauk, *How to Study in College,* 3rd ed. Copyright © 1984 by Houghton Mifflin Company. Adapted with permission.

Evaluating (after taking notes):

Did I achieve my purpose?

Was I able to maintain satisfactory levels of concentration and motivation?

Did I deal with comprehension failures adequately?

Overall, do I feel that I processed the lecture at a satisfactory level? (p. 37)

Taking notes from text or during a lecture is a useful strategy throughout the school experience and in real-life situations. Notetaking helps students concentrate on important ideas and serves as a storage of these main ideas for further reference and study. Middle school teachers who prepare students to take and use good notes help students to meet the demands of high school with more success.

After Reading

After students have surveyed the chapter, asked questions, and read actively, they must organize what they have read to remember it and demonstrate their knowledge at a later time. Five strategies are presented in this remaining section: graphic organizers, outlining, summarizing, report writing, and question-answer relationships. Students choose which strategies meet their needs for organizing information to perform the criterion task.

Graphic Organizers

Graphic representations come in a variety of forms and have been found to be helpful to students for organizing information. Some of these graphic representations are designed to show ideas in a hierarchical fashion (graphic organizers, structured overviews, and pyramids). Others show the relationships and relative importance between concepts, words, or ideas (networks, concept maps, word maps). These graphic representations help students put information into a manageable format, show relationships between ideas, and increase the involvement of the reader (Irvin & Rose, 1995).

Many of the graphic organizers are presented in Chapters 6, 9, and 10, but chapter mapping is discussed in this chapter because it is a powerful tool to help students comprehend and remember the important ideas in a text or lecture (Armbruster & Anderson, 1980). Mapping helps students to understand the important relationships in the text by providing them with a visual outline of the logical connections between key ideas. This strategy helps students become more active readers or listeners, thus facilitating the all-important deep processing. Mapping can also help students organize difficult to understand or poorly written texts. A sample chapter map is presented in Figure 11.2.

Mapping adds a visual dimension to the concepts presented in a text, and thus may enhance comprehension and recall of information. Two or three students can work together to produce a more complete map. Discussion about what should and should not be included helps students to understand the process of distinguishing between important and unimportant information.

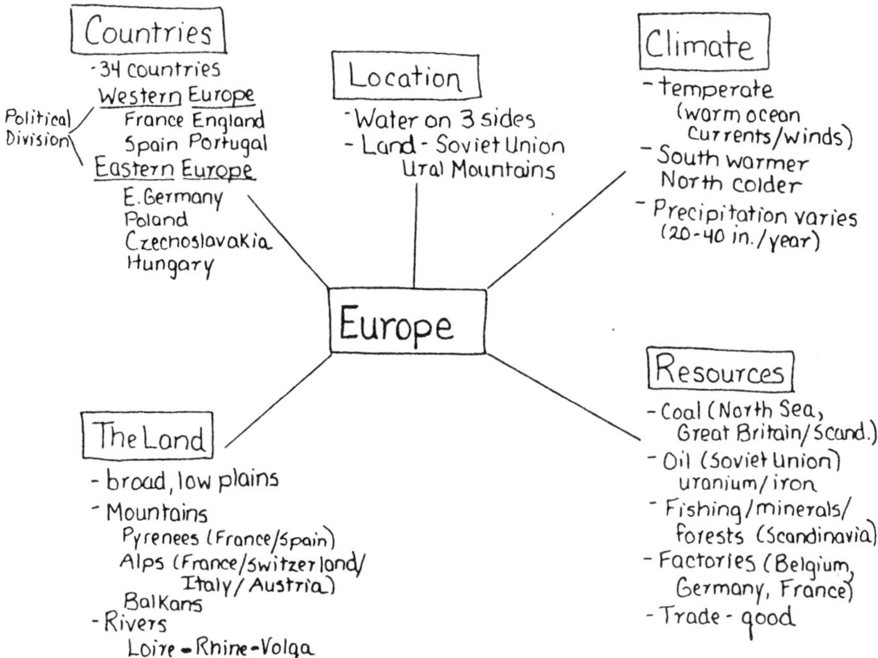

FIGURE 11.2 Map of Europe

Irwin-DeVitis and Pease (1995) suggested that graphic organizers can also serve an assessment function. The graphic organizer shown in Figure 11.3, for example, graphically represents the prior knowledge about AIDS (thin lines) and information learned from the unit of study (thicker lines). The teacher was able to detect misconceptions about the disease and use the map to engage students in self-evaluation of their own knowledge by writing a paper titled, "What They Still Need to Know about AIDS." Maps can also serve as study guides for tests or reports later.

Graphic organizers can be used to test understanding of concepts; for example, students were given thirty-two terms related to geometry and asked to construct a graphic organizer showing their relationships. Figure 11.4 shows two students' attempt to demonstrate understanding. An important feature of this task was the explanation provided about why they organized these concepts as they did, which served to clarify their thinking further.

Recent research "indicates that instructional graphics can help middle grade students learn from reading informational text. The effectiveness . . . is probably due to their role in helping students select and organize information in text. Apparently, involvement of readers in producing the graphics is an important factor in the success of this technique" (Armbruster, Anderson, & Meyer, 1990, p. 4). Many middle school teachers find graphic organizers indispensable for helping students activate and organize what they know and

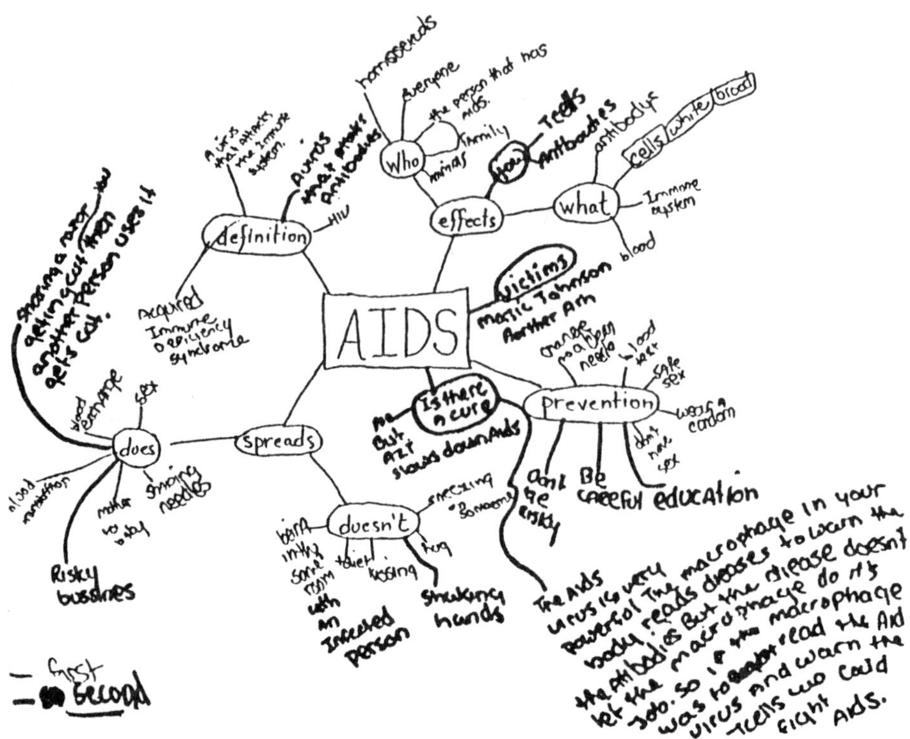

FIGURE 11.3 Map of student knowledge of AIDS

Reprinted with permission from Irwin-DeVitis, L. & Pease, D. (1995). Using graphic organizers for learning and assessment in middle level classrooms. *Middle School Journal, 26*(5), 57–64.

relate that knowledge to new learning. Graphic organizers serve as maps for where they have been and what they have learned and this powerful technique is flexible enough to adapt to a variety of subject matter.

Outlining

Outlining is one of the most popular methods of study. The process of outlining, however, is difficult for students because they must think through the logical relationships in the text before beginning the outline. This task requires analysis and synthesis and some students simply may not be cognitively ready to perform these operations. Some teachers have students make a map first and then move from the map to an outline.

Presuming the text is well organized, an outline can be a skeleton of a chapter, showing the main parts. If outlining is to be taught to middle grade students, the following steps are recommended by Devine (1987):

1. Discuss the plan of a formal outline.
2. Give the students an already completed outline in which the details are printed but the major headings are omitted. Students then fill in these major headings as they read.

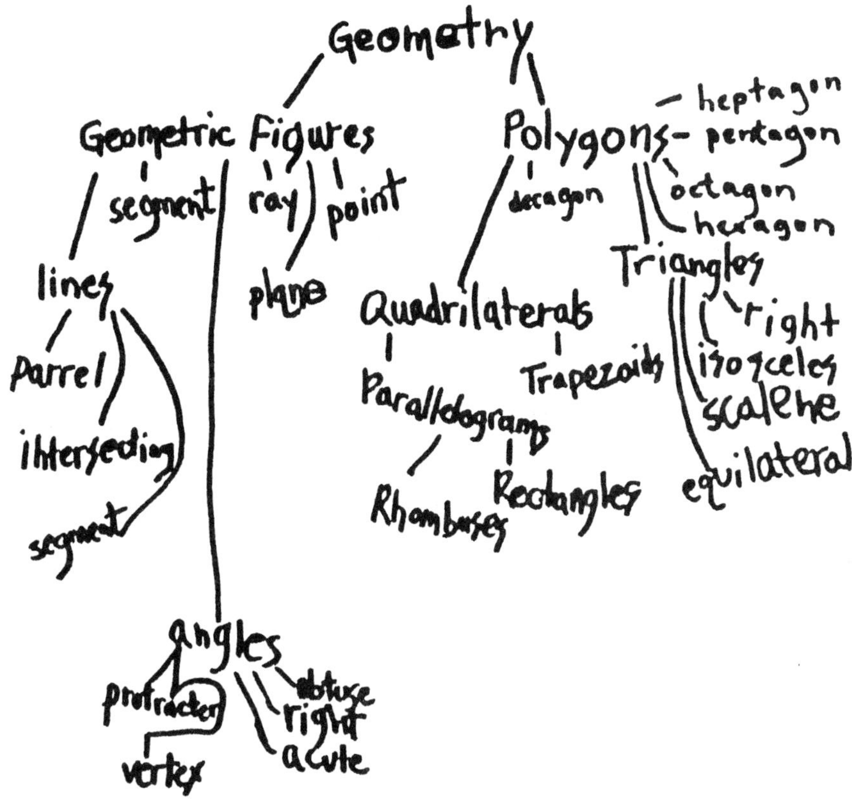

FIGURE 11.4 Concept map of geometry

Reprinted with permission from Irwin-DeVitis, L. & Pease, D. (1995). Using graphic organizers for learning and assessment in middle level classrooms. *Middle School Journal, 26*(5), 57–64.

3. Give the students an outline in which more slots are to be filled.
4. Give the students the outline skeleton, they fill in the information.
5. Tell the students the number of main headings in the chapter.
6. Finally, have students produce a complete outline without assistance.

Summarizing

Writing a summary is a complex activity and involves condensing information to the main ideas and reporting the gist or essence of text. Students must remember the most important ideas and omit the unimportant or irrelevant ideas. Paraphrasing and condensing information are two important skills in writing a good summary. Additionally, sensitivity to text structure is also necessary to identify the most important ideas. The activities involved in summarizing (identifying main ideas, paraphrasing, condensing information, sensitivity to text structure) are important metacognitive skills and, when internalized by the student, naturally lead to more thoughtful reading.

Summarizing information from text is a valuable study technique, but used infrequently in content areas (Vacca & Vacca, 1989). In the past decade, the effectiveness of summarizing as a learning strategy and a study skill is well documented. As with answering essay questions, the process of summarizing facilitates learning and metacognitive abilities and the product is useful to recall information for a later criterion task.

Writing summaries forces learners to use in-depth processing on the more important ideas in the text (Tei & Stewart, 1985) and composing a summary is a complex task that requires considerable skill (Baker & Brown, 1984). Researchers have documented clear developmental trends in summarizing (Brown & Day, 1983; Brown, Day, & Jones, 1983; Paris, Wasik, & Turner, 1991; Taylor, 1986; Winograd, 1984), and report that older and more proficient readers summarize better than younger and less skilled readers. More capable fourth- and fifth-grade summary writers planned before they wrote, used text structure as an aid in selecting and generalizing, recorded important information in their own words, and monitored the text to evaluate their own accuracy.

Effective summary writing is one ability that differentiates good from poor readers, and learning to summarize can improve poor readers' comprehension (Brown & Day, 1983). Teaching students to summarize can facilitate learning by helping readers clarify the meaning and significance of text (Brown, Campione, & Day, 1981; Doctorow, Wittrock, & Marks, 1970). Self-directed summarization can be an excellent comprehension monitoring activity (Hidi & Anderson, 1986). Poor readers, however, do not readily engage in self-directed summarization (Palincsar & Brown, 1983).

Although summary writing is a complex activity, it can be taught and the teaching of summarizing improves comprehension and recall of information. Summary writing is difficult for students to learn, especially for children below the sixth-grade level. Primary grade students often have difficulty identifying the central ideas of a text and condensing it into a concise form (Noyce & Christie, 1989). Therefore, initial attempts to teach summary writing should be as simple as possible. Hidi and Anderson (1986) suggested the following guidelines for teaching students to write good summaries.

1. Use brief passages at first and begin with the more familiar narrative text.
2. Use well organized texts with vocabulary and content that is familiar to students.
3. Keep text in view when young students write summaries. This reduces the burden of remembering information and focuses on the skill of summarizing. As students become more proficient in summarizing, the text can be taken away.
4. Keep initial summaries slightly shorter than the original text, which may involve a retelling of a story with the deletion of only the most trivial details.
5. Make initial summaries writer based; that is, initial attempts should be more like journal entries where the main focus is on content, not on the mechanics of writing. Once students become more proficient at writing summaries, they can be shared with other students and the teacher. Peer-editing groups are a good way to help students revise and perfect summaries prior to publication or grading (pp. 487–491).

Students should have sufficient practice summarizing orally so they can easily and confidently summarize aloud before being asked to compose written summaries. It is important for students to see and hear the teacher model summarizing. Teachers can summarize the day's activities, a story read aloud, or events in the lunch room. Students can be asked to summarize mathematics and science lessons, or give brief oral or written accounts of books they have read. Students who are not fluent writers can use tape recorders to record their summaries (Temple & Gillet, 1989).

Daily classroom activities provide numerous opportunities for teachers to model and students to practice summarizing. Teachers must model what they want students to be able to do. Research clearly indicates that summarizing is an important metacognitive and comprehension skill that deserves systematic attention in the classroom. Granted, students cannot be expected to become proficient at summarizing in the elementary grades, but much can be done to develop the ability during these years.

Hierarchical Summaries Taylor (1986) found that, as mentioned previously, middle grade students typically have difficulty in writing summaries. Summaries seem to present such difficulties because students must include only main ideas and exclude many details. Perhaps details are easier for middle grades students to grasp because they are more concrete than main ideas.

Taylor suggested using hierarchical summaries for middle school students. She contended that this summary-writing instruction is most successful when it is used with textbook material that is organized into headings. The following is an example using social studies content.

Step One: Students skim three to four pages, reading headings only.

Step Two: Students make a skeleton outline using a capital letter for every subsection designated by a heading. After reading three pages on the War of 1812, an eighth grader's summary looked like this:

The War of 1812

A. Causes of the War
B. War in the Northwest
C. The British Strike Back

Step Three: Students read material in full.

Step Four: For each section, students use the pertinent words from the heading that reflect the main idea of the section. Students should underline the main idea.

Step Five: Students write one to three detail sentences under each main idea. A full hierarchical summary is shown in Figure 11.5.

Students should formulate sentences in their own words and not copy from text. Teachers should show students how to generate both main idea and detail sentences used in these summaries. Taylor found that five or six sessions with hierarchical summaries were necessary before middle school students felt confident in making their own summaries.

Taylor also found that cooperative learning (see Chapter 4) techniques can be used effectively when writing summaries. For this strategy, students are divided into groups of three. Students take turns reading short segments from their content textbook. They also take turns generating main idea sentences for each topic and then together develop the best main idea sentence in their own words. Students then suggest two details from the subsection that they

The War of 1812

A. *A major cause of the war was that neither Great Britain nor France wanted the United States to deliver supplies to the other.*
   1. The United States tried to remain neutral.
   2. Great Britain and France both attacked American ships.

B. *Settlers in the Northwest Territory hoped war with Great Britain would give them a chance to claim land in Canada for themselves.*
   1. Land fighting was not successful.
   2. Captain Oliver Perry defeated the British fleet on Lake Erie.

C. *The British attacked Washington, D.C.*
   1. Dolly Madison saved the famous portrait of George Washington.
   2. The president's home was painted white to cover burned places—the White House.

FIGURE 11.5 Hierarchical summary

feel are important to remember. Everyone writes the skeleton outline. The same procedure is repeated for every subsection in the selection. When this process is finished, the group develops one or two sentences that best reflect the main idea of the entire section.

Writing Reports

One of the most difficult tasks for middle grades students is writing informational reports. The problem seems to be that report writing requires a more formal style of language than they are accustomed to writing (Fisher & Terry, 1990). To many students, writing a report means copying out of an encyclopedia. Like answering essay questions and writing good summaries, report writing is complex and involves components such as taking notes, organizing information, and actually writing the report.

Essentially, a report is a piece of writing in which students must take a body of information, interpret and summarize it, give it some personal perspective, and present it in some acceptable form (Nessel, Jones, & Dixon, 1989). Report writing has two purposes: (1) to help learners understand material better by organizing and shaping it for others, and (2) to provide teachers with immediate feedback on the success of lessons (Devine, 1987). Although report writing is often a test of will and tenacity, properly introduced, this task can serve as a vehicle for learning new information and new skills.

A report should not be a task that is carried out only to receive a grade or to prepare for stiffer report requirements the next school year. Rather, a report should be a task to "unearth interesting information and put it in a form that would be interesting to others" (Nessel, Jones, & Dixon, 1989, p. 217). Suggestions for activities that prepare students to write good reports without the usual pain and agony include prewriting activities, recording information, and reporting without words.

Good reports follow from good prewriting activities because report writing is merely an extension of the reading-thinking process (Nessel, Jones, & Dixon, 1989). Before beginning to read about the topic, students should be encouraged to brainstorm the topic using a Know, Want-to-Know, Learn (K-W-L) (Ogle, 1989) strategy or mapping activity. To avoid copying from encyclopedias, teachers should supply only source materials that are easy to read. "Children cannot paraphrase from an encyclopedia they cannot read and understand, they can only copy" (Temple & Gillet, 1989, p. 288). Source material should be displayed and discussed so that going to the library does not become an overwhelming and defeating exercise.

Students can learn much about report writing by collecting and recording their own data before writing. Observations, surveys, measurements, and comparisons both in and out of the classroom provide rich opportunities for students to collect and organize data and construct a written report of the results. Children can use experiences with recording as a basis for more formal report writing later in their school careers.

Devine (1987) suggested that "reporting without words" can be a useful technique to encourage students to decide what is the most important information to present, to organize information, and to present it in a form that lends itself to understanding the material. Visual representations of information include pie graphs, bar graphs, organizational charts, models, maps, and pictographs. A report without words can reveal much about a student's understanding of a topic. Guiding questions can help students read and interpret information. Devine suggested some of the following questions: What is the title? What is its purpose? Why are you using it? What type is it? Are there verbal explanations? Where? Do you understand them? What symbols are used? What do the symbols mean? Is a key given? (p. 272). Visual representations of information can help students organize and synthesize information and can give the teacher insights into what students have learned.

Beach (1983) suggested that students should be taken through the report writing process at least four times a year. Teachers can ensure a successful experience if students have input into selecting their own topic, sources are organized for students, prewriting activities are designed, and immediate feedback is given.

Answering Questions

Answering questions after reading is a common practice in schools. Often, students do not receive much instruction in how to answer these questions successfully. Raphael (1981; 1982; 1984a; 1986; Raphael & Pearson, 1985) developed Question-Answer Relationship (QAR), illustrated in Figure 11.6, to assist students with using information from the text and from their head to answer questions.

QAR instruction begins with students classifying various types of questions according to how they can be answered. Teachers then model the thinking processes required in answering these questions and provide practice opportunities. "Students learn to consider information both in the text as well as information from their experiential background" (Helfeldt & Henk, 1990, p. 510). From her extensive work with QAR, Raphael (1984b) concluded that "it appears that for students from fourth to eighth grade, teaching them about information sources both sensitizes them to task demands of questions and improves the quality of their answers. Students of average and low reading ability tend to demonstrate the greatest improvement" (p. 310).

In the Book	In My Head
Right There: The answer is in the text and easy to find. The words used to develop the question and to answer the question are RIGHT THERE in the same sentence.	**Author and You:** The answer is not in the text. You need to think about what you already know, what information the author provided in the text, and how it fits together.

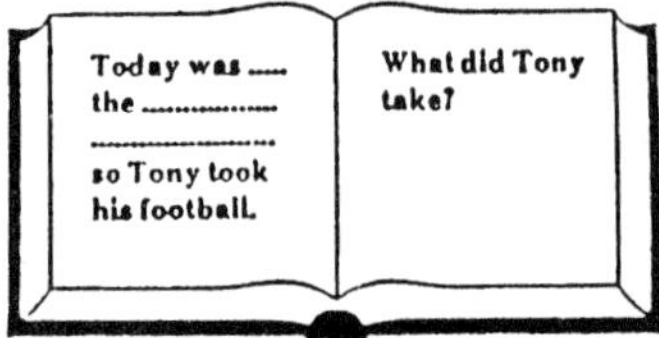

Think and Search *(Putting together)*: The answer is in the story but you need to put together different parts of the story to find the answer. Words for the question and for the answer are not found in the same sentence. They come from different parts of the text.

On My Own: The answer is not in the text. You can even answer the question without reading the story. You need to use your own experiences.

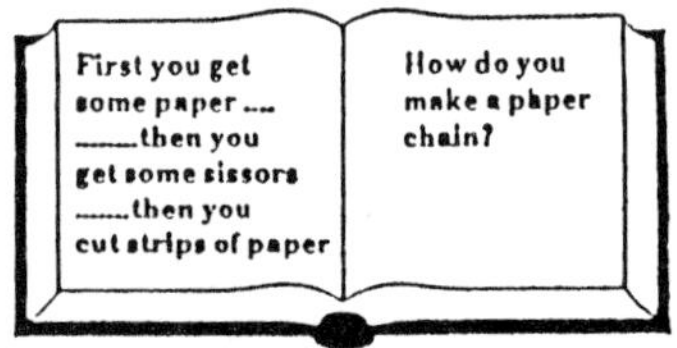

FIGURE 11.6 Question-answer relationship

From Raphael, Taffy E. (1984, January). Teaching learners about sources of information for answering comprehension questions. *Journal of Reading, 27*(4), 303–311. Reprinted with permission of Taffy E. Raphael and the International Reading Association. All rights reserved.

Summary

Students read to pass tests, write reports, and complete assignments; that is, students are reading for a purpose, often a purpose defined by someone else. Study skills are strategies that enable students to meet these purposes. Study skills enable students to learn and remember the material that they read.

To study effectively, students must know *what* to study. The teacher must carefully define the criterion task—the task that students will be expected to perform after studying. Beyond this, students must learn *how* to study effectively and efficiently. Students must learn how to grasp a main idea, how to summarize information, and how to interrelate or synthesize information. They must learn how to check their comprehension and how to adjust their reading rate to the demands of the task. Students must also learn how to take effective notes from text. In short, students must learn how to achieve a deep understanding of the material they are to study. Study skills are the strategies that serve as the means to this end.

References

Andre, M.D.A. & Anderson, T.H. (1978–1979). The development and evaluation of a self-questioning study technique. *Reading Research Quarterly, 14*(4), 605–623.

Anderson, T.H. (1979). Study skills and learning strategies. In H.F. O'Neil, Jr. & C.D. Speilberger (Eds.), *Cognitive and Affective Learning Strategies* (pp. 77–98). New York: Academic Press.

Anderson, T.H. & Armbruster, B.B. (1984). Studying. In P.D. Pearson (Ed.), *Handbook of Reading Research* (pp. 657–679). New York: Longman.

Armbruster, B.B. & Anderson, T.H. (1980). *The Effect of Mapping on the Free Recall of Expository Text.* Urbana, IL: Center for the Study of Reading. (ED 182 735).

Armbruster, B.B., Anderson, T.H., & Meyer, J.L. (1990). *Improving Content Area Reading Using Instructional Graphics.* (Technical Report No. 508). Champaign, IL: Center for the Study of Reading.

Baker, L. (1979). *Do I Understand or Do I Not Understand: That Is the Question.* Champaign, IL: Center for the Study of Reading. (ED 174 948).

Baker, L. & Brown, A.L. (1984). Metacognitive skills and reading. In P.D. Pearson (Ed.), *Handbook of Reading Research* (pp. 353–394). New York: Longman.

Beach, J.D. (1983). Teaching students to write informational reports. *Elementary School Journal, 84*(2), 213–220.

Brown, A.L. (1980). *Learning and Development: The Problems of Compatibility, Access, and Induction* (Technical Report No. 165). Champaign, IL: Center for the Study of Reading. (ED 221 823).

Brown, A.L. (1982). Learning to learn how to read. In J. Langer, & T. Smith-Burke (Eds.), *Reader Meets Author, Bridging the Gap: A Psycholinguistic and Sociolinguistic Perspective* (pp. 26–54). Newark, DE: International Reading Association.

Brown, A.L. (1985). *Teaching Students to Think as They Read: Implications for Curriculum Reform.* (Technical Report No. 58). Champaign, IL: Center for the Study of Reading.

Brown, A.L., Campione, J.C., & Day, J. (1981). Learning to learn: On training students to learn from texts. *Educational Researcher, 10*(7), 14–21.

Brown, A.L. & Day, J.D. (1983). *Macrorules for Summarizing Texts: The Development of Expertise* (Technical Report No. 270). Champaign, IL: Center for the Study of Reading.

Brown, A.L., Day, J.D., & Jones, R.S. (1983). The development of plans for summarizing texts. *Child Development, 54*(4), 968–979.

Brown, A.L. & Smiley, S.S. (1977). Rating the importance of structural units of prose passages: A problem of metacognitive development. *Child Development, 48*(1), 1–8.

Carver, R.P. (1992). Reading rate: Theory, research, and practical implications. *Journal of Reading, 36*(2), 84–95.

Commander, N.E. & Smith, B.D. (1996). Learning logs: A tool for cognitive monitoring. *Journal of Reading, 39*(6), 446–453.

Dansereau, D.F. (1977). How to create and maintain a crummy mood. In D.F. Dansereau (Ed.), *Instructional Packet: Techniques of College Learning.* Fort Worth, TX: Texas Christian University.

Davey, B. & Bensky, S. (1989). Direct instruction in notetaking. *Middle School Journal, 20*(3), 31–33.

Devine, T.G. (1987). *Teaching Study Skills.* Boston, MA: Allyn & Bacon.

Doctorow, M., Wittrock, M.C., & Marks, C. (1970). Generative processes in reading comprehension. *Journal of Applied Psychology, 70*(2), 109–118.

Fisher, C.J. & Terry, C.A. (1990). *Children's Language and the Language Arts: A Literature-Based Approach.* Boston: Allyn & Bacon.

Harris, A.J. & Sipay, E.R. (1990). *How to Increase Reading Ability.* New York: Longman.

Helfeldt, J.P. & Henk, W.A. (1990). Reciprocal question-answer relationships: An instructional technique for at-risk readers. *Journal of Reading, 33*(7), 509–515.

Hidi, S. & Anderson, V. (1986). Producing written summaries: Task demands, cognitive operations, and implications for instruction. *Review of Educational Research, 56*(4), 473–493.

Hoffman, S. (1983). Using student journals to teach study skills. *Journal of Reading, 26*(4), 344–347.

Irvin, J.L. & Rose, E.O. (1995). *Starting Early with Study Skills: A Week-by-Week Guide for Elementary Students.* Boston: Allyn & Bacon.

Irwin-DeVitis, L. & Pease, D. (1995). Using graphic organizers for learning and assessment in middle level classrooms. *Middle School Journal, 26*(5), 57–64.

Jacobowitz, T. (1988). Using theory to modify practice: An illustration with SQ3R. *Journal of Reading, 32*(2), 126–131.

Kiewra, K. (1984). Acquiring effective notetaking skills: An alternative to professional notetaking. *Journal of Reading, 27*(4), 299.

Langer, J.A. (1986). Learning through writing: Study skills in the content areas. *Journal of Reading, 29*(5), 400–406.

McAndrew, D.A. (1983). Underlining and notetaking: Some suggestions from research. *Journal of Reading, 27*(2), 103–108.

McCormick, S. & Cooper, J.O. (1991). Can SQ3R facilitate secondary learning disabled students' literal comprehension of expository text?: Three experiments. *Reading Psychology, 12*(3), 239–271.

Meyer, B.J.F., Brandt, D.M., & Bluth, G.J. (1980). Use of top-level structure in text: Key for reading comprehension of ninth-grade students. *Reading Research Quarterly, 16*(1), 72–103.

Meyer, G. (1934). An experimental study of the old and new types of examination: The effect of the examination set on memory. *Journal of Educational Psychology, 25*(7), 641–660.

Meyer, G. (1935). An experimental study of the old and new types of examination: II. Methods of study. *Journal of Educational Psychology, 26*(1), 30–40.

Meyer, G. (1936). The effects on recall and recognition of the examination set in classroom situations. *Journal of Educational Psychology, 27*(2), 81–99.

Nessel, D.D., Jones, M.B., & Dixon, C.N. (1989). *Thinking Through the Language Arts.* New York: Macmillan Publishing Company.

Nolan, T.E. (1991). Self-questioning and prediction: Combining metacognitive strategies. *Journal of Reading, 5*(2), 132–141.

Noyce, R.M. & Christie, J.F. (1989). *Integrating Reading and Writing Instruction in Grades K-8.* Boston: Allyn & Bacon.

Ogle, D.M. (1989). The know, want-to-know, learn strategy. In K.D. Muth (Ed.), *Children's Comprehension of Text* (pp. 205–223). Newark, DE: International Reading Association.

Palincsar, A.S. & Brown, A.L. (1983). Reciprocal teaching of comprehension-monitoring activities (Technical Report No. 269). Champaign, IL: Center for the Study of Reading.

Paris, S.G., Newman, R.S., & McVey, K.A. (1983). Learning the functional significance of mnemonic actions: A microgenetic study of strategy acquisition. *Journal of Experimental Child Psychology, 34*(3), 490–509.

Paris, S.G., Wasik, B.A., & Turner, J.C. (1991). The development of strategic readers. In R. Barr, M. Kamil, P.B. Mosenthal, & P.D. Pearson (Eds.), *Handbook of Reading Research: Volume II* (pp. 609–640). New York: Longman.

Pauk, W. (1974). *How to Study in College.* Boston: Houghton Mifflin.

Raphael, T.E. (1981). *The Effect of Metacognitive Awareness Training on Students' Question-Answering Strategies.* Unpublished doctoral dissertation, University of Illinois, Champaign-Urbana, IL.

Raphael, T.E. (1982). Question-answering strategies for children. *The Reading Teacher, 36*(2), 186–191.

Raphael, T.E. (1984a). Contexts of school-based literacy: A look toward the future. In T. Raphael (Ed.), *The Contexts of School-Based Literacy* (pp. 295–309). New York: Random House.

Raphael, T.E. (1984b). Teaching learners about sources of information for answering comprehension questions. *Journal of Reading, 27*(4), 303.

Raphael, T.E. (1986). Teaching question-answer relationships, revisited. *The Reading Teacher, 39*(6), 516–522.

Raphael, T.E. & Pearson, P.D. (1985). Increasing students' awareness of sources of information for answering questions. *American Educational Research Journal, 22*(2), 217–235.

Robinson, F.P. (1970). *Effective Study.* New York: Harper and Brothers.

Schmidt, C.M., Barry, A., Maxworthy, A.G., & Huebsch, W.R. (1989). But I read the chapter twice. *Journal of Reading, 32*(5), 428.

Spires, H.A. & Stone P.D. (1989). The directed note-taking activity: A self-questioning approach. *Journal of Reading, 33*(1), 36–39.

Taylor, B.M. (1986). Teaching middle grade students to summarize content textbook material. In J.F. Baumann (Ed.), *Teaching Main Idea Comprehension* (pp. 195–209). Newark, DE: International Reading Association.

Tei, E. & Stewart, O. (1985). Effective studying from text: Applying metacognitive strategies. *Forum for Reading, 16*(2), 46–55.

Temple, C. & Gillet, J.W. (1989). *Language Arts Learning Processes and Teaching Practices.* Glenview, IL: Scott Foresman.

Tierney, R.J. & Pearson, P.D. (1981). *Learning to Learn from Text: A Framework for Improving Classroom Practice.* (ED 205 917).

Tonjes, M.J., & Zintz, M.V. (1981). Teaching Reading/Thinking/Study Skills in Content Classrooms. Dubuque, IA: William C. Brown Publishers.

United States Department of Education (1986). *What Works: Research about Teaching and Learning.* Washington, D.C.: United States Department of Education.

Vacca, R.T. & Vacca, J.L. (1989). *Content Area Reading.* Glenview, IL: Scott Foresman.

Vaughn J.L. & Estes, T.H. (1986). *Reading and Reasoning Beyond the Primary Grades.* Boston: Allyn & Bacon.

Winograd, P. (1984). Strategic difficulties in summarizing texts. *Reading Research Quarterly, 19*(4), 404–425.

Chapter 12

Middle Level Schools

The rhetoric of restructuring in education is pervasive. For middle level educators, however, transforming school organizations into interdisciplinary teams of teachers, creating positive school climates, implementing advisory programs, and shared decision making are not new. Perhaps because this level of education was neglected for so long, middle level educators banded together to form a middle school concept or movement which has become a philosophy of a developmentally appropriate schooling experience for young adolescents.

It is not difficult to convince parents and educators that students aged 10 to 14 are in a unique period of life. This period is characterized by significant changes in physical, emotional, social, and cognitive characteristics of students. The term *middle school* generally refers to a school for young adolescents that is seeking to follow a certain philosophical orientation called the *middle school concept.* Most of these schools consist of grades 6 through 8 but they may be organized in a variety of different ways: grades 5 through 8 or, commonly, grades 7 and 8. In recent years *middle level* has emerged as a term that refers to the full range of grades 5 through 9.

Schools for young adolescents, traditionally the junior high school, were modeled from the high school. These junior high schools adopted rigid departmentalization, competitive sports, and the curriculum of the high school. Middle level educators have for almost three decades worked hard to design and implement schools that are more responsive to the developmental needs of young adolescents. In this chapter, the history of the middle school movement will be traced, efforts by national organizations to provide a vision for middle schools will be described, the status and progress of programs and practices normally associated with the middle concept will be reported, and issues for the future of middle level education will be discussed.

Perspectives of the Middle School Movement

In a predominantly agrarian society, early U.S. schools were small, one room houses that provided the basics of an education for that time. As population increased, some students went to preparatory schools (boys) or finishing schools (girls). Eventually, two distinct levels of education emerged—the elementary school and the high school.

In the early 1900s, however, a number of national committees issued reports relating to the 8-4 plan and a change to the 6-6 plan was often proposed. The 6-6 plan meant that a student would spend six years in elementary school and six years in high school. It was first advocated as a means of improving college preparation but soon was tied to other objectives. High dropout and retention rates, the need for better transition from self-contained system elementary schools to departmentalized high schools, and the newly scientifically discovered extent of individual differences supported the need to reorganize.

Although the initial effort was a downward extension of secondary education (8-4 to 6-6), the notion of dividing the six years of secondary education into junior and senior periods appeared early in the discussions and was specifically recommended in the famous *Cardinal Principles of Secondary Education* (Commission on the Reorganization of Secondary Education, 1918). The rationale for establishing separate junior high schools was rather compelling and not unlike the justification for contemporary middle schools.

In 1910, the first official junior high school opened its doors in Columbus, Ohio. A surprisingly rapid growth of such schools occurred: in 1924, 880 junior high schools were operational, by 1963 the number increased to over 7000 (Lounsbury & Vars, 1978). Junior high schools were just that—*junior* high schools. The typical junior high school soon became largely indistinguishable from the high school in its organization and operation. Departmentalization, competitive athletic programs, and related activities mimicked the high school. The junior high school became big and impersonal and seemed unable to serve young adolescents as intended.

In 1966, Donald Eichhorn wrote *The Middle School* in which he advocated schools that met the needs of students aged 10 to 14 and that provided for a smoother transition from the self-contained elementary school to the departmentalized high school. Lounsbury (1992) cited three major sources for the rapid acceptance of middle schools as a valid educational replacement of the junior high school. First, he cited dissatisfaction with the junior high school as it had evolved primarily from the ranks of educators. Second, Sputnik-induced obsession with academic mastery advocated moving the ninth grade to the high school leaving middle schools free of high school credit and more able to meet the needs of their clientele (Alexander & Williams, 1965). The third factor resulted from "scientific evidence that documented the earlier maturation of young people" (p. 220), arguing that today's sixth grader is more like yesterday's seventh and eighth grader. The new grade configuration of 5-6-7-8 or 6-7-8 began to take hold.

On the surface, one might assume that this massive change in grade configuration was accomplished for programmatic reasons. Other factors, however, seemed to dominate the decisions of school district educators to move to a middle school grade configuration. Many schools reorganized to meet the demands of racial desegregation and population shifts. Moving grades around in a district and busing students often accomplished the goals of desegregation. In addition, the baby boom hit. Elementary schools were bursting and high schools were struggling to remain open. Moving sixth graders out of the elementary school and ninth graders into the high school seemed to alleviate shifting demographic patterns. Unfortunately, with the reorganization, many middle schools were, in name only, retaining the programs and practices of junior high schools. During the next two decades, though, middle schools came of age programmatically. The middle school as a concept, rather than a grade configuration, is now firmly rooted in U.S. education.

The Middle School Defined

Two national organizations—the National Middle School Association and the National Association of Secondary School Principals—have defined and advocated middle level education as it is today. Through their publications, conferences, and work with state and local education agencies, these two organizations not only provided the impetus and support for the establishment of the middle school concept, but also defined it along the way.

National Middle School Association

The first association of middle school leaders, the Midwest Middle School Association, decided in 1973 to go national. By 1976, the membership surpassed one thousand members and National Middle School Association (NMSA) currently has more than ten thousand members. The association also has an array of publications including the popular *Middle School Journal* and *Research in Middle Level Education Quarterly.* The NMSA holds large annual conferences, provides support services, and acts as advocate of issues for young adolescents nationally. The mission of the organization reads:

> *National Middle School Association is dedicated to improving the educational experiences of young adolescents by providing vision, knowledge, and resources to all who serve them in order to develop healthy, productive, and ethical citizens.*

In addition, fifty-three state, provincial, regional, and international affiliates associated with the NMSA enroll additional thousands of members. These affiliates publish newsletters and journals, hold annual conferences, and render other support services.

This We Believe (National Middle School Association, 1982; 1992; 1995) is a position statement first published in 1982 by founders of the organization, revised in 1992, and then, after input from the board of trustees, the council of chairs, and the membership at large, the 1995 edition was released. This edition captured the heart and soul of the middle school concept within the framework of the current context of schooling. Briefly, this important position paper includes the following:

> The National Middle School Association believes: *Developmentally responsive middle level schools are characterized by:*
>
> *Educators committed to young adolescents*
> *A shared vision*
> *High expectations for all*
> *An adult advocate for every student*
> *Family and community partnerships*
> *A positive school climate*

Therefore, developmentally responsive middle level schools provide:

Curriculum that is challenging, integrative, and exploratory
Varied teaching and learning approaches
Assessment and evaluation that promote learning
Flexible organizational structures
Programs and policies that foster health, wellness, and safety
Comprehensive guidance and support services

The National Association of Secondary School Principals

The National Association of Secondary School Principals (NASSP)is one of the nation's strongest professional associations and many of its members have responsibility for the middle level grades. The Association's Middle Level Council, appointed in 1981, has provided extensive services for middle level educators such as special middle level publications (including the journal *Schools in the Middle*), regular conferences, and information sharing. This group initiated the designation of National Middle Level Education Week in 1987 and continues to promote it each March in collaboration with the National Middle School Association. The Middle Level Council authored *An Agenda for Excellence* (1985), a series of publications providing vision for middle school practices.

Three studies were commissioned by the NASSP to collect longitudinal data, each study being more comprehensive than the previous one. *The Junior High Principalship* (Rock & Hemphill, 1966), *The Middle Level Principalship: A Survey of Middle Level Principals and Programs* (Valentine, Clark, Nickerson, & Keefe, 1981), and *Leadership in Middle Level Education: A National Survey of Middle Level Leaders and Their Schools* (Valentine, Clark, Irvin, Keefe, & Melton, 1992) focused primarily on leadership perceptions and roles but also documented programs, practices, issues, and trends in middle level schools.

Impetus for the Middle School

In the summer of 1989, when the Carnegie Council on Adolescent Development released *Turning Points: Preparing Youth for the 21st Century,* the report startled educators and the public alike because of its thorough presentation and analysis of the plight of youth in the United States. The very prestigious task force, including then Governor Bill Clinton, claimed that "early adolescence (aged 10 to 15) is a time when many youth choose a path toward a productive and fulfilling life. For many others, it represents their last best chance to avoid a diminished future" (p. 8). Additionally, they concluded that middle grade schools must be more assertive in the role they play in the lives of young adolescents.

After an examination of the nation's youth and how well middle grade schools, health institutions, and community organizations serve them, the task force formulated eight recommendations:

1. Create small communities for learning.
2. Teach a core academic program.
3. Ensure success for all students.

4. Empower teachers and administrators to make decisions about the experiences of middle grade students.
5. Staff middle grade schools with teachers who are expert at teaching young adolescents.
6. Improve academic performance through fostering the health and fitness of young adolescents.
7. Reengage families in the education of young adolescents.
8. Connect schools with communities (pp. 9–10).

These recommendations coincided with the existing advocacy of middle level educators and associations such as the National Middle School Association. A flurry of new activity relative to middle level schools has resulted in state departments of education and local school districts. Work toward evaluating current practices and implementing changes in line with the Carnegie recommendations is ongoing in nearly every state and school district.

State efforts to reform middle level education have been effective. The California Department of Education published the provocative *Caught in the Middle: Educational Reform for Young Adolescents in California Public Schools* (California State Department of Education, 1987), which presented a reform agenda for the middle grades. In Maryland the department published *What Matters in the Middle Grades* (Maryland Task Force on Middle Learning Years, 1989), and several other states have either legislation or position statements consistent with the goals of national education associations. The local, state, and national efforts in middle level education have escalated in the past decade to support the middle school concept.

Turning Points was the first policy report published by the Carnegie Council, which was followed by *Fateful Choices: Healthy Youth for the 21st Century* (1992a) and *A Matter of Time: Risk and Opportunity in the Nonschool Hours* (1992b). *Great Transitions: Preparing Adolescents for a New Century* (Carnegie Council on Adolescent Development, 1996) concluded the decade of examination of adolescence. In this final report, the authors made recommendations concerning reengaging families, educating young adolescents for a changing world, promoting the health of adolescents, strengthening communities, and redirecting the pervasive power of the media. Sustained efforts by educators and the general community are necessary to implement the Carnegie recommendations if they are to make an impact on the lives of young adolescents.

A Status Report on Programs and Practices

As the middle school evolved, middle level educators found specific programs and practices essential to meet the needs of young adolescents. Interdisciplinary team organization, advisor-advisee programs, and full and rich exploratory experiences became "signature practices" of middle level education. Many of these programs and practices, of course, have been implemented in elementary schools and high schools through the years. Middle level educators, however, have persisted in refining these programs and practices and generally they are systematically and concurrently implemented in middle schools.

In a thorough review of the literature, Ritzenthaler (1993) found "the language used to describe these programs and practices . . . highly consistent in statements of essential characteristics or elements of the middle school program" (p. 20). After reviewing the work of middle level educators (Alexander & George, 1981; Eichhorn, 1966; Georgiady & Romano, 1974; Irvin, 1992), national associations (*An Agenda for Excellence,* 1985; *This We Believe,* 1982; 1992; *Turning Points,* 1989; Valentine, Clark, Nickerson, & Keefe, 1982; Valentine, Clark, Irvin, Keefe, & Melton, 1992), and national studies or programs and practices of middle level schools (Alexander, 1968; Alexander & McEwin, 1989; Cawelti, 1988; Epstein & Mac Iver, 1990), Ritzenthaler concluded that the five most essential elements of a middle level school were (1) interdisciplinary team organization, (2) an advisory program, (3) an exploratory and activities program, (4) varied instruction and assessment procedures, and (5) a program for transition into, within, and out of the middle level school.

Although grade configuration cannot predict programs consistent with the middle school philosophy, many schools moved from a junior high configuration to a middle school configuration to begin the implementation of the concept. The NASSP studies mentioned previously substantiate a clear trend toward 6-7-8 grade configuration: from 5 percent (1966) to 15 percent (1981) to 50 percent (1992). Alexander and McEwin (1989) reported 40 percent 6-7-8 schools, which further verifies the trend to the new predominant 6-7-8 grade configuration.

Interdisciplinary Team Organization

Teams of teachers assigned a common group of students sharing a common planning time generally defines interdisciplinary team organization in a middle level school. At the very least, teams of teachers share information about students, plan team activities, and coordinate grading, homework, and parent conferences. When teams work most effectively together, they function as a unit for their group of students. They schedule and reschedule students, using blocks of time to meet the needs of their students. Fully functioning teams work with unified arts teachers to present an integrated curriculum generally organized around themes of interest and relevance to students. Students are given the opportunity to explore content while at the same time to learn basic skills.

Teams serve an affective function as well; they provide identification with a small group of teachers and students who share common concerns. Ideally, teams provide varied instructional and assessment strategies in an emotionally safe environment and provide for transition into, within, and out of the middle level school.

Alexander and McEwin (1989) reported 33 percent implementing teaming, Epstein and Mac Iver (1990) reported 42 percent and the NASSP (Valentine et al., 1992) reported 57 percent of the schools had partial or full implementation of teaming. Interdisciplinary team organization was implemented most in 6-7-8 schools (66 percent) and least in 7-8-9 schools (40 percent). Teaming is offered to more sixth graders (55 percent) than seventh graders (46 percent), and least to eighth graders (38 percent). Teaming is nearly nonexistent in the ninth grade. Interdisciplinary team organization has taken a firm hold in the nation's middle level schools and "much of the research on teaming points to the potentially positive effects of the team structure on student and faculty affect" (Van Zandt & Totten, 1995).

Most teams have team leaders and many teamed teachers have both a common planning time and an individual planning time. McEwin, Dickinson, and Jenkins (1996) considered adequate team planning time to be a measure of team effectiveness concluding that "where it exists, teams have the opportunity to coordinate curriculum and instruction for their common clients. Where it is absent, teams face a daunting agenda of time and effort without support. When teams without adequate common planning time wither, it is understandable" (p. 40).

Advisor-Advisee Programs

Most adults recognize that early adolescence is a difficult time of life. Not only are students struggling with physical, emotional, social, and cognitive changes, but the stimulating and sometimes confusing society also provides additional pressure. Effective advisory programs provide students with the opportunity to know and be known well by at least one adult in the school. A time is set apart during the day (usually twenty minutes) for students to meet with their advisor. Sometimes team activities are planned, sometimes students discuss current events or personal concerns, sometimes advisor groups read a book together. Whatever the structure, advisory programs provide students a pause during the day to spend some time on their concerns.

McEwin, Dickinson, and Jenkins (1996) reported that advisory programs had increased from 39 percent (1988) to 47 percent (1993). In middle schools having a 6-7-8 grade configuration, 52 percent of the schools reported having advisory programs. Advisory programs are implemented to provide another vehicle for creating a caring learning environment for young adolescents. Although some middle level educators are ambivalent about these programs (Valentine et al., 1992), when implemented properly, as mentioned, they do provide for every student to know and be known by at least one thoughtful adult in the school.

Exploratory Programs and Student Activities

Exploratory opportunities for students are generally defined as unified arts (art, music, technology education), student activities (newspaper, student government), and mini-courses (photography, archaeology). These opportunities, including intramural sports, have a "no cut" policy; that is, all students may participate if they choose. Good middle schools provide all of these exploratory experiences for students. In a study of exemplary middle level schools, George and Shewey (1994) found that 72 percent of these schools implemented an extracurricular program based on the needs of young adolescents, "providing regular success experiences for all students [that] has contributed to the long-term effectiveness of [the] middle school program" (p. 100).

More important, however, than the structured courses and activities is an attitude of exploration that pervades the school. Students are encouraged to pursue topics of interest during social studies, choose among acceptable books to read in language arts, and work on relevant problems in math and science.

In the Valentine et al. (1992) study, most schools (88 percent) reported partial or full implementation of required exploratory courses, cocurricular programs (60 percent), and intramural activities (69 percent) for all students. Student government, career days, musical groups, student clubs, drama, and publications are the most commonly offered cocurricular activities. It is more difficult to access a pervasive attitude of exploration within defined course offerings, but this attitude is shifting toward more student involvement with the implementation of a more integrated curriculum.

Varied Instructional Strategies and Appropriate Assessment Procedures

Much time and energy has been invested in (1) reorganizing teachers into teams, (2) providing meaningful advisory experiences, (3) improving school climates, and (4) providing opportunities for students to explore content and their own evolving nature. Unfortunately, not much has changed inside the walls of the classroom.

McEwin, Dickinson and Jenkins (1996) found that direct instruction (approximately 89 percent) predominated the instructional strategies used by middle level teachers followed by cooperative learning (approximately 52 percent), inquiry teaching (about 35 percent), and independent study (about 19 percent) in middle schools with a 6-7-8 grade configuration.

Recent "shadow studies" (Lounsbury & Clark, 1990; Lounsbury & Johnson, 1988) provided an "inside the classroom" perspective. Prevailing practices seem to indicate that middle grades students (1) are not provided a curriculum that is relevant or integrated; (2) are bored with the endless worksheets, tests, and copying from the chalkboard; (3) are not challenged to think critically or become involved in the decisions of learning; (4) are often "tracked" with the same students all day and all year; and (5) are not given time to interact with peers, especially within a learning context. It is little wonder that young adolescents today do not seem motivated to learn.

Developmentally appropriate assessment procedures at all levels of schooling dominate educational literature and professional conferences. However, Valentine et al (1992) found that the predominant grade reporting procedure remains the letter scale grade (70 to 83 percent). Some schools are using S/U grades (30 to 22 percent) and informal written notes (30 to 24 percent).

McEwin, Dickinson, and Jenkins (1996) compared grade reporting procedures from data collected in 1968, 1988, and 1993. The results are displayed in Table 12.1.

Vars (1992) maintained that the conventional report card falls short of being a developmentally appropriate procedure for reporting the academic performance or progress of middle grades students. The data collected by McEwin and his colleagues indicate a slight move toward more authentic assessment of student progress.

Transition Procedures

George and Alexander (1993) defined a middle school as a "school planned and operated as a separate school to serve the educational needs of students usually enrolled in grades 6 through 8 or 5 through 8 and 10 to 14 years of age, building on the elementary and leading

TABLE 12.1 Pupil Progress Reporting 1968, 1988, 1993

Types of Progress Reports	Percent		
	1968	1988	1993
Letter Scale	86	85	80
Word Scale	6	21	20
Number	13	13	10
Satisfactory-Unsatisfactory	26	39	38
Informal Written Notes	46	64	60
Percentage Marks	36	29	32
Portfolio	—	—	22
Parent Conferences	42	67	62

1968: Alexander definition
1988: Grades 6–8 schools
1993: Grades 6–8 schools

From McEwin, K., Dickinson, T., & Jenkins, D. (1996). *America's Middle Schools: Practices and Progress: A 25-year Perspective* (p. 64). Columbus, OH: National Middle School Association.

toward the high school" (p. 28). Resisting the domination of the high school, some middle school educators have created a separate entity without consideration of experiences before or after the middle school. Effective middle level schools plan carefully for a smooth transition into, within, and out of the middle school.

Articulation within the middle level school is difficult to assess, but in the Valentine et al. study (1992), principals reported persistent problems with transition in and out of the middle school. Major articulation problems with the elementary school were counseling services, pupil promotion policies, subject content and sequence, and teaching methodology. Major articulation problems cited with secondary schools were teaching methodology, orientation of students, and subject content and sequence. Many schools provide visitations and meetings with counselors, and parents, but neglect curricular considerations (George & Shewey, 1994; McEwin, Dickinson, & Jenkins, 1996).

In summary, middle school programs and practices are firmly established in many middle level schools. National associations dedicated to the educational needs of young adolescents are thriving and major foundations such as the Carnegie Council have supported states in their efforts to transform middle level education. The 1980s were a decade of growth and expansion for middle level school identity; the 1990s look even better.

Issues in Middle Level Education

Middle school practices such as interdisciplinary teaming, advisory programs, and expanded exploration programs lend themselves to providing learning experiences that are more integrated and relevant. Some middle level educators refer to this school reform as

"Phase One." Making the leap into a true transformation of curriculum, instruction, learning environments, evaluation procedures, working with health and family issues, and documenting and adjusting practice with research will most assuredly lead to improved student achievement and behavior, which is "Phase Two" (Irvin, 1992).

Curriculum, Instruction, and Assessment

One of the five goals of the National Middle School Association is to define and implement developmentally appropriate curriculum, instruction, and assessment for middle level students (see curriculum position statement in Chapter 3). "The changing nature of young adolescents and the society in which they live, the growth of knowledge and technology, diversity among students and communities, and new information of the ways that people learn are all reasons why curricular reform is imperative at this time" (Irvin & Schumacher, 1990, p. 1). In *A Middle School Curriculum: From Rhetoric to Reality,* Beane (1990; 1993) presented a proposal for a more student-centered, societal-responsive curriculum for middle level students. This provocative monograph is being discussed by faculties across the United States. Since that time, numerous books relevant to developing a more integrated curriculum have been published (see Beane, 1995; Pace, 1995; Siu-Runyan & Faircloth, 1995).

The most credible rationale for transforming the curriculum in middle level schools is that students learn more and better when information is integrated across disciplines, process oriented, and relevant to students. Recent research on "brain based learning involves acknowledging the brain's rules for meaningful learning and organizing teaching with those rules in mind" (Caine & Caine, 1991, p. 4). This learning is based on the fact that various disciplines relate to each other and share common information that the brain can recognize and organize. Meaningful knowledge is "anything that makes sense to the learner and which is generally presented in larger patterns and not in isolated bits of information" (Irvin & Schumacher, 1990, p. 7).

The programs and practices of the middle school concept naturally lend themselves to literacy learning. Teams of teachers can reinforce the teaching of learning strategies, literature can be integrated into units of study, advisory time can incorporate silent reading time, and extended reading can help students explore topics of interest. In exemplary middle schools, literacy learning pervades all corners of the middle school curriculum.

Because middle schools contain an interesting mix of secondary and elementary trained teachers, discussions of curriculum integration around themes relevant to students will not result in a clear direction for some time. These discussions will eventually result in more relevant and integrated curriculum, instruction, and assessment for young adolescents.

Teacher and Administrator Preparation

McEwin (1992) reported that a "small minority of middle school teachers have had specific preparation for teaching at this level, [but] great strides have been made over the last decade to further a separate certification for the middle level" (p. 367). Most middle level educators believe that if the school specifically designed for young adolescents is to endure, then teachers and administrators must be specially prepared to work there.

Valentine et al. (1992) found that middle level certification for teachers remained constant (11 percent) in the 1982 and 1992 studies. More teachers are elementary certified (26 percent), although most are still secondary certified (63 percent). In-service programs (73 percent) were cited as the procedure most used to prepare teachers to work in middle level schools although these programs were often one- and two-day workshops. Principals (44 percent) reported that generally the staff had no special preparation to teach in middle level schools. Student teaching experience in middle level schools decreased from 58 percent (1981) to 32 percent (1992). Teachers involved in university coursework that focused on middle level education decreased from 44 percent (1981) to 36 percent (1992). The majority of principals (90 percent) and assistant principals (71 percent) belonged to the NASSP and many principals (66 percent) and assistant principals (36 percent) belonged to the NMSA. Most principals and assistant principals are involved in state professional organizations or district activities.

Educators who work in middle level schools seem to get on-the-job training. Although middle level teachers and administrators are active and involved in state and national organizations that provide current information on programs and practices, it is discouraging that so few middle level educators are certified or have received systematic training to work with young adolescents. As middle level schooling grows into its own identity, state departments of education and certification boards must recognize the need for a separate middle level preparation.

Connecting with Families to Resolve Health Issues

Two major recommendations of *Turning Points: Preparing Youth for the 21st Century* (Carnegie Council for Adolescent Development, 1989) and *Great Transitions: Preparing Adolescents for a New Century* (Carnegie Council for Adolescent Development, 1996) were to reengage families in the education of young adolescents and to connect schools with communities, which together share the responsibility for each middle grade student's success. Task force members place the responsibility for providing health services for students at the school doorstep. Many middle level educators resist this move to more full-service schools, but the problem can no longer be ignored.

Kochan (1992) advocated schools connecting with families by stating that "middle level educators should take a leadership role in redefining not only the structure of schools but their role and function. This expanded role includes educating children to create strong families and communities in the future and developing and expanding support services to sustain them and their families in the present" (p. 70). All schools, particularly schools serving young adolescents, must find ways to support families and assist them in providing health care for students.

A Middle Level School Research Agenda

Research relevant to middle level education is beginning to proliferate. General recognition of the importance of early adolescence in a child's life, support from foundations such as Carnegie, and system-wide restructuring efforts have increased both the quantity and quality of research in middle level education. In addition, qualitative research methodology lends itself quite naturally to studying teacher interactions on teams, the effectiveness of advisory programs, and a host of other important research questions.

For years, middle level educators implemented programs because they "were good for kids." Initial research confirms their hunches; however, many questions remain to be answered. After a critical review of research in middle level education, Van Zandt and Totten (1995) concluded that "the pursuit of middle level reforms that enhance students' educational experiences and opportunities is well underway. While research prior to 1990 focused on *how* to meet student needs, the current decade is witnessing a shift toward the importance of documenting the *effectiveness* of these programs. In this process, establishing a solid research base to substantiate recommended practices is crucial, not only for increasing movement credibility but for learning how to better address the diversity of needs of today's young adolescent" (p.20).

Summary

After thirty years of implementing the middle schools concept, it has finally taken hold in U.S. schools and is beginning internationally. Restructuring rhetoric for all levels of schooling includes teams of teachers working together, small group guidance activities, integrated curriculum, collaborative planning, and a more exploratory approach to content. Middle schools can share the successes and failures of attempting to implement such practices in schools with educators working in elementary schools and high schools. Of course, what has been advocated for young adolescents is good for all students. In this decade, the term "developmentally appropriate" is taking on new meaning for all educators. At the dawn of a new century, educators can only hope to find ways to improve schooling experiences for all students. Perhaps middle level educators can help in this effort.

References

Alexander, W.M. (1968). *A Survey of Organizational Patterns of Reorganized Middle Schools.* Final Report, USOE Project 7-D-026. Gainesville, FL: University of Florida.

Alexander, W.M. & George, P.S. (1981). *The Exemplary Middle School.* Orlando, FL: Harcourt, Brace, Jovanovich.

Alexander, W.M. & McEwin, K.C. (1989). *Schools in the Middle: Status and Progress.* Columbus, OH: National Middle School Association.

Alexander, W.M. & Williams, E. (1965). Schools in the middle years. *Educational Leadership, 23*(3), 217–223.

Beane, J. (Ed.) (1995). *Toward a Coherent Curriculum.* Alexandria, VA: Association for Supervision and Curriculum Development.

Beane, J.A. (1990). *A Middle School Curriculum: From Rhetoric to Reality.* Columbus, OH: National Middle School Association.

Beane, J.A. (1993). *A Middle School Curriculum: From Rhetoric to Reality.* Columbus, OH: National Middle School Association.

Caine, R.N. & Caine, G. (1991). *Making Connections: Teaching and the Human Brain.* Alexandria, VA: Association for Supervision and Curriculum Development.

California State Department of Education. (1987). *Caught in the Middle: Educational Reform for Young Adolescents in California Public Schools.* Sacramento, CA: Author.

Carnegie Council on Adolescent Development. (1989). *Turning Points: Preparing Youth for the 21st Century.* Washington, DC: Author.

Carnegie Council on Adolescent Development. (1992a). *Fateful Choices: Healthy Youth for the 21st Century.* Washington, DC: Author.

Carnegie Council on Adolescent Development. (1992b). *A Matter of Time: Risk and Opportunity in the Nonschool Hours.* Washington, DC: Author.

Carnegie Council on Adolescent Development. (1996). *Great Transitions: Preparing Adolescents for a New Century.* Washington, DC: Author.

Cawelti, G. (1988). Middle schools a better match with early adolescent needs ASCD finds. *ASCD Curriculum Update.* Washington, DC: Association for Supervision and Curriculum Development.

Commission on the Reorganization of Secondary Education. (1918). *Cardinal Principles of Secondary Education* (Bulletin No. 35). Washington, DC: United States Department of the Interior, Bureau of Education.

Eichhorn, D. (1966). *The Middle School.* New York: The Center for Applied Research in Education.

Epstein, J.L. & Mac Iver, D.J. (1990). *National Practices and Trends in the Middle Grades.* Columbus, OH: National Middle School Association.

George, P.S. & Alexander, W.M. (1993). *The Exemplary Middle School.* Orlando, FL: Harcourt, Brace, Jovanovich.

George, P.S. & Shewey, K. (1994). *New Evidence for the Middle School.* Columbus, OH: National Middle School Association.

Georgiady, N.P. & Romano, L.G. (1974). Do you have a middle school? In L.G. Leeper (Ed.), *Middle Schools in the Making: Readings from Educational Leadership* (pp. 26–29). Alexandria, VA: Association for Supervision and Curriculum Development.

Irvin, J.L. (Ed.) (1992). *Transforming Middle Level Education: Perspectives and Possibilities.* Boston: Allyn & Bacon.

Irvin, J.L. & Schumacher, D.S. (1990). *Curricular Reform in Florida's Middle Level Schools: The Next Step.* Tallahassee, FL: Florida Department of Education.

Kochan, F.K. (1992). A new paradigm of schooling: Connecting school, home and community. In J.L. Irvin (Ed.), *Transforming Middle Level Education: Perspectives and Possibilities* (pp. 63–72). Boston: Allyn & Bacon.

Lounsbury, J. (1992). Perspectives on the middle school movement. In J.L. Irvin (Ed.), *Transforming Middle Level Education: Perspectives and Possibilities* (pp. 3–15). Boston: Allyn & Bacon.

Lounsbury, J.H. & Clark, D.C. (1990). *Inside Grade Eight: From Apathy to Excitement.* Reston, VA: National Association of Secondary School Principals.

Lounsbury, J.H. & Johnston, J.H. (1988). *Life in the Three Sixth Grades.* Reston, VA: National Association of Secondary School Principals.

Lounsbury, J.H. & Vars, G.F. (1978). *A Curriculum for the Middle School Grades.* New York: Harper & Row.

Maryland Task Force on the Middle Learning Years. (1989). *What Matters in the Middle Grades: Recommendations for Maryland Middle Grades Education.* Baltimore, MD: Maryland State Department of Education.

McEwin, C.K. (1992). Middle level teacher preparation and certification. In J.L. Irvin (Ed.), *Transforming Middle Level Education: Perspectives and Possibilities* (pp. 369–380). Boston: Allyn & Bacon.

McEwin, K., Dickinson, T., & Jenkins, D. (1996). *America's Middle Schools: Practices and Progress: A 25-Year Perspective.* Columbus, OH: National Middle School Association.

National Association of Secondary School Principals. (1985). *An Agenda for Excellence.* Reston, VA: Author.

National Middle School Association. (1982). *This We Believe.* Columbus, OH: Author.

National Middle School Association. (1992). *This We Believe.* Columbus, OH: Author.

National Middle School Association. (1995). *This We Believe: Developmentally Responsive Middle Level Schools.* Columbus, OH: Author.

Pace, G. (1995). *Whole Learning in the Middle School: Evolution and Transition.* Norwood, MA: Christopher-Gordon.

Ritzenthaler, B.R. (1993). *An Investigation of Key Programs and Practices of the Middle School Concept in Institutionalized and Noninstitutionalized Middle Schools in Florida.* Unpublished doctoral dissertation, Florida State University, Tallahassee, FL.

Rock, D.A. & Hemphill, J.K. (1966). *The Junior High School Principalship.* Reston, VA: National Association of Secondary School Principals.

Siu-Runyan, Y. & Faircloth, C.V. (1995). *Beyond Separate Subjects: Integrative Learning at the Middle Level.* Norwood, MA: Christopher-Gordon.

Valentine, J., Clark, D.C., Irvin, J.L., Keefe, J.W., & Melton, G. (1992). *Leadership in Middle Level Education: A National Survey of Middle Level Leaders and Their Schools* (vol. 1). Reston, VA: National Association of Secondary School Principals.

Valentine, J., Clark, D.C., Nickerson, N.C., & Keefe, J.W. (1981). *The Middle Level Principalship: A Survey of Middle Level Principals and Programs* (vol. 1). Reston, VA: National Association of Secondary School Principals.

Van Zandt, L.M. & Totten, S. (1995). The current status of middle level education research: A critical review. *Research in Middle Level Education, 18*(3), 1–26.

Vars, G.F. (1992). Humanizing student evaluation and reporting. In J.L. Irvin (Ed.), *Transforming Middle Level Education: Perspectives and Possibilities* (pp. 336–366). Boston: Allyn & Bacon.

Chapter 13

The Reading Program

Change is an integral part of the nature of education. Successful teachers constantly adapt to change—change in schedules, in curriculum, in textbooks. Students change from year to year; in fact, in a middle level school the same students often change from day to day.

Besides the changes that occur naturally in a school or within a classroom, teachers must also respond to the growing body of research on teaching and learning. How does a teacher acquire and apply all this new knowledge so as to meet the needs of the students. The first step in understanding where we need to go is, of course, understanding where we have been. In this chapter, (1) a discussion of the traditional forms of reading instruction, (2) reading development, (3) the components of a successful reading program, (4) suggestions for organizing and managing a reading program, and (5) recommended ways to facilitate change in a middle level reading program will be presented.

Traditional Forms of Reading Instruction in the Middle Grades

Little research on secondary reading practices and programs exists to guide those curriculum planners and teachers who wish to strengthen reading instruction for young adolescents. Most surveys conducted in this area have not drawn conclusions specifically related to the middle level school. One national survey (Irvin & Connors, 1989) was designed to describe the nature and extent to which reading is taught in middle level schools. Using that survey data, and extending it with personal experience with middle level schools across the nation, six patterns of reading instruction seem to be present: (1) no systematic instruction, (2) remedial reading course, (3) developmental reading course, (4) content area reading with a reading specialist usually available as a resource to a team or grade level, (5) integrated language arts, and (6) integrated curriculum using thematic approach.

TABLE 13.1 Extent of Reading Instruction Offered in Middle Level Schools

	Percent of Schools Chosen Randomly n = 154
No reading instruction offered	6
Reading instruction only for students reading below grade level	28
Reading instruction offered only as elective	11

No Systematic Reading Instruction

Although it is unreasonable to expect that students could acquire enough reading competence by the fifth grade to carry them through middle school and high school, many middle level schools offer little or no systematic reading instruction. Table 13.1 shows the extent to which reading was taught in middle level schools in 1988. An above average, average, or slightly below average reader would have no opportunity for reading instruction in almost one-half of the schools in the United States.

"During the middle grades, young adolescents face increasing demands on their literacy skills. They are asked to read and write much more than in the earlier grades, and they are assigned reading and writing tasks that increase in complexity" (Davidson, 1990, p. 74). A departmentalized organization coupled with secondary trained teachers who generally do not feel comfortable teaching reading, partially account for many middle grades students being deprived of systematic instruction in reading beyond grade 5. Surprisingly, many students acquire the reading competence they need to progress academically, but, then, many do not.

Remedial Reading Course

The remedial reading course and reading lab are usually defined as a pullout course for students reading below grade level; it normally includes instruction in skill and vocabulary development, and comprehension. The primary source of reading material is narrative. Few reading labs still exist although many students are still pulled out to work on computer-assisted remedial instruction that resembles the individualization that characterized reading labs. Table 13.2 shows the percentage of students taking remedial and developmental reading courses in 1988.

Often little transfer occurs between what is learned in a remedial reading course and reading required in content area courses. Students who receive isolated skill work and more experience with stories still must face the daily challenge of reading their science and social studies textbooks. Some remedial reading teachers use content area books to help students become more successful readers of expository text by teaching them chapter maps, text structure, and vocabulary strategies. Nelson and Herber (1982) advocated a positive approach to remedial reading instruction in middle and secondary grades based on student strengths of experience, language facility, decoding skills, curiosity, and capacity

TABLE 13.2 Number of Schools Reporting Systematic Reading Instruction

	6th	7th	8th
Developmental Reading Course			
Wheel*	0	8	9
Semester	32	29	19
Year	10	8	7
Remedial Reading Course			
Wheel*	3	14	12
Semester	21	33	30
Year	9	7	6
Reading Lab			
Wheel*	1	5	5
Semester	8	14	11
Year	1	1	1

*The "wheel" is a slot in the school schedule where students may take exploratory courses.

to reason rather than "recycling large numbers of students through basic word recognition and literal comprehension skills" (p. 145).

Developmental Reading Course

The developmental reading course usually includes the development of comprehension, vocabulary, flexible reading rates, and study strategies: it is designed to be a normal part of a student's progression through the curriculum, not as a remedial course. This type of reading instruction seems to be the most popular and the most preferred.

These courses are most heavily emphasized at the sixth-grade level, and the time and the requirement is reduced at the seventh- and eighth-grade levels. It appears that most schools require reading for a semester or a year in the sixth grade. For seventh and eighth grade, reading instruction is commonly offered through "the wheel," which generally refers to a slot in the school schedule when students may take exploratory courses such as art or keyboarding. Students who are below grade level are sometimes advised to take repeated reading courses on the wheel.

Materials used in these courses range from skill materials and worksheets, to basal textbooks, to student-chosen literature. Sometimes learning strategies that help students negotiate text in content areas are taught.

When school budgets are slashed, often the developmental reading class is the first to go. Similar to remedial reading courses, these developmental courses are sometimes isolated from the reading realities of the rest of the student's day. When reading teachers, though, coordinate and integrate the use of learning strategies and vocabulary development with the objectives of content area teachers, students have more authentic reading experiences and have the opportunity to grow into the more complex reading and writing tasks that the middle grades demand.

Content Area Reading

The content area reading orientation to reading instruction has been attempted since the early 1900s (Moore, Readence, & Rickleman, 1983) and was more or less emphasized throughout the first half of the century. Content area reading instruction then reemerged with the publication of Herber's (1970; 1978) *Teaching Reading in the Content Area.* State departments of education began to see content area reading instruction as a vehicle for improving the reading achievement of high school graduates. Despite the efforts of state departments of education and the International Reading Association to promote content area reading instruction, however, this type of instruction did not seem to be widely applied in the schools of our country (Witte & Otto, 1981).

One reason why content area reading instruction was so little implemented may have its foundation in the perceptions of content area teachers. Many of these teachers saw reading as teaching phonics and using workbooks, and as an activity that took valuable time from the content that they were trained and expected to teach. The notion that "every teacher was a teacher of reading" died along with the notion that teaching reading was teaching skills in isolation.

In the Gee and Forester (1988) survey, 18 percent of the respondents reported having or planning a content reading program; 38 percent of these respondents were from middle level schools. The Irvin and Connors (1989) survey supported the findings of Gee and Forester: few middle level schools have a program for content area reading instruction.

Almost half of the educators Gee and Forester surveyed believed that reading instruction was not the responsibility of content teachers. An equally high number of respondents reported that they lacked administrative support or leadership for a content reading program. Although no school administrators were directly asked why they lacked a content area reading program, informal comments indicated that the respondents felt that the developmental and remedial courses offered fulfilled the need for systematic reading instruction.

Although the need for content area reading seems clear, Smith and Feathers (1983a; 1983b) raised the interesting question of the importance of reading the textbook. These authors studied social studies classes and concluded that (1) students needed textbooks only to locate literal answers, (2) although reading was assigned, teacher presentations and worksheets provided other ways of getting needed information to pass a test, and (3) "since students did not value the information being learned, they had little incentive for reading" (1983a, p. 266). Although teachers did not see themselves as the primary sources of information, "students view them not only as the primary sources but, in many cases, as more important than the text" (1983b, p. 353). Student difficulty with text and expediency for covering the material contribute to teacher's "filling in" for the text, making the actual reading of the text superfluous.

If reading in the content areas has been neglected over the years, then writing in content areas has been all but forgotten. Teachers often expect students to complete such tasks as writing essay questions on tests or summaries, but most teachers do not teach students how to write in an expository mode (Gahn, 1989). When students do write, they generally do not have an authentic audience. They write for a teacher for purposes of evaluation. Gebhard (1983) suggested finding real audiences such as peers or younger children to help students learn to write clear and meaningful expository pieces. Webs, semantic feature analysis, or structured overviews can assist students in structuring their writing in the content areas. Reading and writing can certainly be learned together to help students understand the structure of expository text.

In a review of the literature, Alvermann and Swafford (1989) found that a significant research base exists for recommended comprehension and vocabulary strategies generally used in content area classes. Strategies such as study guides, list-group-label, advanced organizers, mapping, and use of text structure have all been substantiated by research as effective for middle grades students. Additionally, these "most frequently recommended and researched strategies are the very ones that teachers report using most often" (p. 394).

The recommended approach to content area reading is one in which teachers collaborate to present content and learning strategies concurrently. Students are given direct instruction in reading strategies as they learn content. This approach enhances reading, thinking, and study skill ability while it increases students' knowledge of content. Thus, one main reason that this method of content area reading instruction is desirable and effective is that it allows direct application of reading strategies to content.

The upsurge in quality research into reading theory and practice and a new comprehension-based view of the reading process have both helped reshape many educators' ideas about reading and writing instruction in the content areas. The gap, however, between current theory and practice continues to gape widely. This incongruence between knowledge and application continues to concern many educators.

Typically, when students enter the middle level school, they meet departmentalization, content textbooks, and teachers who were trained for the secondary school. Thus, students who are accustomed to the security, the narrative-based text, and the skills-oriented teaching of elementary school must suddenly adapt to a much different set of expectations. One of the most difficult parts of adapting to this new environment is making the transition from "reading for story" to reading for content. Unfortunately, few middle level schools have programs that help students to make this transition.

Integrated Language Arts

Based on the premise that reading, writing, speaking, listening, and thinking are interrelated processes, a growing number of language arts teachers are implementing Reading/Writing Workshop. Nancie Atwell (1987) introduced the Workshop in her book, *In the Middle: Writing, Reading, and Learning with Adolescents,* as a way of motivating young adolescents to write about self-selected books, to talk to others about their writing and their reading, and to participate in the evaluation of their work and the work of others. In *Seeking Diversity: Language Arts with Adolescents,* Linda Reif (1992) refined the Workshop by sharing stories of student reading and writing. Atwell (1990) elaborated on writing to learn in her book, *Coming to Know: Writing to Learn in the Intermediate Grades.* These three books and the stories of numerous language arts teachers sharing their

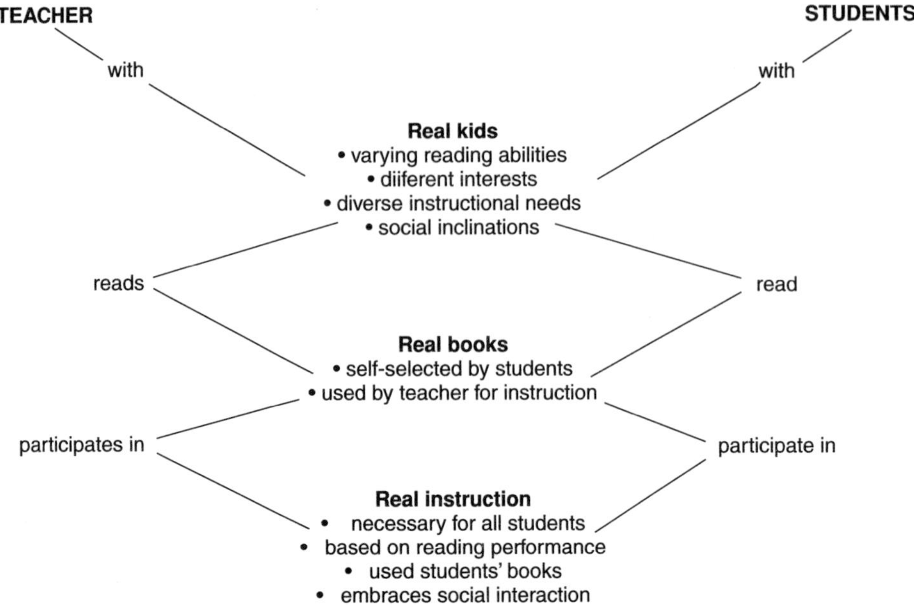

FIGURE 13.1

From Roe, Mary F. (1992, November). Reading strategy instruction: Compexities and possibilities in middle school. *Journal of Reading, 36*(3), 190–196. Reprinted with permission of Mary F. Roe and the International Reading Association. All rights reserved.

experiences through articles and presentations at conferences encouraged teachers to request two-hour blocks of time for students to read and write. Atwell and Reif advocated "mini-lessons" for students in reading and writing process as the need arose, authentic literacy experiences and assessment, and lots of time for reading, writing, and reflection.

Extending the Reading/Writing Workshop, Roe (1992) developed a framework for teaching literacy in middle level schools which is presented in Figure 13.1. This framework facilitates the social nature of young adolescents and centers around real kids, real books, and real instruction.

Workshops and Workshop-like approaches to teaching literacy in the middle school are a giant leap away from the isolated approach of spelling on Monday, reading on Tuesday, grammar on Wednesday type language arts classes that unfortunately continue to proliferate in schools. Some teachers find the Workshop difficult to manage and it seems to be most effective when offered in a longer than one-hour time period. Although a more integrated language arts program such as Reading/Writing Workshop is a vast improvement over the fragmented approach, a middle school literacy program is most effective when students are also taught the learning strategies of content area reading. Helping young adolescents develop literacy abilities consistent with increased demands is a complex task that includes instruction in both narrative and expository materials.

Thematic Learning

A few schools have implemented a curriculum that integrates content around themes. In one middle school, for example, thirty students remain with one teacher for a three-hour block of time to learn social studies, language arts, and reading. Themes derived from social studies content naturally lend themselves to the use of literature which enhances understanding of content. Ideally, learning strategies for both narrative and expository text are taught in relation to learning new content. "By themselves, strategies have no useful function. They exist only as a means of understanding, creating, and communicating information, ideas, and feelings from the knowledge base . . . purposeful integration cannot occur unless teachers understand the relationships among content and strategies" (Roehler, Foley, Lud, & Power, 1990, p. 188). Whole learning holds much promise for middle grades teaching and learning. The pioneers that create meaningful learning environments and experiences for developing literacy abilities and acquiring new content will provide the models for others to emulate and reformulate for their own students.

During the past few decades, literacy learning programs have changed consistently with philosophical changes about language acquisition. Although still alive and well in some middle level schools, teaching reading and writing skills isolated from other language areas and from content instruction seems to be giving way to literacy instruction that is more integrated with the entire curriculum. Reading/Writing Workshop, learning strategies taught in content areas, and literacy instruction integrated with thematic study are promising directions for literacy development during the middle grades. It is imperative that students continue to receive instruction in how to read, write, speak, listen, and think. This instruction is most effective when strategies are taught and applied directly to content being studied.

Reading Development

When proficiency in reading is considered historically, today's students meet or exceed performance of students from any other era (Kibby, 1993). Chall (1983) maintained that "reading, like income, has both an absolute and a relative value. Just forty years ago, an eighth-grade reading level was typical of people twenty-five years old or over, and that was considered about the standard of minimal literacy. Today, the average is eleventh to twelfth grade level. Although it means a much higher reading ability, it probably has about the same relative value as an eighth-grade level had forty years ago" (p. 3).

Responding to a request for analysis of the findings of the National Assessment of Educational Progress, Venezky, Kaestle, and Sum (1987) concluded that "everyday reading tasks will require processing of complex information derived from multiple sources of printed information." These authors recommended "that (a) literacy instruction at all levels should move beyond teaching students to find main ideas and details in texts to the higher-level skills of applying logic, inference, and synthesis to texts, (b) there should be greater use of multiple texts in reading instruction, and most especially, the texts studied should not only be narrative, but also expository" (Kibby, 1993, p. 38).

New technologies have changed the requirements of literacy. Workplace demands now include keyboarding skills, skimming through data on a screen, and making decisions about the location of information. The workplace has shifted to an emphasis on group task performance and problem solving, and collaborative learning is becoming more important.

A new set of strategies is necessary for literacy in the twenty-first century. The lines between "subjects" become less defined. For example, students may use a database to make inferences about migration patterns of early settlers and write and transmit this information to young people in another country via the internet. In earlier times, this activity would have been taught as arithmetic, thinking skills, and writing. Technology facilitates authentic audiences for reading and writing through authentic problem-solving contexts. To meet future needs, the curricula should shift from a "subject centered, disciplinary emphasis to a focus on real-world problem solvings using perspectives and tools from multiple fields" (Dede, 1989, p. 26).

To transform literacy instruction to meet the needs of the future, it is imperative that educators understand the foundational stages of literacy development. These stages are presented in Figure 13.2 and are based on the work of Jeanne Chall (1983).

During the middle grades, students must make a significant shift from "learning to read" to "reading to learn." For some students, this shift becomes a fairly large leap because teachers and materials do not provide for a deliberate transition. Chall described the failure to make a smooth transition from Stage 2 to Stage 3 as the "fourth-grade slump." More silent reading, less reading aloud, more independence, and more expository material are increasingly challenging demands on the reader.

Reading to Learn

Many middle school students who are not proficient readers have not made the transition to reading to learn. They approach a science textbook the same way they do a story. Herber (1984) summarized his beliefs about reading to learn.

1. Reading to learn *is* different from learning to read, both for the learner and for the teacher.
2. Students need to be taught how to read to learn; transfer of skills gained in learning to read is not automatic.
3. Subject matter teachers can provide simultaneous instruction in reading skills and in course content.
4. Subject matter texts are instructional tools; students should not be expected to read them independently.
5. Comprehension is affected but not assured by the organization and content of the text; thus, creating better texts will not automatically produce better readers.
6. Students who are properly placed in a curriculum will find their texts "too difficult" to use independently; if they do not, they already know the subject and are improperly placed.
7. The difficulty of a text should be in its content, not in its organization; and the student need not sacrifice the former to improve the latter.
8. The content of a text determines the processes by which it is read; thus, texts should be organized for the best presentation of content rather than to facilitate the teaching of a given or specific set of comprehension or study skills (pp. 227–228).

	Emergent Reading	
Stage 0 Prereading	Preschool Ages 0–6 years	Child "pretends" to read, retells story when looking at pages of book previously read to him/her; names letters of alphabet; recognizes some signs; prints own name; plays with books, pencils, and paper.
	Beginning Reading	
Stage 1 sounds Initial reading and decoding	Grade1 and beginning Grade 2 Age 6–7	Child learns relation between letters and and between printed and spoken words; child is able to read simple text containing high frequency words and phonically regular words; uses skill and insight to "sound out" new one syllable words.
	Reading for Consolidation	
Stage 2 Confirmation and fluency	Grades 2–3 Ages 7–8	Child reads simple, familiar stories and selections with increasing fluency. This is done by consolidating the basic decoding elements, sight vocabulary, and meaning context in the reading of familiar stories and selections.
	Reading to Learn the New	
Stage 3 Reading for learning the new	**Grades 4–8 Ages 9–13**	**Reading is used to learn new ideas, to gain new knowledge, to experience new feelings, to learn new attitudes; generally from one viewpoint.**
	Reading for Independence	
Stage 4 Multiple view points	High School Grades 10–12 Ages 15–17	Reading widely from a broad range of complex materials, both expository and narrative, with a variety of viewpoints.
	Mature Reading	
Stage 5 Construction and reconstruction	College and beyond Age 18+	Reading is used for one's own needs and purposes (professional and personal); reading serves to integrate one's knowledge with that of others, to synthesize it and to create new knowledge. It is rapid and efficient.

FIGURE 13.2 Stages of Reading Development

Chall, Jeanne S. (1996 Second Edition). *Stages of Reading Development.* Fort Worth, TX: Harcourt-Brace; (1983) New York: McGraw-Hill.

It is clear that the middle grades present a significant change in the expectations of reader development. In addition, students are working on and coping with (1) socioemotional developmental tasks such as developing a self-identity and autonomy, (2) physical growth and development, (3) forming and clarifying moral values, and (4) increased capacity in cognitive functioning. These factors must be considered when planning a program of literacy development for young adolescents.

Goals for a Middle School Reading Program

"The ultimate goal of reading instruction is to develop independent readers" (Wisconsin State Reading Association, position statement, 1991). The critical transition from "learning to read" to "reading to learn" is the point at which learners are becoming more independent. Independence does not mean isolation: teachers have an important role in guiding, directing, and extending the readers to apply and practice their reading abilities in new contexts (Herber & Nelson-Herber, 1987).

Farnan (1996) developed four goals for middle school reading that can serve as the foundation of building a program.

1. *As readers, students will be active constructors of meaning, both individually and in socially structured settings.* The theoretical shift over the past few decades is toward a constructivist view of learning. Using their own personalized schema, readers construct their own meaning from text. Given the vast array of contexts in which reading occurs and the variety in text, this is a complex task. Becoming an independent reader means gaining the ability to construct meaning from text in a variety of settings and with a variety of texts.
2. *Students will learn about themselves and others through a variety of genres and cultural perspectives.* Whether it be a novel, a poem, or a newspaper advertisement, reading provides experiences for students that, in turn, add to their personalized schema and aid in the construction of new meanings. Reading enables students to learn about cultures and events that they cannot possibly experience first hand, but are necessary for a balanced world view.
3. *Students will be strategic readers across a variety of genres and content areas.* Strategic reading is the cornerstone of independent reading. "The strategy is elegant in its simplicity. It provides support that can help all students engage in processes of effective readers—that is, engage in important thinking processes before, during, and after a reading" (Farnan, 1996, p. 441). Readers who internalize strategies that span across genres and content areas become independent learners.
4. *Students will embrace reading as an enjoyable experience.* Work on the interrelationship between affect and cognition (Caine & Caine, 1991; Sylwester, 1995) clearly indicates to educators that "meaningful learning occurs when thoughts and feelings work in tandem as learners make the connections necessary for developing insights and creating new learnings" (Farnan, 1996, p. 443). It is clear that students will not become lifelong readers unless they enjoy reading.

Characteristics of a Middle Level Reading Program

Although the International Reading Association and numerous state affiliates have published position statements on secondary reading programs, only one position statement exists that specifically addresses the needs of middle level schools. The Wisconsin State Reading Association and the Wisconsin Association for Middle Level Educators each appointed members to a committee to study, reflect, and eventually to write *Reading Design for Middle Level Schools* (Wisconsin State Reading Association, 1991). This document has been a useful guide as schools and school districts design literacy instruction for middle grades students.

> *Reading Design for Middle Level Schools*
>
> *The ultimate goal of reading instruction is to develop independent readers. Reading is a tool that spans disciplines, is integrated into all content areas, and addresses diversity. A reading program is not a reading class; it is a school's total commitment to literacy. Therefore, we believe that the essential characteristics of a middle level reading program include:*
>
> 1. *experiential student-centered activities which accommodate the physical, cognitive, social, and emotional needs of the young adolescent;*
> 2. *initiatives which foster positive attitudes toward reading and learning;*
> 3. *attention to cognitive development through higher order thinking processes;*
> 4. *integration of the reading and writing processes;*
> 5. *utilization of interdisciplinary approaches in all curricula;*
> 6. *direct instruction in reading strategies applied to literature;*
> 7. *instruction in a variety of study strategies;*
> 8. *opportunities for self-selection of materials across curricular areas;*
> 9. *recreational reading initiatives;*
> 10. *opportunities to respond to reading through a variety of modes;*
> 11. *utilization of heterogeneous grouping patterns;*
> 12. *assessment of learning which matches instruction.*

This position statement serves four purposes. It (1) reminds educators that the nature and needs of young adolescents are foundational in planning any literacy learning program, (2) gives proper balance between narrative and expository text strategies, (3) takes into consideration cognitive functioning and affective factors, and (4) encourages whole learning, heterogeneous grouping, and authentic assessment. The components presented in the next section describe some tried and true aspects of a program in schools with successful programs.

Components of a Successful Middle Level Reading Program

Those who agree with the tenet that learning to read is a lifelong process and that it is impossible for a student to attain reading maturity in the first six or seven years of school must endorse a secondary reading program. Middle grades students are expected to read increasingly difficult material and increasingly more expository versus narrative material. Textbooks for the middle grades often require students to understand abstract concepts for which they may not be cognitively and developmentally ready.

Middle level students are also expected to do more with what they read, to read increasingly longer assignments, take notes, and do homework assignments based on what they read. Young adolescents cannot be expected to accomplish all these feats on their own. They need guidance.

What, then, are the components of a successful reading program for the middle grades? The following recommendations are based on (1) the testimony of educators who have implemented successful middle level programs, (2) the knowledge of experts in the field of secondary reading, (3) an understanding of the developmental tasks of middle grades students, and (4) personal experience as a teacher and consultant in middle level schools.

Total School and District Commitment

A commitment to improved literacy for middle grades students means providing leadership and support for literacy at both school and district levels. Leadership and support at the district level means that literacy programs will be provided with an overall organization, with funding, and with careful consideration. Such leadership usually involves the appointment of a district reading coordinator who takes full or partial responsibility for the middle level or secondary reading program and who coordinates a staff development and a support system for reading specialists within the district.

Leadership at the building level means providing individual schools with reading or curriculum specialists. These resource specialists then ensure that the school has and maintains a shared vision of the literacy learning program based on an understanding of and appreciation for the nature of young adolescents, language acquisition and developing cognitive processes, and sound theoretical views of reading and learning. "To be consistent with what we know from research, the reading program must be more than another language arts course of which reading is one component" (Peters, 1990, p. 68). A successful reading program includes opportunities for students to listen and read purposefully and write and speak with authentic audiences.

Reading specialists, reading coordinators, content area teachers, building principals, and district level administrators must assist in the planning and share in the vision for a school-wide reading program. "Without administrative support, chances for building a reading program can be severely limited" (Conley, 1989, p. 87). Administrators can hire teachers who share the school vision of literacy, provide for ongoing quality staff development, and share the vision with parents and community members (Binkley, 1989). Administrators can also model authentic reading and writing experiences, and encourage teachers to try new strategies (Siu-Runyan, 1990). School and district support for a reading program are essential components for success.

Content Area Teachers Who Teach Students and Strategies, Not Just Content

To facilitate learning, teachers are expected to understand (1) their students, (2) their content, (3) the learning process, (4) learning strategies—when and how to use them, and (5) the materials they are using and how to adapt the text to their students. In the most effective reading programs, content area and reading teachers work together to teach strategies that students can use across a wide variety of texts. "Domain knowledge is an important component in middle school reading and writing. Without sufficient domain knowledge, comprehension is impeded, strategies cannot be used appropriately, learning is fragmented, and transfer of knowledge is impaired" (Peters, 1990, p. 69). Sole emphasis on content leaves students with isolated information and without strategies for learning new content: sole emphasis on reading process leaves students with little about which to think or write. Students benefit when literacy is enhanced while content is learned and teachers work together.

Instruction That Integrates All Language Areas

Reading and writing have been taught as separate subjects for many years. Reading enhances the ability to write and writing enhances the ability to read (Rubin & Hansen, 1984; Taylor & Beach, 1984; Tierney & Leys, 1984).

The benefits of integrating reading and writing instruction are that (1) students use and expand their prior knowledge through reading and writing, (2) students learn about conventions of print and increase their linguistic competence through reading and have an opportunity to use this knowledge in writing, and (3) all language processes (reading, writing, speaking, listening) require and facilitate thinking, which is the common basis of language. The more language areas a teacher uses to teach content, the more likely the student will be to improve in those language areas and apply these abilities to the content under study.

One or More Reading Specialists in the School

A reading specialist or curriculum facilitator who does not have a student assignment can provide guidance to content area teachers by modeling learning strategies, by assessing text material that may be too difficult for students, or by providing diagnostic information about students. This person can also provide leadership in the recreational reading program by such activities as organizing a book fair or suggesting guidelines for a sustained silent reading program.

These support teachers must have special qualities. They must have (1) knowledge of the latest research and its classroom application, (2) excellent human relations skills and leadership qualities, (3) the ability to function as a catalyst for change, (4) the ability to provide support at the school and district levels, and (5) administrative abilities that contribute to the positive direction of the reading program. Probably one of the most valuable functions of a reading specialist is one of peer coach. "The reading specialist is in an ideal position to act as an observer, rather than a critic, in the classroom" (Lindsey & Runquist, 1983). For teachers trying out a learning strategy for the first time, this feedback and coaching is essential.

Consistent Evaluation and Instruction

Content area teachers who have incorporated the teaching of learning strategies into their curriculum sometimes continue to test in a way that is not consistent with their teaching. In other words, their teaching is for process and main idea; their testing is still objective and detail oriented. The students therefore fail, but for good reasons; the evaluation was not consistent with their instruction. Evaluation and instruction should be tailored to the needs of the students and be consistent with each other.

Reading Committee

Anders (1981) suggested that "people are the key to an effective content area reading program" (p. 316). A reading committee can serve to encourage teachers, administrators, support staff, media specialists, guidance counselors, parents, and students to more and better literacy experiences at the school level. This committee is responsible for planning and executing the reading program in a school.

Recreational Reading and Read-Aloud Program

A school reading committee usually provides leadership for book fairs, reading break time, book exchanges, and any special school-wide reading activities. These activities are usually indicative of a school-wide commitment to reading improvement and carry a strong message to the community. Principals can effectively support a recreational reading program by arranging schedules and acting as a positive role model for teachers and students. How to initiate and maintain a sustained silent reading program is fully described in Chapter 7.

A read-aloud program can occur within language arts classes or it can be a school-wide effort. Young adolescents should be "read aloud to every day, from a variety of texts, including nonfiction" (Anders & Pritchard, 1993, p. 619). This practice creates a common experience and a forum for responding orally and in writing. A full description of how to implement a read-aloud program can also be found in Chapter 7. Recreational reading and reading aloud provide exposure to a wide variety of literature and are the best vehicles for vocabulary development.

Strong Staff Development Program

Once it has been determined by a school, a school district, or a classroom teacher that change is desirable, staff development generally begins. Sometimes the decision to change is made before teachers are consulted. Staff development can consist of teachers reading and discussing a book, peer coaching, or more formal presentations. One key element in the implementation of successful change is ownership or a feeling that the teachers are a part of the change process. "Ownership must be established for any change to survive" (Gallagher, Goudvis, & Pearson, 1988, p. 36). Ownership can be facilitated by teachers setting goals, having input into the process, and mutual respect for all people involved in the process.

It is important in this stage, as with all stages of staff development, that those who are involved in the process consider teacher *growth* and not teacher *deficit.* All people in both their personal and professional lives cherish growth experiences. Professional growth happens in a supportive, positive environment. After ownership and a sense of respect and mutual integrity is established, growth in understanding may occur.

The second key element of change is knowledge. New knowledge may be gained through workshops, reading, discussion, observation, modeling, coaching, or attending conferences. The format is not as important as the support network that is established to help the new ideas grow into eventual application in the classroom.

Parent and Community Involvement

Community leaders and parents have a difficult time resisting the opportunity to offer support to a school-wide effort to improve reading. Parents can help collect books for classroom libraries, work at book exchanges, or talk about their reading interests to a class. Community leaders are sometimes invited to participate in sustained silent reading time as "guest readers": their job is to read with a class for a time and then chat with students about the parent's reading interests and personal history. These sharing times not only provide positive public relations for the school but also give students the opportunity to interact with positive role models.

Administrators can serve as a link between the reading committee and the community. Describing the program at parent meetings, serving as a reader role model for parents and students, and generally supporting the program help ensure the success of a school-wide reading effort (Binkley, 1989).

Classroom Action Research

Although "teachers work hard and are constantly searching for methods and strategies that will help students achieve better, seldom do they receive proof that a different method worked effectively enough to keep at it" (Monahan, 1987, p. 678). Classroom action research consists merely of keeping track of how a particular method—say, graphic organizers—works with one class while continuing to teach other classes in the "old way." Both pre-testing and posttesting may be used to determine which group of students performed the best. Charts can be constructed to dramatize the results. Teachers take ownership of a strategy when they see that its use brings results in improved achievement. Classroom action research is a vehicle for facilitating ownership of new strategies and methods and professional growth.

Facilitating Change

Professional growth is important for all educators but it is especially important for teachers. Ideally, change in a middle level reading program is initiated and supported by district or school personnel. Educational settings, however, are not always ideal. Nothing prevents individual teachers or small groups of teachers from trying some of the strategies that have been supported by research and from sharing these new methods with each other.

Of course, a team of teachers who share the same students can plan more effective instruction than can teachers who do not share the same students. But if one social studies teacher and one science teacher would talk about how to integrate reading and writing instruction in one cooperatively planned unit, professional growth would occur and students would ultimately benefit.

If one reading specialist taught students a strategy for reading their health book and shared that strategy with the health teacher, professional growth would occur and students would ultimately benefit. If one language arts and one social studies teacher worked together to read and write about a piece of literature, professional growth would occur and students would ultimately benefit.

In this chapter, components for a successful reading program have been suggested. If all the components were implemented, students could not help but improve their reading ability. "The necessary ingredients are available for improving the quality of reading programs in our schools" (Samuels, 1988, p. vii). The potential exists to improve the literacy ability in some school organizations such as interdisciplinary team organization. But the lack of these organizations does not prohibit effective instruction and improved learning.

The possibilities for professional growth for teachers and for benefit to students are limitless. But change does not happen overnight. After studying schools in change, Berman and McLaughlin (1975) concluded that successful change often takes six years: two years for needs assessments, establishing priorities, altering the staff beliefs and attitudes, and improved instruction. The next two years are used to implement the plan, and the last two years are used to produce a stable effect (Samuels, 1988).

Summary

Middle level students must adjust to ever increasing demands on their reading abilities. They must deal with increasingly more difficult reading materials, a greater emphasis on expository text, and an increasing expectation that they "read to learn." Despite these increased reading demands, however, many middle level schools still offer little or no systematic reading instruction. Of those middle level schools that do offer such instruction, fewer still offer content-based reading instruction.

An effective reading program for a middle level school has several important components. First, it depends upon support and commitment at both the district and school levels. It also depends upon content area teachers who are willing to teach not only content but also the process of learning. It also depends upon the support of specialists and on community involvement. An effective program is guided by learning strategies rather than materials and integrates all four of the language arts during instruction. Such a program also contains a recreational reading program and is supported and encouraged through staff development. In all, an effective middle level school reading program is a school-wide program that involves both content teachers and specialists and aims at preparing students to meet the demands of the secondary school classroom.

References

Alvermann, D. & Swafford J. (1989). Do content area strategies have a research base? *Journal of Reading, 32*(5), 388–399.

Anders, P.L. (1981). Dream of a secondary reading program? People are the key. *Journal of Reading, 24*(4), 316–320.

Anders, P.L. & Pritchard, T.G. (1993). Integrated language curriculum and instruction for the middle grades. *The Elementary School Journal, 93*(5), 611–624.

Atwell, N. (1987). *In the Middle: Writing, Reading, and Learning with Adolescents.* Upper Montclair, NJ: Boynton/Cook.

Atwell, N. (Ed.) (1990). *Coming to Know: Writing to Learn in the Intermediate Grades.* Portsmouth, NH: Heinemann.

Berman, P. & McLaughlin, M.W. (1975). *Federal Programs Supporting Education: The Findings in Review* (vol. 4). Santa Monica, CA: Rand.

Binkley, M.R.B. (Ed.) (1989). *Becoming a Nation of Readers: What Principals Can Do.* Washington, DC: Office of Educational Research and Improvement, United States Department of Education.

Caine, R.N. & Caine, G. (1991). *Making Connections: Teaching and the Human Brain.* Alexandria, VA: Association for Supervision and Curriculum Development.

Chall, J.S. (1983). *Stages of Reading Development.* New York: McGraw-Hill.

Conley, M. (1989). Middle school and junior high reading programs. In S. Wepner, J. Feeley, & D. Strickland (Eds.), *Administration and Supervision of Reading Programs* (pp. 76–92). New York: Teachers College Press.

Davidson, J. (1990). Literacy in the middle grades. *Educational Horizons, 68*(2), 74–77.

Dede, C. (1989). The evolution of information technology: Implications for curriculum. *Educational Leadership, 47*(1), 23–26.

Farnan, N. (1996). Connecting adolescents and reading: Goals at the middle level. *Journal of Adolescent and Adult Literacy, 39*(6), 436–445.

Gahn, S. (1989). A practical guide for teaching writing in the content areas. *Journal of Reading, 32*(6), 525–531.

Gallagher, M.C., Goudvis, A., & Pearson, P.D. (1988). Principles of organizational change. In J. Samuels & P.D. Pearson (Eds.), *Changing School Reading Programs: Principles and Case Studies* (pp. 11–39). Newark, DE: International Reading Association.

Gebhard, A.O. (1983). Teaching writing in reading and the content areas. *Journal of Reading, 27*(3), 207–211.

Gee, T.C. & Forester, N. (1988). Moving reading beyond the reading classroom. *Journal of Reading, 31*(6), 505–511.

Herber, H.L. (1970). *Teaching Reading in the Content Areas.* Englewood Cliffs, NJ: Prentice-Hall.

Herber, H.L. (1978). *Teaching Reading in Content Areas.* Englewood Cliffs, NJ: Prentice-Hall.

Herber, H.L. (1984). Subject matter texts: Reading to learn: Response to a paper by Thomas H. Anderson and Bonnie B. Armbruster. In R.C. Anderson, J. Osborn, R.J. Tierney (Eds.), *Learning to Read in American Schools: Basal Readers and Context Texts* (pp. 227–234). Hillsdale, NJ: Lawrence Erlbaum.

Herber, H.L. & Nelson-Herber, J. (1987). Developing independent learners. *Journal of Reading, 30*(7), 584–588.

Irvin, J.L. & Connors, N.A. (1989). Reading instruction in middle level schools: Results from a U.S. survey. *Journal of Reading, 32*(4), 306–311.

Kibby, M.W. (1993). What reading teachers should know about reading proficiency in the U.S. *Journal of Reading, 37*(1), 28–41.

Lindsey, J.F. & Runquist, A.D. (1983). Clinical supervision: A tool for the reading specialist. *Journal of Reading, 27*(1), 48–51.

Monahan, J.N. (1987). Secondary teachers do care . . . ! *Journal of Reading, 30*(8), 676–678.

Moore, D.W., Readence, J.E., & Rickleman, R.J. (1983). An historical explanation of content area reading instruction. *Reading Research Quarterly, 18*(4), 419–438.

Nelson, J. & Herber, H. (1982). Organization and management of programs. In A. Berger & A. Robinson (Eds.), *Secondary School Reading: What Research Reveals for Classroom Practice* (pp. 143–157). Urbana, IL: National Council for the Teachers of English.

Peters, C.W. (1990). Content knowledge in reading: Creating a new framework. In G. Duffy (Ed.), *Reading in the Middle School* (pp. 63–80). Newark, DE: International Reading Association.

Reif, L. (1992). *Seeking Diversity: Language Arts with Adolescents.* Portsmouth, NH: Heinemann.

Roe, M.F. (1992). Reading strategy instruction: Complexities and possibilities in middle school. *Journal of Reading, 36*(3), 190–197.

Roehler, L.R., Foley, K.U., Lud, M.T., & Power, C.A. (1990). Developing integrated programs. In G.G. Duffey (Ed.), *Reading the Middle School* (pp. 184–199). Newark, DE: International Reading Association.

Rubin, A. & Hansen, J. (1984). *Reading and Writing: How Are the First Two "R's" Related?* (Technical Report No. 51). Champaign, IL: Center for the Study of Reading.

Samuels, S.J. (1988). *Prologue.* In S.J. Samuels & P.D. Pearson (Eds.), *Changing School Reading Programs* (pp. vii–viii). Newark, DE: International Reading Association.

Siu-Runyan, Y. (1990). Supporting principals. *Journal of Reading, 33*(7), 546–549.

Smith, F.R. & Feathers, K.M. (1983). Teacher and student perceptions of content area reading. *Journal of Reading, 26*(4), 348–354.

Smith, F.R. & Feathers, K.M. (1983). The role of reading in content classrooms: Assumption vs. reality. *Journal of Reading, 27*(3), 262–269.

Sylwester, R. (1995). *A Celebration of Neurons: An Educators Guide to the Human Brain.* Alexandria, VA: Association for Supervision and Curriculum Development.

Taylor, B.M. & Beach, R.W. (1984). The effects of text structure instruction on middle grade students' comprehension and production of expository text. *Reading Research Quarterly, 19*(2), 134–146.

Tierney, R.J. & Leys, M. (1984). *What Is the Value of Connecting Reading and Writing?* (Technical Report No. 55). Champaign, IL: Center for the Study of Reading.

Venezky, R.L., Kaestle, C.F., & Sum, A.M. (1987). *The Subtle Danger: Reflections on the Literacy Abilities of America's Young Adults.* Princeton, NJ: Center for the Assessment of Educational Progress, Educational Testing Service.

Wisconsin State Reading Association. (1991). *Reading Design for Middle Level Schools: A Position Statement of Wisconsin State Reading Association and Wisconsin Association for Middle Level Education.* Schofield, WI: Wisconsin State Reading Association.

Witte, P.L. & Otto, W. (1981). Reading instruction at the postelementary level: Review and comments. *Journal of Educational Research, 74*(3), 148–158.

Chapter 14

Exemplary Literacy Programs

Innovative teachers are helping young adolescents become more literate in schools across the nation. This chapter highlights some exemplary programs. Educators struggling to create, recreate, or revitalize their literacy learning programs may benefit from the following stories and voices. Rathjen and Johnson and Tompkins describe long-term efforts to implement an exemplary reading program district-wide. Dozier and Coomes describe their school-wide efforts and Sherman finishes the contributions with an enthusiastic account of her implementation of a reading and writing program in her classroom.

Reading Across Disciplines Program

NANCY RATHJEN
Parkway School District
St. Louis, Missouri

The Reading Across Disciplines (RAD) program is a systematic integration of reading strategies and study skills into the curricula of social studies, language arts, science, math, and elective subjects. The RAD program began with a pilot at Parkway Central Middle School from 1988–1990, has expanded to all Parkway secondary schools, and is presently being piloted in the elementary schools. The Parkway School District, located in west St. Louis County, encompasses nine different communities and sixty-eight square miles. Parkway's students represent a wide range of ethnic and cultural backgrounds: students speak twenty-seven languages. Approximately twenty-two thousand students are enrolled in the district's eighteen elementary schools, five middle schools, four high schools, and one alternative high school. This enrollment makes Parkway the largest school district in St. Louis County and the fourth largest in the state. The district employs 1350 teachers with an average of eighteen years of teaching experience.

Now entering its ninth year of implementation, Reading Across Disciplines is the formal incorporation of reading techniques and study skills into the content of established curriculum. Figure 14.1 provides a framework for classroom teachers to focus on reading development.

During the 1990 to 1991 school year, eighth-grade interdisciplinary teams across the district implemented the RAD program as a year-long interdisciplinary team project. Expansion began with seventh-grade pilots at three middle schools and 25 percent of the high school staff. The seventh-grade pilots and high school staff participation expanded the following year. An expansion to the sixth grade was piloted in the 1994 to 1995 school year. During the 1995 to 1996 school year, all sixth-, seventh-, and eighth-grade teams at five middle schools (with reinforcement at the high schools) were actively implementing reading and study skill instruction using the Reading Across Disciplines program (see Figure 14.2).

The focus grade levels for RAD in Parkway continues to be the middle school for several reasons. A significant number of students are unable to adapt reading skills learned in elementary schools to reading situations they encounter in secondary schools. In spite of the abundance of research advocating reading instruction as an integral part of the content area classroom, data suggest that in reality content area teachers spend a negligible amount of time showing students how to use such strategies.

Interdisciplinary teaming provides the ideal opportunity for a group of teachers to teach reading using a regular, systematic approach. Interdisciplinary reading units correlated to current curriculum materials are presented in all classes as shown in Figure 14.3.

The ultimate goal of the project is the internalization and application of effective reading strategies. Success of the project was evaluated with various indicators. In addition, subjective evaluation by parent surveys, teacher observations, and student evaluation provided overwhelmingly positive support.

In 1988 and 1989, students on the RAD pilot team were assessed using the *Degrees of Reading Power* test and achieved four times the growth of students on the control team. Special emphasis was placed on helping at-risk students achieve. At-risk student growth results supported the observations of the teachers who believed their students were progressing well. Whereas at-risk students on the control team increased their score two percentile points, at-risk students on the RAD team improved their performance twenty-three percentile points.

During the following year of the project, those results were exceeded by pilot teams. In addition, pilot teams replicated both the average student growth by team and at-risk student growth. During the third year of evaluation, the RAD program again exceeded the average reading comprehension growth shown by eighth-grade students during the previous two years of the program. Subsequent middle schools piloting the program not only met these results in their respective first and second years, but also exceeded the previous results. The reading growth has remained consistent over the life of the program. Clearly the more encouragement and reinforcement students get in the practice of RAD reading strategies and study skills, the more likely their progress in reading will carry over to high school.

An additional follow-up study of the original pilot eighth-grade students was conducted during the year these students should have graduated from high school. The results of this study indicated that compared with similar students who did not receive RAD in eighth

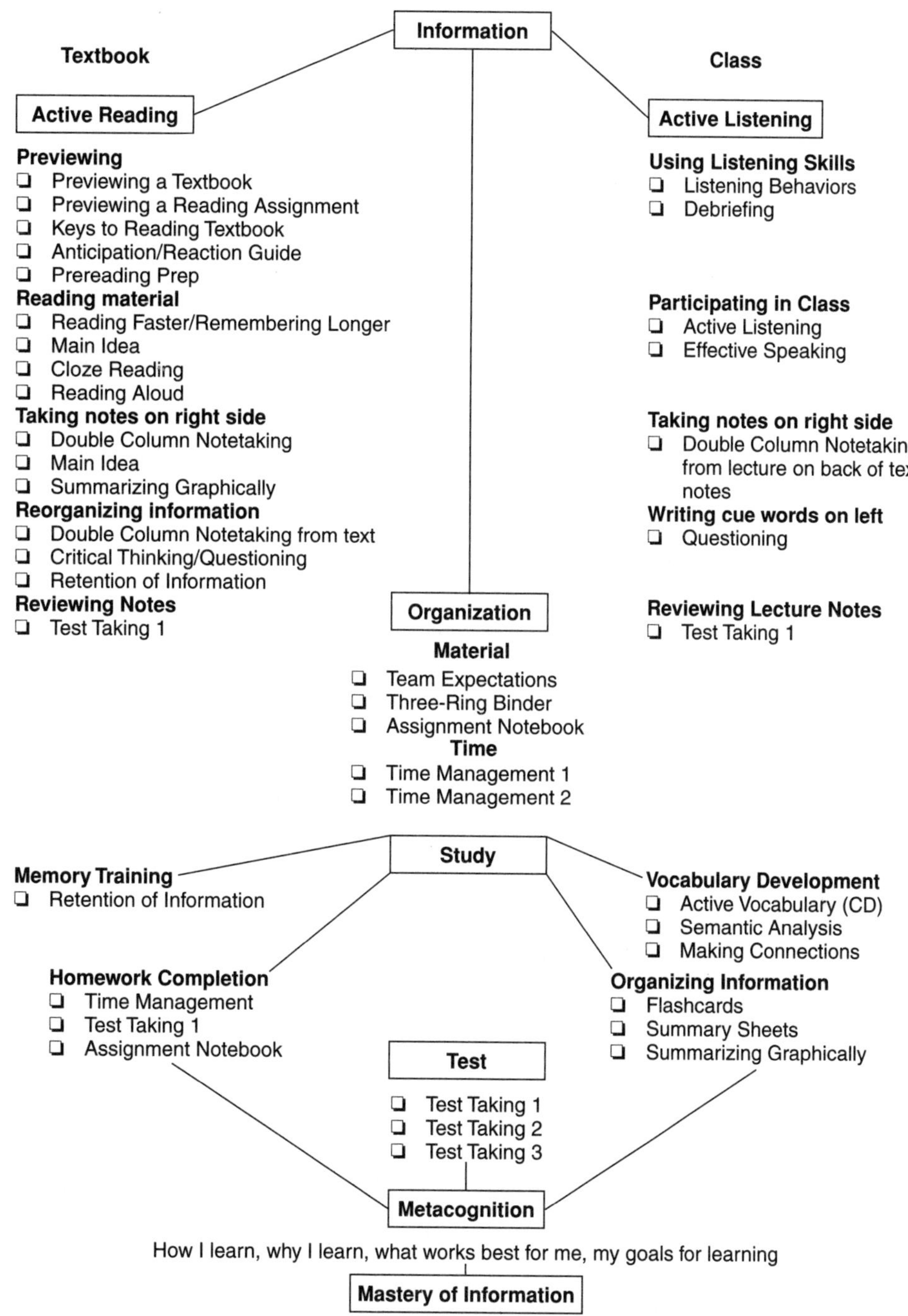

FIGURE 14.1 Reading Across Disciplines: A Look at How RAD Components Work as a System

Copyright © 1995 by Reading Across Disciplines Program.

Month	Skill	Grade Level of Direct Instruction	Reinforced at Grade Levels
September	Team Expectations	6–7	8
	Previewing a Textbook	4–8	9–12
	Three-Ring Binder Organization	4–8	9–12
	Using Assignment Notebook	4–7	8–12
	Organizing Study Space	4–5	6–8
	Previewing a Reading Assignment	4–8	9–12
	Reading Assessment Survey	4–8	
	Keys to Reading Textbook	7	8–12
	Listening Skills	5–12	
October	Organizing Home Study Space	5–6	7–8
	Double Column Notes from Text	6–12	
	Main Idea	8	9–12
	Time Management I	7	9–12
	Reading Faster, Remembering Longer	8	9–12
November	Introduction to Reading Faster	5–6	7
	Retention of Information	7	8–12
	Homework Completion	4–7	8–12
	Test Taking I	8	9–12
	Test Preparation	5–6	
December	Discussion & Listening—Goldfish Bowl	5–8	
	Vocabulary Development-CD	5–12	9–12
	Cloze Reading	5–12	

FIGURE 14.2 Reading Across Disciplines 4–12: Scope and Sequence

Month	Strategy	Grade Level of Direct Instruction	Reinforced at Grade Levels
January	Peer Inspection—Three-Ring Binder	6–8	
	Time Management II	7	8–12
	Catching Up When School Is Missed	5–6	
	Anticipation/Reaction Guide	5–12	
	Comparison/Contrast	6–7	
February	Reading Aloud	4–8	9–12
	Prediction—Preview III	5–6	
	Test Taking #2	8	9–12
	Goal Setting	5–6	7–12
	Preview to Paragraphs	5–6	7–12
March	Mapping-Summarizing Graphically	4–12	
	Memory Training	5–6	
	Vocabulary II-SFA	4–6	7–8
April	Prereading Preparation	8	9–12
	Test Taking #3	8	9–12
	DCN Questioning	6–7	8
May	Recreational Reading—How to Choose a Book	4–6	7–8
	Double Column Notetaking from Lecture	8	9–12
	RAD Study System	8	9–12

FIGURE 14.2 *Continued*

Copyright © 1996 by Reading Across Disciplines Program.

grade, those who did were significantly more likely to be at an age-appropriate grade level and still be enrolled in school. This "RAD effect" was even more noticeable among the at-risk students who participated in the original pilot. Many of the students in the control group who were performing below average in reading as eighth graders were no longer enrolled

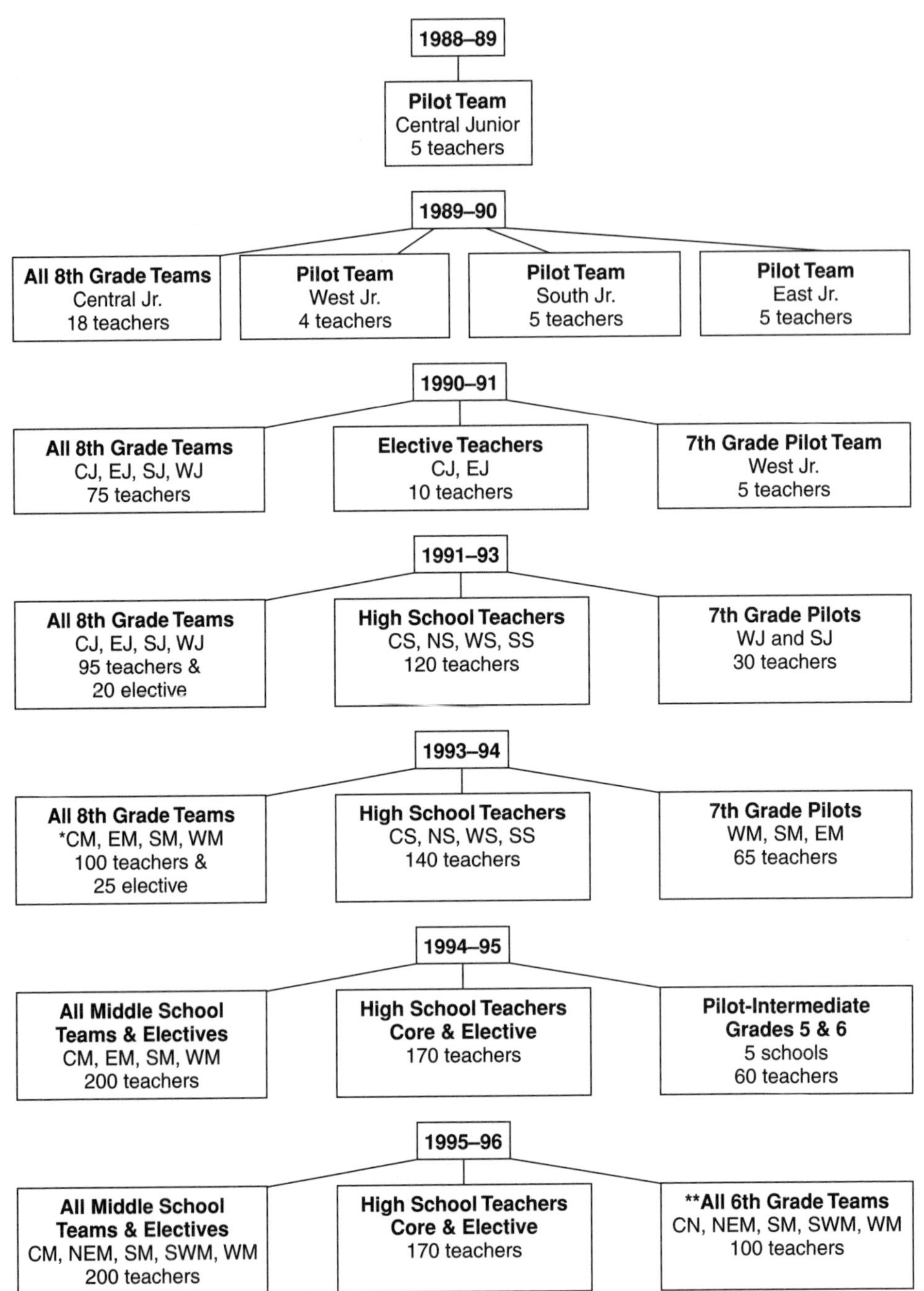

FIGURE 14.3 Reading Across Disciplines Implementation 1988–1996

Copyright © 1996 by Reading Across Disciplines Program.

and less than half made it to the age-appropriate level of twelfth grade. Yet all (100 percent) of the at-risk readers who received RAD training in eighth grade were still in school.

The impact on the budget is minimal to implement and support the program. The only two additional cost items are (1) printing of units developed to correlate study skills and reading techniques with specific curriculum materials, and (2) in-service workshops for all content teachers. Development of the staff as confident teachers of reading and study skills must overlay the already superior job of teaching content. Orientation and training of teachers new to the program at a summer workshop to understand the techniques involved in teaching the units is essential for success. Summer workshops provide the background, knowledge, confidence, and practice with new strategies for teachers to implement the units during the school year. In addition, once a teacher is introduced to the program, follow-up training and assistance help ensure that implementation occurs. Introductory and intermediate workshops have continued through the life of the program.

The parent–child–teacher connection occurs through correlation of the Reading Across Disciplines units with strategies recommended in the Parkway publication, *A Parent's Guide to Study Skills.* Also, *The Principal's Newsletter* highlights learning strategies in regular articles and suggests effective ways for parents to reinforce the strategy at home. The Reading Across Disciplines program is presented to parents at PTO parent forums held regularly throughout the district.

In addition to the Parkway School District where the program was developed with a middle school team of teachers, the program has been implemented at many school districts across the country with similar results. The program appears to be most effective when three variables are in place: (1) interdisciplinary teams of teachers, (2) primary focus at the middle school level and reinforcement at the high school level, and (3) a reading teacher or classroom teacher with a change of responsibility from small group remediation to RAD coordinator. Responsibilities of the reading teachers include working with classroom teachers in planning and presenting RAD units, developing RAD units that correlate with current curriculum materials and textbooks, working with targeted students for frontloading of units, and most importantly, keeping teams on track with the scope and sequence.

With expansion across grade levels, Reading Across Disciplines has made a significant difference in reading and study skills for students. The goal for RAD is for students to learn and apply the most effective reading and study methods in content area classes, and in the process, become reflective, independent learners. Experience and test scores confirm continued achievement of this goal.

Evolution of a Reading Program

CELESTE JOHNSON
AND
DAN TOMPKINS
Volusia County Schools
Daytona Beach, Florida

In East Central Florida lies Volusia County, bordered on its west side by the St. Johns River and on its east side by the Atlantic Ocean. Its sixty-one schools serve fifty-seven thousand students whose median scores rank above state and national averages on standardized tests.

The ten middle schools offer a unique reading curriculum in grades 6, 7, and 8, which has been developed in part using Judith Irvin's book *Reading and the Middle School Student: Strategies to Enhance Literacy.*

The middle school philosophy took hold in the Volusia County School District during 1986 as a pilot program, which grew in succeeding years as more junior high schools became middle schools. The original concept for middle schools, which is still used, included the following classes in a seven-period day: social studies, mathematics, science, language arts, reading, physical education, and an exploratory course. Initially, even though a middle school philosophy was in place, most subjects were still taught in isolation from each other and reading was taught using a basal reader. By the end of the third year of middle school implementation, however, dissatisfaction with the existing basal reading program and the curricular separation of classes was growing: reading scores on standardized tests were questioned and students continued to struggle with text.

In response to these concerns, the district administration formed the first Middle School Reading Task Force (MSRTF) in 1989 to evaluate reading instruction in Volusia County middle schools and to look for new directions in the curriculum. This group began by examining the problems and setting goals. Although the MSRTF owed its beginning to top-level district management, it became clear that effective leadership of the task force would need to be provided by innovative classroom teachers and school-level administrators.

The first year of assessment and goal setting included brainstorming, researching, and attending seminars and workshops. The MSRTF also worked extensively with Judith L. Irvin to refine its vision for the reading program. Soon afterward the MSRTF began writing and piloting a reading program for seventh and eighth grade. From inception through implementation, eleven months of intensive preparation to create a strategic reading curriculum had taken place. Development of a model for the role of the reading teacher was instrumental to guarantee the success of the reading program; few people could identify with certainty what this position entailed.

As it evolved, the reading teacher's role grew to include serving as the team reading consultant and resource teacher in addition to regular classroom duties. Consultation and resource activities included the following:

1. Team consultant.
   - Administer and score *Degrees of Reading Power* test and discuss instructional implications of individual student reading levels with the team.
   - Facilitate discussion of concepts, units, and themes being taught within the team.
   - Suggest to team members strategies that increase students' comprehension of text. For example, as the team's social studies teacher plans a unit about the Civil War, the reading teacher suggests a variety of strategies that can be used throughout the unit of study such as a K-W-L, list-group-label-write, semantic mapping, scavenger hunt, or Cornell notetaking.
2. Resource teacher.
   - Model reading strategies for subject area teachers using students' texts.
   - Observe teachers and offer suggestions in strategic reading instruction.
   - Coordinate strategy instruction across the team.

- Encourage teachers to use reading strategies independently.
- Provide support to teachers who may be apprehensive about new instructional methods.
- Suggest trade or picture books to enrich curriculum.

3. Regular duties of the reading teacher.

- Strategic reading instruction using authentic text.

  —Introduce students to parts of their textbooks.
  —Preview assigned reading.
  —Teach notetaking skills including Cornell notetaking method and semantic mapping.
  —Teach vocabulary skills in context.
  —Reinforce expository writing.
  —Coach students in test taking and study skills.
  —Give instruction and practice in speed-reading techniques.
  —Instill lifelong love for reading novels.
  —Introduce students to popular authors and their books.
  —Write to authors.
  —Videotape book reviews or skits depicting exciting scenes.
  —Offer a variety of literature and give students choices.
  —Set time aside for reading.
  —Set up Reading Workshop.
  —Foster journal writing.
  —Select and read class novels and picture books that enrich the curriculum.

- Use the arts—drama, art, music, and movement—to bring characters and scenes to life.

The Volusia County middle school reading program that grew out of the first year of reflection and planning was implemented as a pilot program in the succeeding year. As that year progressed, the MSRTF members continued to meet to review, adapt, and add to their curriculum. The pilot teachers who served on teams that embraced a strong middle school philosophy were more likely to participate in the three components that made up the role of the reading teacher as envisioned by the MSRTF. The following summer, the task force wrote a curriculum manual and provided in-service for all reading teachers at the six pilot schools. By the fall of 1991, all seventh- and eighth-grade middle school reading teachers had received training from the MSRTF in use of the manual, which was designed to guide instruction in strategic reading using authentic text, literature-based learning experiences, and study and test-taking skills.

During the school years of 1992 to 1993 and 1993 to 1994, there were no further developments or refinements in the middle school reading program; however, under the direction of the reading and language arts supervisor, a second MSRTF was formed in June of 1994. Made up of sixth-, seventh-, or eighth-grade reading teachers from nine of the middle schools in the district, the MSRTF revised the 1990 manual to include sixth-grade reading along with increasing the selection of strategies and resources available to teachers. Oral language and listening activities, portfolio development, and alternative forms of assessment were added to the manual at this time.

Have Volusia County's middle schools demonstrated any significant change in students' reading performance that resulted from the implementation of this reading program? As measured by the Comprehensive Test of Basic Skills (CTBS), students' overall reading scores measured between the years 1991 and 1996 have consistently increased by an average of seven percentile points between grades 6 and 7 and five percentile points between grades 7 and 8. Because these national percentile rankings are normed for grade levels, the overall twelve percentile point increase is most likely due to instruction that utilizes the curriculum developed by the MSRTF. The effort has definitely been worthwhile.

Targeting the Electives to Change the Reading Program

ROSALYN DOZIER
Langston Hughes Middle School
Fairfax County Public Schools, Fairfax, Virginia

Hughes Middle School lies thirty minutes by car from Washington, D.C., and draws eleven hundred seventh and eighth graders from the town of Reston, Virginia. Because Reston is a planned community encompassing all socioeconomic levels, the Hughes population draws students from very low income, government subsidized housing, up to million dollar homes on large tracts of land. With the influx of Southeast Asian refugees beginning fifteen years ago, and the Hispanic population burgeoning in the last five years, the ethnic profile of the Hughes population now stands at 40 percent minority. African Americans and Hispanic Americans comprise the largest portion of this minority student population.

The reading specialist functions as a resource person, teaming with all classroom teachers, to teach reading strategies. The "4-core" (English, science, social studies, and mathematics) teachers form interdisciplinary teams in both seventh and eighth grades.

The Beginnings of the Hughes Reading Resource Role

I was hired to function as a resource reading specialist and asked to design and implement a reading resource program for the school. No written job description was provided, however. It took three years of "coming in the back door," relating to teachers on a one-to-one basis, and a change of principals, before any headway could be made in establishing the role of resource teacher at Hughes, a role that by now had the full support of the Fairfax County school administration. As in any setting, the alliances, backgrounds, and belief systems of the faculty had to be assessed and considered before a resource reading program that would be systematic and welcomed by the faculty could be implemented, and before *all* students could be served effectively.

Clearly, the electives of teen living (the new home economics) and technology education (the new industrial arts or "shop") were good places to begin. No matter *where* I worked with students, the strategies were all the same regardless in which class students encountered them. Starting the reading resource program with elective courses made sense for the following reasons:

1. English-as-a-second-language (ESL) learners and students who are learning disabled or physically handicapped are scheduled into electives with the students in "regular education," with the majority of them going into teen living and technology education. This gives maximum exposure to these special populations for reading instruction away from their special education setting.
2. Low achieving students traditionally choose the electives of teen living and technology education, rather than creative writing, journalism, and drama. This choice provides them instructional time in reading in addition to their "academic" core.

Both of these electives had built-in motivators: *food to eat* and *things to handle.* Therefore, these classes are viewed as "fun" by students. Elective teachers are also accustomed to a freer format and a higher level of mobility in their classrooms. They have traditionally been open to try new things and have generally been more process oriented.

Implementation

My initial efforts began with getting to know more of the teachers personally, which consumed a lot of "chat time," but paid off handsomely as time progressed. The teen living teacher agreed to work with me, and the following weeks were electrifying! Ideas flew back and forth like wildfire, with both of us really excited about the possibilities we saw in combining reading and teen living. After much brainstorming, discussion, correlating our ideas with her curriculum and hours of development time, we developed a number of units over the next several years—and taught them collaboratively. These reading-in-teen-living instructional units have been modified as the needs of scheduling and curriculum have changed. Many of the materials we designed have been revised, but all are still intact in her teen living curriculum ten years later—taught by her, while I have gone on to team with others.

Samples from Reading-in-Teen-Living Instructional Units

The teen living curriculum (now termed "work and family studies") served as the basis for the reading-in-teen-living units developed collaboratively with the teen living teacher. The curriculum has a unit on caring that includes caring for self (personal hygiene and grooming), caring for animals, and caring for others (focuses on baby-sitting).

Teen living unit—**Caring**
Coordinated Reading Components

A. *For self.*

- Notetaking while viewing videos and listening to direct instruction.
- Sharing notes to check for accuracy and completeness.
- Direct instruction on how to write a summary.
- Using completed, accurate notes to write a summary.

B. *For animals.*

- Free brochures from the county animal control are used.
- Direct instruction in the function, format, and reading of brochures.
- Evaluation of the information—authenticating its sources.
- Creating a booklet on an animal care topic of the students' choice, researching numerous brochures on a wide variety of topics.

This project was a real boon to the ESL students who as yet had little proficiency in speaking English. One teacher read the information to the students to let them hear the language, did a lot of miming to explain as much as possible, allowed the students to copy a portion of the brochure, then asked them to create a colorful cover for the report just like everyone else. This quickly revealed the numerous artistically talented ESL students, who made a genuine contribution to the class. We then capitalized on their talents in other work to help integrate them into the group.

- A check-off guidesheet was created to guide the students through the process of researching, writing, and presenting a report, including a bibliography of the brochure used.
- A criteria list was created, with student input, with each student being given a copy before beginning the booklet. This criteria list was used, in turn, for self, peer, and teacher evaluation at the end of the unit.
- Direct instruction was given in composing creative report covers.
- Direct instruction was given in oral presentation skills.
- Booklets were autographed and presented orally by their authors, then proudly hung in the hall!

C. *For others.*

- Child development (how to read an article).
- Child psychology (how to read an article).
- Nutritional snacks for children (reading a recipe—following written directions).
- Sewing safe, soft toys for children (reading a pattern—following written directions).
- Baby-sitting:

  —safety procedures (how to read safety booklets)
  —games to play (nursery rhymes, songs, finger games)
  —appropriate videos (students view videos and evaluate them for suitability to small children, using predetermined criteria based on child psychology and development)
  —activities (how to read to small children—criteria list created by students and teachers as to what makes a good children's book)

Culminating Activity: The teen living teacher has approximately twenty small children (ages 2 to 5) brought in for a day of free baby-sitting provided by the teen living students. They fill out observation sheets based on what they have learned in child development and psychology, give the children the nutritious snacks they have prepared, share the toys they have made, watch the videos that they have approved by viewing and evaluating, play games they have chosen, and read the books that they have written and illustrated to the children.

Samples from Reading-Technology Education Units

Chatting with the technology education teachers provided an opportunity to know what their curriculum plans were and where I might appropriately fit reading into them. I knew enough about the "shop" to talk intelligently about the subject, and found that the seventh-grade teacher wanted to do a "careers in technology" project, but was unsure of how to structure it. I volunteered to design the student guidesheets to walk students through the process, which involved library research, how to use the Reader's Guide, notetaking, organizing the report, writing it, and then presenting it.

Every student completed this careers in technology project. Their presentations were put on video and shown at "Back to School" night. This technology education teacher confessed later that in twenty-five years of teaching, he had never taken a class to the library until this unit. He also learned how to use the Reader's Guide. He is still teaching this unit ten years later.

The eighth-grade technology education teacher had one class of seventh graders and asked me to team with him to do the same careers project. As that was being completed, *Time* magazine ran a cover story on robotics and I asked this eighth-grade teacher if he were up to developing a unit on this exciting technology that was guaranteed to excite students. He was, and we were off and running!

In this six-week unit, students were asked to perform one simple task: design and build a wooden robotic arm that would pick something up, move it to a new location, and put it down. The design, the object to be picked up, and the systems to control it were entirely student choice. It had to be powered initially by hydraulic or pneumatic power, using large syringes or magnetic power, and using self-made magnets from batteries and coiled wire. Many are now being operated by computer, with programs written by the students. The reading portion of this unit focused on

- Vocabulary strategies because of the number of technical words to be learned.
- Following directions in sequence with a check-off guidesheet designed.
- Self, peer, and teacher evaluations (all based on preset criteria).
- Core readings from books on robotics.

Culminating activities:

- Robotic arms are entered in the Fairfax County Technology Fair.
- A field trip to the General Motors plant in Baltimore, Maryland, to see the robotic assembly of cars and delivery of materials to the assembly stations.
- Robotic arms are demonstrated to other classes and to parents on "Parade of Stars" night. This unit, "Put a Little Robotics in Your Life," has received wide acclaim. It has been presented at numerous conferences, including the International Business/Education Partnership conference in Coventry, England, in 1992.

"Robotics" is still being taught by the classroom teacher in the eighth-grade preengineering class, with the (modified) materials that we designed ten years ago.

"Reading in the Content Areas" Spreads to the other Electives

Because most of the "loud, noisy, messy, but fun" electives are located in the same wing of the Hughes building (so as not to disturb students doing "real work"), proximity provided an invaluable asset in spreading the "reading to learn" word to other electives.

Art

- Emotions are interpreted with color, line, shape, and words; the words being a diamanté poem written on a diamond-shaped background and inserted somewhere in the composition created. Instruction is provided by both teachers. Brainstorming for idea generation is an integral part of this unit.
- Articles from art trade magazines are read using learning strategies.
- Colorful, fanciful paper maché masks are created and a very short fantasy myth is written to accompany each, then glued to the inside.

Because this art teacher is now a member of the seventh-grade teams, the integration of reading, art, literature, and writing is being spread into the entire seventh grade!

Music

- The process and materials designed in teen living and technology education were used to design a "careers in music" unit. This repetition is especially helpful in the process of acquiring, processing, and communicating information. The presentation mode was changed to a visual (poster or video) for this unit.
- Reading a feature magazine or newspaper article using learning strategies.
- Writing twelve bar blues songs with lyric writing.

Physical Education

- The sports page from the newspaper is now posted on the gym wall daily for those who finish dressing out early, or who are ready to leave class a little earlier than the others. Many Hughes students do not subscribe to a newspaper at home. This is their one chance to form a habit of turning to a newspaper for information.

Foreign Language

An unusually exciting unit, "Reading in a Foreign Language without Knowing the Foreign Language," leaves students scratching their heads and asking, "How did she *DO* that?" I truly do not know the foreign language and reinforce this at the beginning. The content teacher provides a passage in the foreign language. I go through the reading, set up on a large chart hung at the front of the room, without any explanation as to how I am reading it. Using context clues is the secret, of course, and I think aloud as I figure out the passage using context clues. This works best with the Romance languages and I do not reveal until the very end that I had two years of Latin!

Students are given a difficult passage in the foreign language and are asked to use this strategy to read it cold. No preparation, homework, or study time is given. Students can assist each other with words and explanations of the context clues used. Teachers and students alike are amazed when, collectively, they decode the passage completely without using a dictionary. Some words may miss literal translation a bit, but the meaning always comes through.

What Next?

Over the years, teachers from the core academic areas have become more receptive to building the subject of reading into their curricula, so there has been a progressive transition into arithmetic, language arts, social studies, and science. These units of instruction have come about in many of the same ways as the electives. There are three helpful events that have moved this transition along.

1. An eight-day "Reading to Learn at the Secondary Level" institute involving the reading specialist (who served as part of the teaching staff), and four other content area teachers from the same school. This institute required that the strategies learned be tried in each teacher's classroom, and the results reported back to the group.
2. More and more college graduates in education are familiar with reading in the content areas.
3. Hughes now has a principal who understands the importance of teaching reading in the content areas at the middle school level and supports it. He has built in accountability by requiring teams to include reading and content area initiatives in their team plans and it is now built into the overall school plan. Test scores are another focus as in any reading program, but are viewed as a weather vane directing instruction, rather than an end product to be used as an evaluation of teacher performance.

Whither Goest Thou?

The Hughes reading program reaches outward from its instructional priorities to include several school-wide incentive programs and workshops for teachers, students, and parents. These workshops have covered a wide range of topics including test preparation, test taking, "Groping with Grouping", "Medicine for Academic Success" for low achieving students and their parents and "How To Get Kids to Write Who Won't Write." PTA newsletter articles are written to provide communication with parents, and mentoring of other new reading specialists is considered a professional obligation. School-wide "sustained silent reading" is preached anywhere I can find a pulpit!

Sponsorship of competitions is also provided. A highly acclaimed invention program (teaching research, thinking, and problem-solving skills) is team taught with the eighth-grade science teachers, resulting in an impressive display of student-created inventions on "Parade of Stars" night. A "Reading is Fun" poster contest is integrated into an art graphics unit that teaches the art of effective visuals, and a poetry writing contest follows instruction in a reading and English unit on how to write poetry.

Teachers are encouraged to present these integrated units at conferences, and support is given in the development of these presentations. Publication of teamed reading and content area work is also encouraged. The *Virginia Mathematics Teacher* has published some of the work done at Hughes in reading in math. Attendance at all local, state, and international conferences (all paid for from personal funds) is considered an absolute necessity to keep current with the latest research, materials, and leaders in the field.

When looking at the Hughes program thirteen years ago, and then looking at the point to which it has evolved today, the program is quickly recognized as being "in process," adjusting to changing needs and thinking in response to the latest research and practice in middle school education and in middle school teaching of reading.

Rosalyn Dozier was the winner of the Nila Banton Smith award in 1992. This award is presented by the International Reading Association to a teacher who has made outstanding contributions to reading at the secondary level.

Dakota Meadows Quiet Reading Program

SALLY PAYNE COOMES
Mankato, Minnesota

Each day begins with quiet reading at Dakota Meadows Middle School in Mankato, Minnesota. Students are expected to have a book in their possession when the bell rings and ten minutes are devoted to quiet reading.

During quiet reading, both students and teachers read a book, preferably one that tells a story, such as novels, biographies, or histories rather than books of lists or facts so that readers can sustain attention, build up speed and fluency, and grow to love good stories (Atwell, 1987). The following features of the quiet reading program make it successful:

- Classroom paperback libraries have been provided for each teacher or advisor.
- A staff volunteer reading committee selects and distributes additional suitable books each year. Parent volunteers cover them with clear contact paper.
- An introductory lesson has been created for each teacher to present describing the rationale, the opportunities, and the expectations of the program. The lesson also includes the introductory paragraphs from six appealing books for each grade along with a collage on transparency of the six book jackets.
- Colorful Dakota Meadows bookmarks are provided. The student records the beginning and ending page on the bookmark each day. Books may be abandoned. The student begins another book with a new bookmark. Bookmarks are filed in a conference folder to share with parents.
- Students are expected to have their quiet reading books with them throughout the day to allow further reading when time permits.
- Language arts teachers and some additional teachers promote reading through book talks, reading aloud, passing books around the room, student sharing, or discussion of ways to find a good book.

- Videotaped book talks have been shown featuring staff members' selections.
- A reading survey is administered at the beginning and end of the school year.
- A reading self-evaluation is completed by each student prior to the spring and fall student-led parent conference.

4-Star Book Program

Students recommend outstanding books to one another through the 4-star reading program. The winning student-designed poster is displayed in each advisor's room. If a student reads an especially good book, the student completes a 4-star book card and posts it on the bulletin board around the poster. Other students who agree may add their signatures for extra votes.

Some teachers supply colored stars to make the cards more appealing. A list of the most highly recommended 4-star books is compiled each year to guide reading and further ordering. "When is a book a 4-star book?" lists are posted in each room: The criteria follow:

- The book was a page turner; I couldn't put it down.
- I wanted to stay up late to read it.
- It's a book I wish were longer.
- It's a book I'd like to receive for my birthday.
- It made me want to read another book by the same author.
- I'd like to reread it.
- I keep thinking of parts of the book even after I've finished it.
- It helped me understand something.
- It's a book I'd like to recommend to someone else.

After the first year, surveys indicated that eighth graders' reading increased from the previous year. They reported reading an average of 13.55 books, up from 9.1 the previous year. Eighth graders also reported owning an average of 116.76 books, up from 58.85 at the beginning of the school year. A dislike of reading was reported by 4.6 percent, down from 8.3 percent at the beginning of the year. Teachers and students alike remain enthusiastic about the quiet reading program; it would be difficult to start the day without it.

Trusting the Books—Trusting Ourselves: Implementing the Reading Workshop

MARY JO SHERMAN
Heaton Middle School
Pueblo, Colorado

In my thirtieth year of classroom teaching, while planning for the typical grammar-composition-literature class, something changed my life, and the lives of hundreds of students. Nancie Atwell's (1987) *In the Middle: Writing, Reading, and Learning with Adolescents* opened my eyes to a new world as did Linda Rief's (1992) *Seeking Diversity.*

Their Reading Workshop approach made sense to me; they suggested letting students select their own books. How could I give up the power of prescribing the right book for each student? How could they survive? How could I?

It sounded so effective, however, that I decided to give it a chance to flop. What harm could it do for nine weeks? Several years and hundreds of students later, the only harm done has been to my self-assurance. The approach was miraculous and it has worked too often to be a fluke.

You know something is working when a student writes in her log that R. L. Stine is too predictable now and that Lois Duncan is more her style. More than one young woman has found her way to Cynthia Voigt and Torey Hayden, not because I forced her, but because she tired of the less challenging authors. It takes powerful self-control for me not to suggest something when the suggestion is not invited, but it's worth the wait. I watched one eighth-grade boy struggle with *Goosebumps*—reading only because he had to and proclaiming that he hated every moment—and then see him eventually take Walter Dean Myers' *By Any Means Necessary,* the eminently readable biography of Malcolm X, off the shelf and read it—slowly, yes, but with fascination.

Then he worked his way through the rest of the Myers books in my collection, even the lengthy and challenging *Fallen Angels.* This young man is a reader now, but it never would have happened without letting him have free choice. As I worked through the snags that any new approach has, I found more and more literature supporting this free voluntary reading approach. Stephen Krashen's (1993) *The Power of Reading* summarizes the research; Mary Leonhart's (1992) *Parents Who Love Reading: Kids Who Don't* is full of first-hand experiences of a classroom teacher using this approach. The bottom line, though, experts aside, is that we must trust ourselves.

For free choice reading to work, I believe there are four absolute requirements. First and foremost, the teacher must be an avid reader of young adult literature. Second, students must be given time to read in class. Third, students must have easy access to books. Finally, there must be some vehicle for response—for the kids to respond to the literature and for someone to respond to the kids.

The Teacher Must be an Avid Reader of Young Adult Literature

Young adult literature is my reading of choice now. Stunningly beautiful things are available, but it is not enough that the teacher knows the titles. The teacher must read the books, and then must talk books with the students. For example, Gary Paulsen's *Nightjohn* about a slave who taught others to read should be required reading for the human race. Walter Dean Myers' *Fallen Angels* is possibly the most moving Vietnam book I've ever read. Cynthia Voigt's *Wings of a Falcon* is my favorite book of all time, at any level, and is a hero tale unmatched, in my opinion. The anonymous *It Happened to Nancy* is a nonfiction diary of a young woman contracting AIDS via date rape. Ryan White's *My Story* is unsurpassed as an autobiography. And my reading Torey Hayden's *One Child* in a Georgia restaurant caused the hostess to sit down by my table and tell me how that book had impacted her life. (I don't know what was happening to the other customers.) Sharon Draper's *Tears of a Tiger* combines the themes of drinking and driving with basketball, and yet much, much more as it shows kids coping with stress, guilt, death, and eventually suicide. Janet Bode takes nonfiction to a new level in all her books about teens dealing with violence, with death and dying, with unfortunate love, and many other topics.

I try to hear authors speak at every opportunity, and this means attending conferences, nearly always at my own expense. What could top having Walter Dean Myers sit next to me at breakfast and say, "Please—call me Walter." And I will never ever forget him telling why he wrote *Fallen Angels.* Hearing Gary Paulsen tell the stories he included in *Winterdance* made me laugh until I cried—just as I had done when I read it. Listening to Cynthia Voigt speak about heroes, watching her expressive face, seeing in it the warmth that makes her characters real and lovable, and hearing T. A. Barron tell how he encountered a whale off the coast of Baja while in his sea kayak, in the dark—these are tales I take back to my students and we all are the richer for them.

There is absolutely no substitute for knowing the books firsthand. I once had a student teacher who had read one book by R. L. Stine. She came to me with stacks of book cards she had diligently prepared, but with no first-hand knowledge of young adult literature. She "did me a favor" by reading *Maniac Magee.* The students saw through her in a moment and the credibility she lost was never regained.

Students Must Have Class Time to Read

Just as with the first requirement, there is no substitute for having class time to read—and I, the teacher, need to read right along with them. Sometimes I am tempted to grade just a few papers while they're reading, but my students are rarely fooled. If reading is important to me, then I must read. Period!

Currently we do language arts activities for three days a week; the other two days we read or write in our reading logs. The amount of time anyone devotes to in-class reading is, of course, an individual choice, but it needs to be more than ten or fifteen minutes stuffed in here and there. It needs to be an integral part of the class. Each reading day I take ten minutes at the beginning of the hour for students to name their book and tell on what page they are reading. This reporting accomplishes three things: first, it lets them know I am watching their progress; second, others hear what books their classmates are reading; and finally, it lets me do mini-book talks as different titles are mentioned. I jot down what they tell me on a simple grid. In addition to the in-class reading, I ask that they read thirty minutes a day, five days a week, at home, and have parents sign-off on a little form where this is recorded.

On the reading days or in the reading segments, my students must read—and it must be a book, not a magazine and not a textbook. I've tried to discourage comics, but then a student comes to *Maus: A Survivor's Tale* or to Janet Bode's work that incorporates cartoons. And who could dispute the value of the wonderful picture books available now? I have many in my classroom collection. The source of the book—library, home, department store, the classroom collection—whether it is fiction or nonfiction, serious or hilarious—these matter not.

I put a big poster on my door's window indicating it is reading time. We all read in peace, with kids sitting everywhere, and with absolute silence reigning in the room. There is not much I do in my classroom that is more powerful in terms of making my students enjoy reading.

Students Must Have Easy Access to Books

Nearly every middle school has a respectable media center or library, and mine is no exception. However, I have discovered that nothing replaces a classroom library. Nothing! Currently mine, dubbed Sherman Branch Library by my students, contains more than eight hundred fine young adult books, but it did not start that way. One year at a conference the publisher of Jerry Spinelli's *Maniac Magee* gave me a copy; I read it and fell in love. So when a student (this was before I moved to this approach) would ask if I had read anything good lately, I'd pull *Maniac* off the shelf and loan it out. The result was magical! Never once did a student fail to read the whole thing and then come back and tell me what part he or she liked most.

Building my library was slow going at first, but it is amazing where you can find books if you really look. Did you know that for the cost of a single computer, you can get a good start on a beauty of a classroom library?

My principal has been generous with funds, and he says he gets more return from the money he spends on my classroom's books than on any other investment. Of course my kids write notes to him about which ones they like, and they talk books to him at lunch hour—neither is accidental! I've written articles for which I was given books. I volunteer to review for several organizations and get to keep the books. And of course, I buy lots of the books myself.

My classroom is totally dominated by the books. In fact, my desks face the wall where the library is shelved, so the books form the backdrop for every classroom activity and presentation. The atmosphere, the environment they create is unbeatable. Former students sometimes visit my room because, "I miss the books." Of course I teach other language skills, but it all starts from the books. Without reading, how can we succeed at anything else?

But how do we know which books to buy? The number of young adolescent books is overwhelming, and the quality is very uneven, I'm sorry to say. There are sources, however, to guide in the selection. A favorite of mine is Mary Leonhart's *Parents Who Love Reading: Kids Who Don't.* This book is every bit as much for teachers as for parents, and it has a superb annotated bibliography. Conari Press has a wonderful little volume, *dear author,* in which are printed letters that young adults have written to authors whose books have changed their lives. I have three copies of this, and they are always in demand. The best book talks I give are when I read a letter from it that some young person has written to an author, explaining passionately the impact that author's book has had—and I hold the book in my other hand. I cannot keep that title on the shelf afterward.

Does Sherman Branch Library have every book in it? Absolutely not! I do not want every book! For example, it is one thing for students to read a steamy book they got at the library or at the supermarket—but it is another thing entirely for them to have found that book in Sherman Branch Library!

In addition, lots of current mass-market fiction such as Michael Crichton's and John Grisham's cost a lot but are readily available at public libraries and bookstores. Generally, I try not to tie up my funds on those books, opting instead to buy ones that are not as available. It is most important to remember, though, that a lousy book looks just as good as an awesome one—and the only real way to tell them apart is to read them!

Students Must Respond to Their Reading—and the Responses Must Have Responses

If my students have meaningful experiences with the books they read, then the response must be just as meaningful. I could ruin an absolutely beautiful concept of people sitting around a room reading, with the tried and true book reports, even with the many so-called innovations. These kids are becoming readers, and as middle level students, are young adults. They require a mature approach to the idea of response. Atwell talks about recreating her dining room table in her classroom, where literate people sat around and talked books—gossiping about authors, discussing and debating styles, favorites, and making each other aware of "don't miss" books. She took care of the response requirement by having the students write in logs or journals, but many of my kids are burned out by journaling. However, I am a firm believer in letter writing, and this age-old art came to my rescue.

Each week my students write a letter (to a specific recipient) in a reading log, and the recipient writes back. Each letter must be at least a page long, in ink, on one side of the paper—the usual conventions.

Unlike conventional friendly letters, however, these letters must deal with the reading, and not with summarizing plots. After all, the purpose here is not to check up on the students. It is for the students to respond to the literature, to reflect, to put themselves into the story, to evaluate, to question, to share frustrations at an author's oversight, to give in to hero worship—but it is *not* a place for plot summary.

All those "prove to me you read it" book reports encourage exactly the opposite kind of response to a book. But there are things I can do to encourage reflection. At the beginning of the year, we read a short book together, something simple and touching like John Gardiner's *Stone Fox* or Smith's *A Taste of Blackberries.* These are tailor-made for reflection. We take turns reading, but I read the weepy parts—who cares if I cry, but if a macho eighth grader sounds shaky, he has lost his fan club! We stop every few paragraphs and I ask a reflecting question, "How does Willie feel when he finds out Grandfather is sick and how would you feel in that situation?" or "Write about a special animal you have known who, like Searchlight, would give his or her very life for you." The students write these responses in their reading logs (which are nothing fancy—just a hefty spiral notebook that they will use throughout the year). Every so often we share responses and comment on each other's; but it is low-key and nonthreatening. Periodically through the year, if I notice the quality of reflection slipping, I will stop and redo the all-class activity, perhaps using a story from their literature books or another short book. Everyone needs a tune-up from time to time.

A second way I work on teaching reflection is by my own letters back to the students. Even in answer to the worst of their letters, I make sure my letter reflects, for at least a couple of paragraphs, either on how I felt when I read that particular book or on how I am feeling about whatever I'm reading at the time. I try to make my letter an absolute model of what I want from them. After I have done that, I address directly their shortcomings—what was missing, where they might have added reflective details and insights. Then I always end with a line such as, "I'm looking forward to hearing from you again in a few weeks."

So what do the students get from reflecting? A whole lot more than a reading-language arts grade! First, it supplies them with real-world writing, to a specific audience, and the audience responds. Second, reading and writing are tightly linked. I have a sign in my room taken from Atwell: "Readers Read Writing—Writers Write Reading." Truer words were never spoken. Third, there is an exchange of opinion, insight, discovery about the books they are reading. A peer's recommendation of a title carries much more weight than my best book talk. I watch a particular title make the rounds in my classroom as one after another student suggests it in reading-log letters. Fourth, the letters hook me into the network of reflecting on reading. I become part of the writing process of my students and share my own ideas, joys, frustrations about what I am reading and about what they are reading; in fact, we write as peers, not as teacher-student. Finally, and possibly the most important, these letters forge a link between students and their family members. I have read the most eloquent exchanges between mother and daughter, father and son, and brother to sister. Time after time, the student has motivated the parent to return to reading, even to reading young adult titles. Time after time, they have discovered shared reading when an hour is spent each evening reading aloud to each other; or they spend that time simply reading alone, silently—but in the same room, on the same couch.

Cautions and Caveats

It is not a perfect world, and there are things of which educators must be aware in moving toward free voluntary reading as at least part of a reading-language arts program for their students. Even now I am not sure this is *the* approach for every teacher, but more and more I suspect it is best for the kids. Four areas are of particular concern.

First, one must start slowly and build administrative support. After all, prevailing wisdom is that we must depend on detailed and sequenced anthologies to turn our students into lifelong readers or we are somehow not doing our jobs. This approach has a long history, and you will be proposing something radically different. We need to do our homework, read the experts, and perhaps try it out with a single class in a limited way. If you require out-of-class recreational reading, perhaps you could change from requiring book reports to the letter format; or start devoting one period a week to in-class reading; we can always expand, increase, but it is safer to start small. Once building administration understands what we are doing and is behind it, there is little we cannot accomplish. But we must have that support.

Second, for new teachers, the task of becoming really informed—deep and wide—in young adult literature is a fearsome one. There are so many titles out there—as the shirt says, "So many books . . . so little time!" But if we start, maybe a book at a time, and get to know them along with our students, we can handle it. Students love to recommend their discoveries to their teachers. I have discovered some of my best that way. And surely I can read faster than they can, often finishing a young adult title in one evening. The best news is that the more you read, the faster you get!

Third, the commitment to this approach has to be ongoing. New titles are coming out daily. New young adult authors are appearing just as often. Some of the books are awesome; some, quite frankly, are wretched. If students choose to read the wretched, that is their choice; but I am unwilling to spend my classroom library dollars on purchasing them, so I have to read constantly and I have to attend conferences and haunt author sessions.

Fourth, educators must use common sense and good professional judgment about which titles are in the classroom library. No self-respecting professional is, I suspect, ever totally comfortable in making these decisions. Of course if the student brings a book from outside, and it is particularly rough, at least it did not come from Sherman Branch Library. Sometimes I still request a note from a parent, acknowledging awareness of the book and its content, and giving permission. The "f-word" and his relatives are represented in the books in my classroom library; in addition, "problem books" dealing with AIDS, drugs, suicide, alcohol, various kinds of abuse, and the horrors of war are all there. This past year, when I was teaching only eighth graders, I put quite mature books such as *Go Ask Alice, Do or Die* by Leon Bing, *The Squared Circle* by James Bennett, *Like Sisters on the Homefront* by Rita Williams Garcia, and a whole collection of books on alcoholism right into the general collection. Several parents spoke to me, saying that the students' reading prompted most appropriate discussions with the parent about topics they had been unwilling to bring up. But it could just as easily have gone the other way. This next year I will also be having sixth graders in my classroom. The eighth graders and I decided that some titles should be pulled from the general collection and made available to eighth graders only. At "Back to School" night in the fall, I explain my approach to reading and books and encourage the parents to speak to me if they have concerns. One must read the population where one teaches and, I think, act accordingly.

Conclusion

Caveats aside, I would urge you to try this approach to literacy learning for your students. Even if it becomes only a small part of your literacy program, it richly deserves whatever you can spare. In its simplicity, it requires only four things—a teacher who loves reading young adult literature; class time devoted to reading, easy access to books, and a systematic response vehicle—but most of all, it requires that we trust ourselves, our gut feelings about what makes lifelong readers. In my experience, that means finding that one, that first magical book that shows us into the joys that reading holds for us. Computers are fine—wonderful, even—but there are always those moments in the dark of night, those times when we want to lose ourselves, to escape, to learn, to be inspired, and for those moments there is nothing to challenge the supremacy of a book. I am totally, 100 percent convinced that the person who says, "I just don't like to read," simply has not found the right book. And the best way to find that book is to be involved in free voluntary reading.

Mary Jo Sherman was the winner of the Nila Banton Smith Award in 1987. This award is presented by the International Reading Association to a teacher who has made outstanding contributions to reading at the secondary level.

Summary

Exciting things for young adolescents are happening in these schools, and they represent only a sample of exemplary schools across the country. These programs share some common characteristics: a commitment to literacy learning as a priority, consideration of the developmental tasks of young adolescents, and approaches that connect literacy with the lives of students.

As middle level educators begin to understand the implications that the middle school concept has for improved reading and writing instruction, more schools will improve their programs. The cooperative planning of interdisciplinary team organization naturally leads to thematic units and the integration of social studies and science content with literature and writing. Exploratory courses naturally support the recreational reading activities of a school. Advisor-advisee groups are a logical extension of discussions that began with values issues first encountered in literature. In these descriptions of exemplary literacy programs, middle school programs and practices lend themselves to enhanced literacy learning for young adolescents.

Change is difficult and challenging. But change can also be fun and invigorating, and when teachers feel revitalized they cannot help but pass this enthusiasm for learning on to their students.

References

Atwell, N. (1987). *In the Middle: Writing, Reading, and Learning with Adolescents.* Portsmouth, NH: Boynton/Cook.

dear author. (1995). Berkeley, CA: Conari Press.

Irvin, J. (1990). *Reading and the Middle School Student: Strategies to Enhance Literacy.* Boston: Allyn & Bacon.

Krashen, S. (1993). *The Power of Reading.* Englewood, CO: Libraries Unlimited.

Leonhardt, M. (1992). *Parents Who Love Reading, Kids Who Don't.* New York: Crown.

Rief, L. (1992). *Seeking Diversity.* Portsmouth, NH: Heinemann/Boynton/Cook.

Young Adult References

Anonymous. (1992). *Go Ask Alice.* New York: Avon Books.

Bennett, James W. (1995). *The Squared Circle.* New York: Scholastic.

Bing, Leon. (1992). *Do or Die.* New York: HarperCollins.

Draper, Sharon. (1995). *Tears of a Tiger.* New York: Atheneum.

Gardiner, John. (1983). *Stone Fox.* New York: HarperCollins Trophy.

Hayden, Torey. (1981). *One Child.* New York: Avon Books.

Myers, Walter Dean. (1993). *Malcolm X: By Any Means Necessary.* New York: Scholastic.

Myers, Walter Dean. (1988). *Fallen Angels.* New York: Scholastic.

Paulsen, Gary. (1993). *Nightjohn.* New York: Delacorte.

Paulsen, Gary. (1994). *Winterdance.* San Diego: Harcourt Brace.

Smith, Doris Buchanan. (1988). *A Taste of Blackberries.* New York: Harper & Row.

Sparks, Beatrice (Ed.) (1994). *It Happened to Nancy.* New York: Avon Books.

Spiegelman, Art. (1986). *Maus: A Survivor's Tale.* New York: Pantheon Books.

Spinelli, Jerry. (1990). *Maniac Magee.* Boston: Little Brown.

Stine, R.L. (1994). *Goosebumps.* New York: Scholastic.

Voigt, Cynthia. (1993). *Wings of a Falcon.* New York: Scholastic.

White, Ryan & Cunningham, Ann Marie. (1991). *Ryan White: My Own Story.* New York: Dial Books.

Williams-Garcia, Rita. (1995). *Like Sisters on the Homefront.* New York: Lodestar Books.

Index